Revolution and Political Leadership:
Algeria, 1954-1968

M.I.T. STUDIES IN
COMPARATIVE POLITICS

Under the general editorship of Harold
D. Lasswell, Daniel Lerner, and Ithiel
de Sola Pool.

*The Emerging Elite: A Study of Po-
litical Leadership in Ceylon,* Marshall
Singer, 1964.

The Turkish Political Elite, Frederick
W. Frey, 1965.

*World Revolutionary Elites: Studies in
Coercive Ideological Movements,* Harold
D. Lasswell and Daniel Lerner, editors,
1965.

*Language of Politics: Studies in Quanti-
tative Semantics,* Harold D. Lasswell,
Nathan Leites, and Associates, 1965
(reissue).

*The General Inquirer: A Computer Ap-
proach to Content Analysis,* Philip J.
Stone, Dexter C. Dunphy, Marshall S.
Smith, Daniel M. Ogilvie, 1967.

*Political Elites: A Select Computerized
Bibliography,* Carl Beck and J. Thomas
McKechnie, 1968.

*Force and Folly: Essays on Foreign
Affairs and the History of Ideas,* Hans
Speier, 1969.

*Quantitative Ecological Analysis in the
Social Sciences,* Mattei Dogan and Stein
Rokkan, editors, 1969.

*Euratlantica: Changing Perspectives of
the European Elites,* Daniel Lerner and
Morton Gorden, 1969.

*Revolution and Political Leadership:
Algeria 1954–1968,* William B. Quandt,
1969.

*Revolution and Political Leadership:
Algeria, 1954-1968*

William B. Quandt

THE M.I.T. PRESS
Cambridge, Massachusetts, and London, England

To my parents

Acknowledgments

In the course of my research for this study I have benefited greatly from the aid of other scholars. Some, who will remain unnamed, will recognize the extent of their influence on my thoughts in the following pages. At M.I.T. I was fortunate to receive advice and encouragement from Professors Myron Weiner, Lucian W. Pye and Frederick W. Frey. I am also indebted to Professor L. Carl Brown of Princeton for his careful and helpful reading of an early version of the manuscript. Others who read all or part of the study, and whose suggestions were of great use to me, were Professor Clement H. Moore of the University of California, Professor Alexander George of Stanford, Professor J. C. Hurewitz and Janet Zagoria, both of Columbia.

While carrying out my research in Algeria I was fortunate in the consideration and cooperation I found among scholars and politicians. Marcel Teitler was particularly helpful in introducing me to the complexities of doing research in Algeria. I was aided in my search for obscure documents and facts by Andrée Verdiel, Bruno Etienne, Jean Leca, René Jammes, Abderrahmane Remili, A. Touili, and Father Jean Dejeux. To Nacereddine Guèche I owe a special thanks for help and friendship.

Without the cooperation of numerous Algerian politicians this study would have been impossible. I was fortunate that Algerians

viii   ACKNOWLEDGMENTS

were willing to discuss with me in a direct and frank manner many sensitive issues from their recent past. I am grateful to Mme. Zohra Drif Bitat for helping me establish contacts with other politicians and for describing her own political experiences. While all of my interviewees were most cooperative, I must thank in particular Brahim Mezhoudi for the lengthy hours we spent in discussion, as well as M'Hammed Yazid, Saad Dahlab, Benyoussef Benkhedda, Ferhat Abbas, and Abdelkader Guerroudj, all of whom were willing to take time to try to explain to me the intricacies of Algeria's political development.

For the nearly two years during which this research has occupied my time, I have received generous support from the Foreign Area Fellowship Program. Their constant encouragement and tolerance has been a major factor in bringing this project to a successful completion.

Needless to say, neither the Foreign Area Research Program nor the many scholars and politicians who have contributed to this study bear* any responsibility for the views or interpretations expressed here. Such a disclaimer can be made with less justification toward my wife, Anna, whose comments and criticisms have inevitably worked themselves into the text. I therefore am both pleased to give her credit for certain parts of the text and tempted to hold her jointly responsible for any errors or omissions. In a very real sense this book has been a collaborative venture, and has been much more enjoyable to write because of that fact.

WILLIAM B. QUANDT

April 8, 1969
Santa Monica, California

Foreword

The Algerian struggle for independence captured world attention by reason of its duration, intensity, and drama. The theatrical
tension which emanates from all "wars of national liberation"
was heightened, in the Algerian case, by its impact upon the French
colonial master. Algeria, following hard upon the Suez debacle
of 1956, was the major factor in subverting the Fourth Republic
and installing the Fifth Republic in France itself. As the French,
with their penchant for reducing historical sequences to para-
doxical epigrams, put it: The *socialist* Mollet imposed an imperial-
ist war upon the Algerians from which the *nationalist* de Gaulle
liberated them.

An epoch of accelerated history is obscured by this bon mot, as
often happens when the French indulge their taste for literary
expression at the cost of their need for political analysis. The
interaction between France and Algeria involved nothing less
than three fundamental factors that have speeded historical change
in the postwar arena of world politics: (1) a global factor; (2) a
national factor; (3) a "human" factor.

The global factor was clear by 1947, when Britain "liberated"
the Indian Ocean region of its sunsetless Empire. Once India-
Ceylon-Burma were free to become "new nations," the paradigm
of postwar "decolonization" was historically accelerated. Where

Britain led, others must follow. Some former European empires followed willingly, others reluctantly. Among the reluctant dragons, France was foremost.

The awkward global posture of postwar France was complicated by the national factor of French decline. An elite schooled in the belief that France is the vital center of world civilization found it hard to accept the setbacks that pushed postwar France ever farther into the wings. Ejected unceremoniously from the Middle East, defeated militarily in Indochina, threatened throughout Black Africa, France decided to "keep Algeria French." This, however, was easier decided than done. Such legalisms as declaring Algeria to be a *département,* hence an integral part of French territory, availed nothing against a population demanding their own separate national identity under the leadership of an uncompromising revolutionary elite.[1]

This was the key to the many human factors interwoven in the Algerian drama. French men and women had been settling in Algeria over the past century, and a million or so were living there when the conflict erupted. At the same time, nearly a half million Algerians were living and working in France—and their remittances formed a major component of the Algerian economy. The revolutionary elite itself had been formed mainly in French schools and had been inspired mainly by the *gauchiste* ideologies of the Left Bank in Paris. As they adapted these ideas and techniques to their own nationalist purposes, the revolutionary elite mobilized cadres of their Algerian compatriots into an irresistible force.[2]

Upon this revolutionary elite, then, William Quandt aptly focuses our attention. He traces the historical evolution of political thinking among Algerian leaders from the liberals through the radicals to the revolutionaries. He turns then to the awesome emergence of the military and the intellectuals as "new contenders for power," contenders whose appearance in every postwar struggle for independence has been as regular as death and taxes, and usually associated with both. The Algerian interaction between these two subsets of power seekers eventuated in the conflict between Ben

[1] That the French elite were also skeptical of this legalism is shown in Daniel Lerner and Morton Gorden, *Euratlantica: Changing Perspectives of the European Elites* (Cambridge: M.I.T. Press, 1969).

[2] For comparative materials on revolutionary mobilization, see Harold D. Lasswell and Daniel Lerner, eds., *World Revolutionary Elites* (Cambridge: M.I.T. Press, 1965).

Bella and Colonel Boumedienne and culminated, as it often does, in the ascendancy of the military. This outcome is not necessarily a Thermidorean Reaction nor even a simple regression. It often tends, rather, to inaugurate a new phase in the continuing process of "restriction by partial incorporation" that characterizes the emerging nations-in-a-hurry.[3]

The great merit of Quandt's study is its vivid and intellectually integrated sense of process in history and in the people who make history. By attending to the political socialization of the Algerian elite in their own life history, he is able to differentiate them into five "distinctive types of political actors." By so doing, he can deal with those fundamental predispositions among decision-makers that account for the intraelite conflicts in Algeria's brief past, that specify the "inconsistent orientations" in its present, that foreshadow "both the liabilities and the promises" in its future. This, to paraphrase Monsieur Jourdain's famous discovery, is the nascent language of the policy sciences.

Harold D. Lasswell
Daniel Lerner

---

[3] A vivid case study of the process in Ceylon is Marshall Singer, *The Emerging Elite* (Cambridge: M.I.T. Press, 1964).

Contents

xiii

Tables

Figures

1
The Historical Legacy of
Colonialism and Revolution

In few countries of the non-Western world has the impact of the West been so great as in Algeria. For over one hundred years Algeria was considered to be a part of France, and by the last quarter of the nineteenth century nearly one-tenth of Algeria's population was of European origin. The proximity of France and Algeria made colonial ties particularly close, and eventually the flow of Europeans to Algeria was matched by a sizable migration to Europe of Algerians seeking education and jobs or doing military service in the French army. Many Algerians came to speak French fluently, to dress like Frenchmen, and even to take French wives. A few came to think of themselves as French citizens and desired nothing more than complete assimilation of Algeria into France. For some Algerians, in short, the "civilizing mission" of France was enthusiastically welcomed, and still today a legacy of affection and sympathy for France remains among large numbers of Algerians. This was one side of the enormously complex relationship called colonialism.

But colonialism in Algeria inevitably carried with it the basis for its own undoing, for if the positive aspects of Western domina-

1

tion were particularly strong in Algeria, so also were the negative ones. For every Algerian who profited from the benefits of French culture there were dozens who felt little more than the frustrations, the anger, and the humiliation of being placed in inferior positions by a technically superior culture. Added to this dependency relationship were the all too frequent instances of impoverishment, discrimination, and racism.

In a land long subjected to violence, one might have expected that the stark inequalities produced by French colonialism in Algeria would lead eventually to some drastic efforts by the dispossessed to alter the political structure. And yet when the tides of militant nationalism were beginning to run strong in much of the colonial world in the early twentieth century, Frenchmen could look with satisfaction at their most important colony and note the passivity of the "natives." When some political activity did begin among the Muslims, it was not those who had suffered most under the French who called for change. Rather, it was the small nucleus of French-educated Muslims who had nearly been integrated into French life who found the remaining obstacles to their participation in political and economic activities intolerable.

The tragedy of Algerian nationalism is that France remained aloof from the successive demands for reform presented by moderates seeking to work within the legal system, so that by the time France was willing to make the concessions demanded by the men of the 1930s she was faced with a new generation of nationalists who asked for more and were willing to use more radical methods than their predecessors. These demands were likewise ignored until a third generation of nationalists, this one convinced of the need for the use of violence, had seized control of the nationalist movement from the moderates and had begun a long and painful war for independence. For the Algerians, revolution did succeed in bringing independence but at a frightful cost in lives and in deepened internal conflicts and hostilities. While the human cost of the war was most immediately felt, the legacy of division and distrust left by the prolonged war for independence has had far-reaching consequences in independent Algeria and has seriously impeded the efforts needed to reconstruct the war-torn society and economy. The story of the Algerian revolution is extremely complex, involving the entire range of human relationships and evoking the strongest possible emotions in both participants and observers. While the bulk of this study will examine in detail the principal

Algerian actors in this drama, some sense of the historical developments from the early French presence in 1830 to their final departure in 1962 must be given.

Algeria came to be France's most important colony by the twentieth century, but the beginnings of France's direct involvement in Algeria were modest and even banal. At various points early in the French occupation abandonment of Algeria was considered, but this simple course was never followed, and thus the tie binding Algeria to France was broken 130 years later at the cost of hundreds of thousands of lives and extreme social disruption.[1]

The French decided on the conquest of Algiers in a rather shortsighted and casual manner, and the expeditionary force sent in the summer of 1830 was surrounded by a carnival-like atmosphere, complete with elegant Parisian ladies who had rented space on pleasure boats in order to witness the naval bombardment of Algiers. In anticipation of the conquest of Algiers, a Marseilles merchant ran the following advertisement in the newspaper:

A new enterprise will be established on the occasion of the war against Algiers. A merchant from Marseilles, possessing an attractive ship, will fit it out as a hotel. Those persons wishing to witness the bombardment of Algiers and the landing of our troops will be lodged and fed for 15 francs a day. This ship, which has received legal authorization, will remain at a respectful distance to avoid enemy fire. It will, however, be armed with six cannon so as to defend itself against the corsaires in case of attack.[2]

Initial resistance to the French was vigorous but short-lived, and the Dey of Algiers finally capitulated on July 5, 1830. After sacking the treasury the French hardly knew what to do next, but before long the decision was made for them, as Muslim resistance in the countryside grew around the imposing figure of the Emir Abd al Qadir.[3] Faced with a clear challenge to French supremacy, the French naturally decided that it was necessary to "pacify" the hostile countryside. This decision was the fatal one that drew France into its deep involvement in Algeria, for pacification was

[1] An excellent account of the French conquest of Algeria is found in Charles-André Julien, *Histoire de l'Algérie contemporaine (1827–1871)*.

[2] Quoted in Charles-Henri Favrod, *La Révolution algérienne*, p. 1. Originally published in *Le Sémaphore*, March 30, 1830.

[3] See Paul Azan, *L'Emir Abdelkader*. The Emir Abd al Qadir (Abdelkader) is one of the few heroes in Algeria's past revered today by all groups in the society.

to last for at least seventeen years until the surrender of Abd al Qadir in 1847, and in some areas major resistance was not overcome until after 1870.

In pacifying the countryside, the French rarely spared force, and numerous instances of the worst sort of barbarity of the French troops can be cited. In the era of "colonialism with a good conscience," military officers often kept careful accounts of their victories over the "natives," and clearly the destruction of Muslim life and property was hardly considered beyond the scope of the duties of the bearers of the *mission civilisatrice.* Quotes from two French generals, Bugeaud and St. Arnaud, reflect something of the destructive nature of the "pacification" of Algeria:

"More than 50 fine villages, built of stone and roofed with tiles, were destroyed. Our soldiers made very considerable pickings there. We did not have the time, in the heat of combat, to chop down the trees. The task, in any case, would have been beyond our strength. Twenty thousand men armed with axes could not in six months cut down the olives and fig trees which cover the beautiful landscape which lay at our feet."

"There were still numerous bands of the enemy on the summits, and I was hoping for another engagement. But they refused to come down and I began to chop down the fine orchards and to set fire to the magnificent villages under the enemy's eyes" (1846).

"I left in my wake a vast conflagration. All the villages, some 200 in number, were burnt down, all the gardens destroyed, all the olive trees cut down" (1851).[4]

As the French gained control over the hostile countryside, the Muslim population was often displaced by European *colons,* many of whom came from countries other than France. With Abd al

---

[4] Quoted by Roger Murray and Tom Weingraf in "The Algerian Revolution," *New Left Review* (London), No. 22 (December 1963), p. 23. For a representative selection of quotations describing the French tactics used in conquering Algeria, see Yves Lacoste, André Nouschi, and André Prenant, *L'Algérie, passé et présent,* pp. 300-315.

A certain Dr. Bopichon, author of two books on Algeria in the mid-1840s, wrote: "Little does it matter that France in her political conduct goes beyond the limits of common morality at times; the essential thing is that she establish a lasting colony, and that as a consequence she will bring European civilization to these barbaric countries; when a project which is to the advantage of all humanity is to be carried out, the shortest path is the best. Now, it is certain the shortest path is terror. . . . Without violating the laws of morality, or international jurisprudence, we can fight our African enemies with powder and fire, joined by famine, internal divisions, war between Arabs and Kabyles, between the tribes of the *tell* and those of the Sahara, by brandy, corruption and disorganization. That is the easiest thing in the world to do." From Charles-Henri Favrod, *Le* FLN *et l'Algérie,* p. 31.

Qadir's defeat in 1847, relative security existed in large parts of Algeria and the growth of the European population was rapid. The problem of controlling the Algerians remained, however, and soon the French seemed to realize that they had complicated their task of administering the local population by eliminating many of the Muslims' natural leaders.

The Governor General in Algeria, Jules Cambon, reported to the French Senate in 1894 as follows:

After the Turkish authorities had disappeared . . . there was no day on which we did not try to destroy the great families . . . because we found them to be forces of resistance. We did not realize that in suppressing the forces of resistance in this fashion, we were also suppressing our means of action. The result is that we are today confronted by a sort of human dust on which we have no influence and in which movements take place which are to us unknown. We no longer have any authoritative intermediaries between ourselves and the indigenous population.[5]

If the result of French colonization in Algeria in the nineteenth century was to transform a relatively healthy traditional society into "human dust," the early years of the twentieth century gave some indications that social forces soon to produce new men were acting on the Muslim population. Whether these new men would consider themselves Frenchmen, Arabs, Muslims, or Algerians was unknown, but few seemed to fear that nationalism would become a strong force in Algeria. After all, in the minds of nearly all Frenchmen an Algerian nation had never existed. Much of the drama of the Algerian nationalist movement stems from the fact that large numbers of Algerians shared the belief that an Algerian nation was a fanciful idea devoid of reality.

The stages of the movement which eventually led to Algerian independence can be readily identified, although much is still unknown about some historical events. The earliest manifestations of the forces which in time created the nationalist movement took place in the early years of the twentieth century. These consisted of demands for social and sometimes political reforms. Such demands, usually presented as petitions by the most westernized segments of Algerian society, generally met with failure. The consequences of failure would often be that demands were increased and new means of action were sought. French intransigence seemed to lead

[5] Quoted by Roger Murray and Tom Weingraf in "The Algerian Revolution," p. 29.

inevitably toward the radicalization of the reformist and later of the nationalist movement.

A critical point in the development of Algerian nationalism occurred in the 1930s. During this decade Metropolitan France held out the first promises of substantive reform which would have satisfied many of the moderate nationalists and reformers. These promises of action from Paris frightened the *colon* population in Algeria, however, and great pressures were brought to bear in order to sabotage these liberal plans. As it became clear that the *colons* could determine French policy in Algeria, the Muslim elite began to shift away from a belief that full assimilation of Algerians into French life would be the surest path of progress. Replacing this belief was the conviction that independence, or at least autonomy, would be the best hope for realizing their goals.

A farsighted Frenchman, Maurice Viollette, had warned his countrymen in 1935: "Take care, the natives of Algeria, and through your own fault, still have no country. They are looking for one. They ask us to let them enter the French nation. Let them do so swiftly, for otherwise they will create their own." [6]

Years later, in 1947, a powerful *colon* expressed his contempt for Viollette's warning in the following words:

You appear only to fear the possibility of an Arab insurrection. Try to grasp the fact that there is another danger facing the uncomprehending metropolitan Frenchmen, that of a *colon* uprising. . . . We are tired of this absurd talk of elections for the natives. Even if by some *tour de force* we succeeded once in orienting them in our favor, we could not be forever repeating the operation. There must be an end to all this. We want no more governors drenched in anachronistic sentimentality, but strong men who can ensure respect for our rights by showing force and, if necessary, by using it. In 1936, I sabotaged the Blum-Viollette project and the government capitulated before me. What business had General de Gaulle in meddling once again in this business? Believe me, I know how to bring them to heel." [7]

The era of full assimilation of Algerians into French society was certainly gone by the end of World War II. But the inevitability of violent revolution was not so clearly apparent in the postwar years. One might well have anticipated considerable agitation for change on the part of the Muslim population, but the possibility of a successful armed insurrection seemed slight. And it is well to

[6] *Ibid.*, p. 49.
[7] *Ibid.*, p. 17.

remember that success was not guaranteed to the men who began the revolution in 1954. For the few Algerians who took up arms against France in November 1954, the most probable result of their desperate actions was failure. Nor is it difficult to imagine ways in which France might have greatly increased her chances of holding on to her most valuable African colony. But the thrust of history in the postwar world was toward decolonization, and French leaders finally bowed to this powerful fact as much as they did to the pressures brought to bear by the Algerian revolutionaries. De Gaulle, one of the main architects of Algerian independence, had foreseen as early as 1944 that Algeria would one day become a separate nation from France. But despite his repeated recognition of this fact in private, it was not until September 1959 that he put forward his plan for self-determination in Algeria.[8]

Algeria became an independent nation on July 5, 1962. With the end of the war in Algeria, the attention of people around the world no longer focused on that war-ravaged country. Its leaders' efforts to build a nation out of the society and economy they inherited have been largely ignored. But in a deep sense the consequences of colonialism and revolution in Algeria are best seen in the independent nation formed by these two forces.

The leaders of the Algerian revolution and of independent Algeria are still acting out the lessons they have drawn from their past. And yet these lessons have been so different for individual Algerian leaders that little consensus exists on how the country should be governed, how power should be used, and how political relationships should be ordered.

If Algerian society today is not quite the "human dust" of an earlier era, it is certainly far from being stable or capable of directing sustained efforts toward development and growth. At least part of the stagnation which so dominated Algerian life in the late 1960s was the result of the debilitating conflicts that had divided members of the political elite from at least 1954 to 1968. This has been both the least anticipated and the most persistent legacy of colonialism and revolution. The Algerian people have had little understanding of or sympathy with these internecine disputes.

With deeper examination one can trace the roots of most intra-elite divisiveness to the events of the past four decades in Algeria.

[8] See Jean Lacouture, *De Gaulle,* p. 178.

What appears from such a survey is a picture of many highly motivated men struggling to cope, against great odds, with problems affecting the central values of their society. In this process numerous groups developed distinct strategies of political action, no two of which were fully compatible. Revolution brought these groups together in common cause but also served to deepen the differences that had grown up among them. Independence permitted the full expression of these contrasting views of political reality, but soon tolerance for diversity was replaced by dominance of the powerful who saw in the nation's needs the basis for their claim to legitimacy. No doubt it will be many years before Algerians are able to face the present without constant reference to their traumatic past. An explanation of how that past has impinged upon the men who have been responsible for leading Algeria is thus a first step toward understanding contemporary Algerian politics.

2
Revolution and Political Authority: Concepts and Methods

War and revolution have been the focus of much study by historians, philosophers, and political scientists for over two thousand years. In view of the vast amount that has been written on these topics, it is surprising how little consensus there is on the causes and consequences of these dramatic and destructive events. Part of the explanation for this lack of generalized knowledge seems to stem from the fact that quite often it has been impossible to do careful empirical work on these subjects. Participants are generally inaccessible or unwilling to talk candidly about their experiences. Documents are frequently lacking or irrelevant.

While Algeria hardly provides the researcher with an ideal environment for studying the process of revolution or the consequences of prolonged warfare on intraelite relations, it is presently more open to inquiry than other countries which have recently undergone major revolutions such as China, North Vietnam, or Cuba. Many of the leaders of the Algerian revolution are still alive and are often quite willing to discuss frankly their experiences. While documents are difficult to come by, enough is known of Algeria's recent history so that the broad outlines of development are fairly well known. Eventually it may be hoped that Algerians will write their own history of the revolution, but for the moment this has not been done.[1]

Because of the relatively favorable conditions in Algeria for studying revolution and its aftermath, an analysis of Algerian experiences may lead to the formulation of a few limited hypotheses with relevance for other societies. No hypothesis is proved by a single example, of course, but occasionally a widely held assumption about social processes can be called into question by showing that it fails to account for at least one important case. This study aims both at questioning some commonly held hypotheses and at advancing some tentative conclusions as to general relationships between elite structures and other politically significant behavior.

Hypotheses on Revolution and Political Leadership

One of the most widely held assumptions about revolution and political leadership is that mobilization against a common enemy will unite men who may have had few or even hostile relations previous to this experience. Some have carried this argument even further by claiming therapeutic values for the act of participation in violent activities. Perhaps the foremost spokesman for this point of view was Frantz Fanon. Fanon, although born in the French possession of Martinique, is known primarily as an ardent propagandist of anticolonialism and for his close association with Algeria's wartime FLN. Because of his profound knowledge of Algerian society and of the revolution itself, Fanon's judgment of the effects of violence on the participants in the Algerian war cannot easily be dismissed. In *The Wretched of the Earth*, Fanon passionately presents his case for the use of violence:

But it so happens that for the colonized people this violence, because it constitutes their only work, invests their characters with positive and

---

[1] Good introductions to Algerian history can be found in Charles-Robert Ageron, *Histoire de l'Algérie contemporaine;* Robert Aron, *Les origines de la guerre d'Algérie;* Charles F. Gallagher, *The United States and North Africa;* Yves Lacoste, André Nouschi, and André Prenant, *L'Algérie, passé et présent;* Roger Le Tourneau, *Evolution politique de l'Afrique du nord musulmane, 1920–1961.* Several efforts by Algerians to interpret their own history are worthy of mention, particularly Mostefa Lacheraf, *L'Algérie, nation et société;* Mohamed C. Sahli, *Décoloniser l'histoire;* and Mouloud Gaid, *Tarikh al-jazā'ir al-musaw-war.* On the early period of Algerian nationalism, see also Belkacem Saadallah, *The Rise of Algerian Nationalism: 1900–1930.*

creative qualities. The practice of violence binds them together as a whole, since each individual forms a violent link in the great chain, a part of the great organism of violence which has surged upwards in reaction to the settler's violence in the beginning. The groups recognize each other and the future nation is already indivisible.[2]

Contrary to Fanon's prophecy, however, it is simply untrue that the Algerian revolution produced unity within the political elite. Rather, the revolution not only perpetuated old antagonisms but also created new sources of strain and tension among political leaders.

In Algeria the problem of intraelite conflict has dominated internal politics during the entire period from 1954 to 1968. There has been a constant turnover in top political leadership, and political careers are made and unmade with great rapidity. The men in power in 1968 in Algeria were virtually unknown five or six years earlier, a fact which does not hold true for some other countries that have experienced protracted guerrilla wars. Of the nine "historic leaders" of the Algerian revolution, for example, five were still alive in 1968 but only one played even a minor political role at that time. Between 1954 and 1968, eighty-seven men were in top positions of formal influence within the Algerian political elite, but their average tenure in office was only a little more than two years. (See Appendices B and C.)

Rather than developing into a "political class" that jealously guards its prerogatives and power, the Algerian political elite has been composed of numerous clans, factions, and cliques, none of which has been powerful enough to dominate the entire political system.[3] Nor has a political process evolved which readily accommodates the competing demands and expectations of those contending for political power. Stable alliances or coalitions among these diverse elements within the elite have been notably lacking during the agitated period since the revolution began. Contributing to this instability was the fact that no one within the elite other than the army had the support of powerful groups within the society, and

---

[2] Frantz Fanon, *The Wretched of the Earth*, p. 73.

[3] While it is still too early to tell, it may be that following an abortive coup attempt in December 1967, Algerian leadership is moving toward a more homogeneous coalition of professional military men and technically competent administrators. This would still not provide an example of a single group dominating the political system, but it might prove to be the first relatively stable ruling coalition since independence.

thus incumbency in elite positions depended primarily on personal relations with elite members.

Although it seems that Fanon was incorrect in believing that revolution would produce unity in Algeria, it does not automatically follow that it was the revolutionary process itself that intensified and even created divisions and conflict within the Algerian political elite and between the elite and the masses. Some observers, while either accepting or ignoring Fanon's argument, have nonetheless granted that conflict has been endemic in Algerian politics and requires some explanation. While none of their alternative theories is totally convincing, each deserves to be taken seriously.

The major efforts to explain the problem of intraelite conflict in Algeria have stressed the importance of standard sociological variables, in particular traditional social structure, class, ethnicity, and cultural differences. For example, it is often argued that equilibrium in the traditional Algerian society was maintained by institutionalizing conflict to the point that each village, tribe, and even family was internally divided into rival groupings called *soffs*. The outbreak of conflict was presumably muted by the fact that an attack upon an individual belonging to a different *soff* would be interpreted as a threat to the entire *soff*.[4] Tension ran high in this society, but the actual outbreak of fighting was governed by many restrictions and tacit rules. In contemporary Algerian politics the prevalence of narrow clanlike groups and the many axes of conflict are sometimes interpreted as reflecting the patterns of the *soff*. But in fact it is virtually impossible to test the relevance of this argument, for no Algerian political leader would identify himself as belonging to a *soff*. At best, the *soff* serves as an analogy of limited usefulness.

Conflicts within the political elite have also been traced to ethnic divisions between Arabs and Kabyles.[5] This argument, particularly popular among French scholars, rests on the fact that in Algerian society at large it is quite easy to find examples of tension between these two ethnic groups. But while this axis of division is strong among the masses, it would seem that other experiences or identifications have had a greater impact on the few men who have reached positions of political power since 1954. Kabyles, for

---

[4] Pierre Bourdieu in *The Algerians* gives a description of the workings of the *soff*.

[5] Serge Bromberger, in *Les rebelles algériens,* a book containing much useful, if unverifiable, information, traces disunity to Algeria's Berber character and the Arab-Berber conflict.

example, have rarely acted in unison within the political elite, and one readily finds men such as Boumendjel, Mohammedi Said, Ait Ahmed, Mohand oul Hadj, Boumaza, Abdesselam, and Zahouane opposing each other despite a common ethnic background.

In addition to the emphasis on ethnic particularism, at times a simplistic Marxist argument that class is the basis of most intraelite conflicts is made.[6] But in Algeria one finds many men of modest social origins who hold quite "bourgeois" beliefs. Likewise, some extremely wealthy families have had sons who became ardent spokesmen for the working classes. The difficulty in class analysis is in knowing whether one is talking of "class origin" or "class consciousness." [7] The interesting question of the link between one's social origins and subsequent beliefs is all too infrequently made.

The argument that cultural differences derived from either French or Arab education are the source of much dissension within the elite is often quite persuasive, but it also fails to explain many critical aspects of political behavior. On a few issues, such as whether or how to Arabize the schools or to encourage inter-Arab contacts, the cultural orientations of members of the elite may be extremely important. But on such questions as whether or not a one-party system is most appropriate in Algeria, whether considerations of efficiency should guide economic planning, what degree of tolerance for political opposition should prevail, or whether Algeria should maintain close relations with France, there seems to be little correlation between these types of education and behavior. For example, Algeria's first President, Ahmed Ben Bella, always went to French schools and was illiterate in Arabic but was an ardent propagandist of Arab solidarity and of reviving the "national language." Boumedienne, by contrast, is one of the few Algerian leaders whose education has been almost entirely in Arabic, and yet he has cultivated close relations with France as assiduously as Ben Bella ever did, has been relatively moderate in pushing Arabization, and has surrounded himself with French-educated ministers and graduates of French military academies.[8]

---

[6] This theme is carried in official Algerian statements such as the *Charte d'Alger*.

[7] The distinction between stratum, as the objective part of the economic or social structure from which one comes, and class identification, the subjective feeling of belonging to some group, is developed in Richard Centers, *The Psychology of Social Classes: A Study of Class Consciousness*.

[8] To the extent that education is an important variable in determining Algerian elite political behavior, it seems to be one's absolute level of education rather than one's cultural type of education that matters. While statistically

The Divisiveness of Revolution

If none of the traditional approaches to the problem of political conflict within Algeria seems satisfactory and if Fanon's hypothesis is clearly inaccurate, one is obliged to offer another explanation. The major theme of this study is that the very process that led to revolution in Algeria was the one which created the deep divisions within the political elite. To pursue this theme one must look at the ways in which political leaders were socialized into politics. What emerges from such a study is a picture of a discontinuous process of political socialization whereby each political generation was exposed to radically different experiences while at the same time reacting to what was widely perceived as the failure of the preceding generation to achieve any of its major political goals.

The colonial system in Algeria was so structured that no Muslim political group was allowed to be successful in pursuit of its primary aims. Thus, the demands of moderate reformers for greater equality were rejected by the *colon*-dominated system. The efforts of later nationalists to organize a mass-based political party that would compete for electoral votes were likewise undermined and ended in failure.

Finally, the attempt of a more extremist group to use violence to eliminate the colonial system very nearly ended in failure, and it was only by regrouping all nationalist forces, including the moderates and the party organizers, and by coopting new elements into the political elite, that the Algerian revolutionaries were finally able to gain independence for their country after more than seven years of guerrilla warfare.

The result of the process by which each new group entered the political system as a reaction to the failure of some earlier group meant that there was virtually no recruitment of new politicians into an on-going political process in which the "rules of the game" were relatively well understood and in which the role of the politician was well defined. Rather, each new group rejected the procedures and claims to representativeness of the former political

---

this is difficult to establish, much qualitative evidence supports this interpretation. In an interview, for example, one of the deputies to the National Constituent Assembly who was highly educated in Arabic and was a devout Muslim claimed that his colleagues with Arabic primary or secondary educations would agree with him on concrete economic or social issues. But when it came to such political issues as toleration of opposition, free speech, and checks on executive power, it was only the other university men, most of whom had French educations, who would support him.

activists and became proficient in the skills of opposition while at the same time striving to create a new consensus on what it meant to be a politician or a nationalist. Consequently each group developed rather narrow ideas of its own right to exercise power, and intransigence became a greater value for many than did bargaining and compromise. Toleration for diversity within the political elite was replaced by an aspiration for a homogeneous ruling group.

Given these beliefs, it would have seemed natural for each group to attempt to exclude the others from positions of influence. And yet, ironically, the requirements of the war for independence demanded the efforts of a wide range of political actors—men skilled in violence, bargaining, diplomacy, propaganda, and organization— and thus a heterogeneous political elite formed during the war. Because of a commitment on the part of individuals in each group to the overriding idea of independence, other sources of disagreement were temporarily transcended. This meant that with independence all active participants in the revolution could legitimately expect some share of power in the new political system. The revolution, rather than bringing about the decline of the older nationalist elite, allowed these individuals a chance to overcome earlier failures by effective contributions to the war effort.

The prolonged frustrations of politics within the colonial context and the divisive pressures of organizing a revolution made the elite incapable of adapting easily to change. Individuals were often unwilling to work with others of different backgrounds. Despite an apparent unity of all groups within the wartime FLN, no successful means for handling intraelite conflicts was ever developed. In part it seems as if the failure to adopt means of resolving intraelite conflicts was due to the fact that differences were not based on clearly recognized class, regional, confessional, or communal ties but rather resulted from a combination of historical accidents which had produced men whose views of politics differed significantly. If conflicts had been linked to linguistic or religious affiliations, as in Lebanon and India, the conflicts would have probably been just as intense, but they might have been seen as more natural and inevitable. Then procedures for resolving or accommodating these differences might have arisen. But the conflicts within the Algerian political elite were not of this nature, and consequently they were more difficult to resolve.[9]

9 Lucian Pye, in *Aspects of Political Development*, p. 108, says, "when roles are not well established and fully institutionalized the inevitable conflicts and disagreements of competing interests are likely to be seen as merely the conflict

Subordinate Hypotheses on Revolution and Political Elites

In addition to the major theme of this study which stresses the divisive effects of revolution upon political leaders in Algeria, there are a number of subordinate hypotheses that deal with the causes and consequences of a relatively fragmented elite structure. One of the strongest candidates for further systematic research is the hypothesis advanced in Chapter 8 that enduring political conflicts grow out of reversals in patterns of authority. In a revolutionary situation, where control over recruitment into the elite is not centralized, it is quite common to find rather highly placed leaders being surpassed in the hierarchy of formal influence by their former subordinates. When the authority of another person is accepted, it is usually accompanied by some rationalization concerning his right to rule, his great experience which qualifies him for that position, or his higher social status. But to the man who has been in top positions of influence and who is surpassed by his subordinates none of these arguments make much sense. Therefore, where turnover in elite positions is high, one would expect to find a large number of ex-leaders who find it extremely difficult to accommodate themselves to the current political order. New power-holders are often seen as usurpers, and restoration is hoped for long after it becomes politically impossible. And since revolutions are often the work of young men, there may well be many former premiers, deputies, and ministers in their 30s or 40s who cling to the hope of a return to power more ardently than would a man in his 60s or 70s.

A second hypothesis, presented in Chapter 9, examines the conditions under which political elites are transformed and restructured after the attainment of power. The most generally held idea is that over time the social composition of most political elites will change from dominance by men of relatively cosmopolitan, urban backgrounds toward those with more parochial orientations and stronger local ties. Since the Algerian case contradicts this general hypothesis, an alternate explanation is presented based on the assumption that with the acquisition of power the top revolutionary or nationalist elite will disintegrate because of the incompatible demands for power coming from the large number of contenders for top positions in government. The winner of the power struggle will then actively

---

of personalities. Conversely, the clash of personalities cannot be muted by the respectable assumption that differences are only the result of conflicting impersonal interests."

promote men from the secondary elite, a group that in general differs in social composition from the top elite. Usually this process will bring to power men of lower social status, but the opposite result is also possible if the secondary elite happens to consist of highly educated, cosmopolitan men. In fact, if the top elite is of lower social status than the secondary elite, transformations may be rapid, for there seems to be a strong tendency for power and social status to be positively correlated.

A third hypothesis presented in this study concerns structures of power, recruitment rates, and decision-making.[10] In Algeria there have been essentially three structures of power, each of which has sought to handle problems of authority within a fragmented elite. The first solution is collegial rule in which there is a large amount of mutual influence among political leaders. This structure is associated with a slow rate of secondary elite recruitment and relatively low capacity for making decisions. There is both stability and stagnation in such a system.

A second political structure is that of relatively autonomous centers of power within the elite. This arrangement allows considerable recruitment from the secondary elite, as each power center builds its own base of support. Decisions may be made independent of any consultation with other governmental groups, thus raising many possibilities for conflict and poor coordination of governmental activities. This system seems to be rather unstable, and pressures may develop which lead to either collegiality or authoritarian rule.

This latter solution, the authoritarian rule of a single man or a small group, is associated with a rapid rate of secondary elite recruitment and considerable capacity to act decisively, though often with little consideration of alternatives. The instability of this system stems from the high rate of top elite alienation brought about by the process of concentrating power. A coalition of dissidents may form to overthrow the common opponent, which raises once again the problem of dealing with the question of authority. Movements back and forth among these three systems of authority may easily be imagined, and some logical sequences may even be discovered on the basis of comparative analysis of more cases.

[10] For an insightful analysis of the question of the relation between power structures and decision-making capacity, see Frederick W. Frey, "Democracy and Reform in Developing Societies."

Political Socialization and Political Elites

In a study of the political socialization of the Algerian political elite some clarification of key terms and concepts is necessary. Since "political socialization" is a term frequently used in contemporary political analysis, it is particularly important to define its meaning.[11] As used in this study, political socialization refers to the process by which an individual acquires value-laden political identifications, gains knowledge of the political system, forms judgments of various types of political behavior, and develops skills which are useful in a political career. The process includes both indirect learning from experience as well as overt teaching through some "agency" of political socialization.

It is assumed here that elite political socialization can and does occur at all stages of the life cycle, both well before and after occupancy of a political role.[12] Furthermore, it seems clear that in many ways political socialization of political leaders differs significantly from that of most individuals, if only by the nature of direct participation in positions of top political influence. Most studies of political socialization, however, have dealt with the formation of attitudes and behavioral patterns within the population as a whole and thus provide few guidelines for the study of the same process within that very small portion of the population which becomes highly involved in politics.

Social background analysis is an approach to the study of elite behavior similar to the one adopted here.[13] It is often an abbreviated form of the study of political socialization in which only a few categories such as class, occupation, or education are used to summarize a broad range of experience. But it is also frequently derived from a more Marxist tradition. In this case, the model lying behind social background studies seems to be that certain social "facts,"

[11] Among the more important studies of political socialization, see Herbert Hyman, *Political Socialization;* Gabriel Almond and Sidney Verba, *The Civic Culture,* especially Chapter 12; Robert D. Hess and David Easton, "The Child's Changing Image of the President," *Public Opinion Quarterly,* Winter 1960; Fred Greenstein, *Children and Politics;* and Richard E. Dawson and Kenneth Prewitt, *Political Socialization.*

[12] This point is argued quite forcefully by Kenneth Prewitt, Heinz Eulau, and Betty Zisk, "Political Socialization and Political Roles," *Public Opinion Quarterly,* 30, No. 4 (Winter 1966–67).

[13] Frederick W. Frey and William Quandt, *Social Background Analysis of Political Elites* (forthcoming). Also, Donald R. Matthews, *The Social Backgrounds of Political Decision Makers.*

such as class origin, can predict what interests an individual will have and whether he will behave on the basis of these interests. Thus if one knows the occupation of an individual, for example, one may infer many of his attitudes because of assumed interests related to occupational roles.

In the broader view of political socialization adopted here, social background information is used primarily to indicate types of experiences which in turn tend to produce values and attitudes which then influence behavior. In this view, however, values, behavior, and socialization are linked reciprocally rather than in a unidirectional sense.[14] These two simple models are shown in Table 2.1.

TABLE 2.1 TWO MODELS OF THE EFFECTS OF SOCIAL BACK-GROUND FACTORS ON BEHAVIOR

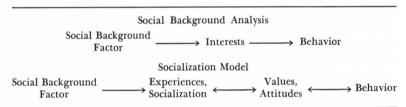

Subordinate concepts in the study of political socialization describe the process and its outcomes in more detail. In this study four "agents" of political socialization will be stressed, namely the family, the school, the occupation, and the political group itself. While what one learns or is taught by each agent is a matter for empirical research to determine, it is assumed that family and school experiences produce more value-laden orientations to politics, while later experiences primarily alter behavior by changing one's knowledge of the political system and political procedures.[15]

It is argued, however, that unique historical events can have a profound influence in altering beliefs and values and may produce sets of attitudes that are hard to change with later experience.

---

[14] Heinz Eulau et al., "Career Perspectives of American State Legislators," in Dwaine Marvick, ed., *Political Decision-makers*, pp. 218–263, stress that in the context of American state politics social background is a good predictor of the point at which an individual will enter politics, but that once involved in the political system an individual is less influenced by his social origins and status credentials than he is by his immediate environment.

[15] See, in particular, Hess and Easton, "Child's Image of the President," and Greenstein, *Children and Politics*.

Unique events of this nature in Algeria are the failure of the Blum-Viollette proposal in 1938, the repression of the 1945 uprising, the revolution itself, and the crisis of summer 1962. These historical events, by the differential impact they had on various groups within the elite, have had a great influence on Algerian politics.[16] Individuals for whom these major historical phenomena constitute a common point of reference in their political formation can be seen as belonging to the same political generation. Very real generation gaps can occur which divide individuals whose chronological age differs by only a few years.

Two outcomes of the process of political socialization are that individuals acquire different political skills and come to hold contrasting images of themselves and others.[17] Four political skill groups have been suggested by Harold Lasswell. Lasswell identifies the "administrator," the "organizer," the "agitator," and the "theoretician" as distinctive types of political actors.[18] Their differing skills are related to the process of political socialization. In addition to these skills, self images and images of others serve as an important basis for an individual's feeling that he has a right to exercise power or that he has a "calling" for politics.[19]

A second major term used in this study is "political elite." The

[16] Harold D. Lasswell, "Agenda for the Study of Political Elites," in Marvick, *Political Decision-makers*, implies that political leaders are largely obliged to deal with problems imposed by historical forces and that the response of these leaders is in part understandable in light of their social origins and routes of ascent to power. In general, the question of whether changes in stage of development or type of system produce changes in the type of men who become influential in politics, or whether it is the change in the type of political actors which leads to changes in the system, is difficult to answer. It is here assumed that no single individual or small group has much influence in changing the type of political system under most conditions but that once systems do change, as from colonial rule to revolution to independence, the personnel in elite positions alters dramatically. This stress on the role of the system as an independent variable finds support in the work of John C. Wahlke et al., *The Legislative System* and in F. W. Frey, *The Turkish Political Elite*. Both studies find that formally competitive systems produce different kinds of elites than noncompetitive systems.

[17] Marvick, *Political Decision-makers*, p. 15, argues that little attention has been paid to "self images" of political leaders and to the opinions they hold of each other. Nor, he adds, is much known of variations in degree of commitment to "rules of the game" and of differences in skill and ability in politics.

[18] Harold D. Lasswell, *Psychopathology and Politics* and *Power and Personality*. For Lasswell the "organizer" is merely a subgroup of the category administrator. Here he is treated as a separate type of political actor.

[19] Max Weber, in "Politics as a Vocation," is particularly informative in his discussion of politicians who believe they have a "mission" or "calling." Hans Gerth and C. Wright Mills, eds., *From Max Weber: Essays in Sociology*.

simplest and most useful way to define a political elite is to say that it consists of those individuals in a society who exercise a disproportionately large amount of influence within the political system.[20] Quite often scholars have used a formal institutional definition of the political elite, but it is also possible to include other "influentials" within this definition. Students of newly independent nations and of authoritarian systems where traditions of citizen participation are weak have frequently stressed the virtual monopoly of the political elite in determining public policy.[21]

Of the many possible definitions of the Algerian political elite, the term as used here refers to a finite set of incumbents of identifiable roles within the authoritative political bodies of the FLN and the Algerian government which existed between 1954 and 1968. Three hundred and sixty individuals who were members of any one of the major decision-making bodies were considered to belong to the political elite.[22] (See Appendix A for a discussion of methodology).

Within the Algerian political elite it is useful to distinguish between top leaders and secondary leaders. Secondary leaders are those who held positions only within the *Comité des 22*, the CNRA, the two Assemblies, and the Central Committee. Those who were part of any of the other major political bodies, whether ministers, in the CCE, members of the Political Bureau or of the Council of the Revolution, are considered to be top political leaders. In all there were 87 top leaders occupying 179 top roles and 133 secondary roles, as well as 273 secondary leaders occupying 379 roles in the political system.

For all members of the political elite an effort was made to group individuals according to the type of political socialization they experienced. Since the resulting categories are not ones commonly

[20] See Harold D. Lasswell and Abraham Kaplan, *Power and Society,* p. 201.

[21] See Dankwart A. Rustow, "The Study of Elites: Who's Who, When and How," *World Politics,* 18, No. 4 (July 1966): 690–717.

[22] Members of the following bodies were studied: the *Comité des 22* and the *Comité Révolutionnaire d'Unité et d'Action* (CRUA) in 1954; the two *Comités de Coordination et d'Exécution* (CCE) of 1956 and 1957; the *Gouvernement Provisoire de la République Algérienne* (GPRA) of 1958, 1960 and 1961; the *Conseil National de la Révolution Algérienne* (CNRA) of 1956 and those known members from later years; the members of the *Conseil des Ministres* of 1962, 1963, 1964, 1965, 1966 and 1968; the members of the *Bureau Politique du* FLN of 1962 and 1964; the members of the *Conseil de la Révolution* of 1965; the members of the *Assemblée Nationale Constituante* in 1962 and the *Assemblée Nationale* of 1964; and the *Comité Central du* FLN of 1964.

used in Algeria (although their meaning would be readily apparent to most informed Algerians) some further explanations are needed.

The smallest group within the political elite is that of the Liberal Politicians. This term designates those men whose early involvement in the nationalist movement took the form of participation in one of the moderate political groups that sought to act within the French parliamentary system. The original group from which the Liberals came was quite influential during the 1930s, but very few remained in positions of influence within the *Front de Libération Nationale* after 1954. Ferhat Abbas and a few of his followers in the *Union Démocratique du Manifeste Algérien* (UDMA) are the most prominent Liberals. During the revolution they typically held important political positions, and after independence some were ministers or deputies during the first two years of Ben Bella's rule. By 1968 their influence within the elite was negligible.

The Radical Politicians form the second group within the political elite. Like the Liberals they received their primary experience in politics during the colonial period, particularly within the *Parti du Peuple Algérien* (PPA) and the *Mouvement pour le Triomphe des Libertés Démocratiques* (MTLD). To be considered a Radical by this definition an individual must have gained some prominence within the PPA or MTLD, such as membership on the Central Committee or candidacy in an election, and during the revolution he must have continued to occupy positions of political influence. This group of Radicals was extremely important within the GPRA, but since independence many have been excluded from politics, though frequently they hold key positions within the state economic system or in the administration.

The third group whose members received a major part of their experience in politics before the war for independence is that of the Revolutionaries. This term is not meant to connote any particular psychological attributes; it is chosen to highlight the key role of this group in beginning the Algerian revolution. The Revolutionaries were men who were active mainly at a secondary level within the pre-1954 nationalist parties, and in particular within the MTLD, but who broke with the ongoing political process in 1954 or soon thereafter and assumed military roles within the revolution. The largest number of the Revolutionaries were members of the *Organisation Spéciale* (OS), a clandestine paramilitary group which formed in the late 1940s, but some members of the UDMA, of the *Parti Communiste Algérien* (PCA) and even of the Association of Reformist Ulama are considered Revolutionaries because of their participation in political roles before the revolution and in military ones following 1954.[23] Ben Bella, the first President of Algeria, is considered a Revolutionary in these terms. The Revolutionaries were extremely important during the war but have fallen rapidly from positions of political influence since 1962. Several now lead opposition in exile groups.

Two groups within the political elite entered top political roles only after the revolution had begun. The Military constitutes the first of these groups, and is composed of men who rose within the *Armée de Libération Nationale* (ALN) to positions of influence during the war and who acquired considerable political power after independence. Among this group of men who entered politics by way of a career in the army, it is useful to distinguish the leaders of the guerrilla war within Algeria, the *maquisards,* from the more professionally trained soldiers who gained influence within the well-organized armies stationed in Tunisia and Morocco. While sharing some important convictions, these two subgroups have often been in conflict. After cooperating in order to remove Ben Bella from power in June 1965, these two groups split in December 1967.

The last group to become part of the political elite is composed of Intellectuals. Like the term Revolutionary, the word Intellectual has some undesired connotations [24] and is here used only to describe those individuals who, largely because of intellectual skills either as theoreticians or technicians, were brought into the political elite during the last years of the revolution. During the war the Intellectuals were primarily confined to secondary roles, but with independence they came to exert considerable influence as ministers, or as lower-ranking administrators, particularly after Boumedienne came to power in 1965. The "technicians" and the "theoreticians," —or the "specialists" and the "generalists"—the latter consisting of some Marxist ideologists, constitute subgroups within the category of Intellectuals. In alliance with the Military, the Intellectuals have dominated important sectors of the administration since 1965.

[23] Some os members never participated in the military effort within Algeria after 1954 but can be considered Revolutionaries because of their association with the os and their role in organizing the war for independence. Ben Bella, Khider, Ait Ahmed, and Boudiaf are included in this group.

[24] A broad use of the term "intellectuals" is found in Edward Shils, "The Intellectuals in the Political Development of New States," *World Politics,* April 1960, pp. 329–368.

To summarize, the five groups around which the discussion of the Algerian political elite will center are defined primarily in terms of earlier organizational membership, skills, and time of entry into various types of political activity. Virtually all members of the political elite can be seen as belonging to one of these groups, although reliable data are available to categorize only about one half of the elite in these terms. Successive chapters will focus on the distinctive experiences of individuals in each of these five groups during the colonial period and the revolution. In addition, the history of the revolution and of the postindependence period will be analyzed in terms of the relationships among Liberals, Radicals, Revolutionaries, the Military, and Intellectuals.

3
The Liberal Politicians

The Algerian Liberal politicians, who constituted the first and most moderate group of nationalists, entered careers in politics in the 1930s by a rather orderly process. Early experiences in the family and in school produced sentiments among Liberals which led them to demand from France both equality and reform. The means adopted by the Liberals to attain these goals were persuasion and petition. The Liberals were the most conciliatory of the subgroups within the elite, the most willing to bargain and compromise, and the most tolerant of diversity. In addition, the Liberals were deeply committed to modernization, taking a rather paternalistic view of their responsibilities for guiding the backward masses to a better way of life.

This chapter focuses on the origins of these ideas among the Liberals and on the first major crisis in their careers, the failure of the goal of assimilation. The inability to achieve this primary demand within the legal colonial system opened the way for more aggressive men with views of politics which differed markedly from those of the Liberals. Who were the Liberals, how did they enter politics, and what were the consequences of their failure to obtain their initial goals?

The term Liberal politician could be applied to a large number of politically active Algerians during the 1930s, but few from this group managed to retain influence after 1954. Nonetheless, because of their formative influence over later generations of nationalists, and because of the contributions of a few individuals during the war and since independence, the Liberals deserve more treatment than their numerical strength might seem to warrant. Their number is small; only five members of the Algerian political elite, as defined here, can easily be considered Liberal politicians. These five are Ferhat Abbas, Ahmed Francis, Ahmed Boumendjel, Abderrahmane Farès, and Ahmed Ghersi. None has been in any position of political power since June 1965, but previous to that date these five men held a remarkable number of offices. The political roles filled by these Liberals include President of the Provisional Government (GPRA), Minister of Finance in the GPRA, President of the Provisional Executive of 1962, President of the National Constituent Assembly, Minister of Finance, Minister of Public Works and Reconstruction, five deputies to the first Assembly, and one to the second Assembly.

The average year of birth for this group is 1907, ranging from 1899 to 1912. At least four of the Liberals were born in villages or small towns, but all received university educations. Two were lawyers, one a notary, one a doctor, and one a pharmacist. All held political office within the French colonial system in some type of parliamentary body, but eventually all but one openly rallied to the FLN. The importance of these social background factors will be apparent as the careers of these men are studied in more detail.

To understand the political beliefs and behavior of the Liberals one must look at their political socialization as a process which began early within their families, continued throughout their school years, and developed further as they actively became involved in politics as adolescents or young adults. At each stage in their socialization new experiences affected their self-image and their political skills, and eventually they received political training that allowed them for many years to play important roles in politics.

Family Political Socialization

Of the Liberals, only Ferhat Abbas has revealed much about his early life, but in many respects his experiences are typical of those of an entire generation.[1] Abbas was born into a society which had been greatly disrupted by the impact of French colonization. Traditional Algerian society by the twentieth century, as represented by large landowners and religious brotherhoods, was far too weak to provide the social milieu for a nationalistic movement of resistance to the French. This meant that the nationalist movement in Algeria could not form around a core of leaders with traditionally high status, both respected by the Muslim community and yet relatively progressive in their ideas and methods of political organization. Nor could the Algerians follow the path of the Moroccan nationalists who were able to use the monarchy as a unifying symbol for the country. Rather, the Algerian leaders of the 1930s were perhaps more products of French schools than of their own societies, and not surprisingly their first political demands were for equal rights with Frenchmen, including French citizenship, rather than independence.

The contribution of the family to the political socialization of the Liberals was much the same as it was for other Algerian nationalists. Within the family the Liberal politicians, most of whom came from moderately advantaged families, learned a limited number of values of great significance for their political careers. The politically relevant values that they acquired primarily concerned questions of personal and group identity. Whether one was born in an Arab family of Constantine or in a peasant Berber family of Kabylia, a young Algerian was sure to become aware that he was a Muslim. What this meant for his daily life differed from family to family, but the simple fact of being a Muslim made him sense the basic differences between himself and the European society he encountered in town or at school. And even if a Muslim tried to ignore this element of his identity, his own society as well as the French *colons* would constantly remind him that Muslim and French were not to be confused.

Overt political socialization within the family was relatively rare for the Liberals, mainly because of the virtual absence of political life among Muslims until about 1930. In this the Liberals differ most from later generations. It seems that the Liberals, although

[1] Ferhat Abbas has written *Le jeune algérien* and *La nuit coloniale.* Jean Lacouture in *Cinq hommes et la France* has a good chapter on Abbas. In addition, the author interviewed Abbas on February 17 and 22, 1967, and on May 17, 1967.

aware' of their separate identity because of family experiences, did not learn from their families the feelings of anger or hostility toward the colonial system which marked following generations. Later they developed some of these sentiments, but more as an intellectual response to oppressive conditions than as early emotional identifications.

While the Liberals certainly knew of the abuses of the colonial system at an early age, many of them seem to have been aware of the economic and social advantages that France could bring to the backward Muslim masses. This may be due in part to the fact that their families had profited from the colonial system. Abbas's father, for example, was the *qā'id* (headman) of a small village and had been made a member of the *Légion d'Honneur* for his services to France.

Family socialization, then, for the Liberals, seems to have been important in three ways. First, the family established the basis of a separate, non-French identity by bringing up children as Muslims and by relating stories and myths telling of the glorious Algerian past before the French came.[2] Secondly, and rather in contradiction to the first point, the family seems often to have transmitted a relatively benevolent image of France to the Liberals. Lastly, family experiences led the Liberals to a concern for modernization, particularly in its western forms. Abbas, living in a somewhat privileged home among poor peasants, developed an almost paternalistic feeling of responsibility toward the masses. In his view the peasants, in order to enter the modern world, must be led by the few intellectuals who were able to obtain western educations. Abbas at one time even believed that economic and social progress was more important than political rights and that these were in fact the necessary prelude to the effective political participation of the masses.[3]

School Socialization and the Concern for Equality

Schools and education, as well as being the key to the Liberals' ideas of social development, were instrumental in transforming these vague family-based sentiments into political beliefs. The Algerian politicians of the 1930s were a highly educated group by

---

[2] An example of the passing down of oral traditions is given by Malek Bennabi, *Memoires d'un témoin du siècle*, pp. 9–11.

[3] Abbas interview, February 17, 1967.

most standards. Virtually all of them managed to complete their secondary education, and most went on to college. In this they differed dramatically from the Algerian Muslim society around them. While most Algerians through their families had developed some awareness of their separate identity and may have even formed a negative image of French colonialism, it was through the schools —almost exclusively French schools for the Liberals—that Algerian Muslims became aware of politics. In school one learned about political issues and became aware of the process of using political influence. If the family created a primitive sense of political identity, it was the schools that created political awareness.

For the Liberal politicians the school experience was particularly important in introducing them to the issue of equality. For a later generation of Algerians school life was more directly related to politics, but for this earliest group school was above all the place where one learned the value of "equality of opportunity." Since equality in one form or another was the primary demand of the Muslim elite for the first three decades of the twentieth century, it is no surprise that a concern for equality led directly to politics.

The awareness of equality as a political issue was the result of at least two processes. One, for those in French schools, was the teaching of French history and the ideals of the French revolution. The contrast between what one learned in school and what one knew to be true in Algeria under the *colon*-dominated system was striking. For some Algerians the conclusion was reached that France, if only she were aware of the injustices in Algeria, would institute reforms.[4] Hence the image, so widespread even today, of a benevolent France in contrast to the narrow-minded, racist *colon* population of Algeria (which, it was often stressed, was largely Spanish, Italian, or Maltese in origin anyway).

The second means toward awareness of the issue of equality came from one's own efforts in school. Ferhat Abbas, the best known of this group of Liberal politicians and one of the few who has played any significant part in politics since 1954, has told how in school he realized that the Arabs were intellectually and morally as good as Frenchmen. As many Algerians of a later generation were also to stress, Abbas claimed that Muslims in Algeria had no feeling of being inferior to the *colons*. Morally, they felt themselves to be superior, in part because their women "did not get into trouble"

---

[4] Abbas, *La nuit coloniale*, p. 115.

as often as French women. And intellectually they felt equal to the *colons,* for, as Abbas proudly said, "I often used to get first place in French language exams." [5]

Another dimension of political awareness concerned the means by which Algerian Muslims might hope to achieve greater equality. This type of awareness seems to have been developed most effectively through newspapers, journals, pamphlets, and books, especially insofar as these reflected the ideas of the nascent groups of reformist Muslims. To appreciate the attitudes and behavior of the Liberal politicians and to understand why they differed from later generations of Algerian Muslims, one must look at the political environment with which they came in contact during their adolescence and early adulthood.

The Political Climate Between the Two World Wars

The years between 1915 and 1925 were largely formative ones for the Liberals who became part of the political elite of the 1950s and 1960s. Before 1915 most were too young to understand politics, and after 1925 most were becoming actors in the political system and in this way forming the new generation of politicians which was to emerge in the 1940s and 1950s. Thus this decade, which began with the First World War, was particularly important for the first group of modern Algerian politicians.[6]

While it would be premature to speak of Muslim political parties during this period, there were nonetheless a small number of individuals and groups who articulated political demands on behalf of the Muslim Algerian population. Of these groups the "Young Algerians" were the most influential in forming the attitudes of the Liberals of the 1930s.[7] As early as 1911 the term Young Algerian was used in the French press to describe a group of politically active young Muslims of French culture. The model for these young men seems to have been the "Young Tunisian" movement more than the Young Turks.

At the time of the First World War there were perhaps 1000

---

[5] Abbas interview.

[6] Jacques Berque, in *French North Africa: The Maghrib Between Two World Wars,* covers the social, cultural, economic, and political changes during this period.

[7] Charles-Robert Ageron, in "Le mouvement 'jeune-algérien,'" *Etudes maghrébines* pp. 217–243, gives the best summary and analysis of this movement.

Young Algerians, a few of them practicing liberal professions such as law and medicine and many others active as teachers. Their earliest coherent political demand was for obligatory military service for Muslims, for in this they saw "a sign of confidence which we shall try to justify." [8] The motivation for this peculiar demand was the feeling that if Algerians served in the French army, France would no longer be able to deny them certain political rights which they desired.

These Young Algerians were not yet nationalists, "an injurious and unjust" term of abuse as they saw it.[9] A contemporary described their attitudes as follows: They are unshakably attached to the French *patrie,* and they do *not* demand the political rights of French citizens except for those Algerians who are willing to abandon their personal religious status.[10] This latter statement does not seem to have applied to all of the Young Algerians, for many were unwilling to give up their religious obligations as Muslims as a prelude to gaining French political citizenship. It was over this issue that the movement eventually was to split.

After World War I the French instituted some modest reforms in Algeria, partly in response to demands of the Young Algerians. The Young Algerians, for the most part, were not satisfied. In 1919 the movement divided, with one wing accepting naturalization as French citizens and giving up Muslim religious status. The other group of non-naturalized Young Algerians looked to the Emir Khaled as its leader. Khaled was the grandson of the hero of Algeria's resistance to France in the nineteenth century, Abd al Qadir, and this must have added to his prestige among some segments of Muslim society. He had also served for many years in the French army and was even a graduate of St. Cyr. Khaled was elected to political office several times, particularly in the *Délégations financières,* an elected body with modest budgetary powers composed of Europeans and Muslims. In 1920, after his election to the *Délégations financières,* the journal *L'Afrique française* labeled him as representing "a tendency which one could qualify as extremist." [11]

Khaled's ideas were spread largely through numerous mass meet-

[8] Robert Aron, *Les origines de la guerre d'Algérie,* p. 61.

[9] Ageron, "Le mouvement 'jeune-algérien,'" *Etudes maghrébines,* p. 230.

[10] Cherif Benhabilès, *L'Algérie française vue par un indigène,* p. 116.

[11] *L'Afrique française,* July-August, 1920, p. 250. For a useful article on Khaled, see Charles-Robert Ageron, "L'Emir Khaled, petit-fils d'Abdelkader, fut-il le premier nationaliste algérien?", *Revue de l'occident musulman,* No. 2, 2ᵉ semestre, 1966, pp. 9-49.

ings and by means of his French language journal, *Ikdam*. Ferhat Abbas explicitly acknowledges his debt to Khaled and his journal. Another young Algerian of this period, Malek Bennabi, whose name was to become more associated with a group of Arab-Muslim intellectuals rather than with the politicians, recalls that during his adolescence he and his family and friends avidly awaited each week the new issue of *Ikdam*. According to Bennabi, "*Ikdam* first introduced me to precise political topics. It denounced the expropriation of the Algerian peasants which was reaching unimaginable proportions at this time. . . . *Ikdam* denounced the abuses of the administration and its obscurantism." [12] Abbas has presented a fuller version of Khaled's demands, including proportional representation in parliament for Muslims, suppression of the "laws of exception," obligatory education, a free press, and freedom for natives to go to France.[13]

These reforms in the 1920s were too audacious for the *colons* to accept, and Khaled was forced into exile in 1923. The reformist tendency was not dead, however, and several journals and newspapers carried on this tradition.[14] Abbas refers to some of these publications, particularly *La voix des humbles,* which stressed equality and education for the Muslims; *Islam; L'étendard* and *La tribune* of Victor Spielman, a liberal European admirer of Khaled; *Le trait d'union,* also edited by Spielman, and notable in part as the journal in which Abbas published his first political essays; *Attakadoum,* another journal for which Abbas frequently wrote; and *Rachidi,* a pre-World War I journal published near Abbas's birthplace, which called for equality and respect for Muslim culture.

Bennabi, whose cultural background was primarily Arabic, also mentions French language journals, such as *La lutte sociale,* of Spielman. Living as he did in the region near Constantine, not far from the Tunisian border, Bennabi also read Tunisian papers such as *Az Zohra* and *Al Asr al Djadid*. In 1920 an Arab language newspaper, *An Nadjah,* was founded in Constantine by an Algerian who had studied at the Tunisian university of Zitouna. Despite the low quality of this paper, Bennabi claims that simply because it was written in Arabic it represented a challenge to the colonial administration. It was read avidly in Bennabi's home town of

[12] Bennabi, *Témoin du siècle,* p. 113.
[13] Abbas, *La nuit coloniale,* p. 117.
[14] See Ali Merad, "La formation de la presse musulmane en Algérie, 1919–1939," IBLA, No. 105, 1st trimester, 1964.

Tebessa.[15] From 1922 to 1924 a more nationalistic Algerian journal appeared, *El Muntaqid,* edited by the future leader of the Reformist Ulama group, Abd al Hamid Ben Badis.

These, then, were the groups and their means of expressing their ideas which were important in shaping the generation of the Liberal politicians. The region of Constantine, the easternmost department of Algeria and the least heavily influenced by *colon* rule, was the area where these ideas seem to have had greatest currency. It is perhaps not surprising then that a highly disproportionate number of Algerian political leaders came from Constantine. Of all those involved in politics before 1954 who played some important elite role following 1954 as well, 60 percent came from the department of Constantine, although only 40 percent of the Muslim population lived there. Ferhat Abbas attributed this to the proximity of Tunisia, the influence of Zitouna University, and the activities of the Old Destour party in Tunisia. Among the politicians of his generation there was a saying, "The light comes from the East," referring to Tunisia.[16] It was presumably by way of Tunisia that information about Mustapha Kemal in Turkey was obtained, and this led to a certain amount of "Turcophilia," as described by Bennabi.[17] Abbas, in fact, used Kemal as part of his pen name, in admiration for Atatürk.

Ferhat Abbas and his generation became involved directly in politics during the 1930s. Their family heritage and, in particular, religious feelings had kept them from following the small group of secularist Muslims who became naturalized French citizens in the 1920s. From their school days they had become concerned with equality and reforms, and these interests were reinforced and given more content as these young men became aware of the other political groups, such as the Young Algerians, and their publications. During this phase of their political socialization they seem to have developed further their already strong commitment to modernization.

In order to obtain a better economic and social status for the Muslims of Algeria they thought that equal political rights must be granted by France. They asked for "assimilation" into the French political community but insisted on maintaining their Muslim statutes for settling such personal litigation as that concerning

[15] Bennabi, *Témoin du siècle,* p. 74.
[16] Abbas interview, February 17, 1967.
[17] Bennabi, *Témoin du siècle,* p. 74.

marriage and inheritance. Political equality would allow the Muslims to evolve socially and economically, and eventually they would take over some political functions in a decentralized French commonwealth. Ferhat Abbas has remarked that to him it did not seem important that Algerians would remain French citizens for some time, for he had noticed that Algerian Jews had become French citizens and that their economic conditions had improved because of it.[18] Assimilation, then, became the key to their hopes, and for this goal they became actively involved in politics in the 1930s.

For Muslim Algerians in the 1930s there were few opportunities to exercise political influence. The best that the Liberals could hope for was to win elections to any of several political institutions which allowed token Muslim representation. The most important of these institutions were the *Conseils municipaux*, the *Conseils généraux*, and the *Délégations financières*. As early as 1847 a few Muslims were appointed by the Governor General of Algeria to be members of the municipal councils. In 1884 these positions became elective, although the number of Muslim representatives was reduced and their power was curtailed. In 1919 the electorate for these positions was broadened slightly, and the number of seats for Muslims was raised to a maximum of one-third the total.[19] Thus a few Muslims were able to participate in local politics but under great restraints and with limited powers.

A second institution which accepted Muslim representation was the *Conseil général*, a parliamentary group which existed at the departmental level. Since 1855 the Governor General had appointed a few Muslims to these bodies, and in 1872 this number was fixed at six *assesseurs musulmans* for each department. In 1919 the reforms of the Jonnart Law raised this number to nine.

The last institutions to be created which accepted Muslim members were the *Délégations financières* and the *Conseil supérieur*, both created in 1898. The *Délégations financières* had 21 Muslim members, less than one-third the total, and the *Conseil supérieur* gave 7 of its 60 seats to Muslims. As with the other legislative bodies mentioned, the powers of these were not particularly important, although the *Délégations financières* could discuss and vote the budget for Algeria.

Within the relatively rigid political framework provided by the

[18] Abbas interview, February 17, 1967.
[19] See Vincent Confer, *France and Algeria: The Problem of Civil and Political Reform, 1870–1920*.

colonial system, the Liberals were able to contend for a few hundred political positions, of which only 55 were not at the local level. The Liberals were, of course, not the only competitors for these offices, since the *colons* actively encouraged more "moderate" Muslims to present themselves as candidates, and indeed most of the incumbents were those called *beni oui ouis*, or "yes men" by the more reform-minded Algerians.

In 1930 the Algerian Muslim members of the *Délégations financières* had the following occupations: large landowners, 15; commerce, 2; administration, 2; liberal professions, 2.[20] Only one of these 21 delegates played a noticeable political role after 1954. This was the Liberal Ahmed Ghersi, a lawyer who was to become a deputy in the National Assembly after independence. The only other Algerian leader of note since 1954 to have participated in these institutions during the 1930s was Ferhat Abbas, who between 1933 and 1936 was a member of the *Délégations financières*, was Municipal Councillor from Sétif and a member of the *Conseil général* of Alger.

It seems clear that, except for a few Algerians whose political careers typically ended by 1954, most politically active Algerians did not pass through this stage of political socialization within the legal parliamentary institutions of the 1930s. Other events were more critical to the developments which came later, so that a brief discussion of alternate means of political participation during this period is needed. The political activities of the Liberals, outside of their elected roles, took place largely within a group formed in 1927 called the *Fédération des élus indigènes d'Algérie*. Its 150 members consisted largely of doctors, lawyers and teachers whose purpose it was to advance assimilationist aims while trying to co-ordinate the efforts of the moderate reformers.[21] By 1933 some organizational changes were made within this group, and under the leadership of Dr. Bendjelloul a *Fédération des élus musulmans* was formed in Constantine, soon to be imitated in the other two departments of Algeria. The journals which expressed the ideas of this group were *Entente* and *La voix indigène*.

The Liberals' Competitors: Messali Hadj and the Ulama

Two other political groups emerged during the 1930s, and though they were not responsible for directly forming the Liberals who are

[20] Maurice Viollette, *L'Algérie vivrà-t-elle?* p. 301.
[21] See André Nouschi, *La naissance du nationalisme algérien,* Chapter 3.

the focus of this chapter, they need to be considered for two reasons. First, they did interact with and in this way influenced the Liberals. Secondly, they were extremely important groups during the 1940s. These two groups, the religious modernists or Reformist Ulama, and the young workers and intellectuals around Messali Hadj, had one important thing in common which distinguished them from the Liberals, namely, a commitment to Algeria as a nation distinct from France. Through the combined action of these two groups the idea of nationalism was introduced into Algeria.

The Algerian Association of Ulama was founded in 1931 and became associated throughout the 1930s with the name of Abd al Hamid Ben Badis. The Ben Badis family for centuries had been influential in Constantine, and Abd al Hamid's own father had been a member of the *Conseil supérieur*. Under the influence of the Islamic reformers of the Arab east such as Muhammad Abduh and Rashid Rida, Ben Badis, who had been educated at Zitouna mosque university in Tunis, became deeply concerned with the status of Islam in Algeria. As early as 1912 he had set up a school in Constantine to teach Arabic and the religious sciences. The influence of the Sufi brotherhoods over the masses was still great, and Ben Badis's first steps aimed at reforming the degenerate and superstitious Islam of the *marabouts,* or holy men.[22] One of the venerable members of the Algerian political elite, Mohammedi Said, was later to say about this period:

> The Ulama were most important on the cultural front. Their actions gave back to the Algerians their national language and helped them to recover their faith from those who had corrupted it. Before the Ulama, every home had a candle burning for the patron saint of the house. Islam was very degenerate in Algeria at that time.[23]

In the 1920s Ben Badis began to propagate his ideas in various Arabic language publications, most importantly in *Al Muntaqid,* followed by *Ash Shihab.*[24] An early follower, Tayeb el Oqbi, founded *Al Islah* in Biskra a short time later. These publications were soon joined by *Al Bassa'ir,* which served as the official organ of the

---

[22] For an introduction to the Algerian Ulama, see L. Carl Brown, "The Islamic Reform Movement in North Africa," *Journal of Modern African Studies,* Vol. 11, No. 1 (1964), pp. 55–64.

[23] Interview with Mohammedi Said.

[24] A study of the role of *Ash Shihab* in the development of Algerian nationalist ideas has been undertaken by Muhammad al Mili, editor of *El Moudjahid* in Arabic in 1967.

Ulama. A modest revival in scholarship in Arabic was also under way, and in 1928 Mubarek al Mili published the first volume of a history of Algeria in Arabic.[25] In 1932 his second volume appeared, as did a history of Algeria by Tewfik al Madani.[26]

The most important political activity of the Ulama was their propagation of the idea that Algerians belonged to a nation with a long and glorious past. With time the idea of Algerian independence also appeared, but in the mid-1930s the major political role of the Ulama was that of articulating the themes of a distinct Algerian identity, as summarized in the slogan, "Islam is my religion, Arabic is my language, Algeria is my fatherland." In 1936, when Ferhat Abbas made his famous statement about his inability to discover the Algerian nation,[27] it was Ben Badis who replied most eloquently, affirming the existence of Algeria and the impossibility of ever becoming part of France.[28] In short, the Ulama fulfilled the double role of weakening the Sufi orders and of preparing the masses for more "nationalistic" ideas in the 1940s.

Since the Ulama's primary emphasis was on education and not politics, especially after the death of Ben Badis in 1940, there were few Algerian leaders of the 1950s and 1960s who had been directly involved with them. Tewfik al Madani is perhaps the best known of the Ulama to have played a political role since 1954. The deputies Mezhoudi, Chibane, and Kheirredine in the first Assembly after independence were also involved directly with the Ulama. Mezhoudi's comments on the importance of the Ulama are representative of the thoughts of many religiously oriented Algerian politicians:

Because of my background in Arab culture, I found myself with the Ulama. Already I had concluded that much of politics is demagogy. Talk of independence at that time was a bit fanciful. Instead, we needed to educate the people first, especially since maraboutism was still very strong.[29]

Many others, including President Houari Boumedienne himself were indirectly influenced by the Ulama because they had attended

25 Mubarek al Mili, *Tarikh al jazā'ir fi-l-qadim wa-l-jadid*, Volumes 1 and 2, The first volume, originally printed in 1928, covered Algerian history before the Arab conquest and was the first treatment by an Algerian Muslim of the pre-Arab period as part of Algeria's national past.

26 See the article by S. Bencheneb, "Quelques historiens arabes modernes de l'Algérie," *Revue africaine*, 1956.

27 Published in *L'Entente*, February 23, 1936.

28 See the translation and commentary by René Jammes, "Cheikh Ben Badis et la France en Avril 1936," *L'Afrique et l'Asie*, 57, 1961.

29 Interview with Brahim Mezhoudi.

their schools. The Ulama's importance, however, is less in having trained the political elite than in having prepared the masses for nationalism and some degree of modernization.[30] Ben Badis is, even today, the only prominent leader of the 1930s whom Algerians of all political tendencies can regard as something of a national hero.[31]

The other political leader of this period, Messali Hadj, has suffered the opposite fate. Despite his great influence both in forming the later political elite and in spreading the idea of Algerian independence among the masses, he is universally condemned by all present political tendencies and has lived since independence in exile in France. He is not a member of what is here considered the political elite, since he has never, since 1954, been among the leaders of the FLN, but his importance is too great for him to be ignored.

Messali Hadj was born in 1898 in Tlemcen, a town near the Moroccan border where traditions had remained relatively strong. The son of a shoemaker, Messali received little education, served briefly in the French army, and worked in France for several years while simultaneously attending classes in Paris at the School of Oriental Languages. During these years he married a French woman who was a member of the French Communist Party, and he too became a member.

In 1924 a new political group had formed among the Algerian workers in the region around Paris. The Emir Khaled after his exile from Algeria had gone to Paris, where he had given a conference which had apparently touched the nationalist sentiments of his listeners, who began to call for an independent North Africa. Among these emigrants a new political group, the *Etoile Nord Africaine* (ENA), found its first recruits.[32] By 1926 Messali Hadj was associated with the ENA, and in 1927 he became its president. From the outset the *Etoile Nord Africaine* was more radical in doctrine

[30] According to Launay, the villages in Oranie where reformist *medersas* (schools in which instruction is in Arabic) had been established were the ones where "nationalism" was strongest. See Michel Launay, *Les paysans algériens,* p. 148. This was also argued by a secular nationalist, Arezki Bouzida, who claimed that nationalist activity was most successful in areas where the Ulama were strong. Interview with Arezki Bouzida.

[31] A clandestine propaganda leaflet published by the radical opposition party, the ORP, on April 14, 1967, simultaneously treated "three anniversaries for the Algerian patriots and socialists," the birthday of Lenin, the adoption of the *Charte d'Alger,* and the death of Ben Badis.

[32] Abbas, *La nuit coloniale,* pp. 135–136; and Amar Ouzegane, *Le meilleur combat,* p. 177.

and tactics than any other Algerian political organization, for it demanded independence and resorted to agitation and propaganda to further this goal. Early contacts with French communists seem to have taught Messali the usefulness of organization among workers and the creation of political cells.

Messali began to propagate his ideas in a journal, *Al Ummah* (The Nation), but his extremism eventually led the French authorities to react by outlawing the party and its press. Thus began a long period of semiclandestine activity during which the party occasionally reappeared under a new name, only to be outlawed again. Meanwhile Messali had gone to Switzerland where, under the influence of the Pan-Arabist Shakib Arslan, he abandoned his communist affiliations and adopted a more Islamic form of Algerian nationalism. Messali and his ideas had a relatively small following within Algeria during the period of the late 1920s and early 1930s, but from 1936 on his influence was increasingly apparent in directing the course of Algerian nationalism.

One last group deserves brief mention, for it was responsible for training a few, but very few, of the future Algerian political elite.[33] The Algerian Communist Party was never particularly strong, even after it received some autonomy from the French party in 1935. It differed from Messali's group in favoring total assimilation of Muslims and Europeans rather than calling for Algerian independence. Its membership included both Muslims and Europeans.[34]

Assimilation and the Blum-Viollette Proposal

In order to understand the political system within which the Algerian Liberals acted during the 1930s, it has been necessary to mention briefly three other groups: the *Etoile Nord Africaine* of Messali Hadj; the Ulama of Ben Badis; and the Algerian Communist Party. The issue which best illustrates the relations among these groups, and which also explains why the Liberals were largely ineffective after 1945, was that of assimilation. The Liberals, it should be recalled, had since Emir Khaled's days favored a policy whereby Algerian Muslims could become French citizens without abandoning

[33] Amar Ouzegane, at one time Secretary General of the PCA until his expulsion in the late 1940s, and Abdelkader Guerroudj are the best-known ex-communists to have played a significant role in the political elite.
[34] See J. Glories, "Quelques observations sur la révolution algérienne et le communisme," (1st part), *L'Afrique et l'Asie*, No. 41, 1958.

their personal religious status. This would have led to full political rights for all Algerians and might have eventually led to total assimilation of the Muslim population into the European community. Conversely, equal rights might have led to much greater Muslim influence so that native Algerians could have pressed for some form of autonomy within a loose French commonwealth. In either case, however, complete independence was neither envisaged nor desired as an outcome of this policy.

The issue of assimilation became suddenly extremely important with the advent in France of the Popular Front government of Léon Blum in 1936. The Liberals, who placed great hopes in Blum's government for granting reforms, were rewarded when a bill, the Blum-Viollette proposal, was sent before the National Assembly, permitting French citizenship for some categories of Algerian Muslims without the precondition of renouncing one's religious legal obligations. In addition to the Liberals, both the Ulama and the Communists supported the bill, although the Ulama seemed rather hesitant to do so. Messali Hadj, however, violently opposed the Blum-Viollette measure, seeing in it a "new instrument of colonialism aimed at dividing the Algerian people, according to the habitual French methods, by separating the elite from the masses." [35] Messali returned to Algeria in August 1936 and with his great oratorical talent as political capital began to organize workers in the region of Algiers.

Meanwhile debate over the Blum-Viollette proposal continued. The *colon* population in Algeria was firmly opposed to the measure, and their protests caused the Popular Front government to hesitate. By 1937 the danger of war in Europe was becoming apparent, and less attention was consequently paid in Paris to colonial problems. Throughout 1937 the proposal remained before the French parliament without ever being discussed. On February 8, 1938, the Federation of Mayors in Algeria threatened to resign *en bloc* if the bill were discussed. The Blum government succumbed to this pressure and withdrew the bill.

The consequences of this action are difficult to determine precisely, but it seems clear that one group, the Algerian Liberals, was greatly weakened by the failure of the Blum-Viollette proposal. Since assimilation had been their primary goal for nearly a decade, the final rejection of this policy meant that the Liberals were

[35] Aron, *La guerre d'Algérie*, p. 72.

obliged either to change their aims or simply be bypassed by other political groups whose concerns were more relevant in the new political conditions of the 1940s.

A few Liberals were able to reformulate their demands and consequently remained important throughout the 1940s and even into the postindependence period. This transformation of goals took place between 1938 and 1943 and was a direct result of the rejection of the Blum-Viollette proposal and the defeat of France in World War II, accompanied by the Allied landings in North Africa. In 1938 Ferhat Abbas split with Dr. Bendjelloul, another moderate leader, and formed a short-lived group called the *Union Populaire Algérienne*. But before this new party could begin to articulate any new program the war in Europe broke out, and Ferhat Abbas loyally rallied to France in her hour of crisis.

With the defeat of France and the installation of the Vichy regime, Ferhat Abbas became convinced that some form of autonomy, rather than assimilation, was necessary for Algerian Muslims. This conclusion was the result of the observation that the *colons* in Algeria could and would prevent liberal reforms emanating from Paris and that Paris itself might not be receptive to Muslim demands, particularly if undemocratic forces governed France.[36]

In November 1942 the Allied Powers landed in North Africa, and Ferhat Abbas, believing that they were the proper authorities to deal with, addressed a petition to them asking for reforms.[37] But these demands were poorly received, and in February 1943 Ferhat Abbas, in consultation with some of Messali's followers, notably Dr. Lamine Debaghine and Asselah Hocine, drafted the Manifesto of the Algerian People. This document, less moderate in tone than his previous petitions, represented Abbas' first break with the idea of assimilation. He concluded his list of demands for reform by saying, "Henceforth a Muslim Algerian will ask for nothing other than to be an Algerian Muslim." [38]

[36] Abbas interview, February 17, 1967.
[37] Jean Lacouture in *De Gaulle,* p. 117, suggests that General de Gaulle never forgave Abbas for dealing with the Americans and British before contacting the Free French during World War II, and that in 1961 de Gaulle still held a grudge against Abbas, then President of the GPRA. Lacouture implies that de Gaulle applied pressure to other FLN members by offering to negotiate if Abbas were removed from the presidency of the GPRA. This was done in August 1961, after which negotiations proceeded rapidly. Abbas in an interview with the author indicated that he believed Lacouture was correct in his interpretation.
[38] See Roger Le Tourneau, *Evolution politique de l'Afrique du nord musulmane, 1920–1961,* pp. 337–343.

With the Manifesto of the Algerian People, Ferhat Abbas and his followers had finally reached the conclusion that Algerian independence in some form was desirable. This new orientation meant that a small group of Liberals would continue to play a part in the independence movement. As the postwar years and the Algerian revolution are discussed further on, the Liberals will frequently be mentioned. But although some Liberals continued to participate in Algerian political life, by 1943 they had received an education in politics which would mark their behavior and attitudes even in the postindependence period. Their political socialization had taught them a respect for legality, a preference for parliamentary procedure, a concern with modernization and equality of opportunity, a relatively pragmatic orientation toward politics, and some skills in compromise.

Those Liberals who were able to accept the idea of independence, for example, Ferhat Abbas and his friends, also came to view themselves as important actors in any nationalist coalition. Their self-image, however, did not preclude sharing power with other groups, for the Liberals seemed willing to accept the fact that they represented one segment of Algerian society, the westernized educated classes. They saw their own right to govern as stemming from their early contribution to the reform movement and their intellectual ability. As true democrats in the French tradition, they seem to have viewed themselves as one of several freely competing groups whose value as a coalition partner lay in flexibility and pragmatism. In short, their skills were those of the parliamentarian, and to a lesser degree the organizer, and their claim to power was based on experience in testing these talents in the colonial setting.

However, the Liberals were not experienced at mobilizing mass political support or preparing for paramilitary actions. Consequently they were somewhat obscured in the late 1940s by a more radical type of politician whose political socialization differed in many ways from that of the Liberals. The Radicals, whose entry into politics coincided with and in part stemmed from the failure of the Liberals' policy of assimilation, represented a new generation of political activists. Formed in reaction to the failures of the Liberals, the Radicals sought to gain control of the nationalist movement after World War II. But despite the relative success of the Radicals in moving to the forefront of the nationalist movement in the 1940s and early 1950s, the Liberals continued to influence the course of political development into the independence period.

4
The Radical Politicians

The Radical politicians in Algeria represented a transitional group that bridged the gap between the legalistic style of the Liberals and the violence of the Revolutionaries. The political formation of the Radicals led them to break with the moderate nationalists, and yet the extremism of the Revolutionaries was almost as uncongenial to these sophisticated politicians. The Radicals, as they entered into politics during the 1940s, were the first group to discover the power of mass organization, of propaganda, and of agitation, skills which prepared them for electoral battles in later years. But also they were tempted by the apparent solution to the colonial question which violence seemed to offer. On several occasions, then, the Radicals sponsored the use of force, but after two disastrous failures with this tactic they withdrew to an awkward position which openly favored legality and tacitly extolled violence.

The school experiences of the Radicals were primarily responsible for their acquiring an intense feeling of nationalism. Political interest was greatly aroused by the French defeat in World War II and the hope that independence, or at least reforms, might be achieved through common efforts of Liberals and Radicals. The promise of a united nationalist front disappeared suddenly, however, with the attempted insurrection of May 1945. The failure to turn violence to their advantage affected the Radicals for at least a decade and led them to conclude that perhaps electoral politics was after all a safer if slower path to decolonization. But the elections of 1948 also destroyed this hope, and the destruction of the clandestine *Organisation Spéciale* a few years later left them with neither the alternative of electoral politics nor force as political methods. In these circumstances the Radicals suffered serious internal crises.

Compared to the Liberals, the Radicals seemed less conciliatory and willing to bargain for reforms. They also appeared more convinced of their own right to exercise exclusive political power. Yet the Radicals, like the Liberals, failed to achieve their major goals, and thus they never created a model of successful nationalist politics which might have brought the next generation of activists into a common political process. Instead, they served as a target for the hostility and frustrations of the next group of nationalists, the Revolutionaries.

The Radical politicians who dominated much of Algerian political life from 1945 to 1954 shared with the Liberals the fact that their basic political socialization occurred almost entirely within the French colonial system. These Radicals were the men who had come under the influence of Messali Hadj during the 1930s and 1940s. Typically, they were younger than the Liberals, their political background had never led them to believe that Algeria could become a part of France, and their confidence in legal political action was ambiguous. Many of the Radicals were temporarily bypassed by the outbreak of the revolution in 1954, but within a few years they succeeded in regaining control of some of the key positions of power within the revolutionary elite. Since independence in 1962 their political influence has been limited, but important administrative and economic functions have been delegated to them.

From 1954 to 1968 approximately twenty Radical politicians played significant political roles. Of these, five were in top positions during the revolution as members of the GPRA, four have been ministers since independence, thirteen were deputies in the first or second National Assembly, and five were members of the Central Committee of the FLN. In 1968, however, none of the Radicals was in a top political position. Two were high in the administration, three headed important sectors of the economy, and two were prominent leaders of exiled opposition groups. The fortunes of this group have clearly changed over time, and to understand these developments one must consider the political socialization of the Radicals.

A composite image of the successful Radical politician would show a man born in the early 1920s, in the region of Constantine or Algiers, of a somewhat advantaged Muslim family living in a small town. From these origins the Radical would have gone on to school, completed a university education, and qualified for a liberal profession in law or medicine. But early involvement in politics would have probably occupied him more than his profession. In the course of his political activity he would have spent some time in prison but would have returned to political life to run as a candidate for election to the Municipal Council or Algerian Assembly. Perhaps he would have become assistant to the mayor in his home town, and most likely he would have eventually risen to a prominent position in the late 1940s or early 1950s within the party of Messali Hadj, the *Mouvement pour le Triomphe des Libertés Démocratiques* (MTLD).

For a limited number of the Radical politicians a more complete picture of their political socialization can be sketched. Since four of the most important members of the Algerian political elite are included in this subgroup, some analysis of their experiences seems warranted. The individuals referred to here are Benyoussef Benkhedda, President of the GPRA in 1961; Saad Dahlab, Minister of Foreign Affairs in the Provisional Government; M'Hammed Yazid, Minister of Information in the GPRA and deputy in the National Assembly after independence; Amar Bentoumi, Minister of Justice in the first government after independence and deputy in the National Assembly; and Abderrazak Chentouf, member of the Provisional Executive in 1962, who, although he does not strictly fit the proposed criteria for inclusion in the political elite, is close enough to the Radicals that his life history is also worth considering.[1]

Family Political Socialization

The family experiences of the Radicals do not seem to differ greatly from those of the Liberals. Like the Liberals, the Radicals

---

[1] Interviews were held as follows: Benyoussef Benkhedda, February 7, 1967; Saad Dahlab, April 13, 1967 and April 25, 1967; M'Hammed Yazid, March 6, 1967; Amar Bentoumi, December 7, 1966; Abderrazak Chentouf, November 29, 1966.

appear to have acquired their feelings of separate Muslim identity from their early family experiences. If one learned little else at home, the simple fact of knowing that one was not French was an important political lesson. Both Liberals and Radicals tended to come from segments of the Muslim population which were relatively privileged, economically or socially. Benkhedda's father, for example, was a Muslim magistrate, a position which allowed him to get his son a scholarship to attend the lycée in Blida. Yazid's father and grandfather had both been in the French army, and because of this he was also able to go to a good school, which in Yazid's case was also the lycée in Blida. Saad Dahlab, a third student at the Blida lycée, came from a family of relatively prosperous sheep herders from the region south of Algiers. His father was apparently involved in nationalist politics, and this perhaps accounts for Dahlab's early political interests.[2]

School Socialization

The distinguishing elements in the political socialization of individuals in this group, however, are drawn not so much from their early family life as from their school experiences. Unlike the Liberals, whose school life only indirectly led them to politics by accentuating their awareness of inequalities between Muslims and Europeans, the Radicals became much more intensely politically socialized within their schools.[3] Not only did they learn that colonialism was bad, but also they learned about the nationalist movement, which by the time of their adolescence was becoming an important force within Algeria. The Liberals, born a decade earlier, experienced nothing during their school days comparable to the direct political involvement of the Radicals.

[2] *El Maghrib el Arabi*, the MTLD newspaper, on October 30, 1948, ran a short notice on the death of Dahlab's father, calling him a "nationalist militant of the first hour."

[3] In 1929, Augustin Bernard gave the following figures on the number of Muslim students. There were 45,000 boys and 3000 girls in "native schools," and 9000 boys and 3000 girls in European schools. These figures refer almost entirely to primary school enrollment, and they make clear how exceptional the Politicians discussed here were in comparison with the uneducated Muslim masses. See Augustin Bernard, *L'Algérie* p. 382. Maurice Viollette, in *L'Algérie vivrà-t-elle?* p. 263, adds that at the University of Algiers in 1929 there were 77 Muslim students, 17 in law, 7 in medicine, 6 in pharmacy, 14 in sciences, and 33 in letters.

Political socialization within the schools seems to have occurred in three major ways for the Radicals. First, the fact of being a small, discriminated-against minority in a French school apparently heightened particularistic feelings. Forced to compete equally with Frenchmen in French language exams and prohibited from studying Arabic, the Radicals became sensitive to the injustices of the colonial system.

A second influence on these young men's political ideas came from the content of what was taught in school. One Radical refers to his study of French history as having made him aware of what had happened to Algeria since the French conquest. Others refer to teachers who were particularly influential. Benyoussef Benkhedda, the President of the GPRA in 1961, mentions a French teacher who occasionally drank too much and would tell his Muslim students how the *colons* exploited the native Algerians.[4] Amar Bentoumi, the first Minister of Justice, recalls one of his teachers, a Muslim Algerian, who had a great influence on his students.[5] During a lesson on French grammar the teacher would illustrate the use of subject and predicate with such sentences as "Colonialism is evil."

A third means of political socialization within the school was through contacts with other politically aware students. At the lycée in Blida, three of the most prominent of Algeria's political leaders during the revolution shared political ideas.[6] Publications of Messali Hadj's political movement, first the ENA and subsequently the *Parti du Peuple Algérien* (PPA), reached the students. *Al Ummah* was particularly influential, and the few Muslim students in the lycée frequently discussed its themes. Another Radical referred to the existence of a youth section of the PPA within the school itself to which some of the students belonged. Under the guise of meeting in a classroom in the evening to do homework, they would discuss politics. The models which seemed most compelling to this generation were less the Young Tunisians, Mustapha Kemal, or the Young Turks than the Arab nationalists in the Fertile Crescent, the Irish Rebellion, and the Indian Congress movement led by Gandhi.[7]

By the time the Radicals had completed their secondary education

---

[4] Benkhedda interview, February 7, 1967.

[5] Bentoumi interview, December 7, 1966.

[6] These three students, Yazid, Benkhedda, and Dahlab, remained in close contact over the years, and their political fortunes were quite similar. All three eventually became ministers in the GPRA in 1961. Such close school ties, it might be added, have served an integrative function in many political systems.

[7] Yazid interview, March 6, 1967.

they were generally already actively involved in the politics of Messali Hadj's nationalist party, the PPA. As they continued their education at the university level, many of the Radicals participated in student politics. Both M'Hammed Yazid and Abderrazak Chentouf led the North African student movement.[8] Other Radicals found that participation in the Muslim Scouts was a means of expressing their recently discovered nationalism. Both Benkhedda and Bentoumi, for example, were involved with the Scouts. These experiences seem to have served as a prelude to more involvement in the nationalist political party, in particular the PPA. It may be that skills in using political organization and propaganda were first developed by some of the Radicals in either student politics or with the Muslim Scouts. In any case most of these young men were deeply involved in politics by their early twenties.

The Impact of the World War

The Radicals were still adolescents or young adults when World War II began. The war appears to have influenced these future political leaders through a combination of two processes. During the war their involvement in politics became more intense, perhaps because some previous controls were loosened after the French defeat. Linked to this was a belief that because of the war Algeria would obtain its independence sooner than had been hoped for. France no longer appeared as powerful, and the Allies, in the Atlantic Charter and elsewhere, were talking of self-determination for colonial countries.

At least one important future political leader, Benkhedda, found his political education during the war advanced because of his refusal to be drafted into the army. For this he was put in jail for eight months. According to Benkhedda this was an important turning point in his life, for prison provided him with an opportunity to study and think. In prison he spent considerable time reading, rather surprisingly, about revolutions, including the American and Russian models. In this way prison helped complete his political education, as it was to do for many other young Algerians in later years.[9]

---

[8] Later recruits to this position included Mohammed Ben Yahia, Belaid Abdesselam and Lamine Khène, all three of whom were ministers in 1968.
[9] Benkhedda interview.

Following the Allied landings in 1942, Algerian politics were in the process of being transformed. The Radicals, who hoped to achieve their ends rapidly, decided to try to work with the Liberals in a broad united front. The Liberals had divided after the failure of the Blum-Viollette proposal, but those who had been able to readjust their beliefs so as to accept the idea of an independent Algeria were still major political actors. And while the younger Radicals were already quite different from the Liberals in terms of their political values, there was nonetheless a brief period during which Liberals and Radicals were able to present a common program. This experience and its failure, however, marked a turning point in the development of the nationalist movement, for after 1945 Liberals and Radicals remained bitter enemies.

Ferhat Abbas, the most prominent of the Liberals, had come to believe in the need for Algerian autonomy during World War II. Thus he was more acceptable to the Radicals as a coalition partner than he had been in the 1930s when he favored assimilation. In 1943 he drafted a Manifesto of the Algerian People after consulting with the followers of Messali Hadj and the Ulama. Most of the younger Radicals agreed with the basic provisions of the Manifesto, although some hesitated to sanction the specific reforms mentioned in a later addition to the Manifesto.[10] Pressures for reform continued. The French, however, responded by arresting Abbas in September 1943. He was soon released, but neither he nor his Liberal followers were as confident as they had previously been of France's good will.[11] When General Charles de Gaulle eventually managed to impose by decree a progressive set of reforms for Algeria on March 7, 1944, the Liberals and the Radicals both rejected the measures as too timid. In fact the reforms corresponded relatively closely to the Blum-Viollette proposal of 1936 which Ferhat Abbas had so strongly supported, but by 1944 times had changed.

In reaction to de Gaulle's reforms, Ferhat Abbas decided to create a united front movement of all tendencies, which could effectively present its demands to the French. On March 14, 1944 he formed the *Amis du Manifeste et de la Liberté* (AML). The Ulama and Messali agreed to support the AML, although Messali was skeptical that any beneficial results would come from it. France, he

10 Yazid interview.
11 Ferhat Abbas, *La nuit coloniale*, pp. 145–146.

claimed, would only give in to force.[12] Abbas, however, still believed
in the possibility of a "revolution by law," for he had confidence in
the liberality of a new France which would grow out of the anti-
Nazi resistance movement.[13] The Radicals, it would seem, were
more unsure of France's good intentions than were the Liberals.
But for the moment it was the Liberals who had seized the initiative
of launching a broad nationalist front, the AML.

Abbas founded a new journal, *Egalité*, to propagate the AML's
ideas and to "render familiar the idea of an Algerian nation." [14]
Within a relatively short time the AML gained impressive mass
support which totaled perhaps 500,000 adherents.[15] Among these
adherents were many of the Radicals and future Revolutionaries.
For some the AML provided a means of reaching the moderates with
Messali's ideas of a more militant nationalism.[16] Other Radicals
seem to have been less reserved toward the AML itself. Amar Bentoumi, the first Minister of Justice, recalls that as a member of the
AML he helped organize a mass demonstration in Algiers, for which
he was arrested and imprisoned for several months. The AML represented for him the moment of greatest unity between the political
elite and the people, surpassing even the wartime FLN in this.[17]

Whatever the motives of the Radicals for joining with the Liberals
in the AML, it is clear that they never disbanded their own political
party, the PPA of Messali Hadj. Evidence of this came in early March
1945 when a Congress was held to strengthen the AML as a common
nationalist front. It became clear that the Congress had been taken
over by Messali's supporters when a motion of Ferhat Abbas calling
for an Algeria federated with France was rejected in favor of one
supporting the idea of total independence. In addition, Messali,
who was in jail at this time, was endorsed as the "incontestable
leader of the Algerian people." [18] Thus, the AML failed to integrate
the Liberals and Radicals into a common movement, and the efforts
of Messali to take over the AML left a legacy of distrust between the
two segments of the nationalist movement.

[12] *Ibid.*, p. 151.

[13] *Ibid.*, p. 151.

[14] See the *mémoire* done at the Faculté du Droit et de Science Economique
at the University of Algiers by Daoud Akrouf, entitled "Les Amis du Manifeste
et de la Liberté," February 1965.

[15] Ferhat Abbas, *La nuit coloniale*, p. 152.

[16] Dahlab interview.

[17] Bentoumi interview.

[18] Roger Le Tourneau, *Evolution politique de l'Afrique du nord musulmane*,
p. 348.

Insurrection and Repression, 1945

The events which followed the apparent PPA attempt to take over the AML have received considerable attention because of the widespread violence which broke out in May 1945, just after the armistice in Europe.[19] Many Muslims had expected that the end of the war in Europe would be followed by reforms and perhaps even by the liberation of Algeria. Tension between Muslims and Europeans had been high for several weeks. On May 8 Muslim crowds demonstrated, especially in Sétif and Guelma, carrying Algerian flags and calling for the release from prison of Messali. A shot was fired by someone, and violence rapidly spread. Muslims began to attack Europeans. French repression was swift and ruthless. For days Muslims were hunted down, strafed from attacking airplanes, and bombarded from French naval vessels along the coast. When order was finally restored about 100 Europeans had been killed. The number of Muslim dead is not known with certainty, but estimates run from just over 1000 to 45,000, with 10,000 being a plausible figure.[20] Needless to say, the AML was dissolved and its leaders arrested.

The brutality of the French repression has often been seen as a major cause in leading the Algerian nationalists to resort to violence in their effort to free their country from colonial rule.[21] For many of the younger nationalists this evaluation is no doubt true, although it should be stressed that some of them had already concluded that force would one day be needed, and the events of May merely confirmed this in their minds. Yet other consequences, more important for the Radicals, can be traced to the massacres of May 1945.

It seems clear that one result of the events of May 1945 was to destroy whatever hope there might have been of uniting Liberals and Radicals within a common nationalist front. Perhaps such unity would never have occurred, as the attempted takeover of the AML by the PPA indicates, but it is conceivable that some form of effective cooperation might have developed had it not been for the violence of May 1945. This final division of the nationalist movement occurred because, contrary to what many accounts of these events indicate, Messali Hadj and some members of his party were clearly preparing for armed insurrection in the spring of 1945.[22]

---

[19] Robert Aron, *Les origines de la guerre d'Algérie* and Manfred Halpern, "The Algerian Uprising of 1945," *Middle East Journal*, No. 2, 1948, pp. 191–202, cover in some detail this event.

[20] Robert Aron, *Les origines*, p. 80, estimates that about 6000 Muslims died.

[21] See, for example, Charles-Henri Favrod, *Le FLN et l'Algérie*, p. 102.

[22] Interviews with Benkhedda, Dahlab, and Ouamrane.

Messali was badly prepared for such action, and it seems that after issuing an initial order to begin the uprising he changed his mind.[23] In some regions, however, the message to revolt apparently got through and may have been responsible for touching off some of the initial clashes between *colons* and Muslims. The French reaction can, of course, be judged apart from whether or not there was a plan among some nationalists for an armed uprising. The important result of Messali's action was that it led to an irrevocable break between the Radicals and the Liberals, around Ferhat Abbas, who made up the two major blocks of nationalists. Abbas believes that Messali, along with the colonial police, purposely tried to instigate the massacres of May 1945 as a means of destroying the AML.[24] Whereas Messali and Abbas had frequently consulted each other before 1945, henceforth their cooperation was minimal.

The second consequence of the failure of Messali's attempt to organize an armed insurrection in 1945 was that the Radical politicians for the next decade were quite hesitant to turn to violence as a means of achieving independence.[25] This meant that the younger PPA members, who were only aware of the scope of the French repression, became more convinced than ever of the need for violence, whereas those Radical politicians close to Messali were more impressed with the dangers of resorting to violence prematurely and consequently were careful to explore all other legal and illegal means of political action. Above all they did not want to resort to violence as Messali had in 1945, out of an apparent belief in the spontaneity of the masses.

Postwar Politics

The Radicals, while weakened by the French repression of 1945, were nonetheless able to dominate postwar politics. Their trust in

[23] Benyoussef Benkhedda has discussed the role of the Radicals in the events of 1945 in his mimeographed study "Contribution à l'historique du mouvement de libération nationale," April 1964, p. 2. It may be, however, that Messali himself did not make these decisions, but rather some of his close associates were responsible for them.

[24] Abbas interview.

[25] Benkhedda, "Contribution," p. 2, states that the Central Committee of the MTLD, of which he was Secretary General, hesitated in 1954 to begin the revolution because they "remembered the events of May 1945 during which the Central Committee of the PPA, after having decided to begin the insurrection, gave the counter order at the last moment."

violent methods had been shaken, but their ability at mass organization and electoral politics had yet to be tested. Competition in elections between Liberals and Radicals thus became a dominant theme in Algerian politics for nearly ten years.

In view of the intense reactions by all Algerians to the French repression of May 1945, it is surprising to note that by 1946 "politics as usual" best describes the dominant tone among the Muslim nationalists.[26] The Radicals and the Liberals were both busy reorganizing their respective followings into new political parties. When Ferhat Abbas was released from prison in May 1946, his immediate instinct was to form a party which called for "a new Algeria, freely federated to a new France." [27] Abbas' ideas were still close to those expressed in his Manifesto of 1943. His new political party, in fact, was called the *Union Démocratique du Manifeste Algérien* (UDMA).

The Radicals, however, would have nothing to do with Abbas's party. Unlike the AML, the UDMA was not a common front of all nationalist tendencies, but rather it expressed the ideals of a small group of Liberal politicians who shared basically the same political attitudes. The UDMA, two weeks after its creation, was allowed to participate in the elections for the second French Constituent Assembly.[28] Since Messali Hadj was still in prison, the primary nationalist group which could rival Ferhat Abbas was out of the competition. In these conditions the UDMA won eleven of the thirteen seats reserved for Muslim Algerians. Thus began a long period of organized electoral participation on the part of the Liberals. The predisposition for parliamentary procedures learned in the 1930s was finally coupled with increased possibilities for Muslim involvement in French political life.

Ferhat Abbas and his friends were not, however, immediately successful in their efforts to convince the Constituent Assembly to form an Algerian Republic federated to France. This first experience of participation in the French legislative system was, in fact, something of a disaster.[29]

Perhaps because of this unhappy initial experience in the French parliament, Ferhat Abbas was willing to stand aside and counseled his followers to vote for the Algerian Communist Party in the elec-

26 Roger Le Tourneau, *Evolution politique*, p. 357.
27 Ferhat Abbas, *La nuit coloniale*, pp. 160–161.
28 Roger Le Tourneau, *Evolution politique*, p. 358.
29 Jean Lacouture, *Cinq hommes et la France*, pp. 299–301.

tions for the French Constituent Assembly in November 1946.[30] The Radicals then seized the initiative, and Messali's party, called the *Mouvement pour le Triomphe des Libertés Démocratiques* (MTLD) demanded the convocation of an Algerian Constituent Assembly and the evacuation of French troops. Messali apparently thought the Muslim masses were ready for independence. He hoped that his new party, which was really no more than a continuation of the outlawed PPA, would receive enough votes to convince the French of this fact.[31] In reality the MTLD did only moderately well, partly due to administrative interference in the elections, winning five of fifteen seats.[32]

The UDMA of Ferhat Abbas, while abstaining in the National Constituent Assembly elections, did compete in the elections to the *Conseil de la République* which were held at the same time. Four of the seven seats assigned to Muslim Algerians were won by UDMA candidates. The new UDMA *conseillers* were all from liberal professions. Two were doctors, one a lawyer, one a professor. None of these four, however, was to play a significant political role after 1954.

By 1946, then, the nationalist movement in Algeria was again divided into two competing parties, one composed of Liberals around Ferhat Abbas, the other made up of the Radicals with Messali Hadj. Both parties were engaged actively in electoral politics, although their belief in the value of this undertaking seems to have differed, as did their ultimate goals. What is remarkable is that after so many signs that legal parliamentary procedures would not bring about Algerian independence because of the intense opposition of the *colons,* the nationalists of both Liberal and Radical persuasions were still willing to try to find a solution to their demands by legal means. Certainly the era of assimilation of France and Algeria was gone, but this did not yet mean that decolonization in Algeria would necessarily be accompanied by a long and costly war. What, then, led the nationalists to forsake parliamentary methods, which seemed relatively congenial to them, in favor of armed force? The answer to this is no doubt complex, but the elec-

---

[30] See Michael Clark, *Algeria in Turmoil*, p. 43.

[31] Ferhat Abbas, *La nuit coloniale*, p. 173.

[32] The successful candidates were Dr. Lamine Debaghine, future minister in the GPRA of 1958; Mohammed Khider, Secretary General of the FLN after independence; Messaoud Boukadoum, a deputy in the first Algerian Constituent Assembly in 1962; and Ahmed Mezerna and Djamel Derdour, neither of whom played important roles in the FLN after 1954. See Ferhat Abbas, *La nuit coloniale*, p. 173.

tions of 1948 certainly were a major reason for the abandoning of efforts at legal reforms, particularly among the Radicals.

The 1948 Elections

On September 20, 1947, the French National Assembly acted in response to demands for reforms in Algeria made by both liberal Frenchmen and Muslim nationalists. A "Statute of Algeria" was voted on that day which would have more than satisfied the Muslim Liberals of 1936.[33] Even in 1947 the Statute could be considered progressive, if only its provisions were actually applied.[34] For the Muslim Algerians the most encouraging feature of the new Statute was the creation of an Algerian Assembly of 120 members, 60 of whom would be Muslims.[35] Despite many limitations on the Assembly's powers, both the UDMA of Abbas and the MTLD of Messali prepared to present candidates in the first elections.

If the Statute of 1947 aroused restrained hopes among some of the Muslims, it clearly frightened the *colons* in Algeria. The threat to their own positions of allowing Muslim "separatists" to be elected to the new Algerian Assembly led them to demand from Paris a "strong" Governor General who could oppose the violent nationalists.[36] The French government answered this request by appointing M. Marcel-Edmond Naegelen as Governor General of Algeria. The stage was thus set for the confrontation of the nationalists and the *colons* in the first elections to the Algerian Assembly in April 1948.

As the elections approached, the UDMA and the MTLD were unable to strengthen the chances of a nationalist victory by presenting a

[33] Ferhat Abbas, *La nuit coloniale*, p. 180, points out that the reforms included in the 1947 Statute were nearly all ones that the Emir Khaled had demanded in 1920.

[34] The Statute did not satisfy the demands of either the Liberals or Radicals. The four UDMA members of the *Conseil de la République* quit in protest after the Statute was passed by the French National Assembly. The Liberals were particularly angered by the provision of two separate electoral colleges, one for Europeans and naturalized Muslims, the other for the remainder of the Muslim population. See Ferhat Abbas, *La nuit coloniale*, p. 178.

[35] Details on the organization of this institution can be found in Ivo Rens, *L'Assemblée algérienne.*

[36] Roger Le Tourneau, *Evolution politique*, p. 365. Also, Michael Clark, *Algeria*, p. 51. Elections in October 1947 to City Councils had shown heavy support for the MTLD and the UDMA.

common list of candidates.[37] Each party accused the other of refusing to unite in a nationalist front. Both parties had scored notable successes in recently held elections to Municipal Councils. The MTLD had done particularly well in the larger cities, with the UDMA winning in many of the smaller towns.[38] Encouraged by these victories, both Liberals and Radicals seemed to expect similar success in the elections to the Algerian Assembly.

Candidates for the 60 Muslim seats to the Algerian Assembly were announced by the UDMA on March 19, 1948, in the newly named party journal, *Egalité: La République Algérienne*. The following week, on March 26, the MTLD published the list of its candidates in *El Maghrib el Arabi*. These lists of candidates are particularly interesting because they permit an approximate comparison of the Liberals and the Radicals in 1948. Many of these men then went on to become members of the Algerian political elite following the outbreak of the revolution in 1954.

Despite the disagreements over both goals and tactics which marked the relations between the two nationalist parties, the candidates of the MTLD and the UDMA seem rather similar in terms of occupational background (see Table 4.1). While the Liberals, as might be expected, were drawn somewhat more from the liberal professions, the similarity of professional backgrounds in the two nationalist parties is more striking than the differences.

The MTLD Radicals, however, do seem to have been somewhat more actively involved in politics than the Liberals. Thirty-two MTLD candidates, or 54 percent, were or had been incumbents of some political office, whereas only 42 percent of the UDMA candidates were readily identifiable as "politicians." The institutions which permitted Muslim political participation were, as already indicated, limited in number. One might be a member of the Municipal Councils at the local level, the *Conseil général* at the departmental level, the National Assembly or the *Conseil de la République* at the national level. One might also be primarily involved in politics as a leader of one of the nationalist parties without holding any elected office. By comparing the MTLD politicians and the UDMA politicians, one immediately notices that

---

[37] Various tracts printed at the time and seized by the French police talk of the problems of forming a united front. For example, an UDMA tract of February 1948 carries a message from Ferhat Abbas in which he objects to allowing both the PPA and the MTLD to have distinct representation in any future Central Committee of a common nationalist party.

[38] Michael Clark, *Algeria*, p. 51.

TABLE 4.1   NONPOLITICAL CAREERS OF CANDIDATES TO THE
ALGERIAN ASSEMBLY, 1948 [1]

	MTLD	UDMA
Liberal Professions	18 (56%)	17 (68%)
Medicine	4	2
Law	3	6
Education	11	9
Economic Professions	9 (28%)	7 (28%)
Commerce	6	1
Agriculture	2	5
Industry	1	1
Traditional Administrative Professions	5 (16%)	1 (4%)
Number = 32		n = 25

[1] This breakdown is derived from the lists of candidates published by each party. The UDMA candidates for the department of Algiers are not included because of lack of information.

the MTLD candidates were primarily active at the local level, whereas the UDMA candidates were more often members of departmental or national political bodies. This difference reflects the relatively recent entry into politics of many of the Radicals as compared to the more experienced Liberals. (See Table 4.2).

TABLE 4.2   POLITICAL EXPERIENCE OF CANDIDATES TO THE
ALGERIAN ASSEMBLY, 1948

Highest Political Office Held	MTLD	UDMA
Municipal Council [1]	22 (74%)	7 (26%)
Conseil général	— (0%)	10 (37%)
Assemblée Nationale	1 (3%)	8 (30%)
Party Leadership Only	7 (23%)	2 (7%)
Number = 30		n = 27

[1] Of the Municipal Councillors, 19 MTLD candidates also occupied the relatively responsible position of assistant to the Mayor, whereas only 3 UDMA candidates were in this position.

These comparisons yield an image of the Radicals as men of approximately the same educational and professional status as the Liberals, but, largely because they were younger, their political experience was limited to local offices or party politics. The Liberals, though less likely to have held any previous political office, tended to have been in higher political positions.[39]

[39] The MTLD candidates who entered the political elite after 1954 were: Ahmed Ben Bella, Mustapha Ben Boulaid, M'Hammed Ben M'Hel, Messaoud

The elections of 1948 were important for future developments largely because both nationalist parties actively participated, and many of the most influential political leaders after 1954 were then candidates to the Algerian Assembly. Still in 1948 the Radicals and the Liberals, while opposing each other, were both willing to try to work within the legal framework of colonial politics. Perhaps this could have become the path to eventual decolonization, but such was not to be the case. When the elections were held in early April 1948, the two nationalist parties, which in the last relatively free vote in October 1947 had obtained well over 50 percent of the Muslim vote, managed to gain only 17 of the 60 seats for Muslims. Nine went to the MTLD, 8 to the UDMA.

Of the 24 candidates in these elections who later played important political roles during the revolution, five were elected, only two of whom were MTLD members. The small number of nationalists elected provided some evidence that the new Governor General had interfered in the elections. This suspicion was confirmed for many Radicals when two newly elected MTLD deputies, along with 30 other unsuccessful candidates, were arrested just before or during the election. Faith in electoral politics among Radicals virtually vanished, leaving behind a feeling of anger and frustration. More than half of the 14 MTLD candidates who later became prominent political figures during the revolution were arrested in the spring of 1948 and were sentenced to imprisonment for terms ranging from a few months to two years. One of these Radicals, M'Hammed Yazid, went on to become Minister of Information in the GRPA and then deputy to the National Assembly after independence. In 1958 he wrote a letter to *The New York Times* in which he said:

The time has long passed for any possibility of achieving Algerian independence through French constitutional means. It was precisely the impossibility of such a procedure which led to the existing state of war between France and us.
I would like to add a personal note which illustrates this. In the spring

---

Boukadoum, Saad Dahlab, Djilani Embarek, Hocine El Mehdaoui, Mohammed Ladjouzi, Salah Mebroukine, Ould Brahim, Mohammed Saadouni, Houari Souyah, Abdelkader Tafraoui, M'Hammed Yazid.

The UDMA candidates who later entered the FLN elite were: Ferhat Abbas, Ahmed Francis, Ahmed Boumendjel.

The Independents were Hadj Hamou and Abderrahmane Farès.

Five others who were candidates but who never entered the narrowly defined post-1954 political elite were: Mohammed Bentiftifa, Chaouki Mostefai, Abderrazak Chentouf, Djamil Bendimered, and Abderrahmane Kiouane.

of 1948 I was a candidate for the Algerian Assembly with fifty-eight other nationalists attempting to work through French "constitutional means"; more than thirty of us were arrested during the electoral campaign and put into jail for years. A look at the list of those then jailed will give you an approximate list of the actual leadership of the Algerian revolution today.[40]

While Yazid's last statement in which he identifies the leaders of the revolution with those arrested is somewhat exaggerated (several candidates who were *not* arrested, such as Ahmed Ben Bella and Mustapha Ben Boulaid, were among the *chefs historiques* of the revolution), the implication that the 1948 elections marked a clear turning point in Algerian political development cannot be escaped.

For the Radicals particularly, the era of legal political participation was about to end, although a certain reluctance to abandon this electoral style of politics persisted until the actual outbreak of the revolution. For the Liberals, who also felt cheated by the results of the 1948 election but who had not faced massive arrest as did the Radicals, political strategy was not changed by the apparent failure of legal reforms. As the leader of the Liberals has stated, even after a long series of prefabricated elections in 1948, in 1949, in 1951, "our group never for a single instant ceased to call for the respect of legality." [41] Thus, while the Liberals were to continue much as before, the Radicals of the MTLD passed through a series of internal crises which eventually resulted in the armed insurrection of 1954.

Before turning to this final stage in the political education of the Radicals, it is worth considering briefly why the French reacted so vigorously, arresting candidates to a parliamentary body which the French National Assembly had created only a few months before. The French Minister of the Interior, speaking before the National Assembly on May 4, 1948, justified the repression by referring to the violence which had marked the MTLD campaign. The MTLD newspaper *El Maghrib el Arabi,* qualified as "separatist" by the Minister, was calling for a "free Algeria." Quite simply, concluded the Minister, those who pursued anti-French activities were arrested. In all Algeria "only" 398 arrests were made.[42]

---

40 *The New York Times,* November 14, 1958, p. 26.
41 Ferhat Abbas, *La nuit coloniale,* p. 183.
42 *Débats Parlementaires, Assemblée Nationale Française,* 2nd session, May 4, 1948, p. 2490.

The Organisation Spéciale

A more revealing reason for the repression was given by Jules Moch later in the month.[43] He defended the arrests of the MTLD candidates by claiming that the MTLD possessed a "paramilitary organization," and that because of this the French government had considered banning the MTLD before the April 1948 elections. In retrospect it is clear that the French police had discovered the *Organisation Spéciale* (OS) of the MTLD which had indeed been formed for paramilitary activity in late 1947. Benyoussef Benkhedda notes that the MTLD had already adopted in 1947 the principle of "fighting by all available means," that is, both "armed fighting" and "political fighting." [44] But Benkhedda goes on to comment on the consequences of the 1948 elections for the OS.

The prefabricated elections to the Algerian Assembly in March 1948 [sic] which took place under the "proconsulate" of Naegelen showed the failure of the electoral path. The Central Committee of the MTLD, meeting at Zeddine [Chéliff] in December 1948 drew the conclusions from this and voted for the principle of priority for the OS. This meant that the OS would benefit from getting most of the cadres, money and munitions as compared to the legal organization of the MTLD. The year 1949 witnessed the building up of the military apparatus.[45]

The *Organisation Spéciale* was particularly important in forming the group of nationalists to be discussed in the next chapter, the Revolutionaries. For the Radicals, who continued to work primarily within the legal political system, the experience of the OS was merely another example of failing to use violence as an effective political weapon. The elections of 1948, despite the evidence they provided for the futility of trying to oppose the colonial system within the French political framework, did not lead the Radicals to reject entirely the political tactics which they had learned during the previous years, for the alternative, mass insurrection, was not a field in which they had proved successful in the past. Like the Liberals, the Radicals were repeatedly to discover the limitations of petitions, elections, mass organization, and propaganda in a *colon*-dominated environment, but no clear substitute seemed available to them.

From 1948 until the outbreak of the revolution in 1954 the Radicals appeared to be caught between their attachment to legal

---

[43] Reported in *Alger Républicain*, May 28, 1948.
[44] Benkhedda, "Contribution," p. 1.
[45] *Ibid.*, p. 1.

political activity and a willingness to investigate the possibilities of resorting to violence. But neither path was chosen with alacrity, for the 1948 elections were a warning for those who trusted the legal path just as the 1945 repression served as a grim reminder to the Radicals of the consequences of a precipitous use of violence. Faced with this dilemma, the Radicals were barely able to maintain a cohesive party, as internal crises succeeded one another in rapid succession. And thus the Radical politicians, whose counterparts in most colonial countries succeeded in leading their countries to independence, were badly weakened and became somewhat in- effectual in guiding the nationalist movement. Their failure meant that leadership was to pass to a different group of political activists, the Revolutionaries.

Crises within the MTLD

But while declining in influence after 1948, the Radicals did survive until the outbreak of the war for independence. The history of the MTLD from 1948 to 1954 is largely one of unresolved internal crises. Each successive crisis resulted in the temporary withdrawal of some of the Radicals from political activity. The profound reasons for these crises, each one more serious than the former, are not always well understood. What is clear, however, is that a sizable number of Radicals became discouraged with the political process during these years, and only with the outbreak of the revolution did they again become active.

The earliest of these crises was based on the ethnic particularism of the Berbers. Berbers, although Muslim, do not speak Arabic as their mother tongue. French scholars have repeatedly stressed the differences between Arabs and Berbers, and in Algerian society this distinction is indeed important in explaining many historical phenomena.[46] But what is true in the society at large is not necessarily true of the select and unusual group of men who become the "political elite" of the 1950s and 1960s. To appreciate the uses and limitations of "ethnicity" as a factor in explaining elite behavior one may examine the "Berberist crisis" within the MTLD in 1949.

[46] An important study of French policies toward Kabyles and Arabs is found in Charles-Robert Ageron, "La France a-t-elle eu une politique Kabyle?", *Revue historique,* No. 223, 1960, pp. 311–352.

The Berberist opposition to the MTLD leadership developed, apparently, among Kabyle workers in France.[47] One of the two major tenets of the Berberists was that Algeria was not Arab but Algerian. By this they meant that all Algerian Muslims, whether of Berber, Arab, or Turkish descent, should participate fully in the liberation movement. Inevitably this opposition to Algeria's asserted Arab nature was interpreted as a particularistic ethnic reaction rather than as a call for unity of all the ethnic groups. The second theme developed by the Berbers was that Messali and the Central Committee were too authoritarian. These criticisms were not well received by the majority of the Radicals, whether Kabyles or not, and the Federal Council of the MTLD in France was dissolved in April 1949.

One consequence of this poorly understood episode in the MTLD's history seems to have been that the first leader of the OS, the Kabyle Hocine Ait Ahmed, was replaced eventually by the Arab Ahmed Ben Bella.[48] But this did not mean that Ait Ahmed was permanently excluded from the nationalist movement, for he and Ben Bella in 1954 were together in Cairo helping to prepare for the coming revolution. Nor did the Kabyles in the MTLD leadership react solidly along ethnic lines. Lahouel Hocine, for example, although he was a Kabyle remained an influential member of the Central Committee. In short, the one example of a crisis inspired by ethnic particularism was neither remarkably profound nor long-lasting in its consequences.[49] More important issues were to divide the Radicals, whether Arab or Kabyle.

The later crises of the MTLD had little to do with Berberism. Rather, they reflected a growing opposition between Messali Hadj and the younger Radicals of the Central Committee. Part of the conflict was due to Messali's authoritarian methods, and part stemmed from differences of opinion as to appropriate tactics.

The origin of these later crises within the MTLD can be traced, as so often seems to be the case, to a clear awareness on the part of the MTLD leadership of having failed in attempting to achieve one of its major goals. This failure was that of the *Organisation Spéciale,* the paramilitary organization of the MTLD. In 1949 and

[47] Roger Le Tourneau, *Evolution politique*, pp. 374–375.
[48] Yazid interview.
[49] Saad Dahlab claimed that "berberism" was generally seen as a tendency which worked to divide the nationalists and thus played into the hands of the French. Interview, April 13, 1967.

early 1950 most of the efforts of the MTLD were focused on strengthening the OS. Undoubtedly the French police were aware of the OS's existence, but it was not until March 1950 that the police were able to destroy the nascent insurrectionary group.[50] The OS was then rapidly dismantled by the French police, and its leaders, including Ben Bella, were either arrested or forced into hiding. The Central Committee of the MTLD in these circumstances could do nothing other than admit that once again preparations for violent insurrection had failed, and consequently the OS was dissolved throughout the country, with the exception of the eastern region of the Aurès. Benkhedda, who by 1951 was Secretary General of the MTLD, indicates that this failure weighed heavily on the MTLD leadership and was a major cause of later crises.[51] Reflecting on this period, Benkhedda was later to say:

I became Secretary General of the MTLD in 1951, just at the time when the crisis with Messali was deepening. Messali didn't allow open discussion or majority rule, nor did he offer concrete solutions to problems. The crisis persisted into 1952 and 1953. The party presented candidates in the Municipal Elections, and we decided to cooperate with the Europeans rather than always fighting them, which had proved to be a sterile policy. Messali reproached us for this position, and finally a second Congress was held in 1953 to try to resolve this crisis.[52]

Some members of the MTLD such as Chentouf, Mostefai, Amrani, Cherchalli, and Belhocine left the party at this time, disillusioned by both the ineffectiveness of the MTLD and the sterility of the quarrel between Messali and the Centralists.

By 1953 the tensions within the MTLD were apparent to all.[53] In an effort to reunite the Party, a Congress was held in April 1953. Two seemingly contradictory decisions were taken at this meeting. The first was to recreate the OS, and to accomplish this a Commission was established which consisted of Ben Boulaid, Benkhedda, Dakli, Lahouel, and Messali. The second decision was to adopt a "realistic" attitude of cooperation with the European members of the Municipal Councils. This policy was favored by Benkhedda but opposed by Messali. Messali soon accentuated the crisis by demanding full powers for himself. Messali apparently had the

---

[50] See, for example, Rabah Bitat's article in *Révolution*, November 1963; Robert Merle, *Ahmed Ben Bella*, Chapter 3; and Benyoussef Benkhedda, "Contribution."

[51] Benyoussef Benkhedda, "Contribution," p. 1.

[52] Benkhedda interview.

[53] Benyoussef Benkhedda, "Contribution," p. 2.

support of the rank and file members of the MTLD, but the party cadres down to the lowest levels sided with the Central Committee. Only three Central Committee members supported Messali.[54]

Both parties to the MTLD conflict tried to avoid a final break.[55] Some concessions were made by the Central Committee in March 1954. But in mid-July Messali held a Congress in Belgium which decided to dissolve the Central Committee and elected Messali president for life. The Centralists held their own Congress a month later and expelled Messali and his followers from the party. The break was irrevocable, and for Messali it marked the end of most of his influence over the nationalists. The Radicals of the Central Committee seem to have been greatly shaken by the crisis, but by fall 1954 they were trying to recapture the initiative by planning for insurrection the following spring. But rather than precipitously engage in armed action against France, the Radicals preferred to make sure that the political preconditions existed for such an undertaking. Could they count on aid from Egypt, and would the Neo Destour in Tunisia and the Istiqlal in Morocco join them if a war began? [56] Such were the questions in the minds of the MTLD leaders. By thus hesitating they were not lost, but they were certainly bypassed by less cautious elements within their own party. Consequently the Radicals, despite their immense contribution to the nationalist movement, were deprived of the moral authority which came from having begun the revolution.

Like the Liberals, the Radical politicians of the 1940s had received their political training almost entirely within the French colonial system. Their socialization into politics had left them with an ambiguous set of attitudes. They had learned to value organization and propaganda, were willing to test their strength in elections, and yet saw no value in legality per se. In this they differed most clearly from the legalistic Liberals. The Radicals, for various reasons, were more willing to resort to illegal methods, including violence, in order to achieve their one agreed-upon goal, national independence. But like the Liberals (and this is why both groups may be labeled Politicians) the Radicals had developed some skills in bargaining, though less than the Liberals, as well as in organization. These two traits were distinctive of their political style even during the revolution. Also in common with the Liberals, the

---

[54] Benkhedda and Dahlab interviews.
[55] Roger Le Tourneau, *Evolution politique*, p. 377.
[56] Benyoussef Benkhedda, "Contribution," p. 2.

Radicals seemed deeply concerned with the socioeconomic betterment of the society, although for the Radicals modernization was a secondary goal to that of independence.

The Radicals shared with the Liberals the feeling of having earned the right to represent the aspirations of the Algerian people, but they were considerably less willing to share power with any other group than were their more moderate competitors. Viewing themselves as more militant than the Liberals, they were more exclusive in their image of their role in the political system. As politicians they might enter coalitions when necessary, but it would hardly be surprising if they tried to dominate any decision-making body they belonged to. As the first nationalists to call for independence, they found it difficult to accept the Liberals as partners in an anticolonial united front. Toward the more extreme group of Revolutionaries, however, their attitude was more tolerant.

The distinctive mark of the Radicals was their ability to appreciate the value of the legal political process as well as the need to break with such rigid forms under special cirumstances. To some this ability seemed like a reflection of opportunism and lack of conviction. But the Radicals, despite their temporary eclipse in 1954, were soon to be found again leading the Algerian nationalists. This time, however, they were to lead an armed insurrection rather than a legal political party. And this time they would be sharing power with a new group of Revolutionaries.

5
The Making of
the Revolutionaries

Unlike most former colonies, Algeria achieved her independence only after a prolonged and costly guerrilla war. One might expect, then, that the men who emerged to initiate and guide the use of violence would be less attached to the legalistic style of colonial politics than other nationalist politicians. The failure of the Liberals and Radicals in Algeria to bring about the liberation of their country by legal methods was strikingly apparent. As Algeria's neighbors, Morocco and Tunisia, began to employ violence in the early 1950s to force France to grant independence, many Algerians felt that honor demanded that force also be used to free their country. In these circumstances it was natural for a third group to make a bid for leadership of the nationalist movement.

Algerian party politics had virtually reached a dead end by 1954. The Liberals continued vainly to appeal for understanding and reforms, while the Radicals were falling out among themselves over their inability to find a successful nationalist program. In these conditions a third group of politically active young men made the decision to break with the ongoing political process and to turn directly to armed insurrection as the only means of both reuniting the badly divided political elite and of obtaining independence from a recalcitrant and threatened French government. Because of their key role in beginning the Algerian revolution, this third group will be referred to as the Revolutionaries. Unfortunately, this term has many other psychological connotations which are not always valid in discussing these Algerians.[1] As used throughout this study the term Revolutionary, as distinct from Liberal or Radical politician, describes those individuals who were both active in politics before 1954, particularly within the paramilitary *Organisation Spéciale* (os), and immediately involved in preparing the armed revolution. All of these men thus occupied both political roles in the colonial period and military ones during the war for independence. In this they differ from the Politicians, whose roles before and after 1954 were primarily political ones, and the Military, who were not involved in pre-1954 politics and who entered leadership roles only as a result of military achievements. The most obvious members of this group of Revolutionaries are the approximately thirty men who are generally credited with beginning the revolution,[2] plus another eleven who were involved in politics before 1954 and who, although not among the instigators of the insurrection, left their political careers and took up arms in order to fight for their beliefs.[3]

---

[1] Several psychological studies of political leaders based on the insights of Harold D. Lasswell have presented an image of the "revolutionary personality." See, for example, E. Victor Wolfenstein, *The Revolutionary Personality: Lenin, Trotsky, Gandhi,* and Alexander L. George and Juliette L. George, *Woodrow Wilson and Colonel House: A Personality Study.* In simplified fashion, the revolutionary is one, in their models, who suffers from low self-esteem based on strained relations with his father. The revolutionary turns to politics, then, in order to overcome low estimates of his own worth. In the colonial setting it might be said that the entire political and social system operates so as to heighten the probability of damaging an individual's self-esteem. It would not then be unusual to find many "natives" entering politics in order to compensate for feelings of inadequacy, and one might even expect them to develop the personality traits mentioned by George and Wolfenstein, namely that they tend to be autocratic, hard for colleagues to work with, and ready to identify with the masses, though hesitant to enter into close personal relations. Some of these characteristics can be found among Algerian Revolutionaries, in particular the unwillingness to compromise and the identification with the masses while avoiding more intimate relations.

[2] See Appendix D for a list of CRUA members.

[3] These eleven non-CRUA Revolutionaries are Dhilès, Mahsas, Batel, Mahmoud Cherif, Ahmed Kaid, Guerroudj, Mendjli, Stambouli, Mezhoudi, Ouzegane, and Saadi Yacef.

The Backgrounds and Careers of the Revolutionaries

The Revolutionaries came to politics by paths much different from those of the Politicians. Their family, school, and occupational experiences did not produce a strong desire for modernization and respect for legality. Rather, they seemed much more sensitive to colonialism as an attack upon their own self-esteem, and in reaction they developed intense feelings of their own right to lead the struggle against France. Likewise, their direct experience in colonial politics was that of failure, and when politics in the sense of elections, bargaining, and compromise seemed futile, violence appeared to provide an answer to feelings of both personal and political impotence.

Of the forty-one Revolutionaries considered here, all were holders of some political elite position between 1954 and 1968. Ten Revolutionaries, however, are included merely for having been among the small "Committee of 22," which was instrumental in beginning the revolution. Either because of subsequent death, arrest, or inability their political influence stopped with this rather limited contribution. At least thirteen of the forty-one had their political careers cut short by death during the war for independence. But the importance of this group is nonetheless apparent when one realizes that the first President of Algeria was a Revolutionary (Ben Bella), as were three of the most powerful members of the GPRA (Boussouf, Ben Tobbal, and Krim), four of the five members of the first Political Bureau (Bitat, Ben Bella, Ben Alla, and Khider), fifteen deputies, and six of the most prominent leaders of opposition in exile groups. But in 1968 only three Revolutionaries remained in high political positions. The extraordinary rise and fall of this group is perhaps the most distinctive feature of Algeria's political development. Consequently it seems worthwhile to discover who these Revolutionaries were, what characterized their socialization into politics, and what roles they have played since 1954.

The Revolutionaries as a group show considerable variety in their social backgrounds and in their experiences. Almost all of them were born between 1918 and 1928, with 1922 being the average year of birth for the entire group. It is important to note that the average year of birth for the Radicals was also 1922. Thus, whereas the differences between the Liberals, whose average year of birth was 1905, and the Radicals were largely accounted for by their belonging to different generations, the Radicals and the Revolutionaries belonged to the same age group. They entered politics at much the same time, and yet their formation and subsequent beliefs were quite different. What was it that distinguished the Radicals from the Revolutionaries?

One would look in vain to find important regional differences in the backgrounds of the Radicals and the Revolutionaries. Nineteen of the Revolutionaries were from the department of Constantine, eight from Algiers, seven from Kabylia, and five from Oran. As with the Radicals, most came from small towns (eleven) or villages (nine), with only a handful from the larger cities (six).

Since most of the Revolutionaries spent many years living in clandestinity, not much is known about their prepolitical experiences. It does seem, however, that by and large they come from more modest origins than the Politicians. There are a few notable exceptions of relatively advantaged Revolutionaries,[4] but even more common are reports of Revolutionaries whose families had once been prosperous but who had lost wealth and prestige over the years, perhaps as a result of French colonization.[5]

But no matter how modest the origins of the Revolutionaries, they were still generally better off than the illiterate peasant masses. The key to this slight advantage was once again education, but in the case of the Revolutionaries education does not seem to have played the dominant political socialization role that it did for the Radicals. This is probably a result of the lower quality of education as well as the more modest educational level reached by the Revolutionaries. Of those whose educational backgrounds are known, only four received university educations, whereas nearly all of the Politicians were so privileged. At least twelve received only secondary education, while four—and perhaps many more—are known to have attended only primary school.

Already one sees that there is a socioeconomic basis as well as a generational one for categorizing the Liberals, Radicals and Revolutionaries. While the Liberals and the Radicals belonged to different political generations, their socioeconomic status and their education were similar. By way of contrast, the Radicals and the Revolutionaries belonged to the same political generation, but their socioeconomic status and their educational level differed significantly.

In addition to a social and educational status lower than that of

---

[4] For example, Abane Ramdane and Mustapha Ben Boulaid.

[5] For example, Boudiaf, Boussouf, Guerroudj, and Mezhoudi are cases of this type of downward family mobility.

the Radicals, the Revolutionaries entered politics differently. Since the definition of Revolutionary used here requires that an individual be prominent in politics before 1954 and active in the military after 1954, all the Revolutionaries were already in relatively important political roles during the colonial period. The largest number, thirty-five, were members of Messali's PPA-MTLD. But in addition to mere membership, most of these individuals were also involved in the paramilitary section of the MTLD, the *Organisation Spéciale*. Seven of the Revolutionaries also participated in politics at the local level, serving as assistants or secretaries to the mayors of various communes. Six were candidates for political office, and one was elected deputy to the French National Assembly. Three more were at some time involved with Ferhat Abbas's moderate party, the UDMA, and two of these were even on its Central Committee.[6] Two more Revolutionaries were primarily associated with the Algerian Communist Party in the course of their political careers, and one was most active with the Reformist Ulama.[7]

The wartime roles filled by the Revolutionaries between 1954 and 1962 cover a wide range of military activities. At least eighteen were at one time or another leaders of a *willaya* (the basic military division in the FLN after 1956, equivalent to a military region), and five were involved with political-military operations in the capital of Algiers. Five were primarily in charge of procuring arms and rallying support abroad as part of the exterior delegation of the FLN.[8] Twelve of the Revolutionaries were in less important military positions within Algeria. In connection with their military or political activities during the war, ten were arrested, nine were killed by the French, and four were executed by the FLN for various "counterrevolutionary" activities.

To fill in this sketch of who the Revolutionaries were and what they did, their political socialization provides a means toward understanding the formation of their attitudes and their resulting behavior. As with the Liberals and the Radicals, the primary socializing agencies were the family, the school, occupations, and direct political participation.

---

[6] Ahmed Kaid and Mahmoud Cherif were both with the UDMA before entering military roles.

[7] Ouzegane and Guerroudj were with the Communists, and Mezhoudi was with the Ulama.

[8] This group suffered somewhat from not being perceived as having been directly involved in the fighting within Algeria.

As a group the Revolutionaries are harder to generalize about than the Liberals or the Radicals. Unlike these Politicians, who were similar to one another in political formation and attitudes, the Revolutionaries had in common primarily their rejection of the colonial political system and their belief that violence was indispensable for achieving independence. This minimal consensus was sufficient to link together the Revolutionaries during the difficult early phase of organizing the war for independence, but as the revolution progressed this core group disintegrated, and despite efforts at regrouping the wartime elite after independence, the Revolutionaries never regained their earlier unity. Some of the reasons for this seem apparent when one examines the variety of paths of political socialization of this group of Revolutionaries who were linked primarily by an intensely felt nationalism.

Political Socialization Within the Family

The contribution of the family environment to the political formation of the Revolutionaries is less clear than in the case of the Politicians. The range of overt family political socialization runs from virtually none to very intense political awareness developed within the family. The best known of the Revolutionaries and the first President of independent Algeria, Ahmed Ben Bella, assigns virtually no importance to his family or his early years in the development of his feelings of nationalism or anticolonialism. He says, "In Marnia, during my childhood, I did not feel the difference between Frenchmen and Algerians as much as I later did at Tlemcen." [9] Marnia, Ben Bella's birthplace, had a small European population and the few relations which took place between French and Algerians were apparently cordial. Ben Bella recalls, for example, that the soccer team he was on was always integrated at Marnia, but that at Tlemcen, where he attended secondary school, Europeans and Muslims had their own teams.

For other Revolutionaries politics and colonialism must have been literally household words.[10] Two important leaders of the revolution, Boussouf and Boudiaf, both had relatives in politics. A

[9] Quoted in Robert Merle, *Ahmed Ben Bella*, p. 24.
[10] Charles-Henri Favrod, *Le* FLN *et l'Algérie*, pp. 275–284, contains Belkacem Krim's own account of his early life. Krim lived in a "nationalist milieu" and described himself as belonging to "the generation of Algerians which had no adolescence," having passed directly from childhood to adult responsibility.

cousin of Boussouf had been active with the Liberals around Ferhat Abbas, and other of his relatives may have been linked to the Algerian Communist Party.[11] Boudiaf came from a family of some consequence in the region of M'Sila, and a relative of his was a communist candidate in the elections to the Algerian Assembly of 1948. Abdelkader Guerroudj, one of the few members of the Algerian Communist Party to enter the political elite, albeit briefly, was distantly related to Messali Hadj and had uncles who were members of the PPA and MTLD. In his case he found the uncles so concerned with merely improving their own well-being that he turned away from the PPA-MTLD and at the age of nineteen became a member of the Algerian Communist Party.[12]

A somewhat less typical Revolutionary, Brahim Mezhoudi, tells how his family instilled in him at an early age a strongly anti-French orientation. Two of Mezhoudi's ancestors had died fighting the conquering French forces in the nineteenth century, and his once rather prosperous family had been forced to abandon the fertile land around Bone for the more remote region of Tebessa. Mezhoudi's father refused to allow him to go to the French school in the nearby village, sending him to the Quranic school instead. Mezhoudi recalls having often fought with French children after his family moved into the *colon* village where he grew up, and his parents sanctioned this fighting because the French were the "enemy." [13]

This image of family political influence on the Revolutionaries is neither clear nor complete. What appears to be lacking, however, are the relatively consistent accounts given by the Politicians of a gradually developed awareness during their childhood of inequalities, of injustices and discrimination. Rather, the Revolutionaries seem to have been either almost oblivious to the colonial system during their youth or intensely aware of both the evils of colonialism and of the actions of nationalist groups seeking to change the system.

While little appears in the biographies of Revolutionaries about their childhood, it is possible to determine the type of birthplace of most of the Revolutionaries, and this can serve as an indicator of the environment in which they were raised. In the 1920s and

[11] This is hinted at in Claude Paillat, *Dossier secret de l'Algérie*, Chapter 2.
[12] Guerroudj interview.
[13] Mezhoudi interview.

TABLE 5.1   PLACE OF BIRTH OF POLITICIANS AND REVOLU-
TIONARIES

Place of Birth	Politicians	Revolutionaries	1954 Muslim Population
Commune de pleine exercice	82%	73%	43%
Commune mixte	18%	27%	57%
	Number = 16	n = 26	n = 7,700,000

1930s a Muslim child would have been slightly more likely to be
born in what the French termed a *commune mixte* than a *commune de pleine exercice*. A *commune mixte* was an administrative unit populated largely by Muslims, most of whom lived in
small villages. The *communes mixtes* tended to be found in relatively isolated areas, away from the large cities, and were free from
much contact with the European population. The *communes de
pleine exercice*, on the other hand, were formed wherever a sizable
European population existed, and here the full French system of
local government operated as it did in France. It has been suggested
that the most remote areas of Algeria produced few of Algeria's
political leaders, and it is no surprise that nearly three-fourths
of the Revolutionaries were born in *communes de pleine exercice*
(73 percent) rather than in *communes mixtes* (27 percent). Nonetheless, the Revolutionaries were less likely than the Politicians to
have been born in the areas of European influence. (See Table 5.1.)
Equally important is the fact that the Revolutionaries were born
in those small *communes de pleine exercice* which were predomi-
nately rural in nature. (See Table 5.2.)

TABLE 5.2 SIZE OF COMMUNES DE PLEINE EXERCICE OF
BIRTH FOR POLITICIANS AND REVOLUTIONARIES

Size of Commune de pleine exercice of Birth	Politicians	Revolutionaries	1954 Muslim Population in Communes de pleine exercice
Under 30,000 (largely rural)	54%	68%	59%
Over 30,000 (largely urban)	46%	32%	41%
	Number = 13	n = 19	n = 4,200,000

These two facts—the tendency, in comparison with the Politicians, for the Revolutionaries to come from areas less influenced by the European presence and from more rural areas in general—lend some support to the impressions gathered from the Revolutionaries' biographies. In the rural areas an Algerian might be unaware of colonialism and national politics. Yet if he were to become informed in some way about the European colonial system, the generally miserable conditions of rural Algerian life might serve to sharpen his sense of grievance and outrage toward the colonial system. Hence one could expect some of the Revolutionaries to have developed their intense political feelings at an early age through the combination of awareness of the pitiful circumstances about them and enlightenment in regard to the reasons for the peasants' poverty and backwardness. Nor is it surprising to find Revolutionaries whose childhood seems to have been spent in relative ignorance of the colonial system. The more unusual type of Revolutionary would be one whose childhood experiences had been like those of the Politicians who developed ambiguous feelings toward the French system because of their early exposure to both the benefits and liabilities of *colon* domination.

In short, it seems as if the intensity of political commitment which characterizes the psychology of the Revolutionaries may be reached in at least two distinct ways. At one extreme it is possible to find individuals who were raised in a highly political environment and whose early concern for political questions was the natural prelude to a very deep political involvement later in life. At the other extreme one encounters the Revolutionary who spent a large part of his early life unaware of political issues and political procedures but who, for some reason, became unusually sensitive to the world of politics later in life. One might speculate that the latter case characterizes people who turn to politics as a way of handling some personal problem (e.g., a felt need for respect, power, deference).[14] These individuals might excel at political agitation but would probably not be effective organizers of sustained political action. Unfortunately, the data of the type needed to substantiate this argument are lacking, and consequently the personality formation of the Revolutionaries remains in part unexplained. What does seem certain, however, is that the Revolutionaries do not fit a single psychological mold and that their personalities, marked by an

[14] See Harold D. Lasswell, *Psychopathology and Politics*, Chapter 5.

intense concern for politics, were formed in several ways, two of which have been suggested here as ideal types.[15]

School Socialization

In discussing the impact of the school environment on the political formation of the Politicians, it was argued that the skills and values relevant to careers in politics were largely those formed during late adolescence within the school setting. In a more general sense it has been indicated that the Algerian political elite differed most clearly from the Muslim population at large in the relatively high level of education attained by its members. Both these assertions are generally valid for the part of the political elite defined here as Revolutionaries, and yet a change of emphasis is needed. The school environment was indeed instrumental in awakening or intensifying nationalist sentiments among the Revolutionaries, but it does not seem to have contributed as directly to their training as future political leaders as was true for the Politicians.

The lesser importance of the school experience in socializing the Revolutionaries into politics stems primarily from two sources. First, some of the Revolutionaries did not pursue their education much beyond the elementary level. Second, few Revolutionaries became involved in student politics or the Muslim scouts, activities which seem to have contributed heavily to the political formation of the Politicians as well as that of the young intellectuals and technicians of a later generation.

A careful investigation of the places of birth of the members of the political elite reveals one of the few nearly universal facts applicable to this heterogeneous group. Without exception the leaders whose birthplace is known were born in towns or villages which had at least one primary school classroom.[16] This does not, of course, mean that all members of the elite attended these schools, but it does help account for the fact that, unlike the population as a whole, most of these leaders received some education. Even the Revolutionaries, who typically came from less advantaged backgrounds, were born in communes where the ratio of population

---

[15] Wolfenstein, *The Revolutionary Personality*, indicates that there are many paths to the creation of a "revolutionary personality."

[16] Data are drawn from the 1948 census in making these calculations.

per primary classroom was about the same as it was for the Politicians.[17]

But even if the Revolutionaries seem to have all acquired some education, few were able to pursue their studies past the secondary level. Once again Ben Bella, as the most prominent of the Revolutionaries, offers an interesting example. After finishing his elementary studies in his home town of Marnia, Ben Bella was sent to the nearby city of Tlemcen to attend the lycée there. At the lycée he became more aware of discrimination against Muslims, particularly on the part of a French teacher who expressed his open scorn for the Muslim religion. Ben Bella claims that about this time he began to feel himself becoming a rebel, but most of his energy seems still to have been channeled into sports.[18] Without much commentary, Ben Bella mentions that in 1934 he failed his *brevet* exams [19] and decided not to try to pass them the next year because he had already concluded that school would only prepare him to enter the colonialist administration.[20] Considering the tremendous stress placed on education by most Algerians, Ben Bella's matter-of-fact acknowledgment of his failure in school is surprising and is quite likely a later rationalization of what must have been an important crisis at the time. In any case, because of his early departure from school, Ben Bella's political education was not much advanced in the classroom.

In a rather indirect way, however, Ben Bella's nationalist formation owes something to the educational system. He explicitly states that his first initiation to politics came through the influence of a friend who was a student in a *medersa*.[21] Through this friend he first made contact with Messali's PPA in 1937. Says Ben Bella, "The nationalist current was much stronger at that time in the *medersa*s,

---

[17] The figure for both groups is about 750 people per classroom in the communes of birth.

[18] A schoolmate of Ben Bella, who later became prominent in nationalist politics and who played on the same soccer team as Ben Bella at Tlemcen, claimed that as a soccer player Ben Bella always wanted to be the one to score the goal and played largely for the grandstands. Many of his later colleagues recognized these same qualities in his political behavior.

[19] The *brevet* exam is generally taken after four years of secondary school. To many better educated politicians, the fact that Ben Bella did not have any secondary degree was seen as a reason for his feelings of intellectual inferiority and for his dependence on leftist intellectuals for many of his ideas.

[20] Robert Merle, *Ahmed Ben Bella*, Chapter 1, covers this period of Ben Bella's life.

[21] A *medersa* is a school for Muslims, where teaching is done in Arabic.

whose clientele was one hundred per cent Muslim, than in the French schools." [22]

Whether in fact the *medersa*s were the training grounds for a large number of Algerian nationalists is unclear, but at least one Revolutionary attended a *medersa*. Brahim Mezhoudi, after finishing his primary education in the local Quranic school, attended the *medersa* in Tebessa for three or four years. The significance of this part of his education was that it brought him under the influence of the Reformist Ulama, especially Sheikh Larbi Tebessi. His deep commitment to Islam, Arabic language, and education stemmed from this period, although little overt political education seems to have been acquired in the *medersa*. Rather, it was when he went to Zitouna Mosque University in Tunis, where he spent six years, that he became associated with a PPA group. And, in his words, the generation of the 1930s at Zitouna "did politics," traveling between Algiers and Tunis, talking of Maghribi unity and independence.[23]

For the remainder of the Revolutionaries the little that is known about their education does not change the general impression that emerges from an analysis of their family experiences. Either the Revolutionaries were politically committed at a young age because of family influences and remained politically aware during their school days, or they were relatively oblivious to politics as children and school did little to change this lack of interest. For those whose families had not made them politically aware of colonialism, the schools appear to have had little added influence. Rather, it seems to be that some of these Revolutionaries first became active in politics after leaving school. To clarify this rather late political formation of individuals who became notorious as committed nationalists it is necessary to examine the occupations and early political involvement of these late developers.

Occupational Political Socialization

In comparing the Revolutionaries to the Politicians in terms of occupational background, one is struck by the remarkable differences between these two groups. Whereas the Politicians had predominantly come from liberal professions, in keeping with

[22] Robert Merle, *Ahmed Ben Bella*, p. 30.
[23] Mezhoudi interview.

both their high level of education and their subsequent political roles, the Revolutionaries were definitely not lawyers, doctors, or pharmacists. No doubt the lower educational level of the Revolutionaries excluded them from these professions. And consequently it is not surprising to find the Revolutionaries, before they became active politicians, belonging to lower-status occupations. Several Revolutionaries at one time or another were workers, either in small industries or on the land.[24] Others were involved in commerce, union activities, or teaching. But most typical of this group were the Revolutionaries who began to make careers in the French army.[25]

Since many Revolutionaries came of draft age about the time of World War II, it is normal that a sizable number would have been compelled to serve in the French army. What is remarkable is that several Revolutionaries actually became officers in the army and even contemplated making a permanent career of the military. Ben Bella, again the prime example, served for over five years in the French army, reached the rank of sergeant, and was decorated for his participation in the Italian campaign of 1943–1944.

Certainly the experience of serving in the French military was of great importance in the later political careers of many Revolutionaries. The military skills acquired in the army were of immense value for Revolutionaries like Ben Bella, Krim, and Ouamrane. And yet it seems strange that men willing to fight with French forces in World War II became ardent opponents of France a few years later. It is apparent that most Algerians who served with the French forces did, in fact, remain remarkably loyal to France, even during the period of the war for independence. At no time from 1954 to 1962 did the number of Algerians fighting with the ALN for independence match the number of Algerians fighting on the French side against the rebels.[26] What, then, led a handful of young Algerians with experience in the French army to become intransigent Revolutionaries, dedicated to eliminating French influence in Algeria by use of violence?

Ben Bella has related in some detail his life in the French army.[27] Throughout most of his account of these years he describes a

---

[24] For example, Khider, Bitat, Guerroudj, Yacef, Ouzegane.

[25] For example, Ben Bella, Krim, Ouamrane, Mahmoud Cherif, Kobus, Hadj Ben Alla, and less enthusiastically, Khider and Boudiaf.

[26] See Arslan Humbaraci, *Algeria*, Chapter 2.

[27] Robert Merle, *Ahmed Ben Bella*, Chapter 2.

fraternal atmosphere in which Frenchmen and Algerians were treated with remarkable equality and fairness. A few isolated instances are mentioned of discrimination toward him on the part of French officers, but these cases are notable because they were exceptional. For Ben Bella, and perhaps for other Revolutionaries, the experience in the French army did not deepen previous nationalist feelings. If anything, it contributed to a sense of self-respect arising from having successfully competed with Frenchmen and having been fairly treated in the process. Perhaps if the relatively egalitarian culture of army life had characterized the Revolutionaries' relations with Europeans they would never have turned to politics. But, of course, these Algerian French officers were bound to be reminded continually that the *colons* of Algeria would never accept them as equals, even if they fought for the liberation of France from Fascism. For Ben Bella the realization that all his military decorations counted for nothing in the eyes of the *colons* came upon his return to Algeria in 1945. Coupled with the stories of the brutal French repressions of May 1945, this awareness of the injustices of the colonial system in contrast to the relative equality which marked French military life contributed greatly to the making of at least one Revolutionary.[28]

For the Revolutionaries who were not members of the French army the effect of their nonpolitical careers on later political attitudes is less clear. The Revolutionaries who spent some years as common workers seem to have developed a rather strong identi-fication with the "impoverished Muslim masses" or the "exploited peasantry." Even among the well-educated Revolutionaries one hears such reflections of this attitude as, "I can never really trust any Algerian leader who hasn't known the misery of the masses [as I have]." Consequently it has become fashionable for members of the Algerian political elite to refer to themselves as "sons of poor peasants," although in many cases this is a great distortion. For those few who really are of very modest origins or have worked as peasants, miners, or factory laborers, these experiences seem to have added to a feeling of a personal "calling" to politics and to a close identification with the "masses." Thus, for some of the Revolutionaries, one of their dominant characteristics—namely an intense conviction that they alone had the right to exercise

[28] *Ibid.*, pp. 63–64.

political power—can be traced in part to their occupational back-grounds.

With the end of World War II and the repression of May 1945 the protorevolutionary workers and the ex-French army officers began to find that they shared perceptions of colonialism and views of what needed to be done. The brief uniting of these highly politicized and individualistic Revolutionaries into a cohesive clandestine brotherhood was a major factor in bringing about the Algerian revolution. How, then, were the political predispositions created by family, school, and occupational experiences acted upon so as to create political leaders of these young Algerian nationalists?

Political Participation of the Revolutionaries

The earliest form of direct political participation of most of the Revolutionaries was membership in the PPA, and later the MTLD, of Messali Hadj. A few were more attracted to Ferhat Abbas, the communists or the Reformist Ulama, but at least three-fourths of the Revolutionaries gained their initial political party experience under the tutelage of Messali and his colleagues. But even though all of the Revolutionaries were active in the pre-1954 nationalist political process, the more significant fact is that nearly all of them by 1954 were deeply alienated from the ongoing legal political system in which the Politicians were participating. This disillusion-ment seems to have had its origins in the repeated failures of the Revolutionaries to work within or even on the margins of the colonial political system. Unlike the Politicians, who achieved considerable personal success within the colonial system (although they were repeatedly thwarted in obtaining their ultimate goals), the Revolutionaries were neither personally successful under this system nor influential in reaching their desired ends. Consequently, when the Revolutionaries finally made their bid for leadership of the liberation movement, they broke violently both with the colonial system and with the existing Muslim political parties.

The Algerian Revolutionaries have often been presented, and have presented themselves, as the one group of nationalists which was free of illusions about the possibilities of reform from within the colonial system. In this view it is stressed that the Revolution-aries passed from early political awareness directly to illegal, clan-destine activities aimed at overthrowing French rule. It has already been argued that early political awareness was not a dominant characteristic of many of the Revolutionaries. Likewise, it is untrue that no attempt to work within the system was made. Rather, for more than a dozen of the best known Revolutionaries an attempt was indeed made, but for most it failed.

Ahmed Ben Bella, for example, upon his return to his native town of Marnia after World War II ran for the office of Municipal Councillor. He was elected along with other Muslims and Europeans, and after some difficulties he obtained an important administrative job that apparently provided considerable satisfaction to this young Revolutionary.[29] Before long, however, he sensed that the administration wanted to eliminate him by means of a "plot" that involved the confiscation of his father's farm by another Muslim. In order to recover his farm, Ben Bella tried legal means first, but when these failed he took direct action. Having dislodged the other claimant to the farm by force, he was obliged to defend it by force. In the course of fighting off a counterattack, he shot at and apparently wounded his opponent. He immediately sensed that under these circumstances he would be thrown in jail, so he left Marnia and his position as Municipal Councillor and became, in his words, "a clandestine militant." [30]

Ben Bella was not the only Revolutionary to be active in local politics before breaking with the colonial political system. Abane Ramdane, Mustapha Ben Boulaid, Belkacem Krim, Ahmed Kaid, and Ali Mendjli are other well-known Revolutionaries in this same category.

A second form of overt political participation within the colonial framework was common for the Revolutionaries. Ben Bella, Ben Boulaid, and Stambouli were all candidates, albeit unsuccessful ones, in the elections to the Algerian Assembly in 1948. Ouamrane ran for office as an MTLD candidate in 1947 but was defeated. Khider was a deputy in the French Assembly until 1951, when his parliamentary immunity was lifted and he was forced into exile in Cairo. Abdelkader Guerroudj was a Communist Party candidate to the *Conseil général* of Oran in 1955 after the outbreak of the revolution, but he was banned from Algeria because of his radical statements

---

[29] *Ibid.*, p. 67.

[30] *Ibid.*, p. 73. Ben Bella claims that his clandestinity began in 1947, but this does not correspond well with the fact that he was a candidate in the elections to the Algerian Assembly in May 1948 from his home town of Marnia. This casts some doubt on the whole story of why he quit as Municipal Councillor, but one may assume that the general outline is accurate although the effects were probably less immediate and dramatic.

and soon organized his own guerrilla fighters before merging with the FLN. Another one-time communist, Amar Ouzegane, had been Secretary General of the PCA but was expelled in 1948 for "nationalist deviations."

All these men, then, had tried in some way to work within the system, but few had been successful. The solution for many of these young Algerians as well as for most of the other Revolutionaries discussed here was to attempt to organize themselves into a new clandestine group dedicated to the use of violence, the *Organisation Spéciale* (os). Those Revolutionaries who joined the os in the late 1940s had already rejected politics as an effective means to independence and were now ready to try military tactics. In this way the Revolutionaries completed their distinctive political-military training which was to set them apart from the rest of the Algerian elite. Amar Ouamrane, an influential Revolutionary during the war, later reflected on his early experiences, saying:

> We were formed by our history—the constant revolts against France, the humiliations, the suffering, the shocking and revolting inequalities —all of this educated us. The nationalist parties sent deputies to the French Assembly, but their actions always ended in failure.[31]

The *Organisation Spéciale* had been created by the MTLD in 1947 at a party congress where it had been decided to fight colonialism "by all means," legal and illegal. The members of the os were young men determined to prepare for what they thought would be the inevitable armed confrontation with France. The first leader of the os was Belouizdad, who died in 1949 and was succeeded by Ait Ahmed, then by Ben Bella. Throughout 1949 a paramilitary organization was created. While the os was nominally under the control of the MTLD, it rapidly became a "party within a party," with its own leadership and procedures.[32] Of the Revolutionaries considered here, nearly three-fourths were members of the os. In addition, a few more Revolutionaries had organized a separate paramilitary group in the Kabylia mountains, which eventually joined the os to form the core revolutionary group of November 1954.

The os experience for the Revolutionaries was not a successful one. Once again it seemed as if these intense Revolutionaries were

---

[31] Interview with Amar Ouamrane.

[32] According to Benkhedda, "Contribution à l'historique du mouvement de libération nationale," p. 1, the *Etat Major* of the os in 1950 consisted of Ahmed Ben Bella, Hocine Ait Ahmed, and Abdelkader Belhadj (Kobus).

to find their careers marked by failure. Such was indeed nearly the case. Despite such minor victories as the robbery of the Oran Post Office, the os was relatively ineffective in its first years of existence. It did, however, organize a sizable group of Algerians who were prepared to risk their lives for Algerian independence. Living in conditions of clandestinity seems to have taught these Revolutionaries some skills appropriate for fighting a guerrilla war—secrecy, reliance on small cells, training with arms—but more importantly it convinced these men that they alone were working for the freedom of their country. Only those in the os, they seemed to think, were personally risking their lives for their beliefs, while the nationalist Politicians remained within the bounds of legality and occasionally even profited from being elected to various French bodies.[33] Also the os members seemed convinced that, despite the 1948 resolutions of the MTLD to give priority to the os, Messali and the Central Committee were too wedded to electoral politics ever to change and were consequently anxious to be rid of the troublesome young Revolutionaries.[34]

In March 1950, following a rather trivial incident, the French police identified many members of the os, and within a short period, most of its top leaders, including Ben Bella, were arrested. Once again the preparation for armed action had led to a disastrous failure that threatened to weaken the entire nationalist movement. Consequently, the Central Committee of the MTLD, with the agreement of the leaders of the os, decided to dissolve the paramilitary arm of the party.[35]

For those members of the os who were not arrested in 1950 the following four years were spent in clandestinity in the more remote zones of Algeria. These were years of practical banishment, during which the os members felt that the MTLD was purposely trying to undermine efforts to rebuild a paramilitary organization regrouping the old os participants. Despite these hardships, some of the os members did remain in contact with each other, including such famous Revolutionaries as Ben M'Hidi, Mourad Didouche, Bitat, Ben Boulaid, Boudiaf, Boussouf, Ben Tobbal, and Zighout Youssef. These were the men who provided the revolutionary core

[33] Batel interview. Also, Lakhdar Ben Tobbal, "Quelqu'en soit le prix, nous triompherons," in El Moudjahid, No. 3, 1956. Some os members, however, were also elected officials, for instance Khider and Ben Boulaid.
[34] Rabah Bitat in Révolution, No. 3, November 1963, pp. 5–6.
[35] Benkhedda, "Contribution," p. 1.

that was the immediate stimulus to the outbreak of war on November 1, 1954. To aid them in this enterprise were a few ex-os leaders in exile in Cairo, including Ait Ahmed, Mohammed Khider, and Ahmed Ben Bella, who had escaped from prison in 1952.

By 1954 a group of nationalistic Algerians had formed which differed significantly from the Politicians described earlier. Most basically, the Revolutionaries, through repeated frustrations and failures, had been led to reject politics within the colonial system as a meaningful way of gaining reforms, let alone independence. By rejecting colonial politics, the Revolutionaries were abandoning elections, petitions, competing political parties, mass organizations, and overt political propaganda. More specifically, they were rejecting the leadership of a group of nationalists, namely the Liberal and Radical politicians around such figures as Ferhat Abbas, Messali Hadj, and Benyoussef Benkhedda. They thought, also, that they were escaping the personal intrigues and struggles for influence which marked the internal life of the legal political parties. The "cult of personality" forming around Messali Hadj was particularly derided by the Revolutionaries.

Even such marginal Revolutionaries as Mezhoudi, who had left the PPA in the 1930s to work with the Ulama at educating the masses, expressed this alienation from politics. Looking back at his early career, he claimed that even when he was a member of the PPA he began to realize that much of politics was merely demagogy.[36] Another marginal Revolutionary, Sadek Batel, expressed his disillusionment with the PPA and Messali. After World War II he believed that the nationalists should not divide their strength by having two parties, the UDMA and the MTLD, which competed in elections. Rather the MTLD should refuse to participate in elections, concentrating more on clandestine organization. When Messali opposed this suggestion, Batel and many others left the party and turned to syndicalist activities for a number of years.[37] Like the os members, these Revolutionaries were disillusioned with the legal political process. After the war for independence finally began in November 1954, under the leadership of the ex-os members, these other alienated Revolutionaries were among the early participants.

In the course of this chapter it has been argued that the Algerian Revolutionaries formed during the colonial period were young

[36] Mezhoudi interview.
[37] Batel interview.

men of modest socioeconomic status who, by various and distinct paths, reached the intensely held belief that French colonialism could only be destroyed by violence. Little united these men other than a common dedication to this belief. They were not in any ordinary sense fanatics, it should be added, though they appeared more committed and singleminded than many of the Politicians. The major consequences of the Revolutionaries' political socialization before 1954 were that they developed a hostile view of the ongoing political process, a deep feeling of their individual right to exercise power, and skills as agitators which would be initially useful in starting an armed uprising but might be of limited value for the later tasks of organizing the revolution and administering a new state. In subsequent chapters the behavior of the Revolutionaries during the war for independence and the postindependence period will be examined. The early political socialization of the Revolutionaries described here will then take on its full importance, for while some attitudes and styles of behavior of the Revolutionaries seem to have been altered by the war or after independence, a large part of their behavior is to be understood best in terms of their political formation between approximately 1935 and 1954.

Liberals, Radicals, and Revolutionaries: Products of Colonialism

Of the members of the Algerian political elite that dominated nationalist politics between 1954 and 1968, a large number of individuals received their primary political socialization within the system of colonial politics. Among those receiving this primary formation before 1954 three groups have been distinguished: the Liberals, the Radicals, and the Revolutionaries. Between 1936 and 1954 the leadership of the nationalist forces within Algeria passed first from the hands of the Liberals to the Radicals, then from the Radicals to the Revolutionaries. Each of these developments was associated with a changing consensus as to the nature of the political problems of a given historical period.

In the mid–1930s it was widely believed by the Muslim Algerian elite that Algerians should associate themselves with France more closely than ever by demanding full political rights, including French citizenship. The major influences on the French to grant those goals stemmed from the actions of moderate Muslims who presented petitions asking for reform. The Liberal politicians, with their French education and training as doctors and lawyers, were well qualified by their political experiences to dominate the politics of this period, for they were skilled in compromise, bargaining, and petitioning.

World War II brought dramatic changes throughout the colonial world, including Algeria. Following the war there was a new elite consensus that assimilation was a dead issue and that some form of independence was required. The means for achieving these goals were seen primarily to be mass organization, propaganda, and elections. The Radical politicians, whose political formation had taught them primarily the skills of organization and propaganda, and whose commitment to a clearly nationalistic ideal was less ambiguous than that of the Liberals, were well placed to dominate the nationalist movement for most of the years between 1946 and 1954. But like the Liberals, the Radicals were ultimately unsuccessful, as even they recognized, and consequently they were relatively quick to acknowledge the claims to leadership of a third group.

The Revolutionaries, from more modest and more diverse origins, had originally organized in order to defend their intensely held belief that independence was only to be won by force and violence. They defined themselves primarily by what and whom they were against. In the course of their political formation they developed considerable skill as agitators, and a few even became effective organizers. When by 1953 and 1954 it was widely recognized that the legal political movements had reached a dead end, the Revolutionaries reorganized and prepared to act. On November 1, 1954, they announced the formation of the *Front de Libération Nationale* (FLN). The Liberals and Radicals were not long in disbanding their own organizations, and many subsequently rallied to the FLN.

Thus, a changing consensus on the possibilities of political action to attain specific goals had allowed one group after another to dominate the nationalist movement. And as each group assumed that role, the challenge was to provide effective leadership or risk being displaced by another set of political actors with other skills and beliefs. By 1954 it seemed as if the Revolutionaries might successfully respond to this need, thereby reversing the long series of failures, both personal and organizational, which had marked their careers. Such was the hope but, as is so often the case, reality was to prove itself more complex.

6

The Early Years of the Revolution

Although the Algerian nationalist movement had been marked by deep divisions preceding the outbreak of the revolution of November 1954, it might have been thought that the decision to resort to armed violence would mean that a small, relatively homogeneous group of Revolutionaries could lead Algeria to independence. Had this been possible, the older, more legalistic nationalist politicians would simply have ceased to be part of the political elite. Perhaps, then, the instability that characterized Algerian political life after 1954 would have been less extreme.

But just as the Revolutionaries were able to seize control of the nationalist movement because of divisions and lack of success among the more established nationalist elite, so also it was the lack of integration among the Revolutionaries as well as their rather modest range of skills which permitted the reentry of the Liberals and Radicals into the political elite after less than two years of the revolution.

In retrospect, many Algerians have seen the diversity of beliefs and values within the wartime FLN as the primary reason for the failure to create a tightly knit party capable of surviving the transition to independence. But while this observation is un-

87

doubtedly accurate, it ignores the fact that the Revolutionaries could not have preserved the FLN as a small, homogeneous party, for they were incapable of leading the war for independence without the aid of the more experienced nationalist politicians.

Why, one may ask, were the Revolutionaries unable to provide effective leadership, and what convinced them of the need to include the Liberals and Radicals, whose politics they had earlier rejected, in the wartime FLN?

The year 1954 was a fateful one for both France and Algeria. In that year France was forced both to admit to a humiliating defeat in Indochina and to devise a strategy to deal with the incipient spread of violence in Tunisia and Morocco. One consolation to many Frenchmen at the time was that Algeria, at least, remained calm. Not only did Algeria seem to be immune from the violent contagion in neighboring countries, but also the radical wing of the nationalist movement, the MTLD, was clearly passing through a debilitating internal crisis.

French intelligence sources, it is safe to assume, were partially aware that a dissident group of nationalists was pressing for armed action. After all, preparations for armed insurrection had been unmasked in 1945 and 1950. Just as certainly, however, the French must have judged that the few committed Revolutionaries in Algeria had no mass following, few arms, and no clear plan of action. This estimate would have been accurate in 1954, and yet within a few years France found herself with more troops fighting in Algeria than she had ever committed in Indochina. The ultimate cost of the Algerian war to France, in terms of men, resources, and political stability was great indeed. But for Algerians, both Muslims and Europeans, the war was even more destructive.

Preparations for Insurrection

The Algerian war for independence began with a few sporadic, though coordinated, acts of violence on the night of October 31–November 1, 1954. Several first-hand accounts of the background and preparations for this historic moment exist.[1] From these

---

[1] See Rabah Bitat, in *Révolution*, No. 3, November 1963; Mohammed Boudiaf, *Où va l'Algérie?*; Rabah Bitat in *L'Express*, November 7, 1963, p. 19; Zoubir Bouadjadj, in *Révolution et Travail*, No. 100, October 1965; Benyoussef Benkhedda, "Contribution à l'historique du mouvement de libération nationale." For secondary accounts of the outbreak of the revolution, both based in part

a relatively coherent picture emerges, although differences in detail mark the various renditions. According to all versions, the MTLD underwent a serious internal crisis in 1953. Messali was clearly becoming increasingly authoritarian, perhaps in response to a threat to his leadership from the Radicals of the Central Committee. Messali appears to have believed that the masses would follow him if a crisis arose, and in this he may well have been right. But the party cadres and the party finances were controlled by the Central Committee.[2]

During 1953 the MTLD was shaken by several disputes revolving around the question of who should effectively lead the party. At meetings of the Central Committee held in mid-September, Messali decided to withdraw his confidence from the acting Secretary General, Benkhedda, while at the same time demanding that the Central Committee grant him "full powers."[3] The Central Committee, however, refused to comply with Messali's demand. A final split with Messali was avoided for the moment, but by January of 1954 the Central Committee was faced with an ultimatum from Messali which once again insisted that he be given full powers, despite the fact that he was then under house arrest in France. The response of the Central Committee was vague but conciliatory. Late in March certain of Messali's demands were met, but the Central Committee continued to retain full control over party finances. Three months later the powers ceded to Messali were withdrawn, and the stage was set for a final split between Messalists and Centralists.

Benkhedda has claimed that this conflict between Messali and the Centralists paralyzed the party and prevented the intended restructuring of the clandestine OS.[4] The vacillation of the Centralists in the face of Messali's growing authoritarianism seems to have encouraged the more revolutionary tendency of the party, the ex–OS members who were in hiding, to consider taking action themselves.[5] The question for these young Revolutionaries was

on captured documents, see Serge Bromberger, *Les rebelles algériens* and Claude Paillat, *Dossier secret de l'Algérie.* More recently, Yves Courrière, *Les fils de la Toussaint,* has written a detailed account of the few months preceding the revolution, based on interviews with both Algerian and French leading personalities.

[2] Dahlab interview.

[3] For a full account of these internal disputes from the Centralist viewpoint, see *La nation algérienne,* No. 1, September 3, 1954.

[4] Benyoussef Benkhedda, "Contribution," p. 2.

[5] Rabah Bitat, in *Révolution.*

whether to try to reunite the party and weld it into an effective instrument of insurrection or to strike out on their own without the benefits or the liabilities of the legal party organization.[6]

As the crisis within the MTLD became increasingly severe, a sizable number of OS militants began to consider the prospects for immediate armed insurrection as a means of escaping from the stagnation into which the nationalist movement had fallen. For several months these hesitant Revolutionaries alternated between trying to mend the rifts within their own party and starting a war for independence which would sharply break with the past political efforts of the Radicals and Liberals. This ambiguous position, midway between revolution and mediation, was underlined in the name given to the group generally credited with having begun the Algerian Revolution, the *Comité Révolutionnaire d'Unité et d'Action,* or more conveniently, the CRUA.

The CRUA has often been considered the prototype of the FLN leadership, a core of Revolutionaries dedicated to the use of violence to liberate Algeria from French colonialism. The members of the CRUA have derived considerable moral advantage from their claim to have begun the revolution, and yet ironically there is no consensus as to what the CRUA really was nor as to who its members were. Various accounts of the formation of the CRUA exist, one of which places its founding as early as autumn 1953. But more often the CRUA is seen as having come into being sometime between March and July, 1954.

It is usually recognized that the primary leader of the CRUA was Mohammed Boudiaf. Consequently, his account of the founding of the CRUA should carry substantial weight.[7] Boudiaf claims that in March 1954 he formed a four-man committee which included two ex-OS members and two members of the Central Committee of the MTLD. This group, which he calls the CRUA, had as a goal the reuniting of the MTLD rank and file to keep them from following either faction of the MTLD. The CRUA hoped to impose a unitary party Congress on Messali and the Central Committee. By August 1954, however, it was clear that nothing could save the party from a final break, as both Messali and the Central Committee held separate congresses which mutually expelled each other from the MTLD. Its mission now irrelevant, the CRUA was

---

[6] Zoubir Bouadjadj, in *Révolution et Travail.*
[7] Mohammed Boudiaf, *Où va l'Algérie?*

dissolved, having already been abandoned by two of its members in favor of the Central Committee.[8] In Boudiaf's version the CRUA was relatively unimportant and certainly unsuccessful.[9]

More often, however, the name CRUA has been applied to a broader grouping of ex-OS militants who met during the spring of 1954 to plan an eventual insurrection. Later this interior group developed links with the external group of Ben Bella, Ait Ahmed, and Khider, which had been established in Cairo for several years with the purpose of obtaining international support and aid for the cause of Algerian liberation. These two groups, then, make up what is commonly termed the CRUA. But it should be emphasized that the entire CRUA never met together and that it was the interior group which laid the plans for the revolution during the spring and summer of 1954 and then communicated their decisions to the exterior group in the fall of the same year.

The interior group of the CRUA included at its core a *Comité des 22*. It was these men, and in particular their six leaders, who were primarily responsible for seizing the initiative from the legal political parties and beginning the war for independence. Sometime during June or July of 1954, and here accounts by participants differ, twenty-two young Algerians met at Clos Salembier near Algiers.[10] According to one member, the group discussed the desirability of starting an armed revolution, whether they should organize before

[8] *Ibid.*, pp. 70 ff.

[9] Other participants in what has normally been called the CRUA gave a different story. Bitat, Bouadjadj, Ben Bella, and Ouamrane all consider themselves to have belonged to something called the CRUA, which indicates that even if Boudiaf's narrow committee was the "real CRUA," the name was adopted by other Algerian Revolutionaries. Boudiaf, in reducing the importance of the CRUA, is probably attempting to discredit the claim of Ben Bella and others of having belonged to the "historic" group that began the revolution. Thus he plays down the CRUA as well as the idea of the "committee of nine," the so-called *chefs historiques*, namely Ait Ahmed, Ben Bella, Ben Boulaid, Ben M'Hidi, Bitat, Boudiaf, Didouche, Khider, and Krim.

The importance of the "nine fathers of the Algerian Revolution" has been built up by many authors, and yet these nine never met before November, 1954, to discuss the war for independence. Not surprisingly, following Ben Bella's ouster in 1965, one rarely sees reference to either the CRUA or the "nine."

[10] Dates given for this meeting are early June 1954, July 10, July 21, July 22, and July 27, 1954. Aside from possible purposeful distortion, it seems that these discrepancies indicate that men living in clandestinity pay little heed to recording dates (or names) carefully. Yves Courrière, *Les fils de la Toussaint*, p. 157, insists that this meeting took place on July 25. Prior to this historic meeting, Ben Boulaid, Ben M'Hidi, Bitat, Boudiaf, Didouche, and Krim had been in frequent contact and had been actively recruiting followers for their "third force," the CRUA.

or after the beginning of the insurrection, and whether such a fight should be limited or unlimited. The "twenty-two" decided upon the principles of an unlimited fight and of organizing after the revolution began. Boudiaf and Ben M'Hidi were nominated to form a directing body for the revolution, and on the second ballot Boudiaf was elected. He in turn named Mourad Didouche, Larbi Ben M'Hidi, Mustapha Ben Boulaid, and Rabah Bitat as coleaders to form a *comité de direction*. In August relations with the Kabyles were strengthened, and Belkacem Krim was formally added as a sixth member of the *comité de direction*. (See Appendix C for a full list of the *Comité des 22* and the CRUA.)

After these decisions had been taken by the "twenty-two," a delegation was sent to Switzerland to meet Ben Bella, who in turn relayed the information to Ait Ahmed and Mohammed Khider in Cairo.[11] The three "externals" in Cairo were given the mission of collecting arms and money to support the revolution. These three, plus the six members of the *comité de direction,* came to be known, somewhat misleadingly, as the *"chefs historiques"* of the revolution.

In preparation for the coming insurrection, Algeria was divided into five zones, later to be called *willayas,* with recognized leaders, plus the Sahara, which was provisionally led by an unreliable minor figure. Boudiaf was responsible for overall organization and relations with the exterior. The zone leadership is shown in Table 6.1.

TABLE 6.1   ALGERIAN WILLAYAS AND LEADERS

Zone	Leader	Second in Command
Aurès	Mustapha Ben Boulaid	Bachir Chihani
North Constantine	Mourad Didouche	Zighout Youssef
Kabylia	Belkacem Krim	Amar Ouamrane
Algerois	Rabah Bitat	Bachir Suidani
Oranie	Larbi Ben M'Hidi	Ramdane Ben Abdelmalek
Sahara	(unassigned)	

Except for the leaders in Kabylia, who had both served as officers in the same regiment of the French Army, all the zone leaders and assistants were exmembers of the os. The five zone leaders plus Boudiaf were considered, along with the three leaders in Cairo,

---

[11] Ben Bella has admitted that he was not directly involved in the preparations for the revolution until fall 1954. See Robert Merle, *Ahmed Ben Bella,* p. 75.

to constitute the collegial directorate of the revolution. According to Ouamrane, two other important Algerian nationalists came to be associated with this group of nine after the revolution had begun, namely Abane Ramdane and Dr. Lamine Debaghine.[12] These eleven, says Ouamrane, were given the mission of leading Algeria on all levels until independence. If any of them were arrested or died, they would be replaced by their second in command. It had also been decided that the *Front de Libération Nationale,* or FLN, would be open to all political tendencies, for only through a broadly based united front could success be assured.

By all accounts, the men who decided to begin the war for independence had few illusions as to the possibility of rapid success. Nor do these men appear to have been motivated primarily by ideological considerations. Rather their decision to act was based on a common agreement that the legal nationalist movement had failed and was disintegrating, that national independence was the primary condition for Muslim Algerians both to regain their honor and to advance socially and economically, and that violence was the only way that the French colonial system could be destroyed in Algeria. Beyond these simple perceptions there was little agreement.

Despite preparations for armed insurrection as early as 1945, the Algerian Revolutionaries of 1954 were miserably equipped and barely organized. Bitat claims that only about 900 men were ready to act on November 1, 1954.[13] Bouadjadj gives the figure of 2400, and Ouamrane mentions 3000.[14] Few arms were available to the first *moudjahids* (fighters in the holy war), as no arms had yet come from abroad, except perhaps in the Aurès region.[15] The western region of Oranie had received almost no military support, as arms shipments by way of Morocco had not arrived.

The leaders of the revolution hoped that through their desperate acts of violence on November 1 they would quickly gain a mass following. Responses among the Muslim population to the news that a few acts of sabotage and several ambushes had been carried

---

[12] Ouamrane interview. Yves Courrière, *Les fils de la Toussaint,* pp. 132-133, claims that Dr. Lamine Debaghine was contacted by Krim, Boudiaf, and Ben Boulaid before the meeting of the "22" and was asked if he would agree to lead the revolutionary movement. Despite his sympathy for the idea of armed revolution, he refused.

[13] Rabah Bitat, in *Révolution.*

[14] Ouamrane interview and Z. Bouadjadj, in *Révolution et Travail.*

[15] Robert Merle, *Ahmed Ben Bella,* p. 95.

out in the name of a *Front de Libération Nationale* were generally ambiguous, except perhaps among the young. Zohra Drif tells that:

When the war began on November 1, 1954, it had the effect of a bomb exploding. My younger brother, age 15, came running home that day and cried, "That's it, we've finally started." My parents thought it was crazy, but we who were young waited eagerly each day for news in the hope that the revolution would continue. Soon the Algerian people got caught up in the revolution and the fighters came to be called by some "the companions of the Prophet returned to earth." Old ladies often cited miracles concerning the deeds of the revolutionaries.[16]

If the Revolutionaries were somewhat disappointed in the initial response of the Muslim masses to the news of the beginning of the revolution, some of them were clearly hoping that when the armed insurrection began the. French would naturally suspect the MTLD and Messali of being involved. Then, as the French had done in 1945 with the AML, the police would disband the MTLD and arrest its leaders, thereby eliminating from influence the politicians, placing the nationalist movement squarely under the direction of the Revolutionaries.[17]

The Weaknesses of the Revolutionaries

Following the initial outbreak of violence, the leaders of the five zones had planned to meet in Algiers, leaving their assistants in command of field operations. They would then assess the situation and decide on next steps. In fact, however, French reaction was swift and effective following the events of early November, and it became extremely difficult for the leaders to meet. By Spring of 1955 the five leaders and their assistants had already suffered serious losses. Ramdane Ben Abdelmalek, the second in command in Oranie, was killed on the first day of the revolution. Mourad Didouche died in January 1955. Rabah Bitat and Ben Boulaid were arrested that same spring, and Bachir Suidani was soon killed.

---

16 Interview with Zohra Drif Bitat.

17 R. Bitat, in *Révolution*, and Robert Merle, *Ahmed Ben Bella*, pp. 96–97. Merle quotes Ben Bella as saying: "We knew that in case of an uprising the French government would not hesitate to dissolve the MTLD and to imprison its leaders. This it did, to our great relief. The French helped us get rid of the *politicards* whom they suspected of being our accomplices, but who in reality greatly bothered us by the confusion they caused among the masses. The FLN, which the *Organisation Spéciale* had founded on November 1, became in this way, and thanks to our enemy, the only political force in Algeria."

Thus by the end of 1955 the original interior leadership of the revolution had all but disappeared. Only Krim and Ben M'Hidi of the five zone leaders were still alive and free.[18] Of the secondary zone leaders, only Ouamrane and Zighout Youssef were still effectively directing armed actions against the French. As the top leadership of the zones fell apart, positions were opened for other Revolutionaries to rise to power, particularly from among the other members of the CRUA. In this way Boussouf, Ben Tobbal, Abane Ramdane, and Benaouda emerged during 1955 and 1956 as important figures in the revolution.

There were few noteworthy military undertakings against the French during 1955, except for the August 20 offensive by Zighout Youssef in the North Constantine area. Nor was the FLN during the first year of the revolution particularly successful in rallying support from the Muslim population or from the international community.[19] The core revolutionary leadership was already badly weakened through death and arrests, and no effort had been made to organize an effective directorate for the entire insurrectionary effort. Disagreements existed among military commanders, especially in the Aurès,[20] and between the interior and the exterior leaders. As yet no broad united front existed grouping all nationalist tendencies, although contact had been made with the UDMA,[21] the Centralists, and the Ulama. The Revolutionaries who had begun the war in November 1954 still monopolized the positions of responsibility in early 1956.

But the Revolutionaries, while men of action, were not particularly effective organizers. The legal political parties for years had been in contact with the masses, creating cells in villages, writing propaganda. The Revolutionaries were novices at this and tended

---

[18] Kabylia, under the leadership of Krim and Ouamrane, was probably the best organized of the zones. The *dairas* within Kabylia had the following leaders on November 1, 1954: Tigzrit, Ali Mellah (Si Cherif) ; Michelet, Said Brirouche; Dra el Mizan, Mohammed Hammouche; Fort National, Ali Zamoum; Azazga, Amar Driss; Lower Kabylia, Mohammed Zamoum (Si Salah). This information was provided by Amar Ouamrane in an interview.

[19] Mouloud Feraoun, in his book *Journal, 1956–1961*, tells of his gradual acceptance of the FLN as the main spokesman of the Muslim population.

[20] See especially Serge Bromberger, *Les rebelles*, Chapter 1.

[21] Some UDMA leaders such as Ahmed Kaid immediately rallied to the FLN. Others such as Abbas did not formally side with the FLN until 1956, although they used their influence to collect money and medicine for the FLN. Within the Algerian Assembly the UDMA leaders continued to call for justice and an end to fighting. From interviews with Abbas and Ouamrane.

to believe that by starting the fight before carefully planning for the future they would be more successful than if they organized first. This attitude, of course, partly reflected the continual frustrations the Algerian nationalists had experienced over the past years. But it also mirrored a feeling on the part of the Revolutionaries that they alone represented the aspirations of the masses, and consequently they could not allow the "bureaucratic" MTLD, even if it was planning for eventual insurrection, to speak for the people. The Revolutionaries were convinced that they alone were the rightful leaders of the nation. In order to receive credit for beginning the war for independence, these men, without a coherent ideology or organization, broke with the better prepared movements and resorted to violence.

In their bid for leadership the Revolutionaries were initially successful. But they appear to have been nearly as content with symbolic rewards—the glory of having begun the revolution—as with material success. Consequently, during the first year of the war they largely ignored the political questions of how the revolution should be directed, what principles of authority should govern decision-making, and what goals other than independence should figure in the leaders' calculations.

The Revolutionaries, who by training and background had been formed as successful agitators, ultimately failed both as theoreticians and as organizers. They did, however, possess the moral and symbolic advantages of belonging to the original group of *moudjahids*. And as long as this symbolic advantage remained, the Revolutionaries were able to stay in power by allying first with the organizers, and later with the theoreticians. In this way they could make up for their lack of skills, while still retaining claims on the positions of leadership.

But in addition to the liabilities and limitations imposed on the Revolutionaries by their narrow range of skills, they also had to cope with each other's claims to power. The original solution to these competing claims had been to form a collegial direction so that no one individual would be more influential than any other. But this had resulted in a virtual absence of overall organization, with each zone commander all-powerful in his own region. The other possibility, the clear dominance of a single individual, was universally rejected. But once the war had begun to acquire some momentum, the desirability of a more adequate coordination of efforts was intensely felt, and when the Revolutionaries, as they had hoped, began to attract a larger number of Algerians to the cause of independence, the need for permanent, authoritative structures became apparent. Alone, the Revolutionaries seemed incapable of creating a broadly based political organization which could legitimately claim to represent all the Algerian people, but with the aid of the Politicians this might be possible. Thus the first alliance of Politicians and Revolutionaries was foreseen, and during 1956 it became a reality.

The Expansion of FLN

From the beginning of the revolution on November 1, 1954, the leaders of the FLN had announced that the FLN would be open to "all purely Algerian parties and movements." [22] This invitation seemed to include all but the Algerian Communist Party (PCA). In fact, only the followers of Messali Hadj were completely excluded from the FLN, simply because they refused to recognize any authority other than Messali's. Within months of the beginning of the Algerian revolution, Messali founded his own counterpart to the FLN, the *Mouvement National Algérien* (MNA). One of the early and enduring tasks of the FLN was to destroy the MNA and its influence, particularly in France among the Algerian workers. Many of the atrocities which characterized the war for independence grew out of this internecine MNA–FLN battle.

Members of other parties were welcomed within the FLN if they agreed to renounce their previous party affiliations. This applied particularly to the communists, who were anxious to join the revolution as a bloc. But the FLN insisted that they could only join as individuals, and even then the communists within the FLN were never fully trusted.[23]

The more important task of the FLN, by late 1955, was to rally the support of the Politicians of the UDMA and the MTLD. With the help of the UDMA, the FLN might more easily gain international recognition. Among the MTLD "Centralists" they could hope to tap a wealth of organizational skills. The men primarily responsible for integrating individuals from the UDMA and MTLD into the FLN seem

[22] The declaration issued by the FLN on November 1, 1954, is reprinted in Arslan Humbaraci, *Algeria: A Revolution that Failed*, pp. 46–49. In retrospect this document does not seem to have projected unrealistic goals.
[23] See Claude Paillat, *Deuxième dossier secret de l'Algérie*, pp. 247 ff.

to have been two Kabyle Revolutionaries, Abane Ramdane and Amar Ouamrane.[24]

As some of the Revolutionaries had anticipated, the Radicals from the Central Committee of the MTLD were arrested soon after the outbreak of the revolution. Benkhedda and Dahlab, for example, were both arrested, the latter several times. Curiously enough, many of the men who came to play important roles in the revolution were arrested, then released during 1955. Perhaps this reflected the hope on the part of the then liberal Governor General, Jacques Soustelle, that a moderate policy toward the nationalists, even toward those in jail, might serve to divide the Politicians from the Revolutionaries.[25] But neither the hopes of the Revolutionaries nor those of Soustelle were to be fulfilled, for within a short time the Radicals had decided to join forces with the Revolutionaries. No other option seemed open to them once the violence had begun.

As the war within Algeria spread, other Algerians felt compelled to come to terms with the FLN. A major event which led many hesitant Muslims to opt for the FLN occurred on August 20, 1955, when Zighout Youssef led one of the first large-scale attacks on French communities in North Constantine. Over 100 Frenchmen were killed. Contradictory accounts of this event exist, and it is not clear to what extent terrorism and threats against moderate Muslims were operative.[26] In any event, the hitherto moderate Governor General, Jacques Soustelle, was apparently shocked by the barbarity of the attacks and soon concluded that he could not deal with criminals.[27] The moderate nationalists, no longer courted by Soustelle and occasionally faced with threats from terrorists, concluded that henceforth the FLN must be taken seriously as representative of the Muslim population, which now aspired to independence rather than assimilation or integration.

On September 25, 1955, at the call of Dr. Bendjelloul, moderate elected Muslim officials, including some Liberals, met to clarify their positions in light of the recent developments. After considerable debate over the validity of Soustelle's policy of integration, a slight majority of the sixty-one officials who attended the meeting voted to

---

[24] Benkhedda and Abbas in interviews both said they were first contacted by these two Revolutionaries during 1955.

[25] See Claude Paillat, *Deuxième dossier*, p. 158.

[26] Roger Le Tourneau, *Evolution politique de l'Afrique du nord musulmane*, pp. 399–400.

[27] See Jacques Soustelle, *Aimée et souffrante Algérie*.

recognize the "Algerian national idea." The minority, which had agreed to accept the decision of the majority, associated itself with the "Declaration of the Sixty-one." [28] Recognizing that "The immense majority of the population presently supports the Algerian national idea," the "Sixty-one" called for autonomy which would allow Algerians "to live their own lives." Henceforth, Algeria would demand to be treated as an associate and not as a "faithful servant." Several months later, on March 20, 1956, those among the "Sixty-one" who had not yet rallied to the FLN asked that the Algerian Assembly be disbanded, which was done by decree on April 11, 1956. Of the "Sixty-one," Ferhat Abbas and Ahmed Francis were later to play important roles in Algerian political life.[29]

With the declaration of the "Sixty-one," some of the Liberals had taken an open stand which came close to revealing their already covert cooperation with the FLN. Likewise the Radicals, once released from jail in the spring of 1955, rapidly made contact with the FLN, as did a few of the more militant of the Ulama. Throughout 1955 the FLN gained some support from the masses as well as from the elite, so that by 1956 a new organization was needed to accommodate the recent recruits and to overcome the problem of dispersed authority.

The Congress of the Soummam

In order to reorganize the now expanded leadership of the Algerian revolution, a Congress was held in late August of 1956 in the Soummam valley. The Congress was attended by approximately 50 delegates and included representation of most of the revolutionary forces within Algeria.[30] However, neither the external delegation nor the zone of the Aurès was represented.[31]

[28] See Michael Clark, *Algeria in Turmoil*, pp. 190–191 for detail. Ghallamallah, a signatory of the Declaration of Sixty-one, claimed in an interview that "about twenty-six" of the "Sixty-one" preferred the formula of integration with Muslim personal status but that they agreed to accept the majority's support of "*le fait national.*"

[29] See Michael Clark, *Algeria*, p. 184 for an important quote from Abbas, defining his position at this period.

[30] Mezhoudi interview.

[31] It is still not clear if Ben Bella and other members of the external delegation tried to attend but were not informed of when the Congress of the Soummam would be held, or whether they sensed that they would be ineffective and remained absent. Mezhoudi claims that he and Benaouda were sent to the Tunisian frontier to meet Ben Bella and that, if he had decided to attend the Congress, it would have been held near Mila. (Mezhoudi interview.)

Although the widely recognized need for a centralized leadership of the revolution helps to explain the holding of the Congress of the Soummam, several specific issues had arisen concerning the conduct of the war which seemed to require decisions. If during 1955 and early 1956 the internal leaders of the revolution had been partially successful in the poltical domain (all parties except the MNA had disbanded and many of their leaders had rallied to the FLN) the same could not be said for military operations. The interior leaders placed the responsibility for the lack of arms and money directly on the exterior delegation, and in particular on Ben Bella. Ben Bella, in addition to being blamed for military insufficiencies, was suspected of trying to arrange a settlement with the French, with the help of the Tunisians and Moroccans, which would largely work to his own benefit.[32]

The widely acknowledged political leader of the internal revolutionary forces at this time was Abane Ramdane.[33] Under his leadership the Congress met on August 20, 1956, and for about two weeks political and military problems were fully discussed. The product of these efforts was extremely important, for the hitherto unorganized revolution was given some structure, an embryonic government was formed, and the rudiments of a political platform were drawn up.

The decisions reached at the Congress of the Soummam represented a clear victory of Abane Ramdane over Ben Bella. Three principles adopted in the Platform of the Soummam confirmed this:

1. Primacy of the interior over the exterior.
2. Primacy of the political over the military.
3. Collegial decision-making.[34]

In several places the Platform condemned the "cult of personality" and asserted the importance of collective leadership. Another implicit criticism of Ben Bella, who was widely perceived as close

[32] Mezhoudi interview. This interpretation is shared by other political elite members, though little clear evidence exists as to what Ben Bella was really attempting before his arrest.

[33] Abane Ramdane, according to many who knew him, was decisive without being authoritarian and was able to command the respect of those around him. Although a Kabyle, Abane is held in high regard by Arabs as well as Kabyles, and several elite members claim that he might have been the one Algerian who could have held the elite together after independence.

[34] See *El Moudjahid*, No. 4, November 1956, for a relatively complete text of the Platform of the Soummam.

to Egypt's Abd al Nasser, came in the form of a declaration of independence from the influence of any foreign power, be it Cairo, London, Moscow, or Washington. The efforts of Ben Bella to find a negotiated solution without having consulted the interior forces were also attacked in the assertion that negotiations could only follow an all-out fight. The formula of "no negotiations before recognition of independence" emerged in this way.

Apart from the external delegation, and in particular Ben Bella,[35] Algerian leaders were nearly unanimous in their agreement on the beneficial nature of the decisions taken at the Soummam. Intellectuals appreciated the outline of a revolutionary ideology contained in the Platform, while Military men felt the positive effects of better organization.[36] For one important Military leader, Mohammedi Said, "The Congress of the Soummam was a second November 1. Up until then I was afraid of dying for fear that the organization of the revolution might collapse. After 1956 I had no fear, since solid structures were rapidly set up."

In addition to the new structures decided upon for the revolution, Abane Ramdane was anxious that the internal forces gain control of the shipment of arms from abroad. This problem was fortunately solved for him. When Ben Bella and his colleagues were unexpectedly arrested in October 1956, the monopoly of the exterior over the transport of arms was partially ended.[37]

---

[35] Ben Bella, who did not attend the meeting, was later extremely critical of the Congress of the Soummam. He was particularly opposed to decisions which he felt led to the creation of an unwieldy bureaucracy and to the admission of "political personalities" into the ranks of the revolution's leadership. Ironically, his major criticism of the leaders who took charge after the Congress of the Soummam was that they left the interior *willayas* without arms and supplies. This led to the weakening of the *willayas,* which soon became little more than fiefs where individual leaders held sway unaccountable to anyone. See Robert Merle, *Ahmed Ben Bella,* pp. 114–116. Also see the *Charte d'Alger,* p. 29, which says, "It [the Platform of the Soummam] developed national ideology without reference to the forces which determined the character of the revolution and it preached the erroneous theory of general insurrection. The social nature of the leadership was, however, decided, which led to the return of leaders who did not believe in the effectiveness of armed fighting and yet were charged with directing the revolution."

[36] Fantazi and Guerroudj interviews.

[37] Ben Bella left behind him Ahmed Mahsas in charge of supplying the interior forces with arms. Abane sent Benaouda and Mezhoudi to oppose him and to take over this function. Eventually the "Mahsas affair" was settled, and Ouamrane was made responsible for supplying the *willayas* with arms. (Mezhoudi and Ouamrane interviews.)

Institutions of the Revolution: The CNRA *and the* CCE

The political structures elaborated at the Soummam Congress consisted of a representative body of seventeen members and seventeen alternates, the *Conseil National de la Révolution Algérienne* (CNRA), and an executive committee of five, the *Comité de Coordination et d'Exécution* (CCE).[38]

The composition of the CNRA is particularly interesting, for it reflects the balance of forces among the various groups within the FLN at the time of its formation. The CNRA consisted primarily of the Revolutionaries who had begun the war for independence.[39] But evidence of the rising influence of the older nationalist politicians could be found in the inclusion of two Liberals from the UDMA and six Radicals of the Central Committee of the MTLD. Two members had even been closely associated with the reformist Ulama.[40] Of the original twenty-seven leaders of the CRUA, seventeen were still members of the CNRA, the others having been eliminated by arrest, death, or incompetence from top political roles.[41]

Although in its first incarnation it never met in plenary session,

[38] See Appendix D for a full list of the CNRA members. The CCE was probably also originally to have included Aissat Idir, who was in jail. See Claude Paillat, *Deuxième dossier,* Chapter 8. In any case, the five men who effectively became the CCE were Abane Ramdane, Larbi Ben M'Hidi, Benyoussef Benkhedda, Saad Dahlab and Belkacem Krim.

[39] At the Soummam Congress, six Revolutionaries were particularly powerful: Abane, Zighout, Krim, Ouamrane, Ben M'Hidi (all full members of the CNRA) and Ben Tobbal. See Benkhedda, "Contribution," p. 3. This is confirmed by an analysis of the signatures on a letter written at the Soummam Congress empowering Brahim Mezhoudi to deal with the quarreling leaders of the Aurès. Zighout, Ben Tobbal, Krim, Si Cherif (Ali Mellah), Ouamrane, Abane, and Ben M'Hidi signed the letter.

[40] Ouamrane, in an interview on May 12, 1967, said that the CNRA members were selected in the following manner: the leader and *adjoint* of each zone, plus two or three members of each of the old parties—MTLD, UDMA, and Ulama—were chosen, with replacements for each full member.

[41] Ben Boulaid, one of the full members of the CNRA who had been in the CRUA, had died in March 1956 and was named to the CNRA in August presumably both to disguise the fact that he was dead and to avoid having to choose among the contenders for leadership within *willaya* 1. Of the non-CRUA members of the CNRA, two were guerrilla fighters from Kabylia, three were ex-members of the UDMA, six were from the Central Committee of the MTLD, two had been with the Ulama, one was an ex-OS member who had escaped from prison with Ben Bella and who served as his alternate, one represented the recently formed trade union, the UGTA, one was a young intellectual who represented the student organization, the UGEMA, and one's background is unknown. In all, then, two were Liberals, six were Radicals, and twenty-one were Revolutionaries; one was a Military man and two were Intellectuals.

the CNRA represented a major step in the direction of defining the authoritative structure of the revolution's leadership. And while its initial membership was subject to substantial changes in later years, the CNRA did play an important, if intermittent, role in the management of the war for independence.[42]

The CNRA, which was created largely to resolve the persistent conflict between the interior leaders and those of the exterior, reflected these two competing centers of power in its membership. Of the top leaders eight were part of the exterior delegation, and seven belonged to the interior forces. Among the alternates five were part of the exterior group, and nine were inside Algeria. In all, the interior was represented by sixteen members, the exterior by thirteen.

Since the Congress explicitly recognized the primacy of the interior over the exterior, it was the sixteen representatives of the interior who seemed most influential in 1956. All but four interior members represented the military forces of the six *willayas*.[43] Of the remaining four interior members, Abane Ramdane was the political genius behind the Soummam Congress, Benkhedda had been politically active in Algiers itself, Dahlab had just been arrested temporarily for the third time since 1954, and Mahmoud Cherif was soon to be placed in charge of the troublesome *willaya* 1.

From among these interior leaders the executive committee, the CCE, was chosen. The CCE was made responsible for making decisions between sessions of the CNRA. The members of the CCE were most likely intended to be Abane Ramdane, plus the four *willaya* leaders on the CNRA—Zighout Youssef, Krim, Ouamrane, and Ben M'Hidi. Zighout Youssef, however, was almost immediately killed in action and Ouamrane was presumably left to head his *willaya*, both because he preferred the military to politics and because his inclusion would have meant that three of the five CCE members were Kabyles. Consequently only Krim and Ben M'Hidi became

---

[42] It may be hoped that future research will reveal more precisely the composition of the CNRA in later years, for it seems clear that membership in this body became an important topic of controversy from 1957 to 1962. At present, complete information on membership in the CNRA exists only for 1956–1957. Up to one-third of the later members are unknown or uncertain.

[43] Two *willayas*, namely the Aurès and the Sahara, were represented by only one alternate. *Willaya* 2, North Constantine, had four representatives, while *willayas* 3 (Kabylia) and 4 (Algerois) and 5 (Oranie) had one full member and one alternate each. The leaders of *willaya* 4 were Kabyles who had originally been with *willaya* 3, but who had been sent to reorganize the neighboring *willaya* 4 during 1955.

part of the CCE, along with Abane Ramdane and the Radicals Benkhedda and Dahlab. The politicians thus came to exercise influence for the first time in the leadership of the revolution. Krim and Ben M'Hidi subsequently joined the other three CCE members in Algiers, leaving their *willayas* to Mohammedi Said and Abdelhafid Boussouf. In addition, Zighout Youssef's death in September had meant that Lakhdar Ben Tobbal became the leader of *willaya* 2. In this way, the rise to power of previously secondary figures was under way.

Once settled clandestinely in Algiers, the CCE members met frequently. According to Dahlab, Abane Ramdane was considered to be something like a "secretary general," even though the five members all had equal votes and practiced collective decision-making. Krim and Ben M'Hidi, he claims, were somewhat handicapped in their tasks by the fact that the French police were actively looking for them. Also, they were less familiar with Algiers.[44]

Some division of labor naturally occurred among the CCE members. Dahlab was primarily responsible for information and propaganda. Benkhedda was in charge of liaisons with French sympathizers and communists and was responsible for acquiring arms. Ben M'Hidi was in contact with the terrorist groups in the Casbah. Krim seems to have coordinated efforts with the *willayas*.

Of the five CCE members, Krim and Ben M'Hidi were the only ones with military experience in the *maquis*. If Dahlab is correct that they were rather less effective in the CCE than the other members, it would seem that, in accordance with the Soummam Platform, political considerations may indeed have taken priority over military ones. Certainly Dahlab and Benkhedda, because of their political background as Radicals, would be expected to be particularly sensitive to political questions of asserting FLN authority over the masses, gaining international recognition, and searching for a negotiated solution to the war. Abane Ramdane, also, while formed as a Revolutionary, was more a skillful politician than a military strategist.

In October 1956 an event occurred which both added to the CCE's decision-making power and further weakened the Revolutionaries in comparison to the Politicians. On October 22, members of the exterior delegation, who were apparently actively involved in pursuing contacts with French liberals with a view toward bringing

[44] Dahlab interview, April 25, 1967.

the war to an end, boarded a plane in Rabat bound for Tunis. The five Algerians on the plane were an impressive group: Ahmed Ben Bella, Mohammed Boudiaf, Ait Ahmed, Mohammed Khider, and an intellectual sympathizer of the FLN, Mostefa Lacheraf. Four of the six "historic leaders" still at liberty were in this group. The pilot of the plane, however, was French, and en route to Tunis he received and obeyed orders to land in Algiers. By this remarkably simple tactic the French army captured four of the top leaders of the revolution, and despite the international clamor over the kidnapping, the French government accepted the *fait accompli.* Ben Bella, Khider, Boudiaf, and Ait Ahmed were to spend the next five and one-half years in French jails, and though their prestige may have risen during those years, their influence over day-to-day decisions was eliminated. Thus from October 1956 on, Abane Ramdane and his CCE colleagues were virtually free to act according to the principles set down in the Soummam Platform.

During its short lifetime, the CCE was responsible for two major decisions on the conduct of the war which reflected the political orientations of its members. The first purely political decision concerned the means of asserting FLN control over the Muslim masses and of proving this hegemony to international opinion. The means adopted were a boycott by the Muslim students enrolled in French schools and an eight-day strike of the entire Muslim population. Muslim students in large numbers at this time quit their classes and either entered the *maquis* or joined the exterior delegation. More important, however, was the eight-day strike organized to prove that the masses were behind the FLN. By all accounts the reaction of the French was brutal and effective. The FLN leadership was virtually dismantled, and the Casbah was occupied by French paratroopers. Yet Benkhedda and Dahlab still view the strike as a success, for it forced the masses into closer cooperation with the FLN than had previously been the case and convinced many questioning Muslims that the FLN represented the lesser of two evils compared to the French paratroopers.[45]

The second major decision, linked to the eight-day strike and similarly motivated, was the adoption of urban terrorism as a more effective use of violence than the guerrilla warfare in the countryside. This conclusion was apparently based on the political cal-

---

[45] Dahlab and Benkhedda in interviews justified these policies. Ben Bella and the *Charte d'Alger* were very critical of them.

culation.that urban violence would draw much more attention to the FLN and could oblige the UN and allies of France to recognize the FLN as a major force with which France should negotiate. Thus the "Battle of Algiers" was undertaken, and for several months sporadic bombing occurred in the hitherto calm capital of Algiers.[46] The "Battle of Algiers," like the strike of eight days, elicited a strong reaction on the part of the French, and by the end of February 1957 the repression in Algiers was so severe that the CCE was forced to flee to Morocco and Tunisia.[47]

The three years from spring 1954 to spring 1957 were the "heroic years" of the revolution. This was the time during which the Revolutionaries controlled the FLN, though by late 1956 the Politicians had already regained considerable influence. The new forces which would soon assert themselves within the political elite were still deep below the surface. The unity of the Revolutionaries had already been weakened by the first major intraelite conflict of the FLN, that between Abane Ramdane and Ben Bella. Behind this personal quarrel, however, lay the deeper issue of authority which plagued the Algerian revolution from its beginning. Its first manifestation came in the conflict between the internal and the external leaders. This issue was to remain unresolved, but with time would be overshadowed by new sources of conflict.

In short, this three-year period provides a case study of the way in which Politicians and Revolutionaries, both products of a colonial political system, were to act in a new context, the war for liberation. It is hardly surprising that the beliefs, values, and styles of behavior developed in earlier years were to mark these first leaders. Thus one finds the Revolutionaries, skilled as agitators and convinced of their own right to represent the nation, breaking with the existing structure and beginning a revolution with little organization and less ideology. Eventually even they realized the need to draw on the skills of the Politicians, so that during the second year of the war both Liberals and Radicals were brought into the FLN. At the Congress of the Soummam, the Politicians were appointed to the CNRA and more noticeably still to the CCE.

[46] The film produced in 1965–1966 by Pontecorvo and Saadi Yacef, "The Battle of Algiers," excellently presents the atmosphere of the time, although it is inaccurate in some historical details. See also Saadi Yacef, *Souvenirs de la Bataille d'Alger.*
[47] During the Battle of Algiers Ben M'Hidi, a member of the CCE, was arrested, tortured, and finally died in prison.

This alliance of Revolutionaries and Politicians was partly a response to the bitter conflict between internal and external revolutionary forces. But whatever the origin of the conflict, the new alliance did produce leaders with a greater concern for organization and political questions such as authority, representativeness, and public opinion. The "Battle of Algiers" and the eight-day strike were typical of the politically inspired decisions of the CCE, just as the early decisions of the Revolutionaries within the CRUA reflected the distinctive political-military formation of the first leaders of the revolution. But by mid-1957, neither the Revolutionaries nor the Politicians, alone or in alliance, had proved fully capable of leading the war for independence. New efforts and new men would be needed if the revolution was to continue.

7

The Military and the Intellectuals: New Contenders for Power

Contrary to a widely held belief, revolution and violence directed against a common enemy do not necessarily provide the basis for political cohesion among former competitors. In Algeria, divisions which had pervaded the nationalist movement before the revolution were perpetuated by the inclusion of virtually all groups within the authoritative structures of the FLN. In addition, divisive pressures were generated by the war for independence itself, and severe conflicts developed between internal and external Revolutionaries.

A second source of heterogeneity and of possible conflict within a revolutionary elite comes from the new recruits who enter top positions of leadership after the war has begun. In a prolonged war there is likely to be both a high attrition rate among early leaders and considerable recruitment of new men whose skills and intelligence are valued by those in positions of authority. Minor leaders may also succeed in securing for themselves positions of influence if the overall structure of authority is relatively loose.

During the Algerian war for independence two distinct routes led previously secondary figures to power. One passed primarily through the army, as capable officers rose within an increasingly complex and autonomous military organization. A second channel of recruit-ment proved to be the political bodies established in Tunisia, which came to be known as the Provisional Government of the Algerian Republic (GPRA). As ministries and subsidiary organiza-tions were established, opportunities for young intellectuals to exercise some influence over the political and diplomatic aspects of the war increased greatly.

Compared to the older nationalists, these new recruits received most of their direct exposure to politics only after the revolution had begun. If indeed one's type of political socialization is linked to distinctive political beliefs and values, then the Military and Intellectuals should differ from the other three groups in important ways. By the end of the war many of these differences in orientations to politics were abundantly illustrated as the Military strove for autonomy and the Intellectuals undertook the tasks of seeking a negotiated settlement and of elaborating programs for the future.

During the first three years of the Algerian war for independence, leadership within the FLN passed from the hands of the Revolution-aries of the CRUA to those of a coalition of Politicians and Revo-lutionaries within the CCE and CNRA. While differing in many re-spects, these leaders all shared the common experience of having participated actively in politics within the French colonial system. Even though the Revolutionaries and Politicians disagreed over tactics and in their evaluation of their own proper role in politics, both groups believed that the overriding goal of the revolution was national independence. To achieve this end the efforts of all capable Algerians were required, and thus a broad united front was eventually formed.

But by 1957 the original leaders of the revolution must have been aware that military victory could not be theirs. The hoped-for "general insurrection" had not occurred, and many leaders of the interior—in particular the CCE—were obliged to flee Algeria and to establish themselves abroad in Tunisia in order to remain effective. The consequences of shifting the leadership of the revolution from Algiers to Tunis were of great importance, for by so doing the Politicians and Revolutionaries created the conditions which per-mitted the formation of two new groups which were ultimately to contend for power. The first of these came from the ranks of the armed forces which until 1957 had largely been controlled by the Revolutionaries. The second group consisted of young intellectuals and technically trained people who gained influence after 1958 within the growing political agencies of the revolution abroad, the ministries, embassies, and FLN-affiliated interest groups.

The Military

Between 1954 and 1968 over eighty individuals whose political careers began in the army occupied positions within the political elite. Relatively few of these, however, reached top positions of leadership during the war itself. Of these Military leaders who might be considered part of the political elite before independence, fifteen were *colonels* in charge of a *willaya,* one became a member of the GPRA in 1959, and approximately twenty were members of the CNRA. Four of these *willaya* leaders were killed during the war, and one was executed after independence.

Despite the crucial role of the *Armée de Libération Nationale* (ALN) during the war, most of the individuals in the Military group first held important political positions only after independence. During the five years between 1962 and 1968 eight ministers came from this group, as did nine members of the Political Bureau, fourteen members of the Central Committee, all five members of the *Secrétariat Exécutif* of the FLN until December 1967, twenty-one members of the Council of the Revolution, at least fifty-seven deputies, and President Houari Boumedienne himself.[1] Of the eighty-one Military considered here, thirty-four can be considered top leaders (ministers, members of the Political Bureau or Council of the Revolution, and ex-*willaya* leaders), while forty-seven occupied less important roles (deputies or Central Committee members).

In common with army officers throughout much of the developing world, the Algerian Military leaders have guarded themselves from public scrutiny. Many of them are known best by aliases, and few have revealed information about their private lives. Even their careers within the army are often unknown. Consequently, it is particularly difficult to describe the political socialization, attitudes, and behavior of the Military who have entered politics. Of the top leaders from this group, just under half are relatively well known,

---

[1] The Military ministers were: Bouteflika, Benhamouda, Boumedienne, Mohammedi, Hassani, Cherif Belkacem, Medeghri, and Benmahmoud. The members of the Political Bureau were: Boumedienne, Mohammedi, Medeghri, Zbiri, Mohand oul Hadj, Khatib Youssef, Bouteflika, and Benmahjoub.

and it is from their backgrounds and careers that a few tentative generalizations will be advanced.

The first characteristic of the Military which distinguishes them from the Politicians and Revolutionaries is that they tend to belong to a different political generation. Whereas the Radicals and Revolutionaries were born about 1922, the Military were, on the average, born in 1928, the median year being 1932. This difference in generation helps explain why the Military were not deeply involved in politics before the revolution. By the time most of them had reached adulthood, the legal political parties were badly divided and clearly ineffective. In 1945 or 1948 it might have seemed possible for a young nationalistic Algerian to work within the framework of the MTLD or UDMA. But by 1952 or 1953, few young Muslims were attracted by colonial politics.

A second trait that characterized several of the Military leaders is that they came from quite modest origins. In this they were most similar to the Revolutionaries, and it may be assumed that their early family life did not differ significantly from that described for the Revolutionaries. On the basis of partial data it seems, however, that the Military were born in slightly larger communes, with larger European populations, than were the Revolutionaries. Schools were also somewhat more common in the communes of birth of the *militaires*.[2]

One enduring member of the political elite who reached politics through his military career, Mohammedi Said, has given a brief account of his early political socialization.[3] Born in 1912, Mohammedi was one of the oldest Military leaders. He came from a family of poor peasants in Kabylia. One of his early memories was of a French officer slapping his grandparents, and from this experience he began to realize the meaning of colonialism. His early awareness of politics was further developed as his family instilled in him a version of Algerian history full of patriotic, nationalistic overtones. Mohammedi also became very religious at an early age. His experiences, in brief, were quite similar to those related by any Algerian nationalist and have little in them that is particular to the formation of the Military group. One may tentatively assume that the family

---

[2] The figure is one classroom per 570 people for the Military, compared to one per 750 for the Politicians and the Revolutionaries. This information comes from calculations based on the 1948 census.

[3] Interview with Mohammedi Said.

environment of the Military was similar to that of the Politicians or the Revolutionaries. For all three groups the fundamental political values established early in life seem to be those related to their identity as Muslims and their sentiments of nationalism.

Education is a critical variable for distinguishing the type of political career one will follow. The Military resemble the Revolutionaries in terms of educational attainment, although they are on the whole somewhat better educated. Of thirteen individuals for whom data are available, five had some university education, six had been to secondary schools, and two did not pass beyond the elementary level. In addition a few from this group went to military schools, such as the French cavalry school at Bou Saada. But even school experiences do not seem to be the major basis for distinguishing the *militaires* from the Revolutionaries, although they do differentiate them from the Politicians, whose more advanced educations often led to careers in liberal professions.

The Military group is most like the Revolutionaries in social origins and education. Where the two groups part ways is in the type of direct political activity engaged in by their members. Thus if the Revolutionaries and the Military are found to differ in their political beliefs and behavior, these differences must be attributed primarily to this later stage in their political socialization, for until late adolescence, at least, individuals from both groups appear quite similar.

As already indicated, the simplest reason for the particular form of political participation that marked the careers of the *militaires* is that most of them were too young to be politically active before the outbreak of the revolution. Those who were members of the PPA remained in minor positions. By definition, the Military first became politically influential only after 1954, whereas the Revolutionaries, also by definition, were already actively engaged in politics before the war. Their less intense political involvement with party politics does seem to have influenced the Military in a number of ways. In general they regarded the ongoing politics of the early 1950s more with indifference than contempt. In this they differ from the os members, though they would doubtless have agreed that force and violence were required to end the colonial regime. Some of the better educated of the *militaires,* however, probably felt that the efforts of the CRUA to reunite the nationalists by engaging in violence before adequate preparations had been made showed lack of organizational skill. But nonetheless, the Military, if not among the first to take up arms, soon rallied to the guerrilla forces of the ALN.[4]

This initial skepticism, followed by active involvement, can be seen in the account by Belkacem Fantazi of his early feelings toward the FLN:

> When the war broke out in November 1954, I didn't immediately join the *maquis* because at that time no one knew what was happening. There were just a few tracts which hardly clarified the goals of the revolution. I wasn't sure that it was really a serious effort, but I decided nonetheless to encourage it by propaganda and by asking for financial contributions for the FLN from the population. By 1956 I was convinced that the cause was just, and by then the French police were watching me closely. I was finally ordered to leave the department of Oran, and eventually I made contact with the organization and joined the *maquis* in North Constantine.[5]

Within the Military group, many individuals followed in the steps of the Revolutionaries who had actively led the insurrection within Algeria. These Military men, however, differed from the Revolutionaries both in their own self-conception and in their political skills. Whereas the Revolutionaries felt strongly that they alone should guide the revolution, the *militaires* in general lacked this strong sense of personal ambition for power. Rather, their feelings of who should properly rule were transferred to the army or to their *willaya*. Institutional or regional loyalty seems to have partially replaced personal ambition and the individual sense of mission characteristic of the Revolutionaries.

At least fifteen Military leaders became *colonels* who led *willayas* which had once been directed by Revolutionaries. Of the entire Military group, another thirty-two reached the rank of *comman-dant,* twenty-three were *capitaines,* and seven secondary leaders were *lieutenants.*[6] Most Military leaders, then, spent some time inside Algeria as guerrilla fighters, and this experience helps to explain some of their characteristic beliefs.

Political life in the Algerian *maquis* during the war has received some attention, though much remains unknown.[7] Accounts by two

---

[4] Some Military men such as Tahar Zbiri, the chief of staff of the ANP until his abortive coup attempt in December 1967, were close to the CRUA and participated in the outbreak of the revolution on November 1, 1954.

[5] Interview with Belkacem Fantazi.

[6] The head of a *willaya* received the rank of *colonel,* the highest rank in the ALN. He was assisted by *commandants.* Zones were led by a *capitaine,* and he was aided by three *lieutenants.*

[7] See Thomas Hodgkin in *The Manchester Guardian,* July 13, 1957, describing his visit to an Algerian military unit inside Algeria.

Military leaders of their experiences in the *maquis* help to clarify the socializing effect of guerrilla warfare on the participants.[8] Belkacem Fantazi, a secretary of *Association des Anciens Moudjahidines* in 1967, has described his introduction to the *maquis*. When he entered into contact with *willaya* 2 (North Constantine) in 1956, he spent twelve days going through careful screening. He was taken to meet the leaders of the *willaya* and was accepted as a new recruit. He was apparently quite impressed with the organization that already existed. For several months he was given no precise function but did learn to handle various weapons.

The effects of the Soummam Congress were rapidly felt in *willaya* 2, and the political officer soon gained in influence alongside the military leader, a pattern repeated in another *willayas* as well. Each *willaya* was independent of the others, but nonetheless similar principles of decision-making seem to have been widely applied. The most common practice, according to Fantazi and Mohammedi, was for decisions to be made collectively. Personal power was distrusted in *willaya* 2, largely because of unfortunate earlier abuses of authority. The military activities of the six *willayas* were rarely well coordinated, and efforts to use force seem to have rested more on tactical planning rather than strategic considerations. Lastly, both Military leaders claim that they received little help from the external forces. As a result the interior leaders felt considerable hostility toward the exterior leaders.[9]

From this scant evidence it appears that the guerrilla leaders of the interior came to adopt some practices and beliefs which differed significantly from those of the Revolutionaries. First, they did not see themselves in the same self-centered terms as the Revolutionaries. They seem, rather, to have developed strong feelings of common identification with the *maquisards* in general and were likely to believe that the peasant masses, who bore the weight of the war, were the rightful beneficiaries of the revolution. The *maquisards* distrusted and disliked the Politicians and were skeptical of the Revolutionaries, especially when the latter tried to direct the war from Tunis rather than from the interior. In contrast to the Revo-

[8] Interviews with Belkacem Fantazi, March 13, 1967, and Mohammedi Said, December 11, 1966.

[9] Mohand oul Hadj, in *Jeune Afrique*, October 14–20, 1963, said that he could never forgive Boumedienne for parading with his well-equipped exterior forces while the interior *willayas* were suffering severe shortages. Nonetheless, in 1965 he joined Boumedienne in opposing Ben Bella.

lutionaries, many of whom clearly had authoritarian tendencies, the *maquisards* seem to have placed greater value on equality, collective decision-making, and self-criticism.[10]

With time and changing circumstances, the *maquisards* no doubt strayed from many of their simple early ideals. And more important, some of the Military were obliged to leave the interior and to organize a more professional army along the Moroccan and Tunisian frontiers. Like the Politicians and Revolutionaries before them, the *militaires* were subjected to divisive pressures in the course of the war, and eventually two rather distinct types of officers came into being in the ALN, professional soldiers and guerrilla fighters. The existence of these competing subgroups meant that the Military might be forced to seek allies among Politicians or Revolutionaries, whereas united, they would have the power to guide events after independence if they so desired. The choice between these alternatives depended greatly on the events of the last four years of war.

The Intellectuals: Generalists and Specialists

The last group of Algerian nationalists to be considered, the Intellectuals, is composed of about forty men, and a few women, who began to gain influence within the political elite during the later years of the war and who after independence came to dominate important segments of Algerian political life. This group had in common with the Military a lack of extensive participation in politics during the colonial period. But unlike the Military, who rose in politics in part because of their military skills and their monopoly over the means of violence, the Intellectuals gained positions of influence because they possessed intellectual or technical skills. Some could offer their broad theoretical training which made them valuable in elaborating the doctrine of the FLN. Others were journalists who could contribute to the propaganda efforts. A few were engineers who could be used by the ministry of information to organize the communications network of the GPRA. Several doctors were attached to units of the ALN and eventually rose to positions of influence in this way. A number of religious leaders and syndi-

---

[10] Exceptions, of course, existed. Colonel Amirouche is reported to have been ruthless and authoritarian in his relations with men of his *willaya*. By contrast, the Revolutionary Ouamrane praised self-criticism, collective decision-making and the "simplicity" which marked the relations among colleagues. (Ouamrane interview.)

calists were called upon to represent their specific clientele within the FLN. Finally, women gained prestige within the FLN because of their service as nurses or, for the more daring, as urban terrorists. In short, individuals without historic claims to political leadership and without military experience initially were brought within the broad framework of the FLN because they possessed some limited skill or knowledge.

The FLN coalition that had existed up to 1957 had been composed largely of agitators (the Revolutionaries) and organizers (the Politicians). With the rise to positions of influence of the Military, few new political skills were brought into the FLN coalition, although the organizers were probably strengthened somewhat. Still, the FLN had neither a large contingent of administrators within its ranks nor many theoreticians,[11] and it was partly to fill these gaps that it began actively to recruit the Intellectuals into the political elite.[12] And although the Intellectuals were obliged to remain in secondary positions during the revolution, with independence and the formidable administrative and organizational tasks ahead they became increasingly important. Who were these men who helped transform the FLN from an insurgent rebel faction into a provisional government preparing to undertake the tasks of modernizing an independent Algeria?

Before independence in 1962 a few individuals from this group of Intellectuals had gained considerable influence within the FLN. One had become a Secretary of State within the GPRA, nine were members of the CNRA, two were associated with the delegation which negotiated the Evian treaty ending the war, three were ambassadors of the GPRA in foreign countries, and five worked within ministries of the FLN. Other Intellectuals were associated with the *Fédération de France* of the FLN (FFFLN), with the student union (UGEMA), or the trade union (UGTA).

Since independence the political roles filled by this group have expanded dramatically. Twenty-two ministries have been led by Intellectuals; three members of the Political Bureau came from

---

[11] These political types are discussed by Harold D. Lasswell, *Psychopathology and Politics.*

[12] Recruiting of Intellectuals was in part a conscious process, especially among lawyers and doctors, both of whom were assigned specific tasks either defending prisoners or caring for wounded soldiers. Abane Ramdane was particularly influential in recruiting Politicians and Intellectuals to the FLN. (Interviews with Haroun, Rebbani, Bentoumi, and Belhocine, four lawyers who joined the FLN.)

this group, seven members of the Central Committee, and about twenty-five deputies. Twenty-five members of this group can be considered to have filled top roles, while nineteen occupied the secondary roles of deputy or Central Committee member.

Like the Military, the Intellectuals represent a political generation different from that of the Politicians and the Revolutionaries. Their average and median year of birth is 1928, which means that most of them were in their twenties when the war for independence began. Youth generally accounts for the low level of direct political involvement that characterizes the prerevolutionary careers of these Intellectuals, though some young activists as well as older nonactivists are found in this group.

The political socialization of the Intellectuals is most similar to that of the Politicians, except that their active political participation generally began after the revolution had started. The Intellectuals, like all the groups discussed, received part of their political formation as children within their families. The themes stressed by the Intellectuals in talking of their family life are similar to those of the Politicians, Revolutionaries, and Military. One Intellectual, whose father was a farmer near Bone, claimed that Algerians naturally learned the differences between Europeans and Algerians when they saw their own parents in comparison to any European. In addition to feelings of separateness, some Intellectuals developed an early hostility to the French colonial system based on perceived abuses and injustices.

The nascent Algerian identity formed in the home prepared these Intellectuals for a more direct form of political socialization during their school years. At about the age of fifteen, while in the lycée, many of the Intellectuals began to read publications of the various political parties. Some joined, or even formed, youth sections of the PPA–MTLD, and at least one became attracted to the Association of Ulama and its impressive leader Ben Badis. In contrast to the Politicians and Revolutionaries, who refer to numerous cases of discrimination in school, this theme is relatively absent from the accounts of the Intellectuals. Perhaps by the 1940s, when most of the Intellectuals were in school, Muslim boys were better accepted by their European colleagues, or at least there were enough Muslims in school so that the sense of being alone in competition with French students was absent.

Another feeling common to many Algerian Muslims, and mentioned by one of the few women Intellectuals in the political elite,

Zohra Drif (Bitat), was that Muslims considered themselves superior to the Europeans even if the latter might be more powerful. In her home Europeans were called *roumi*, a common rather derogatory term for westerners. Within her family she learned that Arab-Islamic culture was great but that it was necessary to learn French in order to be able to use it against the colonial rulers. When World War II came she was a young girl, but she remembers that her parents explained the German invasion of France as God's revenge on the Frenchmen for their treatment of the Muslims.[13]

Zohra Drif, unlike most of the Intellectuals, felt discrimination in her school environment, which deepened feelings of hostility already present. Few Muslim girls had attended French lycées until after World War II, and their treatment by the European girls in the 1940s and 1950s must have been similar to that of the Muslim boys who went to French schools a generation earlier. Of 3000 girls in the prestigious Lycée Descartes, only four were Muslims when Zohra Drif first attended. Because of open and covert discrimination, the Muslim girls felt that their fellow students saw them as *sales Arabes*. When the number of Muslim girls in the school finally grew to nearly fifteen, they were able to form a close group of students who lived apart from the Europeans. For them, as for their male counterparts a generation earlier, it became a matter of honor to be at the top of each class.

Zohra Drif later recalled that:

> In the lycée I became very interested in politics, but I never dared discuss this with the French girls because of the antagonism it produced. I concentrated on getting my baccalauréat. But like the other Muslim girls, I was very concerned with what would happen after graduating from the lycée. Most Muslim families wanted their daughters to return home and marry, but many of my friends and I wanted to enter the university. Unlike most girls, however, I wanted to go to law school instead of to the school of letters.[14]

Despite a general ban on political discussions between Muslim and French girls, events such as the French defeat at Dien Bien Phu and the nationalist violence in Morocco and Tunisia created sharp tensions between the two groups. After repeated exposure to statements of how the French should eliminate all the Muslims in Tunisia and Morocco, Zohra Drif recalls that she heatedly warned the European girls that it would be their turn next when Algerians

13 Interview with Zohra Drif Bitat.
14 *Ibid.*

began their revolution. The sensation and scandal which this remark caused are understandable. But hers was not an idle threat,
for within four years this young Algerian woman was to become
one of the most renowned of the participants in the Battle of
Algiers.

The most distinctive form of political participation of the Intellectuals before the outbreak of the revolution was involvement
in student politics. Their high level of educational attainment helps
account for this type of political activity. Of the more than forty
Intellectuals considered here, thirty-three are known to have had
some university education. A few others were working for the *bac-
calauréat* when the student strike was called in 1956. Probably no
more than half a dozen, largely the trade unionists, had not pursued
their education past the *brevet*.

The occupations pursued by the Intellectuals previous to their
political involvement give some indication of what type of individuals these were. The largest number, twelve, were students at
the time of the revolution, but many of them had not reached the
level of academic specialization. Of those who completed their
education and entered a profession, eight were lawyers, seven were
teachers, five were doctors, three were engineers, one was in commerce, and one was a worker. About 85 percent could thus be considered to belong to free professions, with the remaining 15 percent in economic professions.[15]

An important distinction to be made within the group of Intellectuals is that between specialists, who relied upon particular
skills to acquire political influence, and generalists, who rose in
politics because of broad intellectual ability. The specialists, the
engineers and doctors, brought administrative skills into the political elite, while the generalists contributed to the elaboration of FLN
doctrine as theorists and agitators. Somewhat contrary to expectations, the generalists were proportionately less successful at attaining top political positions, especially as ministers after independence, than the specialists. Table 7.1 makes this clear.

The ascendancy of the specialists will be treated in more detail
in later chapters, although the reasons for their rise are already
apparent. Whereas the generalists often competed with the Revolutionaries in the task of articulating an ideology for the revolution

---

[15] These categories are discussed in more detail by Frederick W. Frey, *The
Turkish Political Elite.*

TABLE 7.1   OCCUPATION AND LEVEL OF LEADERSHIP OF THE
INTELLECTUALS

	Top Leaders	Secondary Leaders	Total
Generalists	10	17	27
Student	6	6	12
Lawyer	1	7	8
Teacher	3	4	7
Specialists	10	0	10
Doctor	5	—	5
Engineer	3	—	3
Commerce	1	—	1
Worker	1	—	1

or for independent Algeria, the specialists could not be easily replaced by any other group. Nor did they constitute an overt threat to the power of the Revolutionaries as did the more ideologically inclined Intellectuals.

By education and profession, the Intellectuals found themselves both united by common political experiences and divided by types of skills. In this respect they were similar to the Politicians, Revolutionaries, and Military. Whether the potential for conflict or integration would be dominant depended largely on the form of political involvement during the war. As was true of the other groups, the Intellectuals experienced primarily the divisive effects of the revolution.

Participation in the war effort took a variety of forms for the Intellectuals. Most common, however, were activities within the student union (UGEMA), the FFFLN, the ministries of the GPRA, and, for a few, service with the guerrillas, particularly during the Battle of Algiers.

Considering the educational attainments of the Intellectuals, it is no surprise that many of them were active in student politics during the revolution. Algerian university students had been organized as early as 1927 into the *Association des Etudiants Musulmans Nord-Africains*.[16] Until the mid-1950s, Maghribi student activity was centered in Paris rather than in Tunis, Algiers, or Fez. With the approach of Moroccan and Tunisian independence, how-

16 Some background discussion on the UGEMA is found in Clement H. Moore and Arlie R. Hochschild, "Student Unions in North African Politics," *Daedalus*, Volume 97, No. 1 (Winter 1968).

ever, the Maghribi student movement became unwieldy, and eventually each national group developed its own association.

When the UGEMA was founded in 1955, less than 2000 Algerian Muslims were pursuing higher education, and two-thirds of these were studying in Metropolitan France. The UGEMA from the outset had considerable autonomy from the FLN, although it clearly supported the war effort and was in contact with various leaders of the revolution. One of its earliest political activities, with the encouragement of the CCE, was to call for a general and unlimited student strike. The UGEMA was successful in this, as most of the Muslim students in Algiers and France left the universities to show their solidarity with the FLN, and many of them joined either the guerrillas or the exterior delegation.

A second goal of the UGEMA, having first established its representativeness, was to enlist international student support for the Algerian cause. This highly successful effort was led by Dr. Ait Chaalal. Parallel to this bid for recognition was a campaign to obtain scholarships for Algerian students to study in other countries. Eventually over 350 scholarships were found for students to study in at least 26 countries. But, according to Moore, this dispersal of students after 1958 had the effect of weakening the UGEMA as an organization, so that by 1962 it was not strong enough to withstand the disintegrative consequences of the disappearance of the GPRA. Nonetheless, the UGEMA had provided an important training ground for a large number of Algerian Intellectuals, especially as it served them in developing their organizational and administrative skills. It is no surprise, then, that a large number of influential political leaders—Mohammed Khemisti, Lamine Khène, Mohammed Ben Yahia, Belaid Abdesselam, Ahmed Taleb, and Dr. Ait Chaalal— were all actively involved in student politics either before or after 1954.

The second organization largely dominated by the Intellectuals was the *Fédération de France du* FLN (FFFLN). The interest of the FLN in establishing a branch organization in France was clearly due to the presence of over 500,000 Algerian Muslims working in France. During the early years of the revolution these workers were mostly under the influence of Messali Hadj's MNA, the FLN's strongest rival for legitimacy. Gradually, the FLN, through a combination of persuasion and terror, was able to organize the majority of Algerians in France within the framework of the FFFLN. One of the leaders of the FFFLN claims that by 1961 about 90 percent of the workers were loyal to the FLN,[17] although other sources indicate that 50 percent might be a more accurate figure. The FFFLN's primary function, especially after 1958, was to raise money to support the revolution. To do this, each worker was taxed 3000 old francs ($6.00) per month. Shopkeepers paid a higher rate depending upon means. One FFFLN leader asserts that in 1961 the operations of his organization brought in 600 million old francs monthly, of which 450 million ($900,000) were sent to the GPRA.[18] In this way the FFFLN was able to contribute more in financial terms to the revolution than any single foreign country.

In addition to raising money for the GPRA, the FFFLN provided judicial services to Algerians in France, paid monthly allowances to the families of political prisoners, set up commissions of hygiene to improve the living standards of the workers, and organized armed groups to carry out police actions against the MNA or repressive landlords. The combination of organizational strength and financial importance made the FFFLN an important part of the revolutionary effort, so that it came to be treated as an equal to the other six willayas. According to Haroun, the CNRA after 1958 was made up of five representatives of each willaya, plus five from the FFFLN, as well as the ex-heads of willayas and the members of the GPRA.

The FFFLN, then, like the UGEMA, provided its leaders with invaluable organizational experience. Its remarkable success was a tribute to the ability of the Intellectuals who became its leaders. Its influence during the revolution was certainly greater than that of the UGEMA, and yet, except for two top leaders who had earlier been in the UGEMA, the FFFLN was not a source of recruits to top elite positions after independence. Table 7.2 indicates the relationship between level of leadership and participation in the UGEMA or FFFLN.

A tentative explanation of this difference in success on the part of equally well qualified Intellectuals seems to lie in the power positions of the UGEMA and the FFFLN. The UGEMA leadership, while influential in student affairs, did not and could not aspire to leadership of the entire revolution or of an independent Algeria. In fact,

---

[17] Haroun interview. Many Algerians in France probably paid dues to both the MNA and the FLN.

[18] Haroun interview. The President of the GPRA in 1961, Ferhat Abbas, agreed, in an interview, that the FFFLN gave more to the war than any one country, but his figures were even higher: 4000 old francs per worker per month, collected from 500,000 workers, yielding 2 billion old francs per month in dues ($4,000,000).

TABLE 7.2 REVOLUTIONARY ROLE AND LEADERSHIP LEVEL
OF THE INTELLECTUALS

	UGEMA	FFFLN
Top Leaders	6	2
Secondary Leaders	1	8
Total	7	10

the UGEMA was greatly weakened by the time of independence, but
its leaders could and eventually did contribute their skills in the
ministries, as ambassadors, and in various sectors of the economy.
The FFFLN, on the other hand, was well organized and experienced
in a wide range of governmental tasks at the time of independence,
since for years it had constituted a virtually independent government. To the real holders of power—the Revolutionaries and the
Military—the FFFLN represented something of a potential threat,
and consequently most of its leaders never rose above the position
of deputy in the first Constituent Assembly following independence.

Conclusion

By 1957–1958 the original coalition of Politicians and Revolutionaries which had led the Algerian war for independence in its early
years was beginning to disintegrate. Added to internal dissensions
was the emergence of two new groups with demands for influence
over the course of the revolution. The first of these, composed of
experienced Military men, commanded the means of violence and
had little tolerance for the interference of Politicians in the business
of fighting a war. For reasons beyond the control of the Algerians,
however, the Military could not establish a united command. Each
willaya remained virtually independent, and it was not until late
in the war that the armies of the frontier were brought under the
control of a single commander, Colonel Houari Boumedienne. The
Military did bring some new talent into the political elite, but it
remained a heterogeneous group of guerrilla fighters and professional soldiers, the first being close to the Revolutionaries in temperament if not experience, while the latter consisted of a highly
disciplined and rather pragmatic group of men with considerable
institutional loyalty and disdain for the individualistic, romantic
vision of the Revolutionaries.

The second group, of the same generation as the Military, entered the political elite because of intellectual and technical skills. Because of their advanced educations, the Intellectuals were drawn into the revolution as propagandists, diplomats, administrators, and ideologists. Within this group there existed both generalists and specialists, and since independence it has been the latter who have been more successful in politics. Many of the Intellectuals gained their earliest direct political experience in the UGEMA and FFFLN, both of which allowed individuals to develop remarkable organizational and administrative skills.

Both the Military and the Intellectuals, because they belonged to the same political generation, shared some attitudes and beliefs. Both were largely indifferent to the intense political battles from the prerevolutionary period and consequently reacted rather scornfully to the personal quarrels of the Politicians and Revolutionaries. National independence and modernization were primary goals for these men, and ideology did not deeply affect most of them. Having entered the revolution later than the Politicians or the Revolutionaries, they tended to avoid the identification of their own efforts with the fate of the revolution. Their individual claims to power were somewhat less, but their institutional loyalties—to the FFFLN, to their *willayas,* to the army—were greater than those of the Revolutionaries or Politicians, both of whom tended to feel personal responsibility for the successes but not for the failures of the revolution.

In 1957 these new groups were welcomed by the FLN as elements with which to build a broader, more all-embracing united front. Furthermore, the skills of the Military and the Intellectuals were sorely needed by the embattled Revolutionaries and Politicians of the FLN. Their adhesion to the leadership of the war for independence added to the FLN's claim to legitimacy and representativeness and thus increased the possibilities of an eventual negotiated settlement favorable to the nationalists.

By 1962, however, both the Military and, to a lesser degree, the Intellectuals were preparing to make bids for power in the independent Algeria soon to emerge. How the FLN leadership was transformed from a relatively integrated coalition in 1956–1957, in which the skills of the Military and Intellectuals could be seen as necessary complements to those of the existing elites, into a loosely joined structure of competing groups anxious to obtain power at the expense of others, is the story of the next chapter.

8
Revolution and the Crisis of Authority

Following the expansion of the FLN to include nationalists of all tendencies during the first two years of the war, the problem of creating new authoritative bodies to guide the revolution became a matter of intense concern. The adhesion of the Liberals and Radicals to the FLN and the rise of the Military and Intellectuals to prominent positions of influence coincided with the weakening of the original core group of Revolutionaries by the combined action of internal quarrels, arrests, and death.

The issue which came to dominate much of the internal political life of the FLN during the last five years of the war was that of how to create a relatively stable and effective political organization out of the many diverse groups which made up the FLN. Could the contrasting images of political life instilled by different experiences in politics be overcome by a common commitment to the idea of national independence? Could an adaptive, relatively collegial political process develop within a political elite faced with the tasks of leading a war for independence?

In contradiction to the expectations of many supporters of the Algerian war for independence, divisive pressures were generated by the revolution itself. These pressures virtually precluded both the concentration of power within the hands of a small, homogeneous elite and the development of a conciliatory political process. Instead, after six years of war the FLN had become a segmented structure consisting of numerous competing and often hostile subgroups. Some semblance of a common front remained, but only at the price of tacitly recognizing that intraelite conflicts could not be resolved until independence was achieved. Since postrevolution politics were deeply influenced by the conflicts which developed during the last years of the Algerian revolution, an understanding of Algerian elite behavior must focus on the events which occurred between 1957 and 1962.

During the first two years of the Algerian war for independence the revolutionary elite was partially successful in attaining several of its immediate goals. The tiny force of badly equipped guerrillas of 1954 had grown substantially into an army able to create great insecurity despite the efforts of several hundred thousand French soldiers. All pre-1954 nationalist political movements had disbanded and rallied to the FLN with the exception of Messali's MNA. The adherence of such well-known public figures as Ferhat Abbas and Tewfik al Madani to the FLN had increased the FLN's prestige and facilitated international recognition. Diplomatic activities at the Bandung Conference in 1956 and at the United Nations were somewhat successful in drawing attention to the demands of the FLN. Also private contacts with French liberals were under way to explore possible means of settling the war.

Leadership of the war effort was still, in 1956, largely in the hands of the original revolutionary elite, although other nationalist politicians had also been coopted into the directing agencies. The Congress of the Soummam in August 1956 represented an important step toward the elaboration of a political doctrine, spelled out the terms for an eventual settlement, provided embryonic authoritative structures for the FLN, and standardized the organization of the army in the various regions of Algeria. A feeling of optimism must have swept over some of the revolutionary leaders at this time, for the Soummam Platform announced that soon a "general insurrection" involving large, pitched battles would be possible. Clearly, many within the elite continued to believe military victory was possible.

Conflict and Conflict Resolution

In the year following the Congress of the Soummam, the FLN experienced frustrations which complicated the political and military organization of the war. First, in October 1956 four top leaders of the external delegation were kidnapped by the French while trying to bring about a negotiated settlement. Second, urban terrorism had been instigated in Algiers, resulting in a massive retaliation by the French which forced the CCE to leave Algeria and establish its headquarters in Tunisia. Third, the hoped-for general insurrection had not occurred.

Thus the FLN by 1957, while showing competence in the political tasks of rallying most of the nationalist elite to the revolutionary effort, had not been militarily successful, nor was a negotiated solution to the war in sight. In many ways the next five years, from September 1957 to September 1962, can be viewed as a prolonged crisis within the political elite generated by the frustrations of leading an insurrection and revolving around the questions of authority and legitimacy. During this entire period the leadership of the revolution remained outside the country, allowing a large degree of autonomy to the embattled *willayas* of the interior. In addition, a complex political structure developed around the provisional government the *Gouvernement Provisoire de la République Algérienne,* after 1958. Following its establishment, a modestly large bureaucracy began to emerge, centering on the various ministries. As the GPRA received the recognition of other countries, Algerian ambassadors were sent abroad, so that soon the FLN through the GPRA acted much like a normal government.

Another significant development was the growth and eventual unification of a large armed force along the Moroccan and Tunisian frontiers. Previous to 1958, Algerian troops had been able to find sanctuary and had trained in the areas along the Moroccan and Tunisian borders. During 1958 the French neared completion of an effective set of barriers, consisting of mines, electronic devices, and barbed wire, which virtually sealed the eastern and western borders of the country. This meant that large numbers of Algerian forces were compelled to remain outside the country for most of the remainder of the war. The justification for maintaining these troops was that they tied down thousands of the best French soldiers who would otherwise have been free to pursue the war in the mountains of the interior. With time and under the unified leadership of the chief of staff of the ALN, these forces came to represent a major center of power within the wartime elite. If constrained to play a passive role during the war itself, these highly trained exterior forces were seen by all as potentially constituting the most powerful force within an independent Algeria. Political leaders of all persuasions kept a careful eye on this group.

The political elite itself during these five years was expanded to include new elements from among the Military and the Intellectuals. The resulting heterogeneity of the political elite greatly inhibited efforts to concentrate on ideological questions, particularly those involving postindependence political structures and the economic and social content of the revolution. Faced with a powerful French opponent, especially after de Gaulle's rise to power in 1958, the Algerian political elite feared that if its own internal divisions became apparent France would refuse to negotiate with the FLN.

The consequences of these structural difficulties, especially the separation between interior and exterior forces and the heterogeneity of the FLN, were felt in numerous ways. Conflicts among the members of the elite became intense and were viewed by nearly everyone as based on "personal quarrels" rather than on ideological differences. Political organs were repeatedly formed or reshuffled in order to resolve paralyzing conflicts within the elite. During these years three major solutions to crises over authority were found by the Algerians, none of which was particularly successful. The first way of handling dissident members of the elite, generally those in lower positions of responsibility, was to coopt them into the higher decision-making bodies. When disputes within a governing body became debilitating, a second means, that of exclusion from the elite, was also utilized. The third temporary expedient for dealing with crises of authority was to allow the competing political groups virtual autonomy within a limited sphere of decision-making. Cooptation, best suited to cleavages between top and secondary leaders, and exclusion and autonomy, more suited to divisions within the top elite itself, were all tried in order to balance the competing claims to power from the Radicals, Liberals, Revolutionaries, and the Military.[1]

---

[1] The Intellectuals, while often occupying such key positions as Secretary General within a ministry or as leaders of the FFFLN, did not generally compete for the top positions within the FLN. At most they became influential within the CNRA.

It is remarkable, given the intensity of many of the intraelite conflicts which developed during the last five years of the war for independence, that the FLN did manage nonetheless to maintain some control over the war effort and eventually gained the support of a large proportion of the Algerian Muslim population. And finally the FLN was able to negotiate a settlement with France that met nearly all of the FLN's demands. What is less surprising is that as soon as independence was achieved the wartime political elite immediately fragmented, resulting in several months of near civil war. The frequently observed pattern of apparent elite unity in the face of opposition, followed by elite disintegration when the opponent withdraws, was thus repeated in Algeria. Within months the mobilized Muslim masses began to fall back into apathy as they witnessed their self-proclaimed leaders struggling with one another over political power.

It is now possible to discover some of the reasons for these disappointing developments that so deeply influenced the early years of independent Algeria. An analysis of the period 1957 to 1962 both illustrates the divisive pressures generated by the revolution and indicates the socializing effects of the war on those who participated in its direction. This stress on conflicts and crises within the elite is not meant, however, to detract from the many admirable instances of unity in confrontation with the French. For surely a most impressive aspect of recent Algerian history is the FLN's role in bringing independence to Algeria. That the FLN and many of its leaders were the first victims of independence does require explanation, especially since the FLN was ultimately successful in gaining independence. Many thoughtful Algerians, as well as a number of inquisitive foreigners, have sought and are still seeking to understand this phenomenon.[2]

The Comité de Coordination et d'Exécution *of 1957*

By May of 1957 the four remaining members of the first *Comité de Coordination et d'Exécution,* Benkhedda, Dahlab, Abane Ramdane, and Krim, had arrived safely outside Algeria. Faced with

[2] Both the *Programme de Tripoli,* written in May 1962, and the *Charte d'Alger* of April 1964, are often extremely perceptive in their analysis of the deficiencies of the FLN during the war. This type of critical realism, if more widely applied, would be a welcome sign for future Algerian historiography concerning the revolution. Benyoussef Benkhedda, in his analysis "Contribution à l'historique du FLN," goes far in this direction.

massive problems of pursuing the war while the French were trying to seal the Tunisian and Moroccan borders, the CCE which had worked well as a unit inside Algeria now found itself divided.[3] Apparently Dahlab, Benkhedda, and Abane Ramdane believed that the CCE should be kept small and mobile and should return to Algeria so as to maintain contacts with the interior troops.[4]

This issue was taken up by the first full meeting of the CNRA, the representative body which had been established by the Congress of the Soummam and whose membership had since that time been changed considerably. The CNRA members, unable to meet within Algeria because of French surveillance, convened in Cairo where they received the sympathetic support of Gamal Abd al Nasser from August 20 to September 18, 1957. There they rejected the proposal of Abane Ramdane, Dahlab, and Benkhedda, apparently fearing that these three were becoming too powerful. They voted instead for the formation of a large and more functionally specific CCE of nine members. Two of the Radical politicians from the previous CCE, Benkhedda and Dahlab, were eliminated in what one described as "circumstances full of intrigue" and the other a "minor coup d'état." [5]

The CNRA also acted to annul two of the decisions of the Soummam Congress, namely the primacy of the interior over the exterior and that of the political over the military. In changing these policies the CNRA was essentially recognizing the fact that the interior could not lead the entire revolution because of French repression and that new elements from within the army had sufficient power to impose themselves on the leaders of the revolution. The composition of the new CCE revealed the rising influence of the military leaders of the interior. The colonels who had once been in charge of willayas 1, 2, 3, 4, and 5, namely Mahmoud Cherif, Lakhdar Ben Tobbal, Belkacem Krim, Amar Ouamrane, and Abdelhafid Boussouf, were all included in the CCE. These five, plus the more "political" Abane Ramdane, were all Revolutionaries. The other three active members of the CCE were the Liberal Ferhat Abbas and two Radicals, Dr. Lamine Debaghine and Abdelhamid Mehri. In addition, five of the chefs historiques in French prisons, Ait Ahmed, Ben Bella, Bitat, Boudiaf, and Khider, were made honorary members. These five were able to communicate intermittently with the

---

3 Benkhedda, "Contribution," p. 3.
4 See France observateur, March 2, 1961.
5 Interviews with Benkhedda and Dahlab.

rest of the CCE and were thus associated with some major policy decisions despite their confinement.

Dahlab has interpreted these changes within the CCE as the elimination of the politicians by the *militaires* who saw themselves as the real *"combattants."* [6] Abane Ramdane was placed in a minority, and power within the CCE, according to most observers, passed to the hands of those who came to be known as the "triumvirate"—Belkacem Krim, Abdelhafid Boussouf, and Lakhdar Ben Tobbal, all three of whom were Revolutionaries of the CRUA.[7] These three men were the only ones to survive every change of personnel within the executive organs of the revolution from 1957 to 1962. But even these three powerful Revolutionaries were unable effectively to use the power attributed to them by many, particularly after the organization of the exterior armies led by Colonel Houari Boumedienne.

The formation of the second CCE is an example of resolving a political conflict by forming a decision-making body through co-optation of new members. Two former CCE members, however, were dropped and immediately came under the authority of their earlier subordinate Lamine Debaghine and, surprisingly, continued to serve as diplomatic representatives for the FLN until they were eventually recalled to positions of responsibility.

One other member of the first CCE, Abane Ramdane, did not fare so well. Abane, while in a minority within the new CCE, must have still represented a threat to the authority of the three colonels who held most power. He certainly must have opposed the reversal of the Soummam principles which he had fought to establish in 1956.

On May 29, 1958, the official publication of the FLN, *El Moudjahid,* announced the death of Abane Ramdane, claiming that he had died after receiving wounds in the course of a battle inside Algeria. While the truth of his death is still unclear, there is probably no informed Algerian leader who does not believe that Abane Ramdane was a victim of personal quarrels with other members of the CCE, and in this belief they are doubtless correct.[8] Assuming that Abane Ramdane was eliminated by his colleagues because of the threat he represented to their power, his death was one of the rare instances of the direct use of physical violence to

[6] Dahlab interview.

[7] Dahlab interview and Gérard Chaliand, *L'Algérie est-elle socialiste?*

[8] A rather irresponsible effort to explain Abane's death is found in Bessaoud Mohammed Arab, *Heureux les martyrs qui n'ont rien vu.* Also see Claude Paillat, *Dossier secret de l'Algérie.*

settle an intraelite conflict. Since Abane Ramdane was a widely admired leader, those generally perceived as responsible for his death, namely the "triumvirate," encountered a great deal of hostility from other elite members.[9]

The fact that physical liquidation was rarely used among the top elite testifies to the widely shared belief that violence of this type would quickly destroy any semblance of elite integration. Henceforth when capital punishments were carried out against prominent political or military leaders, such as during the "colonels' plot" in late 1958, considerable effort was expended to cloak the proceedings with an aura of legality.[10] Assassination and execution did not become widely used methods of resolving elite conflicts.

Organizing the Military

Shortly after the creation of the second CCE a major decision was taken to establish a *Commandant des Opérations Militaires* (COM) which would impose a coordinated command over military operations of the war. The COM was divided into two branches, one with headquarters at Oujda in Morocco with authority over the forces in Morocco and western Algeria, another located at Ghardimaou in Tunisia with authority over the troops in eastern Algeria and along the eastern frontier. The COM may have been handicapped by this dual command, and its effectiveness was certainly diminished by the construction of French barriers on the borders which made communication with the interior *willayas* very difficult, especially after 1958. In fact, the creation of the COM did little to advance the military efforts of the revolution, and it was eventually dissolved in favor of a unified command, the *Etat Major Général*.

But if its contribution to the war effort was small, the influence of the COM and later that of the *Etat Major* on internal politics was substantial. The leaders of the unified army, especially the well-

---

[9] An interior guerrilla leader, Slimane Dhilès, spoke before the National Constituent Assembly: "When we got there [to Tripoli], we weren't concerned with elaborating a Program. It was simply a question of a confrontation between leaders of the interior and of the exterior. Among those at Tripoli, there were some who even wanted to exploit the death of Abane Ramdane in order to reach their goals. They said, 'The time has come to hang war criminals.' Well, the criminals of the revolutionary war are still free, they have filled their pockets, they're not bothered by anyone!" *Journal Officiel, Débats Parlementaires,* November 20, 1962, p. 156.

[10] Claude Paillat, *Dossier secret.*

trained troops along the borders, became men of considerable power and importance.

The forces in Morocco came under the command of a rapidly rising military officer who had been Boussouf's second-in-command in *willaya* 5, a previously unknown young colonel named Houari Boumedienne.[11] The Tunisian COM was led by an older officer who had once been Krim's subordinate before leading *willaya* 3, namely Mohammedi Said. The rise of both Boumedienne and Mohammedi to positions of considerable influence represented one of the early examples of changing authority relations. Those once in subordinate positions were achieving equal power with their direct superiors and, as will be seen, were in many cases likely to overtake them.

Reversals of patterns of authority, where those in power are surpassed by men whose careers they have helped to make, seem to create deep psychological tensions. For just as it appears difficult for people to submit to the authority of individuals of lower social status, so also it seems intolerable for most *chefs* to submit to their earlier *adjoints*.[12] It should hardly be unexpected that enduring personal conflicts have grown out of reversals in patterns of authority, and among these the rivalry of Mohammedi and Krim, as well as that between Boumedienne and Boussouf, deserve special mention. In a revolutionary situation, when careers are made and unmade with astonishing rapidity, where no clear lines of political recruitment exist, there are a large number of these reversals of authority. It would be most unusual if the effects of this process of elite recruitment on the political system were not destabilizing.

In addition to the tensions generated by reversals in authority patterns, there were also the compounded frustrations of trying to survive in the face of a massive war effort on the part of the French. Some successes were registered by the second CCE. The delivery of arms and supplies to the interior was somewhat improved under Ouamrane's direction. The CCE in Tunis, however, could not provide overall direction for the guerrilla leaders, who were left with

[11] Boumedienne's real name is Mohammed Bou Kharouba. René Jammes has pointed out in a personal communication that Boumedienne's alias is a combination of the names of the patron saint of Oran (Houari) and that of a village near Tlemcen (Boumedienne). Since Boumedienne began his army career in western Algeria it is plausible that he consciously selected his name for symbolic value in that region. A useful article on Boumedienne is that by Peter Braestrup and David Ottaway, in *The New York Times Magazine*, February 13, 1966.

[12] See Frederick W. Frey, *The Turkish Political Elite*, pp. 400 and 404–405.

the task of maintaining an atmosphere of insecurity throughout Algeria by undertaking sporadic attacks on French troops in the countryside.

But even these minor military actions of the guerrillas were going badly. The forces in Kabylia were relatively well organized, but their leaders were more concerned with strengthening the hold of the FLN over the population and of fighting potential Muslim opponents than in testing their forces against French troops. A much more critical situation existed in *willaya* 1, the Aurès mountains. There, in the region where the revolution had begun, the capture and subsequent death of the widely respected leader Mustapha Ben Boulaid had set off a serious struggle for succession among his subordinates. Chihani Bachir and Ben Boulaid's younger brother Omar were rivals for the leading role, and when Chihani was executed by his own men on charges of pederasty the fight among the numerous claimants to Ben Boulaid's vacant position increased in intensity. The war effort of the guerrillas in *willaya* 1 therefore collapsed, and the CCE seemed unable to do anything to restore order in this crucial region.[13]

The CCE formed in 1957 had not been able to provide effective leadership of the revolution. Benkhedda, perhaps unjustly in view of the difficulty of the task, attributes this mainly to the personal quarrels within the CCE which rendered it incapable of reaching agreed-upon decisions. According to Benkhedda, the CCE overcame this paralysis only by creating a new governing body, the *Gouvernement Provisoire de la République Algérienne* (GPRA).[14]

The Formation of the GPRA

In September 1958 the second CCE was dissolved. The GPRA which took its place sought to be more than the directorate of the revolutionary movement. It claimed, rather, to be the legitimate government of the Algerian nation. Several reasons have been given for the creation of the GPRA. According to Ferhat Abbas, its first president, the GPRA was formed in order to strengthen the bargaining position of the FLN in case a military regime should seize power in Paris.[15]

The GPRA clearly hoped to gain international recognition that would add to its claim of legitimate representation of the Algerian

13 See Serge Bromberger, *Les rebelles algériennes*, Chapter 2.
14 Benkhedda, "Contribution," p. 4.
15 Abbas interview.

people. In fact, within days of its formation, fourteen countries did recognize the GPRA, and thus on the diplomatic front the Algerian national cause was considerably advanced. This diplomatic success, however, did not hide the fact that the FLN, after nearly four years of war, still suffered from the lack of any overall political and military strategy.[16]

The newly formed GPRA included all of the surviving members of the second CCE except for Ouamrane, who opposed what he called the "gradualism" of the CCE and of the GPRA.[17] In addition to the carry-overs from the CCE there were three new members, Ahmed Francis, a close associate of Ferhat Abbas, M'Hammed Yazid, a schoolmate of Benkhedda from Blida, and Tewfik al Madani, a distinguished representative of the Ulama. Benkhedda, a member of the first but not of the second CCE, was included in the GPRA. Three Secretaires d'Etat, Lamine Khène, Omar Ouseddik, and Mustapha Stambouli, were also named to serve as liaison within Algeria between the GPRA and the willayas. The five prisoners in France were again included as titular members of the directorate of the revolution, this time as Ministers of State. (See Appendix F for the full list of members).

Within the GPRA Lamine Debaghine and the three Revolutionaries Krim, Ben Tobbal, and Boussouf kept the same functions that they had occupied since May 1958 in the CCE. Abbas, who had been in charge of information, became President, and Yazid took his place as Minister of Information. Mahmoud Cherif, who had been in charge of finances, yielded this post to Francis and took over Ouamrane's position as head of armaments and supply. Abdelhamid Mehri, who had been responsible for social affairs, was replaced in this post by Benkhedda and became the new Minister for North African Affairs. Al Madani was named head of the newly created Ministry of Cultural Affairs, a position where his background as an Arab intellectual might serve him well.

A general impression of the formation of the first GPRA is that it continued the process of increasing by cooptation the representativeness of the political elite which had begun at the Soummam Congress in 1956.[18] The number of Liberals in the top executive body of the revolution had risen from none in 1956 to one in 1957

---

[16] Benkhedda, "Contribution," p. 4.

[17] Ouamrane interview.

[18] The *Charte d'Alger* states that the direction of the revolution was enlarged periodically to permit ". . . an integration by cooptation of the elements which challenged the leadership. . . ."

to three in 1958. The Radicals had increased from two in both 1956 and 1957 to four in 1958. The number of Revolutionaries had fluctuated from three in 1956 to six in 1957, then to four in 1958.

From later political developments it is clear that the men who made up the first GPRA were far from united in their views of the Algerian war for independence. Faced with mounting problems due to de Gaulle's vigorous conduct of the war within Algeria, the GPRA could agree on no overall policies. Rather than acting as a unit, the GPRA functioned by tacitly forming three relatively distinct groups. One of these consisted of the "triumvirate" of Krim, Boussouf, and Ben Tobbal, who together held the Ministries of War, Liaison and Communications, and Interior. Mahmoud Cherif, the only other ex-*willaya* commander, was in charge of the Ministry of Armaments and Supplies. These four, then, were largely responsible for the war effort.

Mahmoud Cherif, however, was unusual among Revolutionaries in that he had once been a member of Ferhat Abbas's UDMA party. This old link may have brought him closer to the Liberals Abbas and Francis as well as to al Madani. This more moderate group, three of whom had been with the UDMA, was largely concerned with finances and supply.

The last group, consisting of the Radicals Benkhedda, Yazid, Lamine Debaghine, and Mehri, was in charge of the Ministries of Social Affairs, Information, Foreign Affairs, and North African Affairs. Generally this group handled the diplomatic relations of the GPRA, "the shouting as opposed to the shooting" as one of this group has said. Yazid held forth at the United Nations, Benkhedda traveled extensively, including a trip to China, and Mehri was in contact with the Arab countries.

Divisions within the GPRA can thus be seen to follow lines drawn according to prerevolutionary patterns of socialization. In slightly oversimplified form, one can say that in any large organization there are three functionally distinct activities. One involves internal organization, another is concerned with finances and resource allocation and procurement, and a third deals with external relations.[19]

---

[19] These three organizational problems were found to be the ones least often delegated to subordinates by corporation executives. See Robert A. Gordon, *Business Leadership in the Large Corporation*, Chapters 4 and 6. F. W. Frey, *Turkish Political Elite*, p. 265, finds that the cabinet positions which consistently received the highest power ratings in Turkey were Foreign Affairs, Interior, and Finance.

Within the GPRA the problems of internal organization, including the war effort, came under the control of the Revolutionaries. Those men by training were most adept at organizing the use of violence to obtain political objectives. And with these abilities they alone managed to remain in power throughout the revolution.

The Liberals, who were the least intensely nationalistic and the most politically flexible, were perhaps best suited by their political socialization to the relatively technical tasks of raising money and procuring arms. The Radicals, who as members of the nationalist movement were vociferous agitators, were likewise best endowed for the job of articulating Algerian demands in diplomatic circles.

Since the war for independence was the central concern of the FLN, the three Revolutionaries in the GPRA who controlled the military functions gained the reputation for having the "real power" within the government. In fact, it seems more accurate to conclude that the scope of each group's power lay within the dimensions just defined, resulting in an equilibrium of the three groups rather than in integration under the ultimate authority of a single individual. The role of the President, Ferhat Abbas, seems to have been largely that of a moderator among the various tendencies.[20]

This pattern of authority—namely, functionally autonomous subgroups linked by a skilled mediator—is a recurrent one in Algeria and seems to bring with it the problem that decisions on general questions of orientation or program run the risk of shattering the fragile consensus which exists. Thus it is not surprising to find one member of the provisional government claiming that the GPRA had no military, political, or diplomatic strategy.[21] And virtually all analysts have attributed the lack of ideology of the wartime FLN to the heterogenous nature of the political elite.[22] The danger of this type of resolution of the problem of authority seems to be that it inhibits decision-making by placing a high premium on an almost nonexistent consensus. Since agreement on fundamentals is virtually impossible, there is a tendency to avoid discussion of many topics. A bitter criticism of the GPRA by one of its members, Benkhedda, presents the following picture of the first provisional government's internal workings:

[20] This is the interpretation given by Abbas' administrative assistant for Arab Affairs in the GPRA, Brahim Mezhoudi, in an interview.

[21] Benkhedda, "Contribution," p. 4.

[22] See the *Charte d'Alger;* the *Programme de Tripoli;* and Gérard Chaliand, *L'Algérie.*

A military and political bureaucracy was forged in exile which was characterized by the absence of interior life. Internal democracy, criticism and self-criticism, and serious criteria in the choice of leaders were all ignored, thus opening the door to *arrivisme* and flattery.[23]

The inability of the GPRA to resolve the problem of authority led in July 1959 to a demand by the three Revolutionary ministers in charge of the war that the GPRA turn over full powers to them.[24] Benkhedda, at that time Minister of Social Affairs, claims that the GPRA did give the "triumvirate" a mandate to meet with other military leaders in order to designate a CNRA which would "give to our Revolution a new military, political, and diplomatic strategy." [25] Consequently, Krim, Boussouf, and Ben Tobbal met with the two leaders of the *Etat Major Général*, Mohammedi Said and Houari Boumedienne, as well as with five colonels of the interior *willayas* who were in Tunis.[26] This group of colonels was known as the Committee of Ten, and after more than three months of discussion a new CNRA was finally named.[27]

The Military Strives for Autonomy

From the little that is known of the history of the military structure of the ALN, it seems that the years 1958 and 1959 were ones during which both the interior and exterior forces attempted to organize independently of the GPRA. The military leaders of the interior were the first to meet in an attempt to coordinate the policies of the *willayas* and to confront the CCE and its successor, the GPRA, with a unified demand for internal autonomy.[28] At least two meetings of the interior leaders were held in the latter half of 1958 and were attended by the colonels of *willayas* 1 (Hadj Lakhdar), 3 (Amirouche), 4 (Si M'Hamed), and 6 (Haouès). Two colonels, Ali Kafi of *willaya* 2 and Lotfi of *willaya* 5, did not participate.

The major complaint of the interior leaders seems to have been

---

23 Benkhedda, "Contribution," p. 4.
24 *Ibid.*, p. 4.
25 *Ibid.*, p. 5.
26 *Ibid.*, pp. 4–5. The five colonels were Hadj Lakhdar (*willaya* 1), Ali Kafi (*willaya* 2), Brirouche (*willaya* 3), Slimane Dhilès (*willaya* 4) and Lotfi (*willaya* 5).
27 *Ibid.*, p. 5. Benkhedda says that the "ten" were really two clans fighting over power, and thus they were unable to agree easily on the composition of the new CNRA.
28 This episode is related by Claude Paillat, *Deuxième dossier secret de l'Algérie*, Chapter 19.

that the exterior delegation was not supplying them with enough arms. There also may have been some feeling that the external delegation, immune as it was from the actual fighting of the revolution, was excessively intransigent in refusing de Gaulle's "Peace of the Brave" offer.[29] The results of these efforts at unifying the interior, however, were minimal, and whatever progress might have been made toward the internal military integration of the guerrillas was brought to an end in early 1959 by the death of two of the most prestigious interior leaders, Amirouche and Haouès.

At about the same time as the interior colonels were meeting to establish their independence from the GPRA, a group of colonels with the troops stationed in Tunisia began to realize that military force might be effectively used against the GPRA. Under circumstances which are not clearly known, at least seven colonels planned to overthrow the GPRA.[30] The plot was discovered, however, and the dissident colonels were arrested. A military trial was held, presided over by Boumedienne, with Ali Mendjli acting as prosecutor. Several of the plotters were found guilty of treason and executed.

The result of these two futile attempts by autonomous military units to challenge directly the authority of the GPRA seems to have been the strengthening of one other segment of the army, namely the *Etat Major Général,* and in particular Colonel Houari Boumedienne. By eliminating the dissidence created by the "colonels' plot," Boumedienne gained influence over the entire external army. The interior forces remained relatively autonomous within each *willaya,* though some links may have remained between members of the "triumvirate" and the *willayas* they had once commanded.[31] The GPRA, having relied on Boumedienne to crush the plot of the dissident colonels, probably found it extremely difficult to check his growing authority over the ALN forces in Morocco and Tunisia.

By July 1959, with the formation of the "Committee of Ten," Boumedienne was taking an active part in the selection of a new

[29] *Ibid.,* p. 211. That some interior officers felt demoralized is clear as the Si Salah affair demonstrated in 1960, when an internal guerrilla leader tried to seek a private settlement with de Gaulle.

[30] Most of the participants in this plot were executed in spring of 1959, but a few, most notably Abdallah Belhouchet and Cherif Messadia, were temporarily exiled to obscure posts and after independence held responsible positions, the former in the Council of the Revolution and the latter in the Party.

[31] This seems most likely in the cases of *willayas* 2 and 3, old fiefs of Ben Tobbal and Krim.

CNRA. When the CNRA finally met during December 1959 and January 1960, it seems that a major issue was that of who should control the armed forces of the ALN. The three GPRA ministers, with the support of a few representatives of the willayas on the Committee of Ten, were apparently opposed by Boumedienne and his allies among the colonels. According to Benkhedda, the outcome of this struggle was "the elimination of one clan [the triumvirate] by the other from the military directorate, which was henceforth established as a single military command exercising its authority over all the willayas. A new GPRA was constituted. It relinquished its military powers to the Etat Major Général." [32]

The Second GPRA

The new GPRA named in January 1960 was somewhat smaller than the previous one. Only Mohammedi Said, who had shared authority with Boumedienne within the Etat Major Général of the ALN, was added to the GPRA as Minister of State but without any precise function. This was probably done to allow Boumedienne to centralize his control over the ALN without opposition. A few ministers had new functions within the second GPRA. Krim was no longer Minister of War but rather Vice President and Minister of Foreign Affairs. Boussouf added armaments and supply to his previous functions in a new Ministry of Armaments and General Liaisons. Mehri became Minister of Social Affairs and Cultural Affairs as his previous position of Minister of North African Affairs was abolished. With the GPRA a Comité Interministériel de la Guerre was formed, consisting of Boussouf, Ben Tobbal, and Krim, but it seems that, despite the formation of this group, control of the ALN was effectively with the Etat Major, not with the GPRA. The tension between these two groups, however, remained a constant theme for the remaining years of the war.

Those eliminated from the previous GPRA included Lamine Debaghine, Mahmoud Cherif, Tewfik al Madani, and Benkhedda. The first three, it seems, were dropped because of criticisms of their activities as ministers, whereas Benkhedda chose to resign when his suggestion of forming a single political-military authority within Algeria was rejected.[33]

[32] Benkhedda, "Contribution," p. 5.
[33] Interviews with Benkhedda and Dahlab.

If the formation of the first GPRA represented an expansion of the political elite through cooptation, the second GPRA was formed by excluding several elite members, and the problem of authority was handled once again by recognizing the relative autonomy of the ALN, following the apparently unsuccessful attempt of the "triumvirate" to assert its own authority over the army. From 1960 until independence, then, an increasingly important axis of intraelite conflict was that between the *Etat Major* of the ALN—in particular Boumedienne, Ali Mendjli, and Ahmed Kaid—and the three Revolutionaries of the GPRA—Boussouf, Ben Tobbal, and Krim.

The second intraelite division accentuated by the war was that between the Liberals and the Radicals. Of the Liberals, Ferhat Abbas, Ahmed Francis, and Ahmed Boumendjel were the most influential, even if at times Abbas seemed to be included in the GPRA more in order to add legitimacy than to exercise power. Of the Radicals, the best known and probably the most influential were Benkhedda, Dahlab, and Yazid. The latter two were highly esteemed in diplomatic circles for their abilities as able negotiators and propagandists for the cause of an independent Algeria. The third Radical, Benkhedda, had left the GPRA in 1960 because of his disagreements with Abbas over the conduct of the war, but his reputation for courage and personal honesty remained intact.

From January 1960 to the cease-fire in March 1962 it seems safe to say that the interior military forces were most concerned with mere survival. Military victory was not only widely regarded as a chimera, but also it seemed increasingly unnecessary as de Gaulle gradually elaborated his plans for an "Algerian Algeria" and for self-determination. Meanwhile, the exterior forces, constrained by the effective barriers along the borders, grew into a regular professional army, well equipped, disciplined, and politically indoctrinated with progressive ideas.[34] The GPRA, freed from the major task of supervising military operations, and encouraged by de Gaulle's policies, became actively involved in the search for a negotiated solution to the war.

The Divisive Effects of Negotiations

The first official contacts between the GPRA and France took place in June 1960. De Gaulle had refused the GPRA's earlier suggestion

[34] Bachir Ben Yahmed describes the ALN in Tunisia and Boumedienne in an article in *Jeune Afrique*, July 4, 1965, p. 18.

that the five GPRA ministers held as prisoners in France serve as negotiators with the French.[35] Consequently the GPRA sent Ahmed Boumendjel, a Liberal close to Abbas, and Mohammed Ben Yahia, a young Intellectual, to Melun to begin preliminary negotiations. These first contacts ended in complete failure and resulted in considerable prolongation of the war.[36] The issue of negotiations— how vigorously they must be pursued, what compromises the FLN might be willing to make—became a point of contention among the Liberals, Radicals, Revolutionaries, and Military leaders.

The difficult issues which divided the Algerians as they considered the terms of an eventual settlement with France revolved around the questions of the future status of Frenchmen remaining in Algeria, the degree of economic cooperation with France following independence, residual French rights to military bases in Algeria, and the formal mechanisms for the transfer of sovereignty. The Liberals, it seems, were most conciliatory, despite indications that de Gaulle did not feel that Abbas had sufficient authority to warrant dealing with him seriously. The Military, on the other hand, were quite intransigent, fearing that the Politicians would sacrifice at the bargaining table what they had fought for over six years to obtain, namely full and complete sovereignty over all Algeria. Barring the granting of total independence, the Military seemed willing to fight on indefinitely. More flexible than the Military were the Radicals, and to a lesser degree the Revolutionaries, who were prepared to make some concessions so long as the major demands of the FLN for territorial integrity and sovereignty were met. As negotiations continued, these differences in orientation became increasingly clear to French and Algerian leaders alike.

After the failure of the Melun meetings, negotiations were eventually resumed in May and July 1961 at Evian and Lugrin.[37] At Evian, de Gaulle was willing to drop the formula of *état associé* and to admit Algerian external sovereignty, but he refused to recognize the Sahara as an integral part of Algeria. Once more negotia-

---

[35] This was suggested by the GPRA on November 20, 1959. The issue of *El Moudjahid* in which it appeared had a cover picture of Ben Bella. See *El Moudjahid*, November 27, 1959, No. 56.

[36] The Melun contacts ended in failure because of the Si Salah affair, described in Claude Paillat, *Deuxième dossier*, p. 252.

[37] The official FLN delegation at Evian was led by Belkacem Krim, and included Liberals Francis and Boumendjel; a Radical, Dahlab; the Military leaders Mendjli and Kaid; and two Intellectuals, Ben Yahia and Boulharouf. Reda Malek, another Intellectual, acted as spokesman for the group.

tions were broken off, not to be resumed until the CNRA had met again and had changed the composition of the GPRA.

The Third GPRA: *The Exclusion of the Liberals and the Split with the Military*

From August 9 to August 27, 1961, the CNRA met in Tripoli, and it must be assumed that the topic of negotiations was extensively discussed. A major division still existed between the three ministers of the GPRA and the *Etat Major* of the ALN. The latter was considerably more intransigent than the GPRA in concessions it was willing to make to the French. The *Etat Major* by this time constituted a powerful force with control of its own budget and equipped with specialized services.[38] Nonetheless, the CNRA was apparently able to prevent an open split between the Revolutionaries of the GPRA and the officers leading the ALN. The *Etat Major* may have left the CNRA meeting, which would account for the fact that despite Boumedienne's opposition the CNRA reshuffled the GPRA, replacing the Liberals Ferhat Abbas and Ahmed Francis with the Radicals Benkhedda and Dahlab.[39] Mehri was also eliminated from this last and smallest GPRA (See Appendix F).

In the new GPRA Benkhedda was designated President, Krim was Vice President and Minister of the Interior, Dahlab was Minister of Foreign Affairs, Boussouf and Yazid kept their posts as Ministers of Armaments and Liaisons and of Information. Ben Tobbal lost his position as Minister of the Interior and joined Mohammedi as Minister of State. In fact, however, he seems to have maintained control over the important organization of the FFFLN. The five prisoners in France were, as usual, included as Ministers, with Ben Bella and Boudiaf even rating the title of Vice President.

Several interpretations can be given for the changes of personnel in the last GPRA. A common element to all explanations, however, is that the failure to reach a negotiated settlement weighed heavily on the CNRA members. Abbas believes that de Gaulle, who had never fully forgiven him for an alleged slight in 1943, had hinted indirectly

---

[38] Benkhedda, "Contribution," p. 6. Boumedienne, in an interview with *Al Ahram,* reprinted by *Révolution Africaine,* November 6–13, 1965, criticized the GPRA for having too large a share of the budget for itself.

[39] This interpretation is derived from interviews with Benkhedda, who spoke of the *Etat Major* as leaving the CNRA after an "incident," and from an interview with Abbas in which he asserted that Boumedienne was opposed to his eviction from the GPRA.

to Belkacem Krim by way of Louis Joxe at Evian that negotiations would proceed more smoothly if Abbas were replaced by someone with "more authority." [40] Also, Abbas feels that the Radicals of the old MTLD already had their sights fixed on the postindependence period when they hoped to be able to take power.

The Radicals themselves [41] claim that they believed that Abbas was incapable of pursuing the negotiations with sufficient vigor. There is some hint that they also felt their relations with the GPRA ministers in French prisons were better than those of Abbas. Krim may have even been selected to lead the negotiations with the French partly on the advice of the five prisoners.[42] Whatever the reasons for replacing Abbas by his old rival Benkhedda, it is clear that the inherited Liberal-Radical quarrel from the days of the UDMA and MTLD had not been forgotten. After nearly seven years of war the members of the FLN were still deeply influenced by beliefs and images developed during the long period of the prerevolutionary nationalist movement.

The revolution, rather than overcoming past differences, served to accentuate them as independence approached. Negotiations, unlike fighting a war, meant that clear and coherent positions on a wide range of issues had to be formulated. Negotiating also implied the need to compromise on some points. For both these reasons a more compact and centralized GPRA was seen as desirable by a majority of the CNRA. The three Radical members of the GPRA, once schoolmates at the lycée of Blida, have agreed that the last GPRA worked together most effectively.[43] The "triumvirate" handled some military supply matters, and the Radicals were in charge of political problems. Mohammedi Said's role was undefined and probably of less importance.

Despite the greater homogeneity of the last GPRA, it was unable to end the dispute with the *Etat Major* of the ALN, and consequently it decided to try to preserve the façade of FLN unity by not attempting to resolve the conflict. Thus, the ALN and its *Etat Major* constituted, from August 1961 on, a hostile and powerful independent force opposing the GPRA. Sufficient restraint was exercised by both sides so that the crisis did not erupt publicly to the benefit of the French. As a consequence of this tacit agreement, the *Etat Major,*

---

[40] Abbas interview and Jean Lacouture, *De Gaulle*, p. 117.
[41] Interviews with Dahlab and Benkhedda.
[42] Benkhedda interview.
[43] Interviews with Benkhedda, Yazid, and Dahlab.

which had sent two of its members to the earlier unsuccessful negotiations at Evian and Lugrin, was not represented at the final negotiations at Les Rousses and Evian in February and March of 1962.
As the final negotiations approached, the conflicts within the
political elite were more serious than they had been at any time
since 1954. The Liberals and Radicals were deeply divided as a
result of Abbas's eviction from the presidency of the GPRA. The
internal *willayas* continued to struggle to remain alive and gave
mounting evidence that they felt abandoned by both the *Etat Major*
of the exterior and by the GPRA. Their disenchantment with the
politicians and the professional soldiers, however, was not strong
enough to unite them as a cohesive force which might seek a settlement with France on its own terms.[44] The five prisoners in France
were kept from direct participation in the negotiations, and it was
unclear which groups they would choose to support after independence.

In short, then, on the eve of independence the army was divided
into autonomous *willayas* which generally opposed the *Etat Major*
of the ALN. The Radicals and Liberals were openly hostile to each
other. The Revolutionaries of the GPRA were not sure of the support
of their former comrades imprisoned in France, but they were well
aware of the enmity of the *Etat Major*. In these conditions it is a
tribute to all the members of the FLN that a semblance of unity was
maintained until independence was assured.[45]

The delegation sent by the GPRA to negotiate with the French,
first secretly at Les Rousses, then openly at Evian, differed in two
major respects from the earlier delegation sent to Evian and Lugrin
in 1961. In 1961 the group had included two Liberals, Francis and
Boumendjel, and two members of the *Etat Major*, Ali Mendjli and
Ahmed Kaid. With the changes in the GPRA and the conflicts alluded
to previously, neither the Liberals nor the Military were included
among the negotiators. Instead two Revolutionaries, Krim and Ben
Tobbal, and two Radicals, Yazid and Dahlab, played the leading
roles in the negotiations. All four were members of the GPRA.

44 France had tried in 1960 to bring about just such a settlement with the
leaders of *willaya* 4. This failure probably meant that this alternative was not
seriously considered by France in 1961.
45 In January 1962 these intraelite tensions nearly broke into the open because
of the "dissidence" of the army group in Morocco. Krim, it was reported, played
the role of mediator among Benkhedda, the *willayas*, and Ferhat Abbas. See
Annuaire de l'Afrique du nord, 1962, p. 315. The French were surprised to
see Abbas align himself with the "extremists" in Morocco.

These four Ministers of the provisional government were joined by Intellectuals Ben Yahia and Reda Malek, both of whom had been present at the earlier negotiations, and by a newcomer, Mostefai. At the final Evian meetings another Intellectual, Boulharouf, and one of the early Revolutionaries, Benaouda, were also present. The composition of this all-important delegation reflected well the elimination of the Liberals, the withdrawal of the ALN, and the rising influence of the Intellectuals. The latter, while lacking authority, were well suited to technical discussions and the preparation of lengthy dossiers on such subjects as French minority status, terms of economic cooperation, and the maintenance of French military bases on Algerian soil.[46]

The negotiations proceeded more readily at Les Rousses and Evian than they had earlier, despite serious obstacles and disagreements, particularly over the question of nationality for the Europeans who would choose to remain in Algeria. After the basic elements of an agreement were worked out at Les Rousses, the CNRA met again in February and gave the GPRA a mandate to complete the negotiations. Meeting again at Evian in March 1962, the Algerian and French delegations signed the Evian Agreements on March 18.

The terms of the agreement which ended the long and costly war for independence were largely favorable to the Algerians. Algerian sovereignty was to extend over the entire country, including the Sahara, although France reserved the right to keep for some years an atomic testing site in the Sahara, the modern naval base of Mers el Kebir, and several airfields. French citizens were to have a period of several years during which they could decide to opt for Algerian citizenship or remain Frenchmen. Economic cooperation on mutually advantageous terms between the two countries was foreseen, and France agreed to grant a certain amount of aid to Algeria. A Provisional Executive was set up, consisting of Frenchmen, FLN members, and Muslim moderates, to administer the country from the time of the cease-fire until a legal government could be established. These, then, were the conditions on which Algeria's independence was finally achieved.

The CNRA, including the five prisoners in France, overwhelmingly

---

[46] For an interesting assessment of the Algerian negotiators and for a history of these meetings written by one of the French participants, see Robert Buron, *Carnets politiques de la guerre d'Algérie,* especially pp. 195-264.

approved of the *Accords d'Evian*. There were, however, four dissenting votes cast by members of the *Etat Major*, Boumedienne, Mendjli, Kaid, as well as by *commandant* Nasser. Thus seven and one-half years of war were finally brought to an end. A new battle, however, was about to begin.

9
Independence and the
Disintegration of the FLN

In virtually all the recently colonized countries the transition from nationalist movement to independent governing elite was accompanied by disorder, confusion, and conflict. Some countries, however, seem to have adapted more easily than others to this dramatic change in the nature of the demands made upon the political elite. Success in surviving the transition to independence has often been traced to the training of administrators given by the excolonial power, to the role of a charismatic figure, or to the existence of a large, pragmatic nationalist party that possessed skills in adjusting to the new political environment.

In Algeria none of these presumed advantages existed to ease the transition to independence. Instead, there was within the FLN a backlog of distrust and conflict, and independence merely brought the opportunity to settle accounts that had lain dormant because of the overriding goal of maintaining a façade of unity, at least until the end of the Evian negotiations. Given the heterogeneous nature of the political elite and the low adaptive capacities instilled in individuals by earlier political socialization, it would have been extremely difficult to resolve conflicts peacefully.

The form which the postindependence struggle for power took in Algeria was a direct outcome of the structure of political authority during the revolution. After more than seven years of war, the number of Algerians who had developed a sense of their own right to exercise some measure of influence in the independent Algeria they had fought so long to create was overwhelming. In addition to the many top leaders who had already filled positions of responsibility, there was a large stratum of impatient secondary leaders who might well be suspected of harboring political ambitions. In the few months between the cease-fire of March 19, 1962, and Ben Bella's investiture as President on September 26, the relations among these many contenders for influence were dramatically altered. The nature of the Algerian political system for the next few years was deeply affected by the severe crisis which broke out in July 1962.

The composition of the political elite on the eve of independence provided some hints as to the likelihood of changes in leadership once independence had been secured. The top elite was divided into discernible groups, and an ambitious secondary elite could be identified. But aside from noting that some changes would take place, the analyst might have looked to other successful revolutions for insights into the type of changes in leadership which could occur in Algeria. In surveying other cases of revolutionary change, however, one would find that the Algerian case is unusual and requires a modification of many current ideas of how the political system is affected by the attainment of independence. The crisis of 1962 can be seen as illustrating a more general hypothesis of elite transformation as well as clarifying the specific nature of the Algerian revolution.

Since much of the political life of independent Algeria in the first years after the revolution was colored by the events of this short period, the summer crisis is a necessary component in any understanding of later political developments. The forces set in motion at that time were still influencing Algerian politics many years later.

The Top Wartime Elite

Among the many commentators on the Algerian war for independence, the Algerian participants themselves have often provided the most objective assessments of the strengths and failures of the

FLN.[1] Algerians have been ready to admit the lack of integration within the wartime elite, the absence of a unifying ideology, and the failure to prepare for the problems of economic and social organization in postrevolutionary Algeria. Invariably these weaknesses of the FLN are attributed to the leadership structures which emerged between 1954 and 1962.

The leadership of the FLN was not the preserve of a small group of like-minded men. Indeed, no single institution of the revolution could speak authoritatively for the many groups and individuals who were struggling for Algerian freedom under the banner of the FLN. Amid this diversity, however, the one organization that came closest to being a recognized source of authority and that was most nearly representative of the revolutionary forces was the CNRA. The CNRA from 1956 on functioned as a protoparliamentary body with legal, if intermittent, authority exercised at nearly annual meetings.

While the complete membership of the CNRA after 1957 has never been revealed, at least seventy-seven of its members have been identified. A general image one forms from analyzing the backgrounds of these men is that all the major segments of the revolutionary elite were included in the CNRA. The average member was born about 1926 in the region of Constantine and had a secondary school education. In addition to his position on the CNRA he would have occupied one other top political or military role. This composite image of a CNRA member, however, hides the variety found within the wartime elite. Table 9.1 distinguishes among four groups classed according to political background. The Liberals and Radicals because of their small number are considered together as Politicians.

From Table 9.1 it is possible to identify two main subgroups within the elite. The first, consisting of the Politicians and Intellectuals, is highly educated and somewhat more urban in origin than the second, the Revolutionaries and the Military. The latter are definitely less well educated and more likely to have been born in a village. Additional but less reliable information indicates that the Politicians and Intellectuals frequently practiced liberal professions, whereas the Revolutionaries and the Military were more often workers, peasants, or small traders.

On the basis of this simple statistical evidence it would seem that, roughly speaking, one could classify the elite as, say, cosmopolitans

[1] In particular, see the *Programme de Tripoli,* the *Charte d'Alger,* and Benkhedda's "Contribution à l'historique du FLN."

TABLE 9.1 SOCIAL BACKGROUNDS OF THE ALGERIAN WARTIME ELITE

	Politicians[1]	Revolutionaries	Military	Intellectuals	Total Elite	Percent of Total Algerian Muslim Population (1948)
Education						
University	11 (100%)	2 (8%)	2 (8%)	11 (69%)	26 (34%)	< .5
Secondary	—	19 (73)	4 (17)	3 (19)	26 (34)	1.5
Elementary	—	5 (19)	5 (21)	—	10 (13)	11
Unknown	—	—	13 (54)	2 (12)	15 (19)	
Region of birth						
Algiers	5 (45)	3 (12)	1 (4)	4 (25)	13 (17)	23
Constantine	2 (18)	13 (50)	3 (12)	6 (38)	24 (31)	22
Oran	1 (9)	5 (19)	2 (8)	1 (6)	9 (12)	40
Kabylia	3 (28)	5 (19)	3 (12)	1 (6)	12 (16)	15
Unknown	—	—	15 (64)	4 (25)	19 (24)	
Size of birthplace						
100,000+	2 (18)	2 (8)	—	3 (19)	7 (9)	6
30,000–100,000	1 (9)	2 (8)	1 (4)	—	4 (5)	7
3,000–30,000	4 (37)	10 (38)	1 (4)	5 (31)	20 (26)	25
Under 3,000	3 (27)	10 (38)	6 (25)	3 (19)	22 (29)	62
Unknown	1 (9)	2 (8)	16 (67)	5 (31)	24 (31)	
Average age in 1954	39	32	28	27	29	
Top political roles per individual	2.7	3.3	1.3	1.1	2.3	
TOTAL	11	26	24	16	77	7,600,000

[1] An aggregate of Liberals and Radicals.

and parochials. However, the weakness of such a dichotomy is that it combines within a single category individuals of different political generations and hence of divergent political beliefs. Thus, while in terms of social background the Politicians and Intellectuals are quite similar, they are furthest apart in terms of generation. The Revolutionaries and the Military, while similar in background and close in generation, differ greatly in their paths to power and in the experiences which helped form their dominant attitudes. (See Table 9.2.)

TABLE 9.2 SOCIAL BACKGROUNDS AND POLITICAL GENERATION OF GROUPS WITHIN THE ALGERIAN POLITICAL ELITE

Social Background	Political Generation (average date of birth)		
	1905	1920s	1930s
High status High education	Liberals →	Radicals	Intellectuals
		↓	↑
Low status Low education	(few from this group entered politics)	Revolutionaries →	Military

Note: Arrows indicate the sequence of entry into political positions.

A second weakness of the cosmopolitan-parochial dichotomy is that those Algerians labeled parochials in terms of origin and education came to be perhaps the most ardent of the nationalist leaders. The Revolutionaries, at least, were most prone to identify themselves with the entire nation and in the process acquired a sense of their own right to positions of power in the new state. For the Military, nationalism was an equally strong value, but their view of who should exercise power was more that the army had a right to play a political role than that they as individuals had such a calling. Most of the Military, in fact, went by pseudonyms during the war and some, like Boumedienne, are primarily known by these aliases.

This static picture of the revolutionary elite obscures the developments that had taken place over time. In Algeria the nationalist movement, as in most colonial countries, was originally presided over by men of relatively advantaged origins who were thoroughly educated in the culture of the colonizing country. But in Algeria the hegemony of the "new middle class" over the nationalist move-ment was broken by a series of failures to obtain nationalist de-mands through legal political action. Thus in Algeria the leader-ship of the nationalist movement began to gravitate as early as 1949 toward those Revolutionaries who were committed to the use of violence to obtain independence. This group, more modest in origin though only slightly less influenced by French culture than the Politicians, broke dramatically with the past by organizing a large-scale insurrection in November 1954.

The Revolutionaries were soon joined on the military front by new recruits of modest origins and somewhat less experience and education. On the political front they allied themselves to the old nationalist Politicians. But the continued dominance of the Revo-lutionaries throughout the war is reflected by the fact that they were the largest single group within the top elite and held the greatest number of top political roles per person. The Politicians, while the smallest group, also ranked high in terms of political roles per person, with an average of nearly three. The Military and the Intellectuals were the second and third largest elements in the top elite, and individuals from both groups were generally limited to one political role as members of the CNRA. Many Military officers, however, gained considerable political experience outside the authoritative structures of the Revolution both within the *Etat Major* and as leaders of the interior *willayas*. Likewise the Intel-lectuals, while occupying few top executive political positions, had by the end of the war gained considerable influence within the CNRA or as negotiators.

By tracing developments within the top executive agencies, the CCE and the GPRA, Figure 9.1 shows some of the transformations that took place over time in the political organs of the revolution. For the first half of the revolution the top executive elite expanded

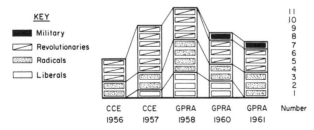

Figure 9.1 Composition of Executive Agencies of the Revolution

and became more broadly inclusive of all political groups, while the Revolutionaries declined somewhat in terms of overall dominance by the time of the first GPRA. From 1958 on, a reverse trend is seen whereby the GPRA contracted slightly and became generally more restrictive. Each addition and subtraction from this top group, it should be recalled, was the subject of intense political concern on the part of the GPRA and CNRA members. Battles raged over the desirable composition of these agencies, and each change was the result of a long process of negotiation, often accompanied by threats or coercion. In 1958 what appears as a simple drop in the number of Revolutionaries represented the outcome of a bitter personal quarrel for power which apparently ended in execution. Other changes, such as the disappearance of the Liberals, had grave consequences in the period immediately following independence. Perhaps only in the addition of one Military man after 1960 is the change of small consequence, since the individual concerned seems to have been "promoted" by the *Etat Major* to facilitate the task of its own reorganization and centralization. But even in this case the presence of one Military officer does inadvertently represent the emergence of a new power center, even if the individual concerned was not its representative within the GPRA.

Changes in the composition of both the CCE–GPRA and the CNRA reflected more fundamental alterations in the style of elite decision-making and in the availability of political skills within the elite. From 1954 to 1961 there was a development from a relatively small, undifferentiated, and collegial decision-making system to a larger, more heterogeneous system in which functionally defined subgroups appeared and collegial decision-making waned. The last stage of development reflected the completion of the process leading to subgroup autonomy with each subgroup becoming more highly specialized and homogeneous.

The first stage coincided with the commencement of a semiclandestine insurrectionary movement. The second stage, reached after considerable cooptation of new elements into the elite, paralleled the drive for international recognition and legitimacy. The third stage, that of subgroup autonomy rather than elite integration, stemmed from failures during the second stage to resolve questions of authority and coincided with the emergence of the Military as a new contender for power. This arrangement seems to have been stable only so long as all groups believed that the danger of openly settling the question of authority would work to the benefit of a common enemy, in this case France. A tacit agreement emerged that conflicts would not be settled until independence was achieved. These changes in the structure of authority during the war for independence are perhaps most likely within a broad united front like the FLN. A more homogeneous, or totalitarian, party or even a more highly articulated ideology might have reduced the pressures that built up among elite members to transform periodically the leadership of the revolution. In the Algerian case, however, there were few rigid controls over recruitment into the elite, and ideology was noticeably absent. Thus changes in patterns of authority were generally accompanied by changes in personnel in elite or subelite positions.

The general trend for influence to pass from the Politicians and Revolutionaries to the Military and, to a lesser extent, the Intellectuals, has been noted. Since individuals in each of these groups differed in terms of political skills and in their own self-images, it is possible to distinguish trends along these dimensions as well. In general there was a tendency during the war to move from dominance by those with agitational skills toward those with organizational and administrative ability.[2] In terms of self-image, the elite was originally composed of those with high claims to power based on either experience (the Politicians) or militancy (the Revolutionaries), but gradually it came to include those whose claims to power were based on actual contribution to the war effort (the Military) or on competence (the Intellectuals).[3] (See Table 9.3.)

The Secondary Wartime Elite

In addition to the top revolutionary leaders, a younger, less experienced secondary elite was formed and mobilized during the

[2] This development lies at the basis of the charge made in the *Programme de Tripoli* and in the *Charte d'Alger* that the GPRA became bureaucratic and nonrevolutionary.

[3] In Table 9.3 the names in parentheses indicate the central tendency of elements within each group. Needless to say, these estimates are not based on quantitative measures. Lasswell, who comes closest to using these categories to discuss individuals, suggests that the implicit scale distinguishing individuals in these skill groups is one describing the generality, or the abstractness, of the objects of displaced affect. For the administrator there is low generality, for the theorist there is high generality. See Harold D. Lasswell, *Psychopathology and Politics*, pp. 127 and 151. Whatever the psychodynamics of the individuals in these groups, it does seem that these four types can be distinguished on the basis of how successfully they deal with specifics or abstractions. The theorist,

TABLE 9.3   DISTRIBUTION   OF   POLITICAL   SKILLS   WITHIN
THE POLITICAL ELITE

Elite Types	Theoretician	Agitator	Organizer	Administrator
Politicians	(Radicals)□□□□□□		(Liberals)□□□□□□□	
Revolutionaries	(Revolutionaries)□□□□□□□		□□□□□□□	
Military	(Maquisards)□□□□□□□		(Professionals)□□□□□□□	
Intellectuals	(Generalists)□□□□□□□□			(Specialists)□□□□□□□

Algerian war for independence. This stratum of political leaders became increasingly important toward the end of the war, largely within the army of the frontiers, the ministries of the GPRA and the FFFLN. An important segment of this elite consisted largely of men who were either students, lawyers, or doctors at the time the revolution began. Some who entered the army reached responsible positions within the *Etat Major,* either at Oujda or Ghardimaou. Others associated themselves more closely with the political agencies of the revolution and became ambassadors, secretary generals of ministries, or directors of propaganda.

Many of these young men rose quickly after independence to positions of great influence. Of those whose careers passed through the army, Abdelaziz Bouteflika, Cherif Belkacem, and Ahmed Medeghri were all top leaders in 1968. Those whose careers began within the political agencies of the revolution, such as Belaid Abdesselam and Ahmed Taleb, also held ministerial posts in 1968. To account for the sudden rise of members from this subelite following independence will be the task of later chapters, but a general picture of the secondary elite in comparison to the top elite is useful for an understanding of these developments.

The secondary elite, as it was taking form in 1961 and 1962, consisted in large part of young professional army officers and a sizable number of Intellectuals. In addition, a few of the older nationalists who had never gained top positions during the revolution added to

it may be suggested, is often a poor politician because his concern for the masses of humanity is too general. The agitator or organizer will appeal to a more manageable constituency and thus is more likely to be effective.

the number of aspiring politicians. In general, this subelite was more highly educated than the top elite and more likely to come from urban areas, particularly in the heavily Europeanized regions of Algiers and Oran. Many of them came from high-status occupations.[4]

The implication which must be drawn from this comparison is that the Algerian political elite on the eve of independence was unusual among political elites in that political power and social status within the elite were not positively correlated. One of the most general findings of elite studies is that the higher the level of authority of a political unit, the larger the percentage of highly educated, urban-born individuals.[5] Generally the percentage of lawyers and other professionals also rises as one moves from secondary to top elite positions. In Algeria it seems clear that those in top power positions during the war were generally less well educated and of more modest social origins than was a major segment of the secondary elite which had developed by the end of the war. In addition, the top elite was made up of men whose skills were largely those of the agitator and organizer, whereas the subelite consisted of individuals most skilled either as theorists or administrators.

The prolonged war for independence, of course, was responsible for this anomaly, for it allowed the top positions to go to those most specialized in the use of violence, namely the Revolutionaries and the Military, who had displaced the more socially advantaged but less militant Politicians and who had not been obliged to step aside to favor the younger Intellectuals. If there is something un-

---

[4] These generalizations are drawn from an analysis of the backgrounds of about 100 men who played some significant political role after independence, but who were not among the top revolutionary elite as defined here. Approximately 75 percent of these men were university-educated, 35 percent came from cities over 30,000 in population, 50 percent came from Algiers and Oran, and over 50 percent were from high-status occupations. For the top revolutionary elite, comparable figures, excluding "unknowns" are 42 percent university-educated, 21 percent urban birthplace, 38 percent born in Algiers or Oran, 32 percent high-status professions of law and medicine. While the absolute magnitude of both sets of figures is open to some question due to incomplete data, there is no obvious bias which does not operate similarly for both the top leaders and the secondary elite. The differences between the two groups are all that is being argued in any case, and in this the secondary elite is clearly more educated, more urban-born, from more Europeanized areas, and more often from liberal professions than are members of the top elite.

[5] This generalization is based on an analysis of hundreds of different elite studies which will form the empirical section of a forthcoming book by Frederick Frey and William Quandt, *Social Background Analysis of Political Elites*.

stable about a political system which allows a subelite with higher social qualifications and new skills to form, one might predict that either the subelite would be dispersed and replaced by more manageable elements or that the top elite would eventually be displaced by the pressures from below.[6] In either event one would expect considerable turnover within the top and secondary elites.

From Nationalist Movement to Independence

Numerous studies, both qualitative and quantitative, describe the transformations of political elites accompanying the change from one political system to another.[7] Nationalist movements have been compared to postindependence governments, revolutionaries to postrevolution elites, and those who articulate an ideology to those who lead ideological movements, In virtually every case the pattern of development seems initially to be from dominance by a highly educated, cosmopolitan elite toward that of a more provincial, regionalist, rather less educated elite.[8]

Throughout much of the developing parts of the world there seems to have been a general emergence of a rural or provincial elite after independence, contrasting sharply with the Western-educated, French- or English-speaking elites of the period of the nationalist movement.[9] Likewise, for the coercive totalitarian movements of Europe and Asia, Lerner has noted that ". . . intellectuals of higher social status founded the movements through which people of lesser status made their way to the top." [10] Historians of revolutionary change have also noted the shift of power from the moderate "men of words" to the more extreme, less educated "men

[6] A general explanation of the instability of such an elite structure is given by F. W. Frey, *The Turkish Political Elite*, pp. 400 and 404–405, where he postulates that it is psychologically intolerable for most people of high status to submit to the influence of those with lower status. Frey also finds in his study of Turkey, p. 268, that high education and professional or official occupation are most highly associated with high levels of power.

[7] Among qualitative studies, see Crane Brinton, *The Anatomy of Revolution* and Lyford P. Edwards, *The Natural History of Revolution*. F. W. Frey in *The Turkish Political Elite* provides quantitative evidence on elite changes in Turkey during the First Republic.

[8] Harold D. Lasswell, in *World Revolutionary Elites*, p. 68, predicts that as identifications broaden there is some "self-reference effect" or reaction which initially appears in the form of parochialization.

[9] Gabriel A. Almond and James S. Coleman, eds., *The Politics of the Developing Areas*, p. 547. See also F. W. Frey, *The Turkish Political Elite*, pp. 396–397.

[10] Daniel Lerner, in *World Revolutionary Elites*, p. 466.

of action." [11] The ubiquity of such generalizations is striking and suggests a common process underlying transformations from opposition movement to governing elite.

Two distinct patterns can be identified within the general trend in which power passes from high-status agitators to lower-status administrators. One pattern is that of the transformation of the nationalist movement or ideological party into an authoritarian regime in which power often lies with a charismatic leader. In this model the ascendancy of a single powerful leader brings about the disintegration of the nationalist elite and opens the way for the rise of lesser elites who succeed in consolidating power through the use of the army and the administration. Variants of this pattern are found in such diverse nations as the Soviet Union, China, Nazi Germany, Fascist Italy, Ghana, Burma, and Indonesia.[12]

A second model that incorporates the idea of a declining incidence of cosmopolitanism among the elite after independence is largely derived from the experience of formally democratic or competitive countries. In these countries one typically finds a highly educated elite guiding the country through the transitions accompanying independence. Gradually, however, a more rural, more parochial elite is able to aggregate local interests sufficiently to rise to political influence through the workings of the electoral system. Countries conforming to this general pattern include the United States, India, the Philippines, Turkey after 1945, and Ceylon.[13] Symbolically this change is seen in the shift of formal or real power from the hands of men like the Founding Fathers in America to the Jacksonians, or, in India, from the Oxford-educated Nehru to the Tamil-speaking Congress party leader Kamaraj.

[11] Crane Brinton, *Anatomy of Revolution* and Eric Hoffer, *The True Believer*
[12] For these countries see Z. Brzezinski and Samuel P. Huntington, *Political Power: USA/USSR*, p. 136; Robert C. North, "Kuomintang and Chinese Communist Elites"; Daniel Lerner, "The Nazi Elite"; and Harold Lasswell with Renzo Sereno, "The Fascists: The Changing Elite," all three reprinted in Lasswell and Lerner, eds., *World Revolutionary Elites;* David Apter, *Ghana in Transition;* Lucian Pye, "The Politics of Southeast Asia," in Gabriel Almond and James Coleman, eds. *Politics of Developing Areas,* p. 131; and Herbert D. Feith, *The Decline of Constitutional Democracy in Indonesia,* p. 25.
[13] See Seymour M. Lipset, *The First New Nation* for the United States; Myron Weiner, "The Politics of South Asia," in Almond and Coleman, eds., *Politics of Developing Areas* as well as his "Changing Patterns of Leadership in West Bengal," *Pacific Affairs,* September 1958, for India; Jean Grossholtz, *Politics in the Philippines,* pp. 223–233; Frederick W. Frey, *The Turkish Political Elite,* p. 188; and Marshall R. Singer, *The Emerging Elite: A Study of Political Leadership in Ceylon.* Samuel P. Huntington, *Political Order in Changing Societies,* pp. 446-461, illustrates the dynamics of "ruralizing elections."

Of these two variants of the model of elite change, the authoritarian example is more relevant to the Algerian case. The early phase of the nationalist movement in Algeria corresponded quite closely to the cosmopolitan period. The Liberals around Ferhat Abbas were all French-educated, and many were lawyers or doctors. The Radicals of the Central Committee of the MTLD were likewise generally well educated and quite open to Western cultural values. In most colonial countries it was the equivalent of the Liberals or Radicals who led their country to independence. In Algeria, however, these groups simply failed to retain control over the nationalist movement, and consequently the predicted trend toward increased influence of less educated, lower-status individuals began before independence.

The Revolutionaries and the Military, both of whom can be seen as representatives of the more socially disadvantaged groups, came to dominate the FLN after 1954. The political survival of the Liberals and Radicals after the outbreak of the revolution was due to a felt need for a broad united front in order to claim legitimacy before the Muslim masses and world opinion.[14] As power passed from the more to the less cosmopolitan elements among the nationalists, so also did those with the greatest capacity for accommodation and compromise give way to those who were least adaptive. According to the models of elite change sketched here, one might anticipate that after independence there would be a tendency for even more provincial and parochial elements to rise gradually to power.

But it should be remembered that in the Algerian case a large part of the secondary elite within the FLN by the end of the war was considerably more educated, urban, and cosmopolitan than the Revolutionaries and the Military. Consequently, in Algeria one might expect a general movement toward more educated, more cosmopolitan leaders after independence if the secondary elite were to gain in influence.

These observations suggest a modification of the cosmopolitan-parochial model of elite transformation. A more general statement of these changes within an authoritarian context would seem to be that the elite members most closely associated with the nationalist or revolutionary movement, whether they be relatively cosmopolitan

14 In an interview Amar Ouamrane, who was instrumental in recruiting Liberals and Radicals to the FLN, explained that it was decided that all tendencies must be brought into the FLN to avoid the failures of earlier anti-French revolts, such as those of Mokrani and the Sidi Cheikh in the nineteenth century, both of which had remained regional in appeal.

or parochial, will develop high feelings of self-esteem and be relatively deficient in accommodative skills. With independence or the conquest of power, the old elite will be unable to agree upon a political process that permits a broad sharing of power, and there will be a tendency for some element among those who feel they have an inherent right to rule to seek clients and allies within the secondary elite.[15] The desirability of this solution is that the secondary elite members have fewer claims to power and generally possess skills somewhat complementary to those of the top elite members.

Eventually those within the secondary elite, by means of their alliances with older, more prestigious nationalists, will find their way to top positions. In most cases, of course, this will still mean that the cosmopolitan nationalists will be replaced by more provincial leaders. But the advantage of this statement of the process is that it accounts equally well for the reverse phenomenon, as occurred in Algeria after independence.

The mechanism of top elite disintegration is that conflicting demands for power cannot easily be mediated or reconciled by individuals with low accommodative abilities, such as those produced by the nationalist or revolutionary process of socialization. The authoritarian solution to these conflicts is for an individual or subgroup to find allies among the secondary elite, whose lesser claims to power and whose complementary, rather than competing, skills are easily accepted. The process, of course, does not stop with the initial transformations accompanying the acquisition of power, and later developments may eventually bring to the fore either more or less educated, urban and cosmopolitan elements.[16]

This modified model of elite change in an authoritarian setting, then, merely predicts that the nationalist elite will disintegrate and that the secondary elite will rise, regardless of whether the latter is more or less parochial. The rapidity of the rise of the secondary elite will depend largely on the structure of the political system.

Each of three possible systems of authority, namely the collegial-accommodative, the centralized-autocratic, and the segmented-

[15] Myron Weiner, in *Party Building in a New Nation: The Indian National Congress,* p. 470, argues that the greater the degree of elite competition, the greater the search for popular support.

[16] Turkey's development since 1945 seems to have been accompanied by both increased localism and increased lawyer dominance following the formal democratization of the political system. See F. W. Frey, *The Turkish Political Elite.*

autonomous systems, seems to produce differing rates of secondary elite mobility. For example, the movement toward a more central-ized system, especially from that of an autonomous one, will be associated with high top elite turnover and rapid rise from secondary elite positions. A tendency toward a collegial or accommodative elite structure will be accompanied by considerable elite stability and gradual, or "capillary" recruitment of secondary elites.[17] Frag-mentation, or movement toward autonomous subgroups, will be associated with relatively low elite turnover but moderate second-ary elite recruitment as each unit within the elite organizes its separate segment of the political system. In Algeria, by the end of the revolution, a relatively segmented elite existed. The rate of secondary elite recruitment would then seem to depend greatly on whether an authoritarian or collegial structure of authority developed after independence.

A necessary qualification to any theory that predicts the dis-integration or alteration of a political elite is a hypothesis which explains the rate and dynamics of change that should be anticipated. Several studies have suggested principles that will govern coalition formation or realignments in ruling bodies.[18] Anthony Downs, for example, has formulated a theorem stating that a coalition will seek under all conditions to maximize its support, and from this he derives a number of important hypotheses. William Riker, by contrast, has argued that coalitions ". . . seek to maximize only up

---

[17] *Ibid.*, p. 393.

[18] William H. Riker, *The Theory of Political Coalitions* and Anthony Downs, *An Economic Theory of Democracy.* While both these models seem designed in large part to explain party politics in formally democratic systems, there is no reason why some of their primary assumptions cannot be applied to developing nations and authoritarian systems as well. A major difference does exist, however, in the degree of certainty that one has gained the support of a "minimal winning coalition." This is true because rules governing the process of winning power, such as acquiring a majority of the electoral votes, are often lacking. What is needed to "win" is generally unclear in developing countries. Thus some incentive to "gain maximal support initially may be more common in such low information systems. Riker takes this into account by discussion the "information effect," pp. 88–89, where he implies that perfect information and perfect rationality would always lead to the formation of "minimal winning coalitions." But neither of these conditions exist in most developing countries, and psychologically it seems more accurate to follow Downs in saying that initially a leader seeks maximum support. Only after he is in power do the costs of maintaining a large coalition become obvious and does information improve so that one can better judge the amount of support required to remain a "minimal winning coalition."

to the point of subjective certainty of winning. After this point they seek to minimize, that is, to maintain themselves at the size (as subjectively estimated) of a minimum winning coalition." [19]

Rather than rejecting one or the other of these models, it seems that each is particularly useful in describing different phases in the formation of coalitions. During the initial period of trying to gain power, an individual or group might well be expected to try to maximize support as Downs would predict. In situations marked by low information, one would rarely be certain that he had just enough support to win and that efforts to gain a broader following were thus unnecessary. During the process of seizing power, then, one may expect a coalition to try to attract as many members or supporters as possible. While Riker's hypothesis allows for this phenomenon in situations characterized by low information, his stress is more on the process of reducing the size of the winning coalition.

The implication of maximizing support during the drive to acquire power is that, if successful, the winning coalition is initially likely to be quite heterogeneous. Once in power, however, the leaders of the winning coalition are probably able to estimate with some confidence the degree of opposition to them and the costs of maintaining a large ruling elite. Since a heterogeneous coalition is expensive to maintain, Riker's suggestion that a winning coalition will seek to reduce its size to the minimum compatible with remaining in power seems valid.

The process by which a winning coalition reduces itself to the minimally effective size can, of course, escape the control of those in power, and what was thought to be a minimal winning coalition may find itself a minority. Nonetheless, it seems safe to predict that a broad coalition will inevitably decline over time in accordance with Riker's "size principle." This phenomenon has been labeled by the French *usure du pouvoir,* the wearing away of power. While *usure* generally refers to the withdrawal from the ruling coalition of dissatisfied elements rather than deliberate exclusion, it does indicate that those who control entry into the top elite are not able or willing to satisfy the demands of all coalition partners, and thus some will leave the coalition. In Algeria the term *usure* is also used to describe the erosion of support for a

[19] William Riker, *Political Coalitions,* p. 33.

given group or individual. At times it even seems that the expectation that the *usure du pouvoir* should be taking place is the stimulus for the actions which insure that it will.[20]

The practical consequences of linking the two models suggested by Downs and Riker to explain the initial seizure of power and the consequent consolidation of power are well illustrated by the Algerian case. In the Algerian context one would anticipate that, following the disintegration of the FLN, the winning coalition that emerged would be broadly based and heterogeneous. Thus, while it might be possible to seize power merely with the support of the army, one could expect that efforts would be made to attract other groups as well. Likewise, one would predict that this coalition might prove somewhat unwieldy because of the large numbers of individuals and groups demanding some "payoff." [21] Thus the process of *usure*, or the move toward a smaller, more homogeneous coalition, would eventually take place. To find evidence for this speculative hypothesis one must turn to the study of the FLN crisis of summer 1962.

Fragmentation and Realignment of the FLN: The Crisis of Summer 1962

Following the cease-fire negotiated at Evian in March 1962, the tensions and divisions within the FLN became increasingly apparent. The release of the five GPRA ministers in France seems to have aggravated the conflict opposing the provisional government and the army, for each minister felt compelled to choose sides in the existing power struggle.

A last attempt to preserve some semblance of unity within the FLN took place at Tripoli during early June, a month before the referendum which brought independence. The CNRA, despite the opposition of many of its members, was once again assembled in what was to be the last attempt of the FLN to work out its internal conflicts without resorting to force. The Tripoli Congress, therefore, represented an important test of the accommodative capacities of the members of the revolutionary elite. Previous conflicts had generally come to be settled by allowing virtual autonomy to each dissident group. No political process for reconciling opposing demands had been formulated. But with independence coming in

---

[20] See Nathan Leites, *Images of Power in French Politics*, June 1962.
[21] Seymour M. Lipset, *First New Nation*, p. 52.

the near future, questions of postindependence political power and structure naturally arose.

The Tripoli Congress and the prolonged crisis that followed illustrate well the ways in which the elite's political socialization and participation in the war for independence had led to the creation of competing subgroups with low adaptive capacity and few bargaining skills. Given these conditions the lack of consensus on political processes virtually insured that the FLN would disintegrate.

At Tripoli two major problems existed. One was to define a program for the future Algerian state and society. The other task was to select the agencies of political power which would govern Algeria until elections could be held. The former problem was seen as one of articulating an ideology, and the Tripoli Program was the successful product of the CNRA's deliberations.[22] The second issue came to be interpreted as the need to name a Political Bureau, and in this matter the CNRA, required by its statutes to invest such a body with a two-thirds majority, found itself paralyzed.[23] The question of ideology, then, was easily dealt with, for it had little relevance, but the question of power was insoluble within the context of the CNRA.

The Tripoli Program, along with the Platform of the Soummam of 1956 and the Charter of Algiers in 1964, is one of the few authoritative outlines of the Algerian elite's political, social, and economic ideas. The authors of the Program were primarily four Intellectuals, Reda Malek, Mohammed Ben Yahia, Mostefa Lacheraf, and Mohammed Harbi. These four were assisted by a number of other Intellectuals and received the encouragement of Ben Bella.

Two themes are of particular interest in the Tripoli Program.[24] The first deals with the inadequacies of the wartime FLN, the second with proposals for the future. The analysis of the FLN identifies

[22] Arslan Humbaraci, in *Algeria: A Revolution that Failed*, p. 67, disputes the common notion that the CNRA at Tripoli unanimously adopted the Tripoli Program. Several participants in the Congress, however, have independently claimed that the Tripoli Program was indeed unanimously accepted. What is clear, however, is that the Political Bureau proposed at Tripoli was never voted upon, although Ben Bella later claimed that individual consultation revealed that a majority of the CNRA supported the Political Bureau.

[23] A pamphlet edited by the *Zone Autonome d'Alger* (ZAA), entitled "Institutions provisoires et l'état algérien," dated June 15, 1962, contains the Statutes of the CNRA.

[24] The text of the Tripoli Program can be found in the *Annuaire de l'Afrique du nord*, Volume 1, 1962, pp. 683–704.

the gap between the revolution's leaders and the masses as the cause of the lack of "ideological firmness." This lack of ideology permitted a "paternalistic" notion of authority to replace the concept of responsibility. This in turn led to "feudalism," "formalism," "romanticism," "a petty bourgeois spirit," "the depolitization of the interior forces," and "the confusion of state and party." These practices and beliefs, if not corrected by "ideological combat," would lead to the creation of a mediocre and antipopular bureaucracy.

Turning to the future problems facing Algeria, the authors of the Tripoli Program foresaw a state subscribing to socialist principles, in which the large means of production would be collectivized and rational planning would be introduced. Algerian culture was to be "national, revolutionary, and scientific," and Islam in its modern, progressive form would be a central component of the Algerian personality. Islam, however, was not to be used for demagogic purposes or as a barrier to progress.

Economic and social problems received some attention, as did foreign policy. What was conspicuously missing, however, was any discussion of the future state's political institutions or the political process that would be adopted in a liberated Algeria. The Tripoli Program has generally been seen as calling for the creation of a single party system, but in fact the closest the Program came to committing itself to any political structures was its call for "a conscientious avant-garde" of peasants, workers, youth, and revolutionary intellectuals. This, then, was the "ideological" program unanimously accepted at Tripoli by the CNRA after a few hours of debate.

The issue of political power was not as easily solved as that of "ideology." At Tripoli it seems that those forces that opposed the GPRA rallied around the *Etat Major* of the ALN.[25] Ben Bella, who perhaps more than any other member of the political elite aspired to top leadership of his country, found in the *Etat Major* a powerful and well-organized potential ally. Under his urging, a Political Bureau was presented to the CNRA for approval as a substitute for the authority of the GPRA. The Political Bureau which was presented consisted of the five exprisoners—Ben Bella, Ait Ahmed, Boudiaf, Khider, and Bitat—plus Mohammedi Said, the least

---

[25] Benyoussef Benkhedda, "Contribution à l'historique du FLN," p. 8.

influential member of the GPRA, and another Revolutionary, Colonel Hadj Ben Alla.

Despite later claims by Ben Bella that the Political Bureau received the support of the majority of the CNRA at Tripoli, it is clear that the Political Bureau was never invested in a formal vote by the required two-thirds majority of the CNRA. Furthermore, Boudiaf and Ait Ahmed refused to be part of the proposed Political Bureau. After Boudiaf, Ouamrane, and others had already left the Tripoli Conference, Benkhedda, preoccupied by the immense problems awaiting solution within Algeria, also quit the Congress before any decisions on the Political Bureau had been reached.[26] In short, the Tripoli Congress failed to resolve any of the political conflicts within the elite and succeeded merely in adopting a Program of generalities. Still, it was not until independence was virtually assured by the referendum of July 1, that the unresolved intraelite crisis erupted into an open struggle for power.

To understand the course of the two-month crisis which opened within the political elite on the eve of independence, it should be recalled that by 1962 the FLN contained within its loose structure at least ten relatively independent centers of authority. The most important of these were the six jealously independent interior *willayas,* the well equipped forces of the *Etat Major* of the ALN in Morocco and Tunisia, the GPRA which was recognized by many countries as the legal representative of the FLN, the FFFLN whose financial contribution to the revolution had far surpassed that of any other source, and finally the five prisoners from among the so-called "historic leaders," who were seen by many to possess considerable moral authority because of their early contribution to the revolution and their long confinement in French prisons. In addition to these contenders for power there were the less

---

[26] *Ibid.* and interviews with Benkhedda and Ouamrane. Benkhedda was widely criticized for walking out of the Conference. An important document condemning him was signed by a number of CNRA members on June 7, 1962, and has been reproduced in Zdravko Pečar, *Alžir do Nezavisnosti,* p. 825. Among the signataries one finds Zbiri, Yahiaoui and Amar Mellah for *willaya* 1; Tayebi (Si Larbi) for *willaya* 2; Mohand oul Hadj and Mahiouz for *willaya* 3; Bencherif and Si Lakhdar for *willaya* 4; Si Othmane and Boubekeur for *willaya* 5; Chaabani, Slimani, Kheirredine and Sakhri for *willaya* 6. In addition, the members of the *Etat Major,* Mendjli, Kaid, and Boumedienne, and the following members of the CNRA also signed: Ben Bella, Abbas, Khider, Francis, Boumendjel, Ben Alla, Bitat, and Mohammedi Said. A photostat of this document is found in *Die algerische Revolution* (Stuttgart, Germany: Deutsche Verlagsges., 1963).

influential auxiliary organizations of students (UGEMA) and workers (UGTA), as well as the Liberals who had been evicted from the GPRA a year earlier. To unify these many divergent forces would have been an extremely difficult task even for the most skilled of diplomats. For the independent and uncompromising subgroups within the Algerian political elite reconcilation of so many conflicting demands was virtually impossible, and thus force was to become the final arbiter.

The nature of the opposing coalitions which were to struggle for power in postindependence Algeria was relatively clear by late June of 1962. The interior *willayas* 2, 3, and 4, those which were furthest from the Moroccan and Tunisian frontiers and the control of the *Etat Major,* reproached Boumedienne and his colleagues for having failed to supply their *willayas* while building up an effective armed force in relative security outside Algeria. Furthermore they resented the attempts of the *Etat Major* to assert its authority over their domains. Thus on June 25, along with the *Fédération de France* of the FLN, these three *willayas* asked the GPRA to use its authority to restrain the *Etat Major* from interfering in their internal affairs. The following day the semblance of GPRA unity was broken as Khider, one of the five prisoners recently released from French prisons, resigned his post as Minister of State in the GPRA. Finally, on June 30, the day before the referendum on self-determination was held in Algeria, the GPRA announced the dissolution of the *Etat Major* of Boumedienne, Mendjli, and Kaid.

The *Etat Major* refused to recognize the GPRA's authority to make such a decision, and its leaders entered Algeria in an effort to mobilize support. The peripheral *willayas* 1, 5, and 6 rapidly rallied to the *Etat Major,* and denounced the GPRA in harsh terms. Ben Bella meanwhile was maneuvering to emerge at the head of the anti-GPRA forces, and thus he dissociated himself from the decision to sanction Boumedienne. Two coalitions were thus formed as the GPRA entered Algiers on July 3. Around the GPRA were the FFFLN and the forces of the three interior *willayas* led by colonels Hassan, Mohand oul Hadj, and Sawt al Arab who were hostile to the *Etat Major.* The second coalition formed around the best organized force in the FLN, namely the frontier armies, and consisted of the *Etat Major* and three *willayas* under the leadership of colonels Zbiri, Chaabani, and Si Othmane. Ben Bella and Khider, as well as the Liberals Abbas, Francis, and Boumendjel also joined this group. The UGEMA and the UGTA remained neutral. In somewhat oversimplified terms, the crisis of summer 1962 resulted in the formation of a pro-GPRA coalition of Radicals and Intellectuals and some of the interior Military forces. The Revolutionaries were divided, some supporting the GPRA and others rallying to the Political Bureau. The key element in the Political Bureau's support, however, was the exterior Military organization. It is worth noting, in considering these alignments, that the two groups which divided most sharply were precisely those which identified themselves most fully with the revolution, namely the Revolutionaries and the Military. The Liberals, Radicals, and Intellectuals were more likely to be all on one side or the other, or perhaps neutral in the conflict. (See Table 9.4.)

TABLE 9.4 COALITION CHOICES OF ELITE TYPES IN SUMMER 1962 CRISIS

	Pro-Etat Major Pro-Political Bureau Anti-GPRA	Neutral	Anti-Etat Major Anti-Political Bureau Pro-GPRA
Elite Subgroups			
Liberals	□□□□□□□□		
Radicals			□□□□□□□□□
Revolutionaries	□□□□□□□□		□□□□□□□□
Military	□□□□□□□□		□□□□□□□□
Intellectuals		□□□□□□□□□□□□□	

In interpreting these patterns of coalition formation, one should note the importance of earlier political alignments. The Radicals, who had entered politics largely in reaction to the failure of the Liberals in the 1930s, found themselves 25 years later again opposed to the Liberals in the crisis of 1962. The Revolutionaries, who had entered politics in part as a rejection of the Radicals, were divided by the crisis, though many did oppose their earlier rivals from the Central Committee of the MTLD.

Rather surprisingly, the Revolutionaries around Ben Bella found the Liberals such as Ferhat Abbas to be relatively congenial coalition partners during this early bid for power. The choices of the Military in the crisis were particularly difficult to understand.

It seems, however, that since the *Etat Major* of the exterior supported Ben Bella, the interior forces fell into an uncomfortable
alliance with the GPRA. The Intellectuals, who had the fewest
claims to power, were the most likely to remain neutral or to
support the GPRA, which had been responsible for their initial
introduction to positions of influence in the elite.

The power struggle continued during the months of July and
August. Following the ineffective dissolution of the *Etat Major*
by the GPRA, an anti-GPRA coalition emerged behind Ben Bella
which came to be known as the "Tlemcen Group." Mohammed
Khider was probably the most active and influential non-Military
member of this group. The forces supporting the GPRA were
centered in Algiers and at Tizi Ouzou in Kabylia. By late July the
GPRA itself was losing its coherence as Dahlab quit and Mohammedi
rallied to Ben Bella. Krim then became the focus of the anti-Ben
Bella forces and a "Tizi Ouzou Group" took form. The hostility
of *willaya* 2 (North Constantine) to the *Etat Major* was overcome
by the "coup of Constantine" on July 25 in which Sawt al Arab
(Boubnider), the leader of *willaya* 2, was temporarily ousted by
Mohammed Tayebi (Si Larbi) who favored Boumedienne and
Ben Bella.[27]

The military forces opposing the *Etat Major* following the "coup
of Constantine" consisted of *willaya* 3 (Kabylia) under Mohand
oul Hadj and *willaya* 4 (Algerois) led by colonel Hassan (Khatib
Youssef). In addition, an Autonomous Zone of Algiers (ZAA) had
been formed under the leadership of pro-GPRA elements. *Willaya*
4 claimed control over this zone, however, and on July 29, with
the consent and encouragement of Khider, *willaya* 4 forcefully
took control of Algiers. The Machiavellian logic prompting
Khider, the powerful political master of the Tlemcen group, to
urge this action was that if *willaya* 4 took over the ZAA, the number
of opponents to the Political Bureau would be reduced.

Amar Bentoumi, who served as Ben Bella's first Minister of
Justice, was close to Khider at this time and has given a detailed
account of this little known incident:

> During the crisis of summer 1962, there were two groups opposing each
> other, one in Tlemcen and the other around Algiers. Khider had most of

[27] More than five years later, in December 1967, Sawt al Arab again opposed
Boumedienne, while Tayebi supported the government and was rewarded
eventually by being named Minister of Agriculture. The persistence of these
early conflicts in subsequent years shows the impact of the crisis of 1962.

the power in the Tlemcen group. At one point he even offered Bitat the presidency, but he refused since he didn't feel he was qualified. During the crisis, Khider came to Algiers to negotiate with the leaders of *willaya* 4, especially Khatib Youssef. Khider, Bitat, Boumaza and I met from 8 P.M. to 6 A.M. the next morning with them. Boumaza, however, left at midnight claiming he was tired. Khider finally offered to help *willaya* 4 take over the autonomous zone of Algiers, the ZAA. They accepted. Khider's reasoning was that, if *willaya* 4 "ate" the ZAA, it would be easier for the Political Bureau to win control. Thus, Khider took responsibility for what was called the "second crisis." Algerians once again fired on Algerians.[28]

By the end of July two anti-Political Bureau groups, *willaya* 2 and the ZAA, had been neutralized. On August 2 an agreement ended the GPRA–Political Bureau dispute, as Benkhedda decided to turn over the GPRA's authority in internal matters to the Political Bureau. This was done on August 7. Elections to a National Assembly were then to be held, and a list of candidates was drawn up and disclosed on August 20.[29]

Opposition to the Political Bureau, however, was merely reduced rather than eliminated. On August 25 *willaya* 4 accused the Political Bureau of breaking the terms of the earlier truce and entered into open rebellion. Elections were then put off and Boudiaf quit the Political Bureau. Open fighting between the troops of *willayas* 3 and 4 and the forces of the *Etat Major* broke out during late August and early September, causing several thousand casualties.[30]

On September 5 the dissident *willayas* accepted the authority of the Political Bureau, and four days later Boumedienne's troops arrived in Algiers. The following week a new list of candidates to the National Constituent Assembly was disclosed, and on September 20 elections were finally held.

This summary of the crisis does scant justice to the complexity of the events but serves to underline the lack of any political process for conflict resolution. The better armed and organized coalition was victorious. The Algerian people, it might be added, played virtually no part in these events, except when mobilized by the UGTA to intervene between warring factions while crying, "Seven years is enough!" [31]

A number of actors in these events have explained their feelings

---

28 Interview with Amar Bentoumi.
29 This list is published in *Alger Republicain*, August 21, 1962.
30 Arslan Humbaraci, *Algeria*, Chapter 4, gives more details on these events.
31 *Ibid.*, p. 80.

and motives and have presented enlightened analyses of the causes for and the effects of the crisis of summer 1962. Benkhedda, in a lengthy article written during the crisis, blamed the decentralized wartime structure of the FLN for the conflict of summer 1962. He wrote on August 5, "The crisis of leadership, which is also a crisis of adaptation among some leaders, has had the effect not only of crystallizing the wartime structures, but also of aggravating the tendency toward the parcellization of sovereignty. This has led to a crisis of authority." [32]

Virtually all members of the elite ascribe the crisis of summer 1962 to personal conflicts rather than to ideological differences. One Intellectual who tried to play a mediating role between the two groups gave the following example of the conflict of personalities.

> Boudiaf and Ben Bella, after spending five years in jail together, couldn't stand each other. They would argue over anything—whether the tea should be served hot or cold, how much sugar should be in it. It was just like a scene out of Sartre's *No Exit*. The crisis was simply a scramble for power. Abbas backed Ben Bella because he was bitter over having been replaced by Benkhedda. [33]

An important participant in these event has quoted Ben Bella, the individual who profited most from the crisis, as saying of the *Etat Major* of the ALN that "I'm not wedding myself to their ideas, I'm wedding myself to their force." Mohammedi Said, the one member of the GPRA to be included in the Political Bureau, and a Kabyle by origin, was asked why he did not side with Krim and the other Kabyles at Tizi Ouzou instead of joining Ben Bella at Tlemcen. With considerable force he responded, "Tizi Ouzou, c'est moi!" [34] Another Kabyle who supported Ben Bella at Tlemcen reported that he did so because he opposed the methods of the GPRA but that he nonetheless felt that Ben Bella's contribution to the revolution had been zero, and told him so to his face. [35]

Abbas himself, the leader of the Liberals, has stated his position during the crisis in the following terms.

> At the time of independence I returned to Sétif to vote. There Boumedienne came and asked me to join the Tlemcen group. After what the GPRA had done to me I couldn't work with them. Nor, after forty years in

---

[32] Benkhedda's "testament" is published in *Le Monde*, August 5–6, 1962.
[33] Interview with Mabrouk Belhocine.
[34] Interview with Mohammedi Said.
[35] Interview with Amar Ouamrane.

politics could I remain neutral. That would have turned Algeria into another Congo. And I've never worked solely for myself. So Ben Bella and the *Etat Major* were the only group I could support.[36]

The ambiguous feelings toward Ben Bella which were characteristic of many Algerians at the time of independence are revealed in remarks such as those of Mezhoudi:

> When the scramble for power broke out in the summer of 1962, I didn't join either side at first, but then once the violence began I joined the group around the Political Bureau. The GPRA included too many anti-socialist and counterrevolutionary types who would have let the poor remain poor. They would have helped the city dwellers and ignored the peasants. Ben Bella seemed to express "our" ideas, and we also thought that the myth of Ben Bella could be used.[37]

Summary and Conclusions

While a few Algerians have analyzed the crisis in terms of differing ideologies, such as democracy versus dictatorship, or in sociological terms, arguing that the GPRA represented an older generation, while the *Etat Major* represented a new generation formed in the *maquis,* most participants agree that coalition choices during the crisis were largely made in personal terms and followed lines drawn by earlier political experiences. After more than seven years of war the FLN had not developed a political process for resolving conflicts on other than a personal basis.

For the first months after independence political conflict was primarily an extension of divisions created within the elite by divergent patterns of political socialization. Liberals continued to fight Radicals, Revolutionaries opposed both while falling out among themselves, and the interior and exterior military forces divided along predictable lines.

Rather than forging a political elite that would be capable of maintaining power after independence, the revolution had deepened existing divisions while bringing to the fore individuals with the tenacity necessary to endure the hardships of the revolution but lacking in accommodative or conciliatory skills. The crisis of summer 1962 found curious alignments forming, and the final resolution of the conflict was to come in military rather than political terms. The apparent victors were elements from among the Revolutionaries and the Military who chose Ben Bella as their

[36] Interview with Ferhat Abbas.
[37] Interview with Brahim Mezhoudi.

spokesman. Whether or not a successful political system could be formed with these components would partially depend on whether a political process would emerge which could aggregate the diverse demands from members of this new coalition.

The crisis within the FLN during the summer of 1962 might have been in part anticipated from a knowledge of the revolutionary process in other societies. As the model of elite transformation presented earlier would predict, the disintegration of the FLN took place immediately after the cease-fire and resulted from incompatible claims to power on the part of individuals and groups who felt that their contributions to the revolution and to the nationalist movement qualified them for dominant positions in the emerging political system. With the top elite warring against one another, many opportunities for the secondary elite to advance rapidly were bound to appear. The speed of their rise to power, however, would depend upon the nature of the political system which Ben Bella would be able to put together.

As might have been expected, Ben Bella came to power in the fall of 1962 with the support of some unlikely allies. Rather than limiting himself to the army, Ben Bella had enlisted as supporters many prominent Liberals and some Revolutionaries. The logic that prompted these choices is not particularly difficult to trace. A large and heterogeneous base of support within the elite would permit Ben Bella to counter the demands of one group with those of another, thus avoiding becoming the captive of any segment of the elite. Lacking any organized base of power himself, Ben Bella's best chances of survival in the face of bitter challenges to his authority would come from this ability to play off various factions against one another. Without deep ideological convictions of his own, Ben Bella could engage in this game by favoring, alternately, the Liberals, the Revolutionaries, the Military, or the Intellectuals. Above all he would resist the emergence of a single group which might become significantly more powerful than any other.

But the costs of retaining the support of so many conflicting groups would be high, and thus one might expect, with time, some reduction in the size of the ruling elite. To achieve this goal without losing his own independence would be the difficult task facing Ben Bella in his efforts to build an Algerian state out of the chaos and anarchy of the summer of 1962.

10

The National Assembly and the Search for Political Process

When Ahmed Ben Bella became Algeria's first President in late September 1962, it was the National Constituent Assembly which selected him, by 141 votes out of 194, to form a government. The Assembly itself had been elected from a single list of FLN-approved candidates on September 20. While the Assembly's stated purpose was that of voting a constitution, its more important latent function was that of ending the debilitating three-month-old crisis within the political elite. Given the heterogeneous nature of Ben Bella's coalition and of the Assembly itself, one might properly have asked whether the Assembly would be able to provide an arena in which conflicting demands and images could be translated into public policies capable of bringing order and development to the war-torn country.

Knowing the history of the divisions within the Algerian political elite in the past, the skeptic could hardly be blamed for predicting in late 1962 that the Algerian Constituent Assembly would fail to develop accommodative political procedures to resolve conflicts. And yet for nearly a year the Assembly served as a forum in which free and often contentious debate took place and in which progress toward reducing intraelite tensions was occasionally made. Ultimately, however, the Assembly failed to serve as the central structure in the development of a conciliatory political system.

Soon after coming to power Ben Bella and other members of the ruling elite found the costs of maintaining a broad, heterogeneous governing elite to be too great, and with time a sizable defection of elite members began. And as the composition and structure of the ruling elite began to change, the political process that was beginning to take shape within the Assembly was deeply affected. From their initial high level of participation and tolerance for opposition, the deputies in the Assembly became less active and assertive as Ben Bella made clear his disapproval of parliamentary procedures. Thus, what began as an admirable attempt to reunite the badly divided FLN ended as a confirmation of previous suspicions and mistrust. The experience of the Assembly during the two years of its existence illustrates how difficult it was for the heterogeneous political elite that emerged from the revolution to develop accepted procedures of conflict resolution and policy formulation.

The National Assembly, while never the key institution within the Algerian political system, did group within it a remarkable number of influential men. Since its proceedings were more open to public scrutiny than those of any other organ of government, the Assembly provides the best arena in which to study intraelite relations in the first two years after independence.

Most of the top elite were members of the Assembly, and many of them have been interviewed concerning their expectations of the role the Assembly could play and of their own roles as deputies.[1] Free debate took place within the Assembly for over a year, and these speeches provide one of the most important documentary sources for studying the values of the political elite.[2] Also, several votes were taken and recorded on important issues, and these sup-

---

[1] Twenty interviews with available ex-deputies were conducted during 1966–1967. Those who were willing to be interviewed tended to be the more articulate, better educated deputies, particularly those who came to be associated with the opposition. Only five of those interviewed, for example, were reelected in 1964 to the National Assembly.

[2] Parliamentary debates were published in the *Journal Officiel, Débats Parlementaires* for the *Assemblée nationale constituante* and the *Assemblée nationale*. Hereafter this will be referred to as *Journal Officiel*.

plement the speeches as useful behavioral indicators. Finally, whether or not a deputy was reelected to the second Assembly in September 1964 provides an important test of the government's tolerance for specific types of political behavior.

The Composition of the Assembly: Structural Sources of Conflict

During the crisis of summer 1962 each party to the conflict called for the convening of the CNRA to find a political solution to the many divisions within the elite. But despite this apparent consensus, the CNRA never met. Instead, the creation of a National Constituent Assembly responsible for naming a government was decided upon. Clearly the control of the nomination of individual deputies would be of greatest importance for the composition of this Assembly. On August 2, 1962, a compromise between the Political Bureau and the GPRA was reached, and soon thereafter consultations began to select FLN-approved candidates for the Assembly. Since the interior *willayas* still exercised effective territorial control over large sections of Algeria, they demanded the right to nominate their own candidates. Electoral districts corresponding to the French departments were formed, the number of candidates being determined primarily by the size of the population in the department. Sixteen European candidates were selected and were included on the lists of the various departments.

The process of selecting the non-European candidates involved lengthy negotiations between the Political Bureau and the *willayas*. The opposition *willayas* 2, 3, and 4 covered the departments of Algiers, Medea, El Asnam, Tizi Ouzou, Sétif, and Constantine. These heavily populated departments were represented by 105 of the 180 Muslim candidates. The Political Bureau, which had control over the other areas, directly selected the candidates for the remaining departments. In addition, the Political Bureau seems to have obtained the right, by the compromise of August 2, to select two-thirds of the candidates proposed for each department by the *willayas* while reserving the choice of one-third of the seats to nominees of its own choice.[3] This arrangement considerably reduced the potential opposition to the Political Bureau but would have nonetheless resulted in a large and hostile group within the

[3] Interviews with Belkacem Fantazi and Mohammed Haroun. Mohand oul Hadj, it seems, named most of the candidates in the departments of Tizi Ouzou and Sétif.

Assembly. Also, members of the GPRA, the FFFLN (which considered itself deserving of equal representation with the other *willayas*), and the UGTA demanded some representation in the Assembly. On August 20, 1962, a first list of candidates was published for elections to be held on September 2.[4] This list of candidates is particularly interesting, for it contains the names of virtually all the major leaders of the significant groups within the political elite at the time of independence. The Liberals, for example, were represented by Abbas, Francis, Boumendjel, and Farès, the Radicals by Benkhedda, Yazid, and Bentoumi, the Revolutionaries by Ben Bella, Boudiaf, Krim, and Boussouf, the Military by Mohammedi Said, Khatib Youssef, and Boubnider, and the Intellectuals by Malek, Ben Yahia, Ait Chaalal, and Harbi. The interior *willayas*, the *Etat Major*, the GPRA, the FFFLN, the UGEMA, and the UGTA all were represented by a few candidates. Noticeable among those missing from the list were such well-known Revolutionaries as Ait Ahmed and Ben Tobbal, both of whom refused to be members. Boudiaf soon announced that he would not be a candidate and simultaneously left his position on the Political Bureau. Khider and Bitat were not candidates but were part of the five-man Political Bureau. Boumedienne, likewise, was not a candidate, but his control over the ALN and the large number of ALN candidates insured that his influence would be felt.

Within five days of the publication of this list of candidates, however, a new crisis developed which forced the Political Bureau to put off the elections. *Willayas* 3 and 4 forcefully opposed the Political Bureau and obliged it to evacuate Algiers. On September 3 Ben Bella in a classic understatement declared that "The only problem is that of authority." But a few days later troops under Boumedienne were able to reach Algiers and to enforce a settlement upon the dissident *willayas*. On September 13 a new list of candidates to the National Assembly was published.[5]

Of 196 candidates on this new list, 50 had been added since mid-August. Those on the first list who had been dropped came essentially from two groups, *willaya* 2, and the GPRA and its close allies.[6]

[4] *Alger Républicain*, August 21, 1962.
[5] See the *Annuaire de l'Afrique du nord*, Vol. 1, 1962, pp. 714–716 for a list of these candidates.
[6] The departments corresponding to areas of opposition to the Political Bureau had 31 percent of their candidates removed from the second list and 10 percent transferred to new departments. The "loyalist" departments, on the other hand, had 24 percent of their candidates changed and 1 percent transferred.

Both these groups, it will be recalled, were the first opposition elements to compromise with the Political Bureau in early August. The more intransigent opponents of the Political Bureau, *willayas* 3 and 4, were much less affected by the changes. Thus the more conciliatory groups, the GPRA and *willaya* 2, were eliminated, whereas the more rigid opponents of the Political Bureau were included in the list of candidates to the Assembly. In this way the National Assembly was deprived of the talents of such well-known individuals as Benkhedda, Benhabylès, Ait Chaalal, Lacheraf, Reda Malek, Abdesselam, Ben Yahia, Boussouf, Harbi, Ali Kafi, Boubnider, and many others. Of those added to the new list, only Ait Ahmed was a well-known figure, though Heddam and Khobzi soon gained some influence as ministers. The new candidates were an undistinguished group, and most were probably included because of anticipated servility toward the Political Bureau. In short, by the time of the elections to the Assembly, the Political Bureau had already acted to reduce the influence of the Radicals, the Intellectuals, and the *maquisards* of *willaya* 2. The remaining opposition elements were a substantially smaller minority than they would have been if the first list had been elected.

The FLN-approved candidates named on September 13 were all elected on September 20, and in this way the National Constituent Assembly was formed. The composition of the Assembly gave some indication of how it was likely to function. Of the 194 deputies who finally became members of the first Assembly, 16 were Europeans and 10 were women.[7] The average age in 1962 of the deputies was 39, the same as the average age of the Radicals and the Revolutionaries. The occupational backgrounds of the deputies are not particularly good indicators of probable behavior, since many deputies had not practiced their professions since the beginning of the revolution and were much more marked by their political participation during the war years than by their previous occupational socialization. Nonetheless, the statistics on occupations do indicate the social milieu from which the deputies came. Roughly speaking, about two-thirds of the deputies in the Assembly had practiced relatively low- or medium-status occupations, while about one-third came from the more advantaged, higher-status occupations. (See Table 10.1.)

An analysis of the occupations of 70 of the best-known and proba-

[7] Boudiaf, although elected, refused to be a deputy, and Guerras resigned to work with the Party after the first two sessions.

TABLE 10.1   OCCUPATIONAL BACKGROUNDS OF DEPUTIES TO
THE NATIONAL CONSTITUENT ASSEMBLY, 1962

Military	18%
Liberal Professions	18
Commerce	14
Teachers	12
Agriculture	11
Workers	7
Other [1]	10
Unknown	10
	100%
Number =	194

[1] Includes *cadres, employés,* and *fonctionnaires*
Source: Figures derived from Anisse Salah Bey, "L'Assemblée nationale constituante algérienne," in *Annuaire de l'Afrique du nord,* Vol. 1 (1962), p. 115.

bly the most influential deputies indicates that, in comparison to
the secondary leaders in the Assembly, the top leaders were more
likely to have been lawyers, doctors, teachers, or students, and less
likely to have been engaged in commerce, agriculture, or manual
labor.[8] About 25 percent of the deputies were known to have had
university-level education, while the majority seem to have received
some secondary schooling.[9]

More revealing than the occupational backgrounds of the new
deputies is information regarding the type of political training
which they received. Data concerning this variable are available for
somewhat over half the Assembly and thus permit only a rough
approximation of the entire Assembly. Those whose political formation was like that of the Liberals and Radicals accounted for only
15 percent of this sample of deputies. Another 15 percent can be
considered to have developed politically as Revolutionaries. Slightly
more than 20 percent were Intellectuals who began their political

[8] These conclusions are based on the analysis of the backgrounds of 70
well-known deputies. This group is only a rough approximation of the "top
elite" within the Assembly, but the findings are probably accurate. The figures
for the various occupations of these deputies are: law, 21 percent; medicine,
16 percent; students, 16 percent; teachers, 19 percent; commerce, 9 percent;
agriculture, 9 percent; workers, 5 percent.
[9] Tensions between intellectuals and nonintellectuals within the Assembly
were revealed in the following remark of Amar Ouamrane in the course of
an Assembly debate: "Now when those who are illiterate like myself [*sic*] see
someone more educated than himself, they try to cause him trouble. It's too
bad to have to say this, but it's true. This complex which opposes intellectuals
and illiterates should disappear. . . ." (*Journal Officiel,* first year, p. 258.)

careers during the last years of the revolution. By far the largest number, about 50 percent of the total, entered politics by way of the Military, primarily with the rank of *commandant* (major) or captain.

On the basis of this information concerning the occupation and political background of the deputies it seems fair to conclude that about one-third, because of previous parliamentary experience, legal training, or particularly close identification with western political norms, might be expected to function effectively in a French-style parliamentary system.[10] Roughly 20 percent of the Assembly was composed of Revolutionaries and *maquisards* from opposition areas. These deputies would probably find the Assembly an uncongenial arena for policy-making or opposition activity, for both groups were opposed to "legalism" and were rather ineffective as bargainers. About half the Assembly, consisting primarily of the Military from areas favorable to the Political Bureau, could be expected to participate only marginally in the life of the Assembly and to offer little opposition to Ben Bella. Finally, it should be added that well over three-quarters of the deputies spoke or understood French, whereas the number of educated Arabists was close to fifteen percent.[11] Thus political discourse within the Assembly would almost certainly be primarily in the language of the ex-colonizer.

Expectations of Deputies

An analysis of the composition of the Assembly indicated that its members came from a wide variety of backgrounds and had received quite different preparations for the role of deputy. It was also apparent that a sizable potential opposition group existed but that the majority of deputies could be expected to vote for the Politi-

---

[10] Three figures confirm this estimate: the number of Politicians and Intellectuals in the Assembly (35 percent); the number from liberal professions and teaching (30 percent); and the number of deputies with university educations (25 percent).

[11] This estimate is based on judgments of several deputies who claimed that about 30 or 40 members of the Assembly were somewhat educated in Arabic. Claude Estier, *Pour l'Algérie,* estimates on the basis of his observations of the Assembly that about nine-tenths of the deputies spoke French and that 20 or 30 deputies used the simultaneous translation system when Arabic was spoken. One Arabist, Chibane, claimed in an interview that about 40 deputies had a "national culture," (i.e., Arab), while Mezhoudi thought that only about half a dozen Arab-speaking intellectuals, meaning university-educated men, were in the Assembly.

cal Bureau. Opposition seemed most likely to come from deputies previously associated with *willayas* 3 and 4 and the FFFLN. Another group, namely the Politicians and some Intellectuals, might be willing to support the government so long as the Assembly was allowed to play a reasonably important role in the political system. If the Assembly failed to provide the forum for the development of an accommodative political process, this group might also express opposition to the Political Bureau. These judgments are supported by the expectations held by deputies at the time of entering their new political roles.

According to the legal documents which brought the National Assembly into existence, the Assembly was to last for one year, during which time its only precisely defined function was to adopt a constitution for the country. Such a narrow definition of the purpose of this newly created institution failed to specify the relations between the Party, the government, and the Assembly.[12] Nor was it clear that the Assembly would write as well as adopt the Constitution. Likewise, the Assembly's role as a legislature was left undefined. Consequently, the newly chosen deputies could legitimately hold widely differing expectations as to both the power position of the Assembly within the political system and to its more general functions in policy-making. In the absence of any precise legal definition of these powers and functions, the deputies' expectations seemed to reflect attitudes developed in other contexts concerning parliamentary systems and the political process.[13]

Two contrasting images of the Assembly's proper power position can be identified. One group of deputies, probably a minority, saw the Assembly as the ultimate source of authority in the political system, with control of the executive much in the tradition of the French Fourth Republic. One of the strongest proponents of this view was Ferhat Abbas, whose long experience in French parlia-

[12] "Government" is used here in the French sense of the Prime Minister and his Cabinet.

[13] Kenneth Prewitt, Heinz Eulau, and Betty Zisk, in "Political Socialization and Political Roles," *Public Opinion Quarterly* 30, No. 4, pp. 569–582, argue that, "Differences in orientation toward significant actors in the legislative arena and differences in self-evaluation are not rooted in experiences associated with the genesis of the political career" (p. 582). The opposite hypothesis seems to hold for the Algerian National Assembly, but this is doubtless due to the fact that American legislators are brought into an ongoing system with relatively clear rules and procedures, whereas the Algerians were obliged to create the roles and processes appropriate to parliamentary life with few clear models and little prior relevant experience.

mentary bodies had left its mark. Unlike most of the deputies, Abbas was experienced in parliamentary procedures and believed that the Assembly should play an important legislative role. Abbas, who became the first President of the Assembly, clearly believed in some version of separation of powers, with the Assembly in charge of making laws which would be applied by the executive.[14] The Assembly, in this view, should also choose the government and by a vote of nonconfidence could overturn that government.[15] While the specific proposals of Abbas were not widely approved, many deputies, particularly Liberals, Intellectuals, and those Revolutionaries opposed to Ben Bella, seem to have felt that the Assembly should operate as a check on the powers of the Party and of the executive.

Another deputy who expressed similar feelings was an Intellectual, Mouloud Gaid:

> When I was elected as a deputy, my image of how the Assembly should work was based on the French Assembly—it should be democratic, with deputies representing the people, with free expression permitted, and everyone should be working for the reconstruction of the country. The existence of a single party meant mainly that there would be unity of ideas on some basic principles, and as long as these principles were respected I thought that considerable latitude should be left in applying these ideas. There had been no rigid discipline in the Party—as in a communist party—and this is still true.[16]

A second view of the power of the Assembly was that it could have relatively little importance in a one-party system. Policy and legislation, in this view, would originate within the Political Bureau, and the essential task of the legislature would be to elaborate and perhaps occasionally to revise these proposals before legitimizing them through a formal vote. Deputies who stressed this role for the Assembly were those who believed in the need for a strong one-party regime, whereas those who held the former view tended to believe that Algeria should eventually allow a plurality of parties. But even the deputies who thought the Assembly's power

[14] Abbas's image of the emerging political system was revealed on the day of his election to the Presidency of the Assembly, when he said ". . . as for your constitution, it should, among other things, respect the separation of powers—the legislative, the judiciary and the executive." (*Journal Officiel*, first year, p. 2.)

[15] See Abbas's "Projet de Constitution," mimeographed, May 1963. Interviews with Abbas, Bouzida, and Mezhoudi provided further examples of this orientation.

[16] Interview with Mouloud Gaid.

would necessarily be limited would admit that the FLN was too weak at the time of independence to exercise proper control over the Assembly. Some, in fact, believed that deputies should have spent their time trying to build up the strength of the Party rather than in the often sterile process of debate.[17] These images of a limited role for the Assembly were found most frequently among the Military and the few Radicals and Revolutionaries who supported Ben Bella.

The expectations of deputies concerning the functions that the Assembly might serve indicate rather more variety than beliefs concerning its power. Many deputies, particularly those Politicians and Intellectuals with some legal training, believed that the Assembly should draft as well as adopt the Constitution.[18] The idea that the party would write the Constitution and that the Assembly would then merely ratify it was not widely held. One deputy, a lawyer by profession, described how, soon after his election, he checked out numerous books from the library to prepare for drafting the constitution. Other deputies, particularly those who had been associated with the FFFLN, had already worked out proposals for a possible constitution.[19] For most deputies, however, it seems that their expectations were merely that the constitution would be elaborated within the Assembly and that their comments would be taken into consideration.

A more controversial idea prevalent among some deputies was that the Constituent Assembly should also assume legislative functions.[20] In this view the Assembly should be allowed to take the initiative to draft legislation and to vote bills. This legislative function, however, was not approved by all deputies. Some thought that laws should originate within the Political Bureau and merely be ratified by the Assembly. Others believed that the eventual legislative role of an Assembly would depend upon the specifications included in the constitution. Until a constitution was written, the government, it was assumed by some, would rule by decree.

A less legalistic role was also envisaged for the Assembly by many deputies. Quite common was the belief that within the Assembly

[17] Interview with Zohra Drif Bitat. Others interviewed with similar views were the deputies Batel, Chibane, and Yazid.
[18] Interviews with Rebbani, Bouzida, Belhocine, Guerroudj, Haroun, Mezhoudi, and Abbas.
[19] The contents of the FFFLN project can be found in Le Monde in a summary published on August 9, 1962, p. 2.
[20] Interviews with Gaid, Bouzida, Belhocine, Guerroudj, Mezhoudi, and Abbas.

deputies should attempt to overcome old antagonisms and learn the procedures of parliamentary process which could help to reconcile conflicts.[21] Free debate and expression were seen as practices that would in some sense resocialize the deputies into new political practices. Opposition to the government should be permitted, and it was believed that if free expression were allowed in the Assembly then opposition would be expressed in debate and by voting rather than through the violence and armed confrontation which had filled the summer of 1962.[22]

Ending the violence of the summer crisis had been, after all, the fundamental political reason for naming the Constituent Assembly. Whether the Assembly could reintegrate a badly divided elite, whether political styles and processes adopted in earlier circumstances could be transformed, were open questions in the fall of 1962. The important fact is that a sizable portion of the Algerian political elite, and in particular many of those who made up the most obvious opposition groups, did hold such expectations. As the Assembly began its work, there were signs that these hopes might be realized. But after one year this initial promise was betrayed, and the Assembly became increasingly ineffective at mediating intra-elite conflicts. The reasons for these failures are deeply embedded in the ways in which the political predispositions of elite members were operative in the context of a relatively free Assembly.

The Assembly in Action

The deputies elected to the Constituent Assembly in September 1962 were originally to have remained in office for one year. In fact, the mandates of the deputies were extended for a second year, although during the second year several deputies had resigned, been expelled or been arrested. In retrospect, deputies typically distinguished between the first and second years when assessing the quality of Assembly life. Those who wanted an important role for the Assembly in balancing the power of the executive tended to see the first year of the Assembly's existence as one full of promise. A prominent opposition spokesman referred to the first year as

[21] During the early sessions of the Assembly many deputies mentioned the need to "do their apprenticeship" in order to learn how to act as parliamentarians and how to overcome divisions.

[22] Interviews with Gaid, Bouzida, Belhocine, Haroun, Ouamrane, and Mezhoudi.

"impeccable," and another called the Assembly the freest in all Africa. A European deputy termed Abbas a great president of the Assembly, and this sentiment was shared by many other deputies. Numerous deputies referred to "free debate" and "free expression" to describe the first year.

The second year of the Assembly was frequently seen as one of restrictions on discussion, the use of threats and arrests to intimidate deputies, and the decline of the opposition centering around the old guerrilla fighters.[23] The first year of the Assembly, it should be noted, was presided over by the Liberal Ferhat Abbas. During the second year two Revolutionaries, Hadj Ben Alla and Ali Mendjli, guided the Assembly's work. The former was a close ally of Ben Bella, the latter was a colleague of Boumedienne.

A second group of deputies, primarily Military men who had little use for politics, viewed the initial year of the Assembly as one of too great a tolerance of the opposition, excessive time spent in endless discussions of procedural matters, and the exacerbation of conflicts through open debate. The second year, during which some of the opposition was eliminated and some won over was viewed as a period during which the Assembly could work effectively. Both these groups of deputies, despite their differing evaluations of the first and second year, agree that tolerance for opposition declined over time. Their agreement on this point is not fortuitous, for both practice and government policy during the first year allowed nearly total freedom for debate and opposition, whereas official policy during the second year stated that differences should only be discussed within the Party. Opposition within the Assembly was rarely tolerated after Abbas quit as President at the end of the first year.

Participation Within the Assembly

During the first year of the Assembly at least five major political debates occurred. The first, lasting five days, was over the procedural rules the Assembly should follow. A shorter debate on foreign policy followed, as did an eight-day discussion of internal policies. Later in the year a lengthy debate took place over the issue of what the *code de nationalité* should be. Finally, the first year ended with a five-day debate on the proposed constitution.

[23] Deputies expressing this view in interviews were Gaid, Rebbani, Bouzida, Belhocine, Mezhoudi, and Abbas.

During the second year of the Assembly only one major political debate took place; this concerned the question of whether or not capital punishment would be allowed in Algeria. On this issue, as on the previous five, the Ben Bella government was always supported by the majority of the voting members of the Assembly, but sizable opposition was frequently voiced. As political debates became increasingly rare in the Assembly following the adoption of the constitution in August 1963, the large part of Assembly debate was focused on economic questions. On these issues there was much less opposition to the government. Clearly politics in the general sense of power and authority was a more divisive issue than economics.

Deputies to the first Algerian National Constituent Assembly were, in the majority of cases, totally lacking in previous parliamentary experience. Perhaps as many as one-third, however, had been members of the CNRA, but that body had met infrequently and had been less concerned with drafting legislation or political programs than with resolving difficult intraelite conflicts by naming new executive agencies for the revolution. From the little that is known about participation in the CNRA, it seems that members were free to speak without fear of sanctions.[24]

It is easier to discuss participation in the Constituent Assembly, since sessions were public and the record of the debates has been published. Unfortunately only remarks made in open sessions of the Assembly are recorded, so that it is impossible to establish whether or not the work of the numerous parliamentary committees provided a significantly different forum for participation.[25] In any case, participation in open Assembly debates is a useful measure of an individual's belief in the value of the parliamentary process, of his willingness to rely on persuasion rather than force, and of his skills in debate. It is possible to judge both the frequency of a deputy's participation and the amount of his speaking in the Assembly.[26]

An indication of the initially high degree of participation in

[24] Interviews with Haroun and Ouamrane. Ben Bella supported this view indirectly by referring to the unconstructive nature of CNRA debates. (*Journal Officiel*, first year, p. 312.)

[25] There is some reason to think that those deputies who believed in the supremacy of the Party did not often speak in public debates but were more active in committees. (Batel interview.)

[26] The amount of speaking is estimated from a 20 percent systematic sample of all the published debates, measured in column inches.

Assembly debates and of the gradual decline over time can be seen in Figure 10.1.[27]

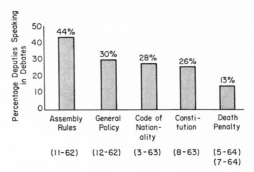

Figure 10.1　Deputy Participation in Selected Debates

Each of the five political debates considered here lasted over five days, and feelings ran high on all sides as these topics were discussed. The first debate, over the internal rules of the Assembly, witnessed the participation of 85 different deputies. The debate on the constitution, a far more important issue, attracted the participation of 51 deputies. The proposed law on capital punishment, which received less support than any other government measure, was the only political debate during the second year. A mere 26 deputies participated in it. These figures indicate rather clearly the declining willingness to engage in debate and to rely on persuasion to obtain political goals. As will be seen, this trend was not paralleled by a decrease in opposition voting. It seems, rather, that those who opposed Ben Bella gradually recognized that persuasion and discussion in the Assembly could accomplish little.[28] Silence, or a resort to other means of political influence, and in particular force, were the typical responses of these alienated deputies.

Participation in Assembly debates, as measured by the amount of

[27] A similar development can be traced by examining the number of speakers in the 20 percent sample in each *séance* in the five sessions of the Assembly. The figure for the first session is 3.5, for the second through fourth it is 2.3, and for the last it is 1.1.

[28] One opposition deputy, Haroun, has stated in an interview that only once in the two years of the Assembly did the opposition succeed in blocking a government measure. This occurred over the seemingly insignificant issue of how to carry out capital punishment. The opposition managed to table the government's proposal until a debate and vote was held to determine whether capital punishment would be permitted in Algeria. In the end the government managed to get its bill adopted by a plurality of the deputies.

speaking in a 20 percent sample of all debates will be used as an indicator of a deputy's willingness to rely on persuasion as a form of political influence. If speaking does provide some measure of this political value, one would assume that amount of speaking would correlate with other variables that refer to previous political socialization. In fact, correlations are found for the following variables: socialization type, education, cultural background, age, and previous political role.

Earlier it was argued that a useful way of looking at the Algerian political elite is in terms of the paths by which individuals reached power. This approach emphasizes distinctive patterns of political socialization as being responsible for the major political orientations and values found among the Algerian leaders. Politicians, Revolutionaries, the Military, and Intellectuals have all been seen to differ in terms of their early experiences with politics, and thus one would anticipate that deputies from each of these groups would be distinguishable in their participation in Assembly debate. Table 10.2 indicates the degree of these differences.[29]

TABLE 10.2 TYPE OF POLITICAL SOCIALIZATION AND AS-SEMBLY PARTICIPATION

| | | Elite Subgroups | | | | |
		Politicians	Revolutionaries	Military	Intellectuals	Entire Assembly
Amount of Speaking	None	6 (37%)	5 (31%)	25 (48%)	1 (4%)	83 (43%)
	Moderate	3 (19%)	5 (31%)	19 (37%)	13 (54%)	69 (36%)
	High	7 (44%)	6 (38%)	8 (15%)	10 (42%)	40 (21%)
	Number = 16		n = 16	n = 52	n = 24	n = 192

From this table it seems fair to conclude that the Politicians and Intellectuals participated most in Assembly debates, followed closely by the Revolutionaries. The Military were least likely to speak in the Assembly. To some degree this correlation is due to the differential incidence of highly educated individuals in each of these groups.

[29] Since appropriate data are lacking which would permit the classification of all 194 deputies according to their political socialization, this table is based on the 108 deputies whose political careers are fairly well known. The same practice is followed in later tables, and thus the total number of deputies is rarely included in a single cross tabulation. It is not clear what bias this inevitable procedure may introduce, but none is immediately apparent. Conclusions, of course, must be tentative and could be modified by more data.

Table 10.3 suggests there is a strong positive relationship between level of education and amount of participation.

TABLE 10.3   EDUCATION AND ASSEMBLY PARTICIPATION

		Level of Education	
		University-Educated	All Others
Amount of Speaking	None	7 (19%)	76 (49%)
	Moderate	11 (31%)	58 (37%)
	High	18 (50%)	22 (14%)
		Number = 36	n = 156

An analysis of participation and cultural background reveals that deputies identified as Kabyles were the most active participants, followed closely by those non-Kabyles who had received French educations. Those who were primarily formed by Arabic culture and who chose to speak Arabic were least likely to speak in debates.[30] (See Table 10.4.)

TABLE 10.4   CULTURAL ORIENTATION AND ASSEMBLY PARTICIPATION

		Cultural Orientation		
		Kabyle	Arabic	French
Amount of Speaking	None	5 (21%)	6 (33%)	10 (18%)
	Moderate	8 (33%)	10 (56%)	28 (49%)
	High	11 (46%)	2 (11%)	19 (33%)
		Number = 24	n = 18	n = 57

Age also is related to participation; the generation born in the 1920s participated most fully, those born before 1920 more moderately, and those born after 1930 least of all. (See Table 10.5.)

[30] Numerous comments by deputies during debates indicated that it was commonly believed that deputies who spoke only Arabic were hindered in their work in the Assembly. See, for example, Heddam's comments on page 99 of the *Journal Officiel*, (first year), and Kara's on p. 543. "Cultural orientation," it should be added, was derived as follows. Any deputy known to be a Kabyle was included in that category, regardless of education. "French" types were those who had received secondary and university educations in French schools and who chose to speak French, while "Arabic" types were those educated in Arabic and who chose to speak that language. These latter have been the most difficult to identify because they participated least in debates.

TABLE 10.5   AGE AND ASSEMBLY PARTICIPATION

		Date of Birth		
		pre-1920	1920s	1930s
Amount of Speaking	None	4 (17%)	8 (23%)	8 (38%)
	Moderate	13 (57%)	10 (28%)	7 (33%)
	High	6 (26%)	17 (49%)	6 (29%)
		Number = 23	n = 35	n = 21

Finally, type of political elite position is also linked to participation. Those who were part of the top elite during the revolution were the most active participants, those entering top elite positions only after independence were the next most active deputies, and the secondary level elite was the least involved in Assembly debates. (See Table 10.6.)

TABLE 10.6   ELITE STATUS AND ASSEMBLY PARTICIPATION

		Elite Status		
		Revolutionary Elite	Postindependence Elite	Secondary Elite
Amount of Speaking	None	5 (23%)	7 (32%)	71 (48%)
	Moderate	9 (41%)	11 (50%)	39 (26%)
	High	8 (36%)	4 (18%)	38 (26%)
		Number = 22	n = 22	n = 148

From these tables it seems that the categories based on type of political socialization are the most useful in predicting the amount of participation in Assembly debate. Politicians and Intellectuals, the two groups who were most closely in tune with French political traditions, were most willing to use the forum of the Assembly to express their political ideas. The Revolutionaries, while less sanguine about the prospects for conducting the business of government through free discussion, did feel compelled to express themselves on nearly all issues, and thus they participated nearly as much as the Politicians and the Intellectuals in the life of the Assembly. However, in the case of the Revolutionaries it seems that self-importance was the primary reason for participation, and they appear to have had little faith that the process of free debate was an important value in itself. The Military, like their laconic leader Colonel

Boumedienne, attended the Assembly debates in a silence which reflected well the skepticism that they must have felt toward the usefulness of this type of politics.[31]

The groupings of deputies based on prior political formation are, of course, essentially products of some combination of the variables of education, age, elite position, and cultural orientation. These four subordinate variables are all related to participation but with varying degrees of intensity. The data are not trustworthy enough to justify powerful statistical manipulation of these variables, but they do indicate that high participation, apart from the association with the general socialization categories just mentioned, is most related to education, elite position, and perhaps cultural background, while particularly low participation was affected most by elite position and age. Multiple correlations and simultaneous controls of several variables would reduce the already small number of cases too greatly for intelligible analysis, but these simple cross tabulations do seem to point to the major factors influencing amount of participation.

Type of participation in Assembly debates can also be related to numerous social background variables. For example, deputies from the Military spoke almost exclusively on political topics, while Politicians restricted themselves primarily to economic debates. Both these associations reflect well earlier patterns of socialization, particularly the Politicians' concern for development and the Military's interest in power.

Less educated deputies tended to specialize in political debates, whereas the more educated ones dealt with economic and political matters with equal frequency. Other relations can be found between area specialization and background factors but, as with amount of participation, the broader categories based on political socialization provide the most significant relationships.

Opposition Voting within the Assembly

Given the circumstances in which the Assembly was formed and the backgrounds of the deputies, it was inevitable that some opposition to the government would be expressed within the Assembly. During the very first sessions, in fact, individual deputies began to

[31] Boumedienne's own role in Assembly debate, in the few instances in which he participated as a member of the government, was that of suggesting that long and inconclusive debates be ended and that the issue be put to a vote, since further discussion would not change the existing differences of opinion.

assert their independence from and hostility to the government of Ben Bella. Krim, for example, warned of the dangers of "personal power," and Ait Ahmed spoke of the role of the Assembly in withdrawing confidence from the government. Ben Bella responded by speaking openly of "my brothers in opposition" and promised the Assembly absolute sovereignty in drafting the future constitution of the Republic. Mezhoudi spoke early in the session to support the Tripoli Program but warned that if necessary he would offer "constructive opposition." Bouzida argued that deputies should be free to disagree with the government. Finally, after a particularly naive speech on unity and reconciliation, Mahiouz intervened to say:

The radio, the newspapers talk of unity, but that is mere bla-bla-bla! Of all the leaders who were abroad, I haven't seen any of them visit the mountains or the ruined villages. Not one! They prefer to quarrel. Few have taken any steps toward reconciliation, not toward real reconciliation. There are only intrigues on all sides! [32]

How long the government would tolerate such open criticism was not clear. On December 12, 1962, after an exhaustive and often hostile discussion of the government's proposed policies, Ben Bella replied.

There is a tendency to use this forum to discuss publicly the affairs of the Party, to judge the Party, whereas one should limit oneself here to discussions of government actions. It would be an error to imagine that we could overcome our mutual incomprehensions by coming here to discuss them. . . . The elaboration of the nation's political thought is reserved for the Party.[33]

Despite this overt warning by Ben Bella as to the limits of free debate, deputies continued to "discuss matters reserved for the Party." When Ben Bella spoke of the Party, it was clear that he meant the Political Bureau, which after the dispute with Khider in early 1963 effectively consisted of three men. Aside from the Political Bureau there was little formal Party organization, and thus deputies rightly interpreted Ben Bella's insistence on handling controversial policy questions within the framework of the Party as a call for personal power. Many deputies, sharing the Algerian's natural individualism and disputatiousness, resisted the implications

[32] These statements are all in the *Journal Officiel*, first year; Krim, p. 15; Ait Ahmed, p. 15; Ben Bella, p. 22; Mezhoudi, p. 27; Bouzida, p. 28; Mahiouz, p. 29.
[33] Ibid., p. 312.

of one-party rule when this meant in fact the granting of power to a single man.

As criticism continued, Ben Bella again spoke on June 25, 1963, just after the arrest of his old prison mate Boudiaf. While announcing that the government had discovered a "plot" against it, Ben Bella went on to say: "There isn't a single country in Africa which, after conquering its independence, has allowed people to speak so much, and even to lead criminal actions contrary to the interest of their country.[34]

The period of relative tolerance for opposition reached its end in August 1963. At that time it was learned that the Politicial Bureau had prepared a draft constitution and had presented it for approval to Party members in a local cinema without consulting the Assembly. Several deputies, angered by the fact that the Assembly had been taken over by Ben Bella's hand-picked Party, denounced the new constitution in Assembly debate. The government's response came in a speech by Benabdallah who defended the Party's right to "elaborate" a draft constitution. He went on to say,

Can one honestly reproach, especially in public—I think one might have done so by addressing complaints to the Party—but can one reproach the Party, which has the responsibility of elaborating the policies of the government, the policies of the nation, for having thought of and for having conceived of a plan for a constitution? [35]

Abbas, who was presiding over the session, replied acidly:

My dear colleague, I don't want to intervene in this question, but I might agree with you if the Party did exist. For me, the Party does not exist! The Party does not exist, and there are no other FLN militants than those in this Assembly, in the administration, and in the army. The day when a party is democratically constituted, I will applaud with both hands!

A few minutes later he concluded by saying: "I regret that the constitution has been discussed in a cinema instead of in the Assembly. The constitution of a country is too important for it to be prostituted in a cinema." [36] Ben Bella's reply came on August 27, a week after Abbas had resigned as President of the Assembly.

My colleagues will excuse me for drawing their atttention to a fact which, unfortunately, is often neglected in this Assembly—the Party is insufficiently installed, it has great weaknesses, but you forget that your presence here is due only to that Party!

[34] Ibid., p. 676.
[35] Ibid., p. 869.
[36] Ibid., p. 869–870.

After repeating the argument that criticism could only be tolerated within the Party, not in the Assembly, Ben Bella concluded with the warning:

To all those who do not want to accept the Party, under the pretext of "democratism" or for other reasons, to those who want a permanent debate and who profit from this Assembly which has an altogether different function than searching for weaknesses in order to begin a debate that the people do not want, which they denounce—well, I will say that it is precisely for such individuals that certain articles in our constitution have been conceived.[37]

So ended the first relatively free year of Assembly debate. Nonetheless, such open threats to the deputies to cease their opposition were not effective. True, fewer dared to speak in debates, but voting continued to reflect opposition. Figure 10.2 shows the percentage

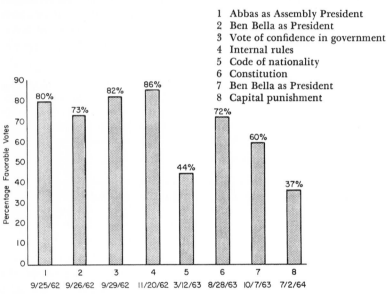

1 Abbas as Assembly President
2 Ben Bella as President
3 Vote of confidence in government
4 Internal rules
5 Code of nationality
6 Constitution
7 Ben Bella as President
8 Capital punishment

Figure 10.2   Progovernment Votes on Selected Issues

of votes favorable to the government on eight different key issues. Deputies who did not favor the bills either abstained, voted against them, or were absent.[38]

[37] Ibid., pp. 978–979.
[38] Abstention most often reflected opposition and was denounced early in the Assembly by the Minister of Justice, who referred to a CNRA precedent which forbade abstention. Absence is a less accurate measure of opposition, but absent deputies could, if they so desired, delegate their vote to another

An analysis of what factors influenced opposition voting can be undertaken on the basis of three major votes for which detailed results are recorded. The issues involved in these votes were whether to grant a vote of confidence to the first Ben Bella government, whether to adopt the Code of Nationality, and whether to vote for the proposed constitution.[39] Of the 194 deputies 60 percent never voted against the government or abstained on any of these three issues. Nineteen percent voted against the government once or abstained, and 21 percent opposed the government more than one time. These three divisions can be labeled "loyalist," "moderate opposition," and "strong opposition."

Of the four groups within the elite, the Politicians during the first year were the most likely to be "loyalists," followed by the Military. For the Politicians this finding is rather unexpected, but it must be remembered that those Politicians most hostile to Ben Bella had been eliminated during the summer crisis. Most of those who remained in the Assembly were there on the sufferance of the Political Bureau. Also, with their beliefs in the values of parliamentary democracy, some Politicians may have felt that in order to insure an important role for the Assembly in the evolving political system they would have to avoid overt opposition. Compared to the Politicians and the Military, the Intellectuals and Revolutionaries were considerably more likely to express their hostility to the government by voting against its bills. (See Table 10.7.)

TABLE 10.7   TYPE OF POLITICAL SOCIALIZATION AND OPPOSITION IN THE ASSEMBLY

	Politicians	Revolutionaries	Military	Intellectuals
Opposition				
None	11 (69%)	8 (50%)	30 (58%)	12 (50%)
Moderate	3 (19%)	3 (19%)	9 (17%)	5 (21%)
Strong	2 (12%)	5 (31%)	13 (25%)	7 (29%)
	Number = 16	n = 16	n = 52	n = 24

deputy. Thus absence reflects apathy, if not opposition. After October 1963 there were only 189 deputies in the Assembly, and the percentages are based on this total.

[39] In addition, the sponsors of the amendment to outlaw the death penalty were considered to have opposed the government. The full vote on this issue was not made public or it would certainly have been included here as a measure of opposition.

Since the Revolutionaries are among the least-educated and the Intellectuals among the best-educated segment of the elite, the relation between education and opposition seems ambiguous. As Table 10.8 indicates, those with higher education are more likely to show some opposition to the government, but this opposition tends to be moderate. Those with lower education are less likely to oppose the government at all, but if they do their opposition is strong. The less educated deputies, when moved to attack the government, were not notable for their temperance.

TABLE 10.8   EDUCATION AND OPPOSITION

	Level of Education	
	University Level	All Others
Opposition		
None	23 (49%)	94 (64%)
Moderate	19 (40%)	17 (11%)
Strong	5 (11%)	36 (25%)
	Number = 47	n = 147

Both cultural background and age also appear to be related to type of opposition in the Assembly. On the basis of partial information it seems that Kabyles were most likely to oppose the government, whereas those with Arabic educations were least likely to oppose the government.[40]

The relationship between age and opposition is less pronounced, but the data are more reliable than those concerning cultural orientations. There is a tendency for those born in the 1920s to be more likely to oppose the government, while those born either before or after 1920 were less likely to do so.[41]

Finally, position within the elite is related to opposition in predictable ways. Those who were in the top revolutionary elite were most likely to be in opposition, followed by the secondary elite. The postindependence top elite, naturally enough, showed the least amount of opposition to the government.[42]

[40] The figures for "loyalists," based on incomplete data, show that 90 percent of the Arabists were in this category, 26 percent of the Kabyles, and 50 percent of the French-educated.

[41] The percentages "loyalist" for these groups are: born before 1920, 60 percent; born in the 1920s, 55 percent; born in the 1930s, 64 percent.

[42] The percentage in strong opposition runs from 27 percent for the top revolutionary elite, to 22 percent for the secondary elite, to 9 percent for the postindependence elite.

The data on opposition within the Assembly seem to indicate only a partial relation between type of political socialization and political behavior. Given the close relationship between prior political experience and participation and between experience and specialization on certain issues, this finding requires some explanation. In general, it seems that those types of behavior over which one does not exercise conscious control are most likely to be related to enduring character traits or personality formation. Acts such as voting may well be strongly affected by circumstantial considerations of costs and benefits so that the impact of earlier experiences is weakened. In the Algerian Assembly it is reasonable to conclude that opposition as expressed in votes cast in public sessions is not generally an expression of early political socialization but rather is closely linked to proximate circumstances. Several deputies, such as Abbas and Francis, never voted against a government measure, but they made their opposition to Ben Bella clear before the first year of the Assembly was over.

Opposition to the government during the first year was in many cases a direct extension of opposition to the Political Bureau during the summer crises of 1962. Of the 81 deputies from the departments which had once been part of *willayas* 3 and 4, 72 percent expressed some opposition to the government, compared to 12 percent of the deputies from the other departments. More generally, those who had been candidates on the first list drawn up in August 1962 were more likely to vote against the government (38 percent) than were those candidates added by the Political Bureau in September (22 percent). For example, the 19 deputies who were added to the list from Constantine in September never opposed Ben Bella. It would seem that Ben Bella's alteration of the list of deputies during late August 1962 had indeed reduced the potential for opposition to his programs by bringing into the Assembly relatively docile men.

During the second year of the Assembly the nature of the opposition to the government changed considerably. It has already been shown that speaking declined during the second year. Public votes during that period were not recorded, but on the basis of interviews with deputies there seems to be wide consensus that in the second year the old opposition from the interior *willayas* became more willing to support Ben Bella. Several members of the Assembly claim that the poorly educated deputies who had originally opposed Ben Bella began to worry about their political careers as the time for reelection approached. Most of the deputies had no profession outside of politics and, so the argument goes, they gradually ceased their opposition to Ben Bella.

In comparing the wartime CNRA to the Constituent Assembly, one deputy, Mohammed Haroun, argued that:

In the CNRA, no one had yet begun to think in terms of political careers, and since any of us might die the next day we weren't worried about alienating powerful figures. Some very low placed militants would speak very harshly to highly placed people. But in the Constituent Assembly, people began to worry about careers and what would happen to them if they spoke out. Many of them, of course, had no careers to return to if they were eliminated from politics.[43]

Parallel to this partial reintegration of the original opposition there was a growing dissatisfaction with Ben Bella's methods among the Politicians and Intellectuals, beginning with the manner of preparing the constitution and reaching its peak in the debate over the death penalty. To many deputies it seemed incongruous that Algerians who had fought and suffered for so long should in turn institute such a repressive form of justice. Emotions were raised even more by the awareness that Ben Bella did not desire the death penalty as a punishment for major crimes but for use against political opponents.[44] During the second year of the Assembly's life this issue was by far the most divisive one the deputies were asked to vote on.

Participation, Opposition, and Reelection

Some evidence does exist for the inferences concerning the relative permanence of opposition groupings during the first year and their alteration during the second. Elections to a second National Assembly were held in September 1964. The number of deputies was reduced from 194 to 138.[45] By most accounts, those deputies perceived as being in opposition to Ben Bella at the time of this election were eliminated from the second Assembly. But perhaps

[43] Interview with Mohammed Haroun. Mezhoudi and Abbas expressed similar judgments in interviews.

[44] Interview with Amar Bentoumi.

[45] The old opposition areas during the 1962 crisis, namely the departments of Algiers, Medea, Al Asnam, Tizi Ouzou, and Constantine, lost the largest number of deputies in these changes. Among the new deputies, only Mohand oul Hadj, Mohammed Harbi, and Ait al Hocine were important figures. These three men had already been named to the Central Committee in April 1964.

a more accurate judgment would be that only two types of deputies were allowed in the second Assembly: those who had been actively loyal to the government and those who had been passively hostile and who had some independent power base, such as the ex-guerrillas of *willayas* 3 and 4.

Whereas one might have expected a clear negative linear correlation between opposition and reelection, this was not the case. A small group of intransigent deputies were expelled from the Assembly or quit before reelections were held. But of the remaining strong opposition 52 percent were reelected, as compared to 20 percent of the moderate opposition and 36 percent of those who showed no opposition. It seems clear that the strongest opposition group was important enough, or powerful enough, that it was deemed wise to include it in the second Assembly. Moderate opposition, however, was punished. Intransigence, then, was rewarded, particularly if one was not too vocal in expressing this opposition. For example, those opponents who remained silent in Assembly debates were reelected more readily than were vocal opponents (44 percent as compared to 25 percent). The lesson that through intransigence one is successful in Algerian politics had been learned during the war for independence and in the lengthy negotiations that followed. The reaffirmation of this lesson in the postindependence period must have been discouraging to those who had hoped that the Assembly would teach Algerian politicians how to bargain and compromise in order to overcome their differences.

In this connection it is interesting to look at the overall reelection rate for deputies in the first Assembly. About two-fifths, 43 percent, were reelected to the second Assembly. A number of variables are associated with a particularly high reelection rate. For example, 65 percent of the Military were reelected, 60 percent of those born in the 1930s, 50 percent of those speaking only in political debates, 56 percent of those in the top elite who never opposed the government, and 53 percent of those on the list of candidates of August 1962.

Low rates of reelection were found among the Intellectuals (17 percent), those who moderately opposed the government (20 percent), those added to the list of candidates in September 1962 (23 percent), those who only spoke on economic issues (27 percent), and those few deputies of European origin (7 percent). The widest range of reelection rates is seen when deputies are grouped by type of political socialization, as is evident in Table 10.9.

TABLE 10.9   REELECTION RATES OF ELITE SUBGROUPS

	Politicians	Revolu-tionaries	Military	Intel-lectuals	Entire Assembly
Reelected	8 (50%)	7 (44%)	34 (65%)	4 (17%)	83 (43%)
Not Reelected	8 (50%)	9 (56%)	18 (35%)	20 (83%)	111 (57%)
Number =	16	n = 16	n = 52	n = 24	n = 194

A second nonlinear correlation exists between participation in political debates and reelection. Figure 10.3 shows that a little par-

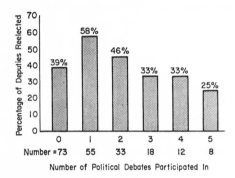

Figure 10.3   Participation in Political Debates and Reelection

ticipation was better than either none at all or much. Silent but loyal deputies could be dispensed with since they neither posed a threat to the regime nor actively supported it. The rewards of membership in the Assembly could be better used to coopt potential dissidents into the system or to retain the support of important incumbents.

In economic debates there is a more direct negative correlation between reelection and participation, with nonparticipants being reelected in 49 percent of the cases and high participants only 31 percent of the time. Politics in moderation was a safer topic, it seems, than was economics. Perhaps this merely reflects that those concerned with power, especially the Military, were more able to survive in the second Assembly than were the Politicians and Intellectuals who concerned themselves with economic development.[46]

[46] One might infer from this finding that as long as major problems of political authority persisted, specialists in economic matters were deemed dispensable. The "rewards" which could be distributed by the government went to those who were concerned with power. Later, when a greater degree of

In any case, after two years of independence Algerians were still struggling to reach some agreement on who was to exercise power. Then, it was believed, the tasks of economic development could be faced.

Summary and Conclusion

Many of the facts which characterized the Algerian Assembly were brought out years later by the deputy Mouloud Gaid, who summarized his feelings as follows:

Tendencies existed within the Assembly because deputies had different basic political formations. Some had been with the PCA, some with the MTLD, some with the UDMA, or Ulama, and this basic education had left its mark. With my French schooling I couldn't easily give up my Cartesian way of reasoning, and those from Arab schools were different in some ways. But when faced with specific problems we could usually understand each other easily. The first year of free discussion contributed to a sense of realism, but those who spoke too freely were eliminated from the second Assembly.[47]

Despite the fact that a large number of deputies who initially opposed Ben Bella were reelected to the second Assembly in 1964, there is no reason to believe that the Assembly itself contributed to this partial reconciliation. Rather, those hostile deputies who were reelected were precisely those who participated least in the work of the Assembly.

The more obvious consequences of the operations of the Assembly in its first two years of existence were that most of the Intellectuals, as well as many Politicians and Revolutionaries were alienated from the Algerian political system. Some left the Assembly, some were expelled or arrested, and many more were not reelected. The Assembly, then, generally lost the talents of the best educated men, the specialists in economic affairs, those who voiced moderate opposition, and those who participated most actively in the Assembly's work. Deputies who remained in the second Assembly were primarily those who had participated only moderately, who had opposed the government either not at all or a great deal, and whose primary political formation had been with the Military. Those who were loyal to the government were more likely to be reelected if they participated actively, while deputies who opposed the government were reelected only if relatively silent. This conclusion follows

political stability was achieved under Boumedienne, Intellectuals and technicians rose rapidly in influence.
[47] Interview with Mouloud Gaid.

from Table 10.10, based on a 20 percent sample of all published debates, measured in column inches.

TABLE 10.10   REELECTION RATES RELATED TO DEGREE OF OPPOSITION AND AMOUNT OF SPEAKING

	Strong Opposition	Moderate Opposition	No Opposition
Reported Speeches in Column Inches			
Averages of All Deputies	23"	12"	15"
Average of Those Reelected	12"	4"	35"
	Number = 31	n = 34	n = 117

Thus reelection to the Assembly was used by the Government to eliminate important groups from an arena where criticisms were voiced publicly, to reward loyalists, and to win over some previously hostile and powerful elements of the elite. Clearly, however, the Assembly did not perform the function of reintegrating all or part of the political elite through the development of a political process which tolerated diversity and resolved conflicts through voting and persuasion rather than force.

With the failure of the Assembly to provide the means by which a segmented autonomous elite could develop into a more coherent governing body, there remained the possibilities of continued elite division and functional autonomy or the concentration of power in the hands of an individual or small group. The former structure of authority might have permitted a degree of stability but at the cost of compromising effective decision-making. The latter required the subordination of numerous subgroups and risked a high degree of elite alienation. But whatever the costs, Ben Bella and his colleagues, having rejected the accommodative solution offered by the Assembly, chose to undertake the immensely difficult task of concentrating power by altering the structure of the political elite. It had proved too difficult, as this study of the Assembly shows, to change the political process in order to reintegrate the elite. Whether structural changes could cope more successfully with the difficulties caused by intraelite divisions was the essential question which faced Ben Bella and his followers during their few years in power.

11

The Search for Political Authority: Ben Bella in Power

When the Algerian war for independence came to an end in the spring of 1962, the tasks of nation-building and of creating authoritative political structures seemed beyond the capacity of the badly divided FLN elite. During the summer these divisions nearly brought civil war to Algeria, and a prolonged crisis of authority insured the disintegration of the FLN. The men who finally emerged from this chaos to lead independent Algeria formed a heterogeneous coalition led by Ahmed Ben Bella.

In his struggle against the GPRA and the dissident *willayas,* Ben Bella had sought to gain as much support within the rest of the revolutionary elite as he could. Although his decisive support came from Boumedienne's exterior troops, he also came to power with the aid of many prestigious Politicians and Revolutionaries. That this mixture of Military men, Revolutionaries, and Politicians would work together effectively was to be doubted from the beginning. Each held some hope of gaining power for himself, and many of the Revolutionaries could claim to have contributed at least as much to the national cause as had Ben Bella. At no time in the past had such a heterogeneous group of Algerians worked together without rivalry and disagreement, and the attainment of independence did not promise to increase their ability to bargain and compromise.

Through a process of collegial decision-making Ben Bella might have hoped to retain the support of those who helped him to power. Instead he chose to centralize influence in his own hands, and those who did not submit to his authority were soon excluded from government positions. As the top leadership began to disintegrate, high positions were opened for members of the secondary elite, especially for those Intellectuals who were often better educated and more cosmopolitan than Ben Bella and his military allies.

Ben Bella's few years in power witnessed important transformations in the composition of the political elite. Older, prestigious Revolutionaries and Politicians quickly fell from positions of influence as younger, less experienced Intellectuals and Military men rapidly rose as ministers or regional army commanders. At the same time Ben Bella's initial coalition of Liberals, some few Radicals, Revolutionaries, the Military, and a number of Intellectuals was soon transformed into a more homogeneous group consisting primarily of the Military and the Intellectuals plus Ben Bella. Nearly all those who had received their basic political formation before the revolution were replaced by men who entered politics only after 1954.

The concentration of power undertaken by Ben Bella had two results of theoretical interest. First, the process of concentrating power led to the widespread alienation of other elite members. Second, by bringing many relatively autonomous centers of power under his own control, Ben Bella greatly augmented his regime's capacity to act decisively, although implementation of new policies was often difficult because of the lack of support from other elite members and because of the serious organizational weaknesses of the FLN.

Ben Bella, who found that he could not collaborate effectively with the well-known Politicians and Revolutionaries, soon discovered that his new allies were hardly more manageable. After eliminating many of his early supporters with the backing of the army, he risked becoming a virtual prisoner of the forces supporting him. To break this dependence he sought to divide the Military along the lines of the *maquisards* of the interior versus the professionals trained in Morocco and Tunisia, but such tactics ended in failure. On June 19, 1965, the Military acted in unison to remove Ben Bella from power.

When the Political Bureau of the FLN established itself in Algiers in September 1962, the problems of creating new political structures were immense. The most powerful groups at the time were the frontier armies under Colonel Boumedienne, the six independent *willayas*, and the trade union (UGTA). Less important, but still possessing some influence, were the FLN itself, the student union (UNEA), the women's union (UNFA), the Algerian Communist Party (PCA), the various publications of the Europeans and of the PCA, and some rather traditional religious leaders. The Political Bureau added to this diversity of contenders for power by creating a National Assembly, by reorganizing the FLN and its branch in France, the *Amicale*, and by naming a new government which would take over the administrative tasks of the country.

Even though a few key rivals for power had been eliminated by the Political Bureau during the crisis of the summer, there was a multiplicity of groups and organizations with actual or potential influence in the fall of 1962. A pluralistic political process might have evolved to accommodate and aggregate the demands of these diverse groups. But such a process, which perhaps could have developed within the National Assembly, was notably absent during the nearly three years of Ben Bella's rule. Instead the Political Bureau, and Ben Bella in particular, sought to establish the authority of the Party and the state by taking direct control of virtually every autonomous political group within Algeria.

One can only speculate on the reasons that led Ben Bella to attempt the difficult task of centralizing power in Algeria. The decision, however, was certainly in accord with his personality and his earlier political experience. Ben Bella since his adolescence had never respected the quarrels of political parties, the elections, debates, and ineffectiveness which he associated with the French political system. By 1954 he had rejected these methods and had witnessed with the outbreak of the revolution how the bold action of a few men could accomplish more than years of political bargaining, voting, and petitions. For these reasons he must never have believed that the National Assembly was a viable means for initiating reforms. Rather, he seems to have thought that decisions should come from the top, and if the Politicians would be offended by this procedure, "the people" at least would applaud.

Ben Bella's personality also lent itself to flamboyant leadership. Like many of the Revolutionaries in 1954, he not only wanted to gain independence for his country but wished to be at the front of the independence movement. The desire to lead was probably part of Ben Bella's character long before 1954. An old acquaintance from Ben Bella's school days was to recall years later:

> When I was at the lycée in Tlemcen, Ben Bella was also attending school there. We played on the same soccer team. Ben Bella was a good soccer player, but he never forgot the galleries. He wanted to be number one. Ben Bella always wanted his teammates to pass him the ball so that he could score. He was the same way in politics.[1]

By 1962 there were many who felt that the situation called for the decisive leadership that Ben Bella might provide. After more than seven years of war, Algerians were anxious to achieve some of the goals for which they had suffered so long. Expectations were high that by zeal and good intentions many things could be accomplished. That much needed to be done could hardly be doubted. The economy was in grave danger due to the departure of most of the technically trained European population. Preparations needed to be made for opening schools and for finding teachers for Algeria's large number of children. War veterans expected some form of compensation and rarely hesitated to burst into offices staffed by better educated but less militant young men to demand their just reward for having fought the revolution. Agricultural land was being taken indiscriminately by peasants who felt that independence should at least mean that they could take ownership of land that the Europeans were abandoning. Vacated apartments and villas were being occupied by peasants who poured in from the countryside. Decisive action was needed. Thus in Algeria, as in many other developing countries, authoritarian political structures were developed in the belief that this would create authority itself. Such, however, was not to be the case.

When the Political Bureau of the FLN came to power in September 1962, many members of the political elite believed that the Political Bureau, in consultation with other groups, would draw up a list of candidates to a National Constituent Assembly. This, in fact, was done. It was also widely assumed that Ben Bella would be chosen head of state and the Assembly would approve his nomination and his choice of ministers. This also took place. But the role of the Party proved to be a more controversial issue. Many Algerian

[1] Interview with Abderrazak Chentouf.

leaders expected that a congress, modeled after the CNRA, would be held to reorganize the virtually nonexistent FLN. This congress, then, would be responsible for deciding on a new Political Bureau. A constitution, drafted by the Assembly, perhaps on the basis of recommendations from the Party, would then define the role of the FLN and of the government. In any case, the five-man Political Bureau and the government selected by it were widely viewed as provisional until the decisions of a Party congress could define more explicitly the nature of the political system.[2]

The First Political Bureau of the FLN

The Political Bureau, it will be recalled, had been proposed to the CNRA at Tripoli before independence. The original list of members consisted of Ben Bella, Ben Alla, Khider, Bitat, Moham-medi, Ait Ahmed, and Boudiaf. Ait Ahmed and Boudiaf, after some vacillation, refused to be members, and the five remaining candidates were never able to get the prescribed two-thirds vote needed to invest them legally as the Political Bureau of the FLN. Nonetheless, in the course of the crisis of summer 1962 these five men were accepted as the arbiters of Algeria's immediate political future.

Four of the five members of the Political Bureau were Revolutionaries who had spent most of the war in French prisons. The fifth, Mohammedi, had led *willaya* 3 for some time, then commanded ALN troops in Tunisia before becoming a member of the last GPRA. As a devout Muslim and as a Kabyle who ardently believed in Arabization, Mohammedi's inclusion in the Political Bureau had at least symbolic value.[3] There was little question, however, that Ben Bella and Khider were the dominant leaders of the FLN.

---

[2] These assertions are based on interviews with several deputies, from statements by Ben Bella himself, and from speeches or interviews of other elite members. Boudiaf, in his preface to *Où va l'Algérie?* argues that the agreement of August 2, 1962, foresaw the formation of a provisional Political Bureau which would convene the CNRA or a Congress of the FLN in the near future.

[3] Mohammedi in an interview claimed that he supported Ben Bella only after extracting a promise from him that Ben Bella would work for the construction of a Muslim Algeria. Mohammedi consistently opposed the socialist leanings of Ben Bella but said that he believed he could be more effective inside the Political Bureau than in opposition.

According to H. Bourgès, *L'Algérie à l'épreuve du pouvoir*, p. 95, both Ben Bella and Khider were searching for majorities within the five-man Political Bureau. Given the alignment of forces, Mohammedi Said held the decisive vote, and his decision to support Ben Bella shifted the balance in favor of the President and against Khider and Bitat.

The members of the Political Bureau of 1962 were all long-time nationalists. Four of them had been involved with the clandestine os, and four were members of the early CRUA which began the revolution. Three had led *willayas* within Algeria during the war. Their average age in 1962 was 42, ranging from 50 for Khider and Mohammedi to 30 for Ben Alla. Three had been primarily workers before entering politics, and two had been officers in the French army. None of them had university educations, and three had attended only elementary school. All five came from modest origins in rural areas. Two were from the region of Oran, two from Constantine, and one from Kabylia. Such, then, were the men who assumed the task of creating the Algerian state.

Ben Bella's First Government

Following elections to the National Assembly on September 20, 1962, the Political Bureau's immediate task was to select Algeria's first government. On September 26 Ben Bella was authorized by the Assembly to form a cabinet, and the following day he released the names of the new Ministers. Two days later the Assembly invested Ben Bella and his cabinet as the first independent government of modern Algeria.

The composition of Ben Bella's first government is particularly interesting because it reflects the diversity of support which he received from the major groups within the political elite at that time. Cabinet positions, in Algeria as elsewhere, are one form of repayment for political support. Ben Bella, in fact, freely offered cabinet positions, or even membership on the Political Bureau, to individuals whom he thought he could neutralize or reward in this way.[4]

The cabinet formed by Ben Bella differed significantly from the Political Bureau in its composition. Of the five major types of Algerian politicians, all were found within the cabinet. The Liberals

[4] Haroun, an early opponent of Ben Bella, claimed that Ben Bella offered him a place on the Political Bureau at Tripoli. Bouzida, the spokesman for the Tizi Ouzou group during the crisis of summer 1962, said that Ben Bella offered him the ministry of Justice and Krim the ministry of Foreign Affairs. They both refused because they feared that as members of the government they would be unable to criticize Ben Bella. Bentoumi, when under arrest on Ben Bella's orders, was approached by a government representative who said that Ben Bella was willing to let Bentoumi back into the cabinet if he would help to oppose Boumedienne. None of these offers was accepted. (Interviews with Bouzida, Bentoumi, and Haroun.)

were represented by Francis and Boumendjel, the Radicals by Bentoumi and Boumaza, the Revolutionaries by Ben Bella himself, also Ouzegane and Bitat, the Military most notably by Boumedienne, Medeghri, and Bouteflika, and the Intellectuals by Khemisti and Benhamida. Although there was a preponderance of ministers from the Military and the Intellectuals, important ministries, such as Information, Finance, and Justice were led by more experienced Politicians of the old nationalist movements. Of the nineteen ministers, at least eleven had either previous experience or training which suited the new functions they were to perform.[5] It might be added that the only ministers with a powerful "constituency" outside of the elite were those from the Military. Other ministers were primarily dependent upon personal relations for their position within the government.

The cabinet, then, was heterogeneous in terms of the political formations of its members. Compared to the members of the Assembly and the Political Bureau, the ministers were generally better educated and more likely to have practiced liberal professions. Whereas the members of the Political Bureau seemed to be chosen largely because of their revolutionary roles, the ministers tended more to be selected according to criteria of technical competence. But like the deputies to the Assembly, the ministers were also included in the cabinet as part of the compromise which ended the summer crisis. Although the positions on the Political Bureau were restricted to the victors in that crisis, cabinet positions were somewhat more generously distributed. Whether these initial steps by Ben Bella would be seen as a step toward reconciliation depended in large measure upon the degree of autonomy allowed each minister. In any case, the potential for conflict between the Party and the government seemed apparent from the composition of these two bodies, the one dominated by Revolutionaries and the other by more technically oriented men.[6]

[5] Francis, the Minister of Finance, had held the same post in the GPRA. Boumaza, the Minister of Social Affairs and Work, had performed similar functions in the FFFLN. Bentoumi, the Minister of Justice, was a lawyer. Hadj Hamou, the Minister of Information, had been Secretary General of that ministry in the GPRA. Boumedienne, the Minister of Defense, had been head of the ALN. Mohammedi, the Minister of War Veterans, had been influential in the army. Khemisti, the Minister of Foreign Affairs, was a cosmopolitan ex-UGEMA leader. Benhamida, the Minister of Education, was well educated in both French and Arabic. Khobzi, the Minister of Commerce, was a Mozabite merchant. Nekkache, the Minister of Health, was a doctor.

[6] The social backgrounds of these ministers are fairly well known. Their average age was 39, placing them as a group slightly below the Political Bureau

Structures of Power: Party, State, and Army

In September 1962 most observers would have selected Ben Bella, Khider, and Boumedienne as the three most influential political actors in Algeria. Khider was Secretary General of the FLN, Ben Bella was President of the Council of Ministers, and Boumedienne was Minister of Defense. Khider and Boumedienne had been the architects of Ben Bella's victory over the GPRA, and both seemed determined to retain a large share of influence for themselves. Khider, in numerous public statements, referred to the need for a mass party that would control the activities of the state and for the withdrawal of the army from politics.[7] Boumedienne, while more laconic, made it clear that the army intended to play a political role.[8] Ben Bella spoke of the need to reinforce the authority of the state, of forming an avant-garde party restricted to tested *militants,* and of the economic and social role which the army might play.[9] It seemed, then, from the outset that the major figures in the political elite differed in their conceptions of the appropriate patterns of authority which should guide the Algerians in the process of creating a political system.

Khider, while lacking the power base that Boumedienne had in the form of an army, seemed nonetheless anxious to assert his own influence and to build up personal support through the FLN.

and equal with the Assembly. The youngest minister was 26, the oldest was 63. The region of Constantine was the birthplace of 7 ministers, Oran of 6, Kabylia of 4, and Algiers of 2. Five came from large urban areas, 5 from small villages, and 9 from modest towns. Eleven of the ministers had received university level educations, and 3 were known to have attended only elementary school. Seven had been in prison during some part of the revolution, and 10 had been in some military role during the war. Three ministers had been lawyers, 3 doctors, 2 teachers, 2 students, 2 journalists, 1 engineer, 2 "politicians," 2 workers, and 1 merchant. All but 3 ministers were also deputies, and 3 were members of the Political Bureau. Six of the ministers had held top elite positions during the revolution, while the others had belonged to the secondary elite. Already in this first government one can see the rise of new elements, well-educated men if often politically inexperienced.

[7] Khider, in a press conference in Cairo, October 10, 1962, expressed these sentiments.

[8] Boumedienne, more by his actions than his words, indicated the political role he foresaw for the ANP. Later statements after Boumedienne came to power in 1965 indicated more clearly the political role he envisaged for the army. Hervé Bourgès, *L'Algérie à l'épreuve du pouvoir,* p. 51, says that "Ben Bella was halfway between the conceptions of Khider, who hoped for the return of the ALN to the barracks, and of Boumedienne who never accepted, even after the war was over, the distinction between civilians and the military."

[9] Ben Bella's early ideas are well expressed in his "Déclaration ministerielle," September 28, 1962, reprinted in *Discours du President Ben Bella.*

In September 1962, however, Khider revealed, somewhat ambigu-
ously, that he did not oppose a multiparty system so long as other
parties worked within the framework of the constitution.[10] Presumably he was indicating that the Algerian Communist Party, the
PCA, would be able to continue its legal existence if it did not
oppose the state.[11] Two months after Khider's overture to the communists, however, the Minister of Information announced that the
PCA would be banned in Algeria, not because of anticommunism,
he asserted, but simply because no other parties would be allowed
to organize. Already it seemed as if Khider was losing his ability to
guide the course of Algeria's political development.

Khider was more successful in his attempt to subordinate the
UGTA to the FLN. As early as November 1962 the UGTA had referred
to conflicts between it and the Party over control of the trade union
movement. Some form of agreement seemed to be reached the
following month, but at the first UGTA Congress in January 1963,
Khider packed the audience with his hand-picked men and succeeded
in electing leaders of the UGTA who would accept the authority of
the Political Bureau.[12]

Khider's next move toward asserting the authority of the FLN
came during the first week of April 1963.[13] Following a meeting of
Party members in Algiers, Khider declared that the Party should
be enlarged, that it should have authority over all political structures in the state, and that a Party Congress should be held before
the end of the first Assembly. Despite Ben Bella's denial of divergences between himself and Khider, Khider finally announced his
resignation as Secretary General of the FLN on April 16, explaining
his action as "the result of fundamental divergences in points of
view within the Political Bureau concerning the value of holding a

[10] Khider, in an interview to the Italian communist party newspaper, *Unità*,
September 23, 1962.

[11] The day before Khider's statement, the first clandestine opposition party,
the *Parti de la Révolution Socialiste* (PRS), generally linked to Boudiaf's name,
was formed. Khider, it would seem, was not referring to this party when he
suggested that a multiparty system might be acceptable.

[12] Gérard Chaliand, in *L'Algérie est-elle socialiste?* p. 25, tells of this incident
and implies that Ben Bella was opposed to Khider's action.

[13] During this time Boumedienne was leading a large Algerian delegation
on a visit to several Arab countries. Among the members of the delegation was
the Minister of Justice, Amar Bentoumi, a close associate of Khider. In an
interview he claimed that Ben Bella urged the delegation to prolong its stay
abroad rather than returning on schedule.

national Congress of the FLN before the end of the present Assembly's mandate." [14]

Ben Bella was immediately named Secretary General in Khider's place. A major step in the centralization of power in his own hands was thereby taken. He later explained the origins of the dispute with Khider in the following terms:

Algeria needs a respected power which is not always challenged by some other authority. We have reached the point today where a duality of power has grown up everywhere. The Party representatives attack the representatives of the central government, denouncing their activities, and by their actions they greatly weaken the government. . . .[15]

From this statement, it would seem that Ben Bella wished to reduce even further the influence of the FLN over the state. In any case, as head of both the government and the Party, he no doubt thought that frictions could be reduced in the future between these two centers of power.

In slightly more than six months Ben Bella had clearly centralized power in his own hands. Other political parties had first been banned, then the FLN itself came under his control. Furthermore, perhaps in preparation for the showdown with Khider, Ben Bella had made a series of decisions, known as the March Decrees, which nationalized French lands and legalized the system of self-management *(autogestion)* which peasants had spontaneously instituted after independence.[16] These decisions undeniably won Ben Bella some popularity in the UGTA circles.[17] But other members of the political elite were already worried about the course of events. Mabrouk Belhocine, a moderate supporter of Ben Bella, was later to say:

The FLN during the war was a front grouping all tendencies, not a party, which is the political expression of a given social class. I would have preferred that the FLN remain a front, but instead it became a tool for either Khider or Ben Bella, depending upon who controlled it. Ben Bella, instead

[14] *Le Monde*, April 19, 1963, carried an interview by Khider explaining his decision. See also, Arslan Humbaraci, *Algeria: A Revolution that Failed*, pp. 99–100.

[15] Quoted in *L'Observateur du Moyen Orient et de l'Afrique*, April 26, 1963, p. 7.

[16] See A. Humbaraci, *Algeria*, p. 144, for an account of these decrees. While Ben Bella played for the support of the left, Khider had been exhorting all Algerians to respect the fast of Ramadan as good Muslims, thus gaining the favor of the religious conservatives.

[17] Mohammed Harbi, it seems, was influenced by these decrees in deciding to support Ben Bella.

of trying to reconcile the various factions, wanted to increase his own personal power. There were others, like Ait Ahmed, who also exacerbated tensions. I felt that we needed to tackle the concrete tasks of reconstruction rather than getting involved in "politics" in the worst sense of the word.[18]

Khider's resignation symbolized the first wave of elite alienation from Ben Bella. As might be expected, individuals least able to accommodate themselves to Ben Bella's authoritarian style were those who by their political formation felt most entitled to positions of power, namely the Revolutionaries. By the time of Khider's resignation such prominent Revolutionaries as Ben Tobbal, Boussouf, and Boudiaf were out of politics or in opposition. Others, for example Ait Ahmed and Krim, had expressed open criticism of the government and were soon to join the ranks of the opposition. Likewise, Bitat eventually withdrew from active participation in the Political Bureau. In brief, those whose experiences in politics most clearly paralleled Ben Bella's were least able to work with him. For Ben Bella the process of eliminating latter-day allies had begun, and soon the search for new sources of support would be under way.

The question of the proper role of the Party in the Algerian political system had been partially resolved when Ben Bella became Secretary General following Khider's resignation. The uncertainties concerning the army's role were less easily resolved. Boumedienne, it seems, concentrated most of his efforts during the first months after independence on unifying and "reconverting" the army into a coherent force, now named the *Armée Nationale Populaire* (ANP). Little is known of the means by which Boumedienne accomplished the reconversion of the army, but he appears to have been eventually quite successful in creating a modern, well-trained army out of the ALN. New military regions were formed to cut across the old *willaya* boundaries, and some ex-*willaya* commanders were replaced by trusted professionals. For example, in February 1963 the military commander of the sixth military region, Mohammed Tayebi (Si Larbi), was relieved of his command and was replaced by Chadli Bendjedid.

Ben Bella, meanwhile, never one to become the unwilling captive of any group, had begun to promote the interests of a number of intellectual leftists closely associated with Mohammed Harbi. The March Decrees had been an early effort to consolidate this new alliance. A second indication of Harbi's growing influence came in

[18] Interview with Mabrouk Belhocine.

May 28, 1963, when the Political Bureau announced that the press was to be reorganized. The three editors of *Révolution Africaine,* including Zohra Drif, Bitat's wife, and the editor of *Le Peuple,* all of whom had been named by Khider, were replaced by the Intellectuals Harbi and Zerdani. With Harbi and the UGTA as new sources of support and with Boumedienne in control of the army, Ben Bella was prepared to continue the process of centralizing power.

Unrelated to Khider's resignation but occurring at the same time was the assassination of Mohammed Khemisti, the young, affable, and cosmopolitan Foreign Minister who had grown up in Ben Bella's home town.[19] The circumstances surrounding the assassination remain unclear, but it is generally thought Khemisti was shot by a mentally deranged man and that the act was not part of a larger plot. The result of this tragedy, however, was that a key position within the government was now vacant. Who Ben Bella would appoint as his foreign minister would give some hint as to the balance of forces between his recent Intellectual allies and the army.

Events moved quickly in the next few months, and elite turnover became rapid. Previous supporters broke with the government, and Ben Bella sought simultaneously to eliminate possible threats to his regime, to build new alliances with the Intellectuals, and to strengthen his position with regard to the Military.

The week after Khemisti's assassination, Minister of Information Hadj Hamou resigned and was replaced by Mouloud Belaouane, a former UGEMA leader and a trained psychiatrist. On April 20, a man who had clashed with Khider, the Minister of Posts and Transport, Hassani, also resigned. He was succeeded by a young technician, Abdelaziz Zaibek. Of greater significance however, was Boumedienne's promotion to the position of first vice president and Bitat's demotion to third vice president. In addition, Mohammedi Said was named second vice president.[20] The net result of these changes was to eliminate some of Khider's residual influence and to replace his supporters by more manageable Intellectuals. At the same time the Military increased its influence as Boumedienne's power was overtly recognized.

---

[19] Khemisti was Ben Bella's *"frère du lait,"* meaning that when he was an infant he was orphaned and it was Ben Bella's mother who nursed him.

[20] Bitat and Khider seem to have been fairly close in personal terms, if not always in beliefs. Ben Bella clearly wanted to be rid of Bitat, and on May 19, 1963, Ben Alla took over Party functions from Bitat within the Political Bureau. A minister who was associated with both Khider and Bitat was told by Ben Bella at this time to drop Bitat because "he was finished."

The rupture between Ben Bella and the alienated Revolutionaries soon became public. On June 22 the announcement was made that Boudiaf, one of the earliest leaders of the CRUA, had been arrested, and three days later Ben Bella revealed the discovery of a "plot" against the state.[21] On July 9, Ait Ahmed, one of Ben Bella's companions from the French prisons, disclosed that he would open a fight against the government, and this sentiment was echoed by Krim a few days later in *Le Monde* when he said, "We have a duty to fight again." [22] In their dispute with Ben Bella some of the Revolutionaries were turning to armed insurrection, that political tactic in which they had once before been successful.

Apparently there were others in the country who agreed with the Revolutionary dissidents. On such suspicion the *maquisard* Sawt al Arab (Boubnider) was arrested. In August rumors came of a small guerrilla band forming in Kabylia around Dra el Mizan under the curious leadership of a pro-Zionist Marxist who was a descendant of the Emir Abd Al Qadir.[23]

At the same time that some of the Revolutionaries were entering into opposition, Ben Bella parted ways with his Liberal supporters. On July 9 Ferhat Abbas angrily denounced the army newspaper *El Djamahir* for calling him a traitor. Ben Bella briefly attempted a reconciliation by suspending the publication of *El Djamahir*. This truce did not last long, however, especially after Ben Bella presented a ready-made constitution to the members of the FLN before consulting the National Assembly. On August 5 Ahmed Francis, Minister of Finance and a close friend of Abbas, left for Switzerland for "health reasons," and on August 16 Ben Bella announced Abbas' expulsion from the FLN.

The opposition to the government was clearly growing in strength. But as the danger seemed to increase, Ben Bella was all the more free to bring power into his own hands or into those of his close supporters. After the departure of Ahmed Francis, for example, Ben Bella appointed a more loyal ally, Bachir Boumaza, to head the new ministry of National Economy. The constitution, which granted great power to the President, was accepted by a

---

[21] Boudiaf, *Ou va l'Algérie?* relates the circumstances of his arrest and detention. Along with Boudiaf, three others were arrested, namely Ali Allouache, the ex-spokesman of *willaya* 4, Moussa Kebaili, and Mohand Akli Benyounes. The latter two had been with the FFFLN during the war.

[22] *Le Monde*, July 12, 1963.

[23] See Abderrazak Abdelkader, *Le conflit judéo-arabe; juifs et arabes face à l'avenir.*

majority of the now docile Assembly on August 28. Opposition from those out of power was voiced by a new clandestine opposition party, representing primarily Kabyle dissidents, the *Front des Forces Socialistes,* which flatly rejected the constitution. The FFS's opposition had little immediate effect. On September 8, 1963, a constitutional referendum was held throughout the country, and except for the region of Kabylia participation was high. Two days later Ben Bella was nominated as the only candidate for President in the forthcoming elections, and on September 15 he was elected.

In the course of one year Ben Bella, with the help of Boumedienne, had brought under control many of the major independent forces of the Algerian revolution. The internal *willayas* were largely reintegrated into a relatively unified ANP, the UGTA and the FFFLN (or *Amicale*) were under the direction of the Party, Ben Bella had become Secretary General of the FLN, the press had been brought into line, the Assembly had lost most of its illusions of playing an independent role, and a constitution had been adopted which placed virtually all power in the hands of the Party, even though the Party itself was poorly organized outside the large cities.

The Constitution

The provisions of the constitution seemed to legitimate the concentration of power already undertaken by Ben Bella during his first year of rule. A preamble to the constitution declared the goals of the Algerian state to be social and economic development within the perspective of socialism and Islam. Stability, it was argued, could only be assured by a single party regime, and this "avant-garde" party was to be the ultimate source of authority. The army, however, was also to play a political role, but within the framework of the Party. Islam was declared to be the state religion, and the President was required to be a Muslim.[24] A few articles of the constitution declared that the FLN would be the only party in Algeria, that it would define the policies of the nation and would

[24] This provision was included in the constitution only after a stormy session of the "Commission on the Constitution" of the Assembly in which the deputy Brahim Mezhoudi ardently defended the Islamic nature of Algeria. Ben Bella, who had previously argued that a modern state should be secular, was convinced by Mezhoudi's arguments, and Islam was made the state religion. Mezhoudi also opposed the provision of the constitution granting the army a political role, but in this he was voted down. (Mezhoudi interview.)

supervise the actions of the Assembly and of the government.[25] Very limited powers were granted by the constitution to the Assembly (Article 38), while broad powers were given to the President, including emergency powers (Article 59). On paper, then, Ben Bella had managed to concentrate as much power in his own hands as any constitution can grant. But by doing so he had already forced many influential political figures into opposition. It was the process by which Ben Bella had accomplished this as much as the final result which had alienated many of his colleagues. Zohra Drif's comments are typical of those made by many other deputies:

> I didn't mind that the constitution was made by the Party instead of the Assembly, but the method they used wasn't a legitimate one. The constitution was discussed at the lower levels by Party members, but important principles were avoided in these debates. Each Party federation discussed the constitution. There was a façade of democratic centralism, but because of the lack of formation of the Party militants, many of the real problems were never brought up. A plenary meeting was held in Algiers, but individual discussion and debate were not permitted on the text of the constitution. Rather, there was a rule that each Federation could have a representative present suggestions and criticisms which were then considered by the Party and were answered all at the same time. The constitution was completely based on the Party—it really institutionalized it for the first time. But the Party had no *legal* existence. There had been no constitutional Congress for the Party. Thus the form of the Party was not yet defined and when voting on the constitution no one knew what the Party would in fact be like.[26]

The Second Ben Bella Government

Ben Bella's new cabinet, named on September 19, 1963, reflected the rapid political turnover of the previous year, the disaffection of the Politicians, and Ben Bella's growing reliance on the Military. Earlier in September, Ben Bella had appointed a new Foreign Minister, Abdelaziz Bouteflika, a friend of Boumedienne from the Oujda group. Now he added three more men who were considered to be Boumedienne's protégés. Cherif Belkacem became Minister of National Orientation (regrouping the ministries of Information, Education, and Youth and Sports). Nekkache became minister of Social Affairs, a new ministry combining Health, Social Affairs, and Work, and Boumedienne's colleague in the *Etat Major* of the ALN, Ahmed Kaid, became minister of Tourism. Other new ministers

[25] The French term used was *contrôler*.
[26] Interview with Zohra Drif.

were named from among those who were thought to be loyal to Ben Bella. Bachir Boumaza headed the new ministry of National Economy which regrouped the previous ministries of Finance, Commerce and Industry. Another old colleague and friend, Ahmed Mahsas, became minister of Agriculture. An Intellectual, Hadj Smain, became minister of Justice.[27]

Ben Bella now found himself in an awkward dilemma. Although he had successfully asserted his authority over the Party and the Assembly, he was unable to exert the same kind of control over the army. In a speech before his election Ben Bella had declared, "The ANP only exists within the framework of the FLN." But such assertions of authority were little more than rhetoric.

In his attempt to consolidate power, Ben Bella had aroused strong and occasionally violent opposition. As the opposition organized and threatened the regime with armed conflict, Ben Bella became more and more dependent on Boumedienne. This dependence must have alarmed him, and thus throughout the next year Ben Bella played a dangerous game of using the army to put down the opposition while at the same time seeking to weaken Boumedienne's influence. The groups which he relied on most in this latter task were the ex-willaya leaders and the Marxist Intellectuals. Ben Bella's conflict with Boumedienne came to be garbed in much ideological phraseology—the proponents of scientific socialism opposing those who favored a specifically Algerian form of socialism inspired by Islam[28] —but the more basic issue seems clearly to have been that of "who governs?"

The question of power eventually came to look more like an ideological issue as Ben Bella sought to capitalize upon his prestige abroad, primarily in socialist countries, to bolster his own position. Thus, the opponents of Ben Bella became sensitive to the issue of

[27] Sadek Batel became Undersecretary in charge of Youth and Sports on September 23. Bitat, who was named third vice president, refused to accept this position. The average age of these 15 ministers was slightly higher than that of the first cabinet, namely 42 years. Liberal professions were less well represented, and the number of ministers with some military experience increased somewhat. The level of education dropped slightly, with 7 of 15 ministers having university educations. Ten of the ministers were also deputies, and 6 had held top elite positions during the revolution.

[28] Mind-bending discussions of many paths to one socialism or many paths to many socialisms, etc., left some Algerian politicians both confused and alienated. Either one concluded that the whole discussion was absurd, that Ben Bella and Harbi were communists, or that the army represented traditional Islamic reaction. (Interviews with Belhocine, Mezhoudi, and Guerroudj.)

outside interference in Algeria's affairs and focused considerable hostility on foreign Trotskyite advisers of Ben Bella such as the Greek Raptis and the Egyptian Lotfallah. With the aid of hindsight, however, it seems that much of the ideological verbiage was simply a mask for maneuvers of various groups within the elite which aimed at securing or bolstering their own positions of influence.[29]

Shortly after the elections in September 1968, the clandestine opposition movements were seen to be growing in strength, and events seemed to be moving toward armed conflict. Soon after the formation of Ben Bella's second government, the National Assembly excluded five deputies from its ranks, including two Kabyles, Krim and Ait Ahmed. A week later the clandestine party, the FFS, was banned, and the following day FFS-sponsored antigovernment demonstrations took place at Tizi Ouzou in the heart of Kabylia. Ait Ahmed and the regional military commander, Mohand oul Hadj, were then joined in their denunciations of the government by several deputies, in particular Ali Yahia, Mourad Oussedik, Dhilès, and Arezki Hermouche.[30]

The same day Ben Bella relieved Mohand oul Hadj of his military functions, which provoked the FFS to reply that, "By this act the government has made clear its desire to eliminate all the revolutionary militants of the interior in favor of ex-officers of the French army." [31] The allusion to the officers of the French army no doubt referred to the growing influence of such professional soldiers around Boumedienne as Chabou and Slimane Hoffmann. Later in the crisis Mohand oul Hadj was to reaffirm his solidarity with other internal military leaders in the following terms: "I felt that one day I would be eliminated like all the other leaders who fought till the end of the war inside Algeria. Look at Sawt al Arab, the ex-colonel of North Constantine, he's now in prision." [32]

On September 30 Ben Bella, noting the concentration of Moroccan troops along the frontier, denounced the collusion between the FFS and the Moroccan monarchy. The same day Boumedienne left

---

[29] Exceptions to this statement, of course, exist. Perhaps Harbi was one of the most obvious "ideologues." Also, some of those influenced by their Arab-Islamic background saw some issues in ideological terms, as did the deputies Mezhoudi and Chibane. Gérard Chaliand, *L'Algérie,* indirectly supports this argument of the irrelevance of ideology by showing how opportunistically Ben Bella would use ideology. Humbaraci, *Algeria,* comes to much the same conclusion.

[30] Most Kabyle deputies, it should be stressed, signed a declaration in the Assembly denouncing the FFS.

[31] Quoted in the *Annuaire de l'Afrique du nord,* 1963, p. 309.

[32] *Jeune Afrique,* October 14–20, 1963, p. 8.

on a previously arranged trip to Moscow, probably to procure arms. The following day, profiting from Boumedienne's absence, Ben Bella named an ex-guerrilla leader, Tahar Zbiri, as head of the *Etat Major* of the ANP. This was done without Boumedienne's knowledge or approval and was interpreted at the time as an attempt to undermine Boumedienne's hold on the army. Boumedienne two years later confirmed the accuracy of this interpretation.[33] Simultaneously, Said Abid, a young officer who had served in the same *willaya* as Zbiri, was named to replace Mohand oul Hadj as head of the seventh military region. By promoting the *willaya* leaders, Ben Bella was trying to rekindle old rivalries in the army and set the guerilla fighters of the revolution against Boumedienne's professionals. In order to gain popular support in this crisis, Ben Bella made the last dramatic decision of the day by declaring the nationalization of all French-owned lands in Algeria.[34]

External threats intervened at this point, requiring some measure of unity and facilitating a reconciliation between Ben Bella and some of the opposition. Tensions with Morocco had finally reached the point of impending conflict, and on October 3, 1963, Ben Bella invoked a constitutional clause which granted him full powers in a national emergency. Within a week, fighting had begun along the Moroccan border. At first, Mohand oul Hadj announced that only the destruction of the Ben Bella–Boumedienne regime could end the crisis in Kabylia. But on October 24, as the war with Morocco deepened, Mohand oul Hadj announced that he would rally to the regime and help fight off Morocco's attack. Thus, Ait Ahmed was deprived of his major source of military support. This phase of the internal crisis ended on November 12 with a signed agreement between Mohand oul Hadj and Ben Bella which foresaw the reintegration of opposition groups into the FLN, the release of political prisoners and the preparation of a full-scale Party Congress within five months.[35]

[33] Boumedienne interview with Hassanein Heykal, originally published in *Al Ahram*, October 8, 1965, and reprinted in French in *Révolution Africaine*, November 6–13, 1965.
[34] *Révolution Africaine*, October 5, 1963, carried an article entitled "Du GPRA à Tizi Ouzou," which analyzed the Kabyle crisis in historical terms and ended by strongly condemning, as Ben Bella had done some days earlier, the GPRA "triumvirate" of Krim, Boussouf, and Ben Tobbal. On page 8 of the same issue a detailed list of opposition moves over the preceding year was published.
[35] *Jeune Afrique*, November 25–December 1, 1963, p. 8, gave the terms of the agreement as follows: (1) One-third of the Preparatory Commission of the FLN Congress should be made up of members of the opposition. (2) The *chefs historiques* should return to positions of power. (3) The government

A less immediately apparent result of the brief war with Morocco seems to have been the modernization and reequipment of the army under the pretext of defending against further Moroccan attacks. Boumedienne, it appeared, focused his attention on building a modern army. Equipment and advisers were soon forthcoming from the Soviet Union.[36] Ben Bella, on the other hand, largely neglected the organization of the major centers of power within Algeria. Just as the members of the CRUA had placed their faith in the spontaneity of the masses in 1954, so now Ben Bella relied on the masses to support him, no matter what the politicians or the military men thought of him. Ben Bella's first Minister of Justice has provided the following example of Ben Bella's populist orientation:

Ben Bella really believed that the people were behind him. I once accompanied him to a meeting with peasants where he spoke about the need for reforestation. At the end of his speech they applauded loudly. On our return trip to Algiers, Ben Bella said to me that he wasn't concerned with the growing signs of opposition to him from his colleagues since the masses were with him. After all, he said, their applause is worth more than troops.[37]

The Party Congress in April 1964

On November 16, 1963, Ben Bella named a forty-four member commission to organize the Party Congress which had been promised in the agreement with Mohand oul Hadj. Ben Bella hoped to increase his own authority and the stability of his government by building up the Party, which might then serve as a counterweight to both the opposition and the army. While organizing the Congress, an attempt was made to regain the loyalty of some of the elite who had moved into the opposition. At the same time, Ben Bella was careful not to concede too much to the opposition. Those most actively courted were the *maquisards* who might have some military following. Few concessions were offered the Politicians, although many of them were allowed to attend the Party Congress.

In its task of bringing some degree of unity to the postindependence elite, the Party Congress was only partially successful. When

should be completely reshuffled before the Party Congress. Boumedienne and his friends, as well as the Kabyle ministers, should be dropped. (4) A new ANP should be established which would be led by the ex-*willaya* commanders.

[36] See Stuart Scharr, *The Arms Race and Defense Strategy in North Africa.* American Universities Field Staff Reports, December 1967.

[37] Interview with Amar Bentoumi.

the Congress convened in April, many of the opposition leaders were present. Guerrilla leaders who had been in defiant opposition, such as Lt. Allouache, Mohand oul Hadj, Sawt al Arab, Commandant Lakhdar, and Khatib Youssef were all in attendance. Likewise, many of the old GPRA members were there, including Radicals Mehri, Dahlab, and Yazid, Revolutionaries Boussouf, Ben Tobbal, and Krim, and Intellectuals closely associated with the GPRA such as Malek and Ben Yahia. While allowed to speak at the Congress, none of these men emerged with official positions of influence on the Central Committee.

Certain other leaders did not attend the Congress. The Liberals Abbas and Francis and all four of Ben Bella's former prison mates were absent. Ait Ahmed was still in armed opposition in Kabylia; Khider had returned to Algeria earlier in the year to fan the Islamic sentiments of the *Al Qiyam* Association but had decided not to attend the Congress.[38] Bitat was represented by his wife but remained personally aloof, and Boudiaf as usual refused to seek any accommodation with Ben Bella.

What was to be the key issue of the Congress, the struggle for influence between Boumedienne and Ben Bella, had started well before the Congress opened. On March 4, 1964, Ben Bella had taken another step toward trying to weaken Boumedienne by reorganizing the *Etat Major*. The major change was that Colonel Chaabani, who had been responsible for the military region of the Sahara since independence, was named to the *Etat Major*. Boumedienne was later to point to this incident as another attempt to destroy the unity of the army.[39]

Meanwhile the preparatory commission of the Party, and in particular Mohammed Harbi and his colleagues, had drafted an *avant-projet* of a Party program heavily laced with Marxist jargon and tending to play down the Arab-Islamic heritage of Algeria.[40] Shortly before the Party Congress convened, Boumedienne, Bouteflika, and Medeghri reacted to these measures of Ben Bella to

---

[38] Khider had attended a meeting held by Al Qiyam Society at the UGTA headquarters in Algiers on January 5, 1964, where "enemies of Islam" were vigorously attacked. A. Zerdani, and others, writing in *Le Peuple* on January 17, 1964, had condemned this conservative stance. Raymond Vallin (pseud.), "Socialisme Musulman en Algérie, " *L'Asie et l'Afrique*, 1st trimester, 1965, gives other examples of traditionalist assertions in early 1964.

[39] Boumedienne interview, *Al Ahram*, October 8, 1965.

[40] Boumedienne had refused to participate in the drafting of this *avant-projet*, according to *Le Monde,* April 17, 1964.

undermine their influence by offering their resignations in what must have been seen as a thinly veiled threat.[41] Their resignations were not accepted, and in this less than fraternal atmosphere the first Party Congress met on April 16, 1964.

At the Congress, the dispute between Ben Bella and Boumedienne took on ideological overtones as Harbi defended scientific socialism, and the members of the Ulama seemed to support Boumedienne by stressing Algeria's Islamic roots. On the opening day of the Congress a respected leader of the reformist Ulama, Bachir Ibrahimi, vigorously attacked Ben Bella's socialist doctrines in the following terms:

> Our country is slipping more and more toward unavoidable civil war, toward a moral crisis without precedent and insurmountable economic difficulties. Those governing us do not seem to realize that our people wish above all for unity, peace and prosperity, and that the theoretical bases of their action should be drawn from our own Arab-Islamic doctrines, not from foreign ones. . . .[42]

This question of the degree of compatibility of socialism and Islam was apparently vigorously debated during the Congress, and after a denunciation of Ibrahimi by Ben Bella, a deputy, Amar Chibane, defended the President of the Ulama ardently enough to lead to a seeming reconciliation a few days later.[43] A compromise on this issue resulted, to be seen most clearly in the Party Program that emerged from the Congress.

The second disputed issue at the Congress involved the growing strength of the army, Boumedienne's primary source of power. The tension between the ex-*maquisards* and the professional army, which Ben Bella hoped to exploit, came into the open at the Congress. Boumedienne was severely criticized for ignoring the fighters who had won the revolution and for relying instead on officers who had been trained in French military schools. Boumedienne, however, was able to defend himself from this charge. He replied by saying that he would rather work with Algerians no matter how late they

---

[41] Boumedienne interview, *Al Ahram*, October 8, 1965, also *Le Monde*, April 18, 1964, and David Gordon, *The Passing of French Algeria*, p. 147.

[42] Quoted in R. Vallin, "Socialisme Musulman," p. 17. Humbaraci, *Algeria*, p. 237, also quotes this but erroneously dates the statement April 16, 1965, instead of 1964. The Arabic edition of the UGTA's journal replied in an article entitled "The Ulama of Evil," *Ath-thawra wal-'amal*, No. 16, April 29, 1964, p. 20. At the same time Benkhedda issued his "Contribution à l'historique du FLN" in which he warned against accepting "imported" socialist doctrines.

[43] Interview with Amar Chibane.

had joined the revolution than rely on foreigners, an apparent allusion to Ben Bella's Trotskyite advisers.[44]

Another attempt to weaken Boumedienne's monopoly over the armed forces was Harbi's suggestion that popular militias be set up. Harbi's reasoning in putting forward this idea seems to have been that the "progressive" elements within the government needed their own armed power base in order to offset Boumedienne's exclusive control over the means of violence. While the role of popular militias in case of any conflict with Algeria's neighbors might partially justify their existence, the more critical function foreseen for the militia was that of deterring the army from any attempt to take over the government. As was to be expected, Boumedienne was resolutely opposed to the formation of such independent forces. Once again the issue was resolved by a compromise. Militias were to be formed, but their training would be provided by the regular army, and in case of conflict they would be placed under the authority of the ANP. Also, Harbi, the originator of the idea, was not made a member of the Political Bureau as had been expected, although he was named to the Central Committee.

The "Charte d'Alger" and the New Political Bureau

The results of the Congress in reaching compromises over divisive issues are best judged by the *Charte d'Alger* and the composition of the newly named Political Bureau and Central Committee of the FLN. The *Charte d'Alger* contained the most complete doctrinal statement of Algerian socialism to date, falling short of a clear-cut affirmation of scientific socialism by stressing Algeria's Arab-Islamic past.[45] The published "Resolution of General Policy" seemed to reflect the beliefs of both the Islamic socialists and the Marxists, ending with a section on foreign policy to which all could subscribe. The role of the FLN as supreme authority in Algeria was strongly asserted in the Charter, and the army was formally subordinated to the FLN. In addition, popular militias, which Boumedienne

[44] See Humbaraci, *Algeria*, p. 227. Hervé Bourgès, in *L'Algérie à l'épreuve du pouvoir*, p. 112, gives a somewhat different version of Boumedienne's speech.

[45] See the section entitled "Fondements idéologiques de la Révolution algérienne" in the *Charte d'Alger*, Chapter 3, which begins by asserting Algeria's Arab-Islamic nature.

opposed, were to be formed, but the army would be able to control them in time of war.[46]

These doctrinal compromises between the Marxist intellectuals and the army, the latter supported by some of the more religious elements in the political elite, were also reflected in the composition of the new organs of the FLN. Those who seem to have advanced most in influence within the Political Bureau were neither the Intellectuals, represented by Ait al Hocine, Zahouane, and perhaps Benmahjoub, nor the Military men like Boumedienne, Mendjli, Bouteflika, or Medeghri, but rather the ex-guerrilla leaders such as Zbiri, Mohand oul Hadj, Chaabani, and Khatib Youssef. This group of *maquisards* from the interior *willayas* seems to have been the key to Ben Bella's plan to undermine Boumedienne and his allies of the so-called "Oujda group."

In addition to the Military and the Intellectuals, the Political Bureau contained the three still-active members of the first Political Bureau, Ben Bella, Ben Alla, and Mohammedi Said, as well as three influential ministers, Nekkache, Mahsas, and Boumaza. The Political Bureau now consisted of one Radical, four Revolutionaries, nine Military leaders, and three Intellectuals.[47] If the Military remained divided, with the *maquisards* siding with Ben Bella as seems to have been his hope, the Secretary General with the support of the Intellectuals could probably be assured of a majority on the Political Bureau.[48] (See Figure 11.1, Table 11.1 and Appendix H).

The Central Committee of the FLN

The Central Committee was a much more broadly inclusive body than the Political Bureau, consisting of 80 full members and 23 alternate members. Many opposition leaders were members of the Central Committee, although no prominent Liberals or Radicals from the GPRA were included.[49] Nor were men like Ben Tobbal,

---

[46] See the *Charte d'Alger*, Part 3, Chapter 2, Section 13.

[47] See Appendix H for the full membership of the Political Bureau.

[48] It was generally assumed that Ben Bella could count on the support of Ben Alla, Ait al Hocine, Zahouane, Benmahjoub, Mahsas, Boumaza, Zbiri, and perhaps Mohand oul Hadj, Khatib Youssef, and Chaabani. The "Boumedienne clan" was seen as composed of Mendjli, Bouteflika, Medeghri, and Nekkache. As will be seen, these judgments went wrong with respect to Mahsas, Boumaza, Mohammedi, Zbiri, Nekkache, Mohand oul Hadj, Khatib Youssef and Chaabani.

[49] Yazid's absence from the Central Committee after his active role in helping to draft the *Charte d'Alger* was most surprising. Several others on the Preparatory Commission were not made members of the Central Committee—for instance, Temmam and Belhocine.

TABLE 11.1 CHARACTERISTICS OF POLITICAL BUREAU
MEMBERS

	First Political Bureau, 1962	Second Political Bureau, 1964
	Number = 5	n = 17
Average age	42	37
Percentage University-Educated	0%	35%
Member of Top Wartime Elite	100%	59%

Boussouf, Krim, and Boudiaf found at this secondary level of power, even though five other CRUA Revolutionaries were on the Central Committee. Other important Central Committee members were Intellectuals, for instance, Harbi, Zerdani, and Ali Yahia; Military men favorable to Boumedienne, Benmahmoud, Cherif Belkacem, Yahiaoui, Boudjenane, Bencherif, Bensalem, Draia, and Benhamouda; and ex-*willaya* leaders Tayebi, Sawt al Arab, Si Othmane (Benhaddou), and Si Lakhdar.[50]
Many of the members of the Central Committee, however,

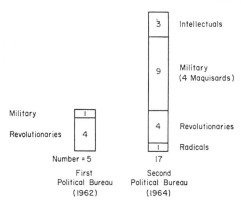

Figure 11.1 Composition of the Two Political Bureaus

[50] A *commission idéologique* was also formed, consisting of members of both the Political Bureau and the Central Committee. The members from the Political Bureau were Ben Bella, Boumedienne, Mendjli, Mahsas, Benmahjoub, and Zahouane. Those from the Central Committee were Harbi, Zerdani, Ali Yahia, Ouzegane, Louanchi, and Hachem.
Hervé Bourgès, *Algérie*, p. 114, has argued that although Boumedienne had been relatively conciliatory with regard to the contents of the *Charte d'Alger*, he was insistent that all his men be named to the Central Committee. This reflects his greater concern for building a power base than for ideology.

were relatively unknown representatives of the regional FLN federations or of various national organizations like the UGTA. As Secretary General of the FLN, Ben Bella seemed to be trying to establish relations inside the Central Committee with new men whose claims to power were less and who might be more easily controlled than the coopted opposition leaders who had already made their desires for power sufficiently clear. In short, Ben Bella appears to have been trying to balance off the influence of the army by reintegrating previously hostile elements into the FLN leadership, while at the same time searching out virtually unknown subelites to bolster his own unstable position as head of the Party. The main losers of the FLN Party Congress were most obviously the Liberals, Radicals, and Revolutionaries who had played important roles during the war for independence.

The Party Congress, then, can be seen as achieving only a limited success at overcoming the divisions within the elite. Of the opposition, only those Military elements who had resorted to arms to oppose Ben Bella were now brought back into power. And this was largely done, it seems, to balance the influence of Boumedienne and the army. Once again, some of the most moderate Liberals and Radicals were excluded. The Revolutionaries, whose highly individualistic claims to power were virtually impossible to reconcile, were also excluded by their ex-colleague Ben Bella. Thus as Algeria entered its third year since the cease-fire of March 1962, the political elite was already somewhat less heterogeneous than it had been earlier, with Ben Bella managing to retain his position by playing off Intellectuals, ex-guerrilla leaders and the professional Military men against each other.[51] How long this game could last was unclear, but some future challenges to his authority could easily be predicted.

The Crisis of Summer 1964

The paradox for Ben Bella of having to rely upon the army to remain in power while at the same time seeking to undermine Boumedienne's influence became painfully clear in the summer of 1964. By late May, terrorist attacks in the countryside were occur-

---

[51] Tahar Zbiri, in *El Djeich*, No. 30, October-November, 1965, p. 9, said that Ben Bella ". . . constantly sought to create clans, opposing one to the other, so that when one clan was destroyed, he would create a new one to destroy those remaining."

ring with sufficient frequency that Ben Bella could speak of a "counter revolution." Earlier opponents, such as Ait Ahmed in Kabylia, were still active, and new threats were beginning to appear in other regions. An early reaction to these challenges was to reorganize the army. Ben Bella, on May 31, 1964, removed Chaabani, now a member of the Political Bureau, as head of the fourth military region of the south. A few days later a government decree officially named the commanders of all five military regions.[52] A further military measure to oppose armed threats to the regime was proposed in mid-June by Mohammed Harbi, the editor of *Révolution Africaine,* in a vigorous article calling for the formation of popular militias.[53]

The incipient crisis which had stimulated these military measures reached its peak during July. On June 30 Chaabani's exclusion from the Political Bureau was announced. Ben Bella's attempt to use Chaabani against Boumedienne had failed, and Chaabani retreated to the south to form another center of armed opposition to Ben Bella's endangered regime. The following day Mohammed Khider announced from exile that all opposition groups were uniting against Ben Bella, and a few days later he declared that FLN funds in his name deposited in Swiss banks would be made available to the regrouped opposition, the CNDR.[54]

On July 4, the Central Committee of the FLN expelled five of its members, asked that eleven deputies be removed from office,[55] excluded Boudiaf, Ait Ahmed, Khider, Hassani, and Chaabani from the FLN, and asked Ben Bella to take special powers to deal with the crisis. Numerous arrests, particularly of Liberals and those suspected of Islamist or pro-Khider sympathies, followed shortly. Ferhat Abbas

---

[52] Those named as regional military commanders were Said Abid, Chadli Bendjedid, Salah Soufi, Amar Mellah, and Belhouchet.

[53] See *Révolution Africaine,* June 3, 1964. These militias were eventually formed under the direction of Mahmoud Guennez, an officer who had served under Boumedienne in Tunisia.

[54] On July 6, Hassani announced that the PRS and the FFS had formed the CNDR (*Comité National pour la Défense de la Révolution*), which included as members Ben Ahmed (Si Moussa), Boudiaf, Ait Ahmed, Hassani, and Chaabani. Two days earlier *Révolution Africaine,* July 14, 1964, p. 6, said that ". . . either the revolution will defend itself by using revolutionary terror or the revolution will hesitate and be lost. . . . We are not involved in a juridical debate—he who renounces the use of violence, renounces revolution."

[55] The eleven deputies were Dhilès, Laadjel, Saci, Mezhoudi, Ali Cherif, Ahmed Benbrahim, Amar Bentoumi, Abdelkader Bentoumi, Cheikh Kheirredine, Amar Sakhri, and Moussa Hassani. The five Central Committee members expelled were Djerabi, Laadjal, Saci, Abadou, and Chenoufi.

and Abderrahmane Farès were put under house arrest, as were ex-ministers Khobzi and Bentoumi. Commander Azzedine and the deputies Boualem Oussedik and Mezhoudi were also imprisoned.[56] In the midst of this crisis the Minister of the Interior Ahmed Medeghri, one of Boumedienne's closest allies, announced his resignation.[57] His decision had doubtless been prompted by a move made by Ben Bella which required all prefects to report directly to the President rather than to the Minister of the Interior.[58]

Meanwhile, as Ben Bella sought to remove Boumedienne's allies from power, the army was successfully destroying the various centers of resistance to the regime. Chaabani was captured on July 8 and was executed a few days later in one of the rare uses of capital punishment. The leader of the armed opposition in western Algeria, Mohammed Ben Ahmed (Si Moussa) was arrested on the same day that Ben Bella announced the formation of popular militias. A few days later Ben Bella took over the critically important functions of the Minister of the Interior. Two more clashes with Boumedienne's allies occurred in late July as Bouteflika's *chef de cabinet* was arrested and Ahmed Kaid resigned as Minister of Tourism.[59]

As the summer crisis came to an end during August, the contest for influence between Ben Bella and the army continued.[60] A significant event which indicated that Boumedienne still had considerable power took place in September when Harbi was dropped as editor of *Révolution Africaine*. Ouzegane, who replaced him,

---

[56] Before his imprisonment, Mezhoudi had largely withdrawn from politics, but on the night of his arrest he attended a formal reception at Ben Bella's invitation. In the presence of ambassadors and other dignitaries, Ben Bella called Mezhoudi aside and asked him to take a walk with him in the gardens. When they were out of sight of the guests, Ben Bella said that he had heard that Mezhoudi was plotting against him. Mezhoudi denied this and argued that his views were known since he openly expressed them in the National Assembly. Ben Bella called him a liar and threatened to have him arrested. Mezhoudi laughed and reminded him that his own constitution guaranteed parliamentary immunity. At that, Ben Bella called out, "Arrest him!," and from behind the bushes security officers appeared and led Mezhoudi off to prison. (Interview with Brahim Mezhoudi.)

[57] Mezhoudi, who was arrested at this time, claimed that Medeghri and Draia had both refused Ben Bella's orders to arrest him. (Interview with Brahim Mezhoudi.)

[58] See David Gordon, *French Algeria*, p. 151.

[59] Some arrests continued, most notably that of Ahmed Taleb.

[60] At about the same time, on July 24, an Egyptian ship carrying arms to Algeria exploded in the Port of Annaba. Some Algerians have said that the arms were destined for Ben Bella's "popular militias" and that the ship was secretly blown up on orders from the army.

immediately reaffirmed Algeria's Islamic nature and stressed the important strides made in constructing new mosques in the countryside. Harbi was nonetheless elected to the second National Assembly on September 20.[61] Finally, on October 17, the opposition to the regime was badly weakened by the army's arrest of Ait Ahmed. Thus at the end of Algeria's third serious crisis since independence Ben Bella was still in power, but his dependence on Boumedienne was increasingly clear.

Ben Bella's Third Government

Ben Bella had survived a severe threat to his authority in the summer of 1964, but his own position was still shaky. On December 2, he acted to increase his influence by naming a new government. Ben Bella's third cabinet was somewhat larger than the previous one, primarily because three powerful ministries—National Orientation, National Economy, and Social Affairs—were divided into smaller ones.

Four ministers from the previous government were no longer in the cabinet, namely the Liberals Boumendjel and al Madani, and Medeghri and Kaid, allies of Boumedienne who had resigned earlier. Cherif Belkacem, another colleague of Boumedienne, was relieved of some of his functions but remained Minister of Education, Boumaza suffered a similar trimming down of his authority but was left with the Ministry of Industry and Energy. Most important, Ben Bella added to his own duties as President those of Minister of Finance, Information, and Interior. Thus three of the most essential ministries came under his direct control. (See Appendix G.)

Seven new ministers were added to Ben Bella's third cabinet, namely, Cherif for Arab Affairs, Bedjaoui for Justice, Dellici for Commerce, Heddam for Habous (religious foundations), Ghozali for Public Works, Boudissa for Work, and Amrani for Administrative Reform. These new recruits had occupied no top elite positions during the revolution, but with a few exceptions they were competent, technically trained men who could qualify more as intellectuals than as experienced politicians. Heddam, Dellici, and Bedjaoui, for example, were university-educated men. The cabinet members as a whole were somewhat younger than their predecessors;

---

[61] The second National Assembly had 54 new members, most of whom were unknown. The most important of the new deputies were Ait al Hocine, Mohand oul Hadj, Hadj Smain, and Harbi.

their average age was 39 while that of the second cabinet was 42. There were no longer any Liberals in the cabinet, though there were two Radicals, four Revolutionaries, four Military, and nine Intellectuals. Figure 11.2 and Table 11.2 trace the changes in the

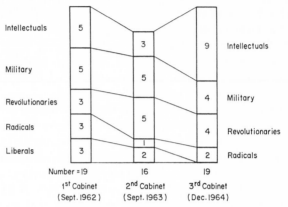

Figure 11.2   Composition of Ben Bella's Three Governments

TABLE 11.2   CHARACTERISTICS OF MINISTERS IN THREE BEN BELLA GOVERNMENTS

	First Cabinet (September 1962)	Second Cabinet (September 1963)	Third Cabinet (December 1964)
Average age	39	42	39
University-educated	58%	44%	42%
Liberal professions	42%	25%	26%
Born in Oran region	32%	38%	37%
Kabyles	21%	25%	16%
Born in village or town	74%	63%	58%
Belong to top revolutionary elite	68%	56%	42%
	Number = 19	n = 16	n = 19

composition of the three Ben Bella governments and illustrate both the rise of the secondary elite and the growing homogeneity in the political background of the cabinet members. In Ben Bella's first cabinet, for example, all five types of Algerian politicians had been included in approximately equal numbers. By Ben Bella's third cabinet, half of the ministers were Intellectuals, men relatively new to politics who shared many common experiences in the course of their political training.

The reduction in the number of ministers from the old nationalist elite, and especially the Liberals and Radicals, is apparent from Figure 11.2 and Table 11.2. This, in part, accounts for the decline in the level of education and in the number of men from liberal professions from the first to third government. The corresponding rise in the influence of the Intellectuals has not yet compensated, in terms of the level of education, for the exclusion of the old elite. But the influx of Intellectuals into this last cabinet seems to indicate that Ben Bella, having tried to limit the influence of the Military on several occasions, was now attempting to balance their influence by that of the less politicized Intellectuals.

Following the formation of his third government, Ben Bella, who now directly controlled virtually the entire administrative apparatus of the country, seemed both less threatened by opposition and less dependent on the army. During December and January several noteworthy opponents of the regime, particularly Bitat and Hassani, abandoned their open hostility to Ben Bella.[62] Little open political activity was in evidence during the next few months, as Ben Bella traveled about the country with some regularity. Numerous appointments were made to civilian positions, new ambassadors were named, and the image of a more stable political system began to emerge.[63]

In April several political prisoners, particularly Ait Ahmed and Si Moussa, were brought to trial, condemned to death, and then had their sentences commuted by Ben Bella. Behind this façade of order and benevolence, however, Ben Bella's struggle with the Military continued. Preparations were under way for the holding of the Afro-Asian Conference in July, and Ben Bella seemed determined to play the starring role. His foreign minister and ally of Boumedienne, Abdelaziz Bouteflika, seems to have resented Ben Bella's assumption of many of his duties, and rumors of his impending resignation were circulated.

---

[62] At this same time Ben Bella's emissaries were contacting prisoners such as Bentoumi and offering to let them return to power if they would help oppose Boumedienne. Bitat, only two months earlier, had spoken of the large degree of opposition to Ben Bella within the FLN. See *Le Monde*, October 7, 1964, p. 5.

[63] In March 1965, the organization of the army underwent a few changes with the naming of Ahmed Draia to head the *Corps National de Sécurité* (CNS) and with the replacement of Amar Mellah, the head of the fourth military region, by Commandant Abdelghani. The identity of the new commandant is unclear, however, and there is reason to think that this name has been incorrectly reported.

During early June 1965, Ben Bella announced several new initiatives that reinforced the image of growing stability and self-assurance. First, it was announced by the Political Bureau that the newspaper *Alger Républicain,* previously the organ of the Algerian Communist Party, would be fused with *Le Peuple* to form a new Party newspaper. A few days later many of those arrested during the crisis of the previous summer, such as Abbas, Farès, Bentoumi, Tayebi, Oussedik, and Mezhoudi, were released from prison. On June 15, the Kabyle opposition group, the FFS, announced that an agreement had been signed between it and the government putting an end to their conflicts. The reappearance of the imprisoned Ait Ahmed as the new Foreign Minister replacing Bouteflika was anticipated by some.

The following day, during a visit to Oran, Ben Bella proclaimed optimistically that, "In Algeria there is a socialist revolution, a regime and leaders who are more unified than ever, more decided than ever to oppose plots from any quarter. . . ." Then, three days later, on June 19, 1965, Ben Bella was removed from power in a well-planned and virtually bloodless coup. The new ruler of Algeria, to the surprise of very few, was Houari Boumedienne.

Conclusion

Ben Bella's efforts to create authoritative structures of government out of a divided political elite ended in failure. And yet major steps had been taken to change the composition of the political elite. Ben Bella had alternately relied on exclusion and cooptation to secure his own position at the top of the structures of influence, but within a short time these maneuvers succeeded in alienating most of the old nationalist elite, as well as in creating deep suspicions concerning Ben Bella's motives among his new allies.

Structural changes, and in particular the concentration of power and the reliance on less politicized intellectuals for support, had been Ben Bella's solution to the problem of elite diversity and conflict. But just as it had proved difficult to develop a political process to integrate the elite, so also it was impossible to achieve such integration by changing the structures of power.

Neither the reduction in the heterogeneity of the original ruling elite nor the recruitment of new elements from the secondary elite had produced a small, homogeneous coalition capable of remaining in power. A solution to the crisis of authority caused by the diversity in the backgrounds and formation of Algerian political leaders still had not been found. The autonomous structures of the period of the revolution had been rejected, accommodation had failed, and Ben Bella's efforts to concentrate power had likewise not succeeded. How Algeria's new President, Houari Boumedienne, might solve these same problems was unknown in June 1965, but there was no reason to believe that the task of creating a governing elite would be an easy one.

12
The Limits of Collegiality: Boumedienne in Power

When Houari Boumedienne came to power in June 1965, a question often asked was how this change in ruling coalition would be reflected in political practices and in policy. To answer this query it was necessary to know who Algeria's new leaders really were, but weeks passed before the composition of the Council of the Revolution, of the Council of Ministers, and of the Party leadership was announced. Finally it became clear that power was shared by the professional Military officers, the *maquisards,* and the Intellectuals, all of whom had entered politics only after the revolution had begun. Few familiar names from the 1940s or 1950s were found among these new power-holders.

While the political elite after Ben Bella's fall was somewhat more homogeneous than it had been earlier, there were still several apparent axes of conflict dividing the new leaders of Algeria. As Ben Bella had done in 1962, Boumedienne came to power with rather broad support, including that of many former opponents. This diversity within the ruling group had both the advantage of insuring relative stability for some time and the disadvantage of virtually paralyzing decision-making.

To avoid the kind of alienation of the top elite from the political process that had been produced by Ben Bella's concentration of power, the new regime opted for collegial decision-making and the abolition of the "cult of personality." With time, however, these practices degenerated into a tacit recognition of autonomy for the major subgroups within the elite. The price of stability thus became something close to stagnation, particularly with regard to the political life of the country. In total contrast to Ben Bella's rule, top elite relations were relatively orderly under Boumedienne, but the secondary elite, and in particular the trade union and the students, were persistent sources of trouble.

Whereas the capacity of Ben Bella's regime to adopt new policies was relatively high, it had proved difficult to implement effectively many of the new programs. Boumedienne's coalition was rarely able to adopt new policies, but implementation was likely for the few efforts that did gain sufficient elite backing. One major structural political reform, the communal elections of February 1967, illustrated both the limits and possibilities of decision-making in the Boumedienne regime. But finally, the pressures to reduce the size of the existing coalition grew as conflict became increasingly apparent, and the political elite went through one more alteration in late 1967. A more homogeneous elite emerged from this crisis, but its capacity to bring both order and progress to Algeria was still uncertain during 1968. As efforts to create an effective political party progressed, tensions seemed to be developing within the core leadership group over the respective roles of the State and the Party. Questions of authority still plagued the Algerian leaders.

The Coup of June 19, 1965

The coup which deposed the prominent world statesman Ahmed Ben Bella in favor of the mysterious and unknown Colonel Boumedienne caught nearly all observers by surprise. Ben Bella, it had seemed, was at the pinnacle of his career, and the impending Afro-Asian Conference to be held in Algiers promised to boost his international renown. In retrospect, many thought that the Military acted when it did precisely to avoid the possibility that Ben Bella would increase his prestige by cultivating contacts with his third-world guests.

The coup itself was carried out in the early morning of June 19, 1965, with remarkable ease.[1] The futility of Ben Bella's attempts to divide the army by naming Tahar Zbiri as *chef d'Etat Major* in October 1963 and by creating popular militias in summer 1964 was readily seen when Zbiri himself helped arrest Ben Bella, and the head of the militia quickly sided with Boumedienne. The ex-*willaya* leaders, the third element in Ben Bella's strategy to counterbalance the army's influence, also joined forces against the President.

Resistance to the coup among the political elite was so slight that only two members of the Political Bureau, Ben Alla and Nekkache, were immediately arrested along with Ben Bella, as was one other minister, Abderrahmane Cherif. Popular demonstrations in favor of the supposedly charismatic Ben Bella were virtually nonexistent apart from the actions of some students in the capital. The trade union, the UGTA, initially greeted the coup with some reserve, expressing its satisfaction with the end of "personal power" but hoping that "self-management" and union autonomy would be respected.[2] The only expressions of organized opposition to Boumedienne came from the leaders of the *Amicale* of Algerian workers in France and from the Parisian section of the student union (UNEA). By contrast, the Algerian Association of Ulama enthusiastically greeted Ben Bella's downfall.[3]

The reaction of Ben Bella's opponents, particularly the Revolutionaries, to news of his overthrow was almost predictable. Khider expressed satisfaction and said that he would return to Algeria if the new government would adopt his ideas. Boudiaf remained skeptical, claiming that the entire Ben Bella system had to go, not just a single man. Boussouf in Geneva expressed his approval of the coup and his confidence in Boumedienne.[4] Bitat returned to Algiers and announced his intention to "resume his responsibilities."

The virtual unanimity of the political elite's condemnation of Ben Bella after the coup revealed the low degree of loyalty which

---

[1] Arslan Humbaraci, in *Algeria: A Revolution that Failed*, Chapter 10, gives a detailed account of the coup.

[2] See the UGTA's response to the coup in *Révolution Africaine*, No. 128, July 10, 1965, p. 4.

[3] Mohammedi Said in a letter to *Révolution Africaine*, published in the July 17, 1965 issue, page 6, claimed that all the Ulama in Algeria supported the coup. On May 29, 1965, *Révolution Africaine*, No. 122, p. 3, had run an article honoring the past president of the Ulama, Bachir Ibrahimi, who had just died.

[4] Boussouf gave his evaluation of the coup in an interview to the *Gazette de Lausanne*, June 21, 1965.

Ben Bella had been able to inspire. Elite alienation was widespread, even among those who were often considered his close supporters. Attacks on Ben Bella took several forms, the most prominent of which focused on the political structures he had created, his political practices, his beliefs and his background.[5]

Perhaps the most frequent criticism was aimed at Ben Bella's excessive concentration of power in his own hands, resulting in a "cult of personality" which eliminated many "real militants." A second common reason for dissatisfaction with the deposed President alluded to Ben Bella's political behavior. Many disliked his improvisation and his demagogy, his failure to consult others when policies were made, and his unwillingness to respect even his own laws if they restrained his ambitions. A deputy to the National Assembly who had been arrested by Ben Bella expressed the opinion of many of his colleagues when he said:

Ben Bella was neither particularly bright nor stupid. He did, however, seem to be sincere at first, but soon he began to exceed all limits. Even the law, including ones he made, couldn't stop him. Boumedienne and his team played an essentially negative role. They didn't accept Ben Bella's caprices but they didn't do anything to stop him either.[6]

A number of other members of the elite felt Ben Bella was too "adventuresome," was not a "real Muslim," was too close to "foreign advisers," or was "false" and hypocritical in the way he treated both friends and enemies. A few pointed to his background as a reason for their alienation, stressing that he was not an "old time militant," that "his contribution to the revolution had been zero," and that he never fought within Algeria and could thus never understand the desires of the masses.

Algeria's new President, Houari Boumedienne, on several occasions explained the basis of his dissatisfaction with Ben Bella.[7] Boumedienne believed that much of Ben Bella's behavior was a result of his "complex of not having effectively participated in the fight for liberation." Because of this, Ben Bella was, among other things, intolerant of criticism from others. Boumedienne also stressed that,

---

[5] The comments referred to here are derived from interviews with numerous members of the political elite.

[6] Interview with Mezhoudi.

[7] In particular, see Boumedienne's interview with *Al Ahram*, October 8, 1965, reprinted in *Révolution Africaine*, November 6–13, 1965; his speech of July 5, 1965; and his declaration on June 19, 1965.

. . . we soon discovered that because of his formation, his mentality and his preferences, he belonged to the "school of careerists" and not that of revolutionaries. After all, didn't he grow up in a setting favorable to political maneuvering within the traditional parties which preceded the Revolution, the very parties which never had the least success? [8]

Boumedienne also criticized Ben Bella for being too open to foreign influences, for squandering scarce resources, for his improvisation, for his "liquidation of revolutionary cadres," and for his excessive desire for power. A close collaborator of Boumedienne, Cherif Belkacem, added to this list of failings Ben Bella's ideological confusion, exemplified by his "five socialisms": socialiasm à la Castro, specifically Algerian socialism, scientific socialism, Arab-Islamic socialism, and "I accept Marxist economic analysis, I reject materialism. . . ." [9]

The early declarations of Boumedienne indicated that Algeria's goals and policies would not be radically changed but that political practices and political structures might be profoundly altered. Emphasis was placed on the need for order, stability, planning, efficiency, legality, economic development, hard work, the reinforcing of state authority, consultation, and technical competence as a criterion for recruitment.[10] Finally, Boumedienne declared that verbal socialism and the cult of personality were to be banished and that the new regime should be judged by its acts, not by its rhetoric.

The new political structures formed after Ben Bella's overthrow differed somewhat both in personnel and in functions from those which had been created during the first three years of Algerian independence. In general there was a simplification of political structures, a greater degree of functional specificity for each institution, and a move toward greater homogeneity within the political elite. Despite several overtures on the part of both Boumedienne and members of the older nationalist elite, it is striking that virtually none of the Liberals, Radicals, or Revolutionaries who had been expelled from positions of influence by Ben Bella were reintegrated into the new political elite.[11]

---

[8] *Al Ahram* interview, p. 11.

[9] *Révolution Africaine,* October 23, 1965.

[10] These terms are selected from Boumedienne's speeches of June 19, 1965, July 7, and July 12, 1965, all reprinted in *Actualités et Documents,* July 1965.

[11] See *Jeune Afrique,* July 11, 1965 on contacts with Boussouf, and *L'Observateur du Moyen Orient et de l'Afrique,* October 29, 1965, on a possible role for Boumendjel.

The Council of the Revolution

The first institution to become known after the coup was the Council of the Revolution. The Council was to replace such institutions as the National Assembly, which had been suspended along with the constitution, and the Political Bureau of the FLN, which had been disbanded. The Council was intended to function as the "supreme instance of the Revolution" until a new constitution might redefine structures of authority.[12]

The composition of the Council of the Revolution was not revealed until July 5, more than two weeks after the coup. Of the twenty-six members of the Council, only two had never occupied military roles during the revolution. Also, two of those who had been actively engaged in military operations during the war had also participated prominently in the prerevolutionary political process, thereby qualifying as Revolutionaries. In short, the Council consisted of one Radical, three Revolutionaries, and twenty-two Military. These latter were almost equally divided into one group which had led the interior *willayas* and a second one consisting of professionally trained officers, some of them graduates of French officer schools.

Ten of the seventeen original members of the defunct Political Bureau became members of the Council of the Revolution. Intellectuals like Zahouane and Ait al Hocine were excluded, as was Omar Benmahjoub. All survivors who had commanded interior *willayas* at the end of the war were made members of the Council.[13] Military men on the General Staff of the ANP and those in charge of the gendarmerie, the security police (CNS), and the officers' school at Cherchell were likewise included, as were the commanders of the five military regions.[14] The Secretary General of the Ministry of Defense, Commandant Abdelkader Moulay (Chabou) was made a member of the Council, and two ministers without military backgrounds who had been on the Political Bureau, Boumaza and Mahsas, were also included despite recent criticisms of their actions

[12] Deputies to the National Assembly, even though they never met after the coup, still received salaries and various privileges of their office in 1967.

[13] Zbiri for *willaya* 1, Sawt al Arab (Boubnider) and Mohammed Tayebi for 2, Mohand oul Hadj for 3, Khatib Youssef for 4, and Bouhadjer Benhaddou (Si Othmane) for 5.

[14] Said Abid, 1st military region; Chadli Bendjedid, 2d military region; Salah Soufi, 3rd military region; Mohammed Ben Ahmed, 4th military region; Abdallah Belhouchet, 5th military region.

as heads of the two key ministries of Industry and Agriculture.[15]

The most obvious lines of cleavage in the Council of the Revolution, on the basis of the political background of the members, were those dividing the professional Military and the ministers close to Boumedienne from the ex-*willaya* leaders and the "civilian" ministers. The group closest to Boumedienne, often referred to as the "Oujda group" because of the common training received by several of these men during the revolution at the *Etat Major de l'Ouest* at Oujda in Morocco, consisted of Medeghri, Bouteflika, Mendjli, Kaid, and Cherif Belkacem. The ex-*willaya* leaders, some of whom had expressed deep hostility to the Boumedienne clan in the past, consisted primarily of Zbiri, Mohand oul Hadj, Boubnider, Khatib Youssef, Si Othmane (Benhaddou), and Si Moussa (Mohammed Ben Ahmed).[16] The civilian ministers Boumaza and Mahsas had been thought to be close to Ben Bella, and many observers found them the most unlikely participants in the new coalition. Table 12.1 (page 244) shows the composition of the Council of the Revolution and the backgrounds of its members.

The remarkable fact about the new Council of the Revolution was that it included representatives of virtually all tendencies within the Military. Men who had once been extremely hostile to each other—interior guerrilla leaders versus the wartime *Etat Major,* for example—were able to agree on the need for removing Ben Bella from power. Whether or not they would be able to work together to attack the many problems awaiting solution was a different matter. Boumedienne, by coordinating the efforts of the various factions within the army in preparation for the coup, had proved himself an able mediator. His answer now to the question of how to overcome the differences in outlook and ambition of the members of the Council of the Revolution was to propose collective decision-making and to put an end to the concentrated power structure formed by Ben Bella.

[15] Gérard Chaliand, "De Ben Bella à Boumedienne," *Partisans,* November 1965, argues that Mahsas and Boumaza had been criticized for their actions as ministers just before the coup. He correctly predicted that they would not last long in the cabinet. *Jeune Afrique,* July 4, 1965, pp. 16–17, says that before the coup Mahsas and Boumaza had criticized Ben Bella's *pouvoir personnel* as being responsible for the bad economic situation and that in reply Ben Bella defended himself by saying that it was the economic crisis which required the concentration of power in his hands.

[16] The position of Mohammed Tayebi, who had often expressed hostility in the past to Ben Bella, was more ambiguous, but he generally seemed to be rather close to Boumedienne.

The heavy representation of the Military on the Council of the Revolution indicated that the primary function of the Council would be to insure order and security by including nearly all individuals with influence inside the armed forces. Maintaining the unity of the army would certainly be a major guarantee that the new regime would be more stable and resistant to opposition than Ben Bella had been. Since the army was by far the strongest and best organized force within Algeria, it must have been clear to Boumedienne and his close allies that the greatest danger to the regime might be a second coup from within the army. The logical leaders of such a move would be those ex-*willaya* commanders who on numerous previous occasions had indicated their dislike and distrust of the professional army officers around Boumedienne.[17]

Boumedienne's First Government

Whatever the new functions of the Council of the Revolution, it seemed clear that these men could do little alone other than organize and train the well-equipped armed forces of Algeria and determine the general outlines and orientations of Algerian domestic and foreign policy. The administrative tasks of the government were to be left to the members of the Council of Ministers named on July 10. Boumedienne, in a speech on July 12, defined the somewhat indirect links between the Council of the Revolution and the ministers in these terms: "Ministers will be responsible to the Council of Ministers which will judge them on their work, it being understood that a minister should carry out decisions made by superior authorities [e.g., the Council of the Revolution]. . . ." [18]

Following a practice already developed under Ben Bella, a number of key ministries were headed by men who also held positions within the highest authoritative institution, the Political Bureau in 1964 and the Council of the Revolution in 1965. The President of the Council of the Revolution was also President of the Council of Ministers. The important Ministries of Defense, Interior, Foreign Affairs, Information, Finance and Agriculture were also presided

(continued on page 246)

[17] Two influential French-trained officers not included on the Council of the Revolution were Mohammed Zerguini and Slimane Hoffmann, the latter a St. Cyr–educated commander of the tank batallions. Along with Chabou, these officers were influential professional soldiers.

[18] Boumedienne speech of July 2, 1965, reprinted in *Actualités et Documents*, July 1967, p. 20.

TABLE 12.1 COMPOSITION OF THE COUNCIL OF THE REVOLUTION, JULY 1965

	Date of Birth[1]	Political Positions under Ben Bella						Revolutionary Role				Active Member 1968
		PB	CC	Min.	Dep.	Op.	Mil.	TE	Wil.	EMG	Ouj.	
Houari Boumedienne	1932	□	□	□	□			□	□		□	Yes
Ahmed Medeghri	1934	□	□	□	□			□			□	Yes
Abdelaziz Bouteflika	1937	□	□	□	□						□	?
Ali Mendjli	1922	□	□		□						□	Yes
Ahmed Kaid	1927		□	□	□					□	□	Yes
Cherif Belkacem	1933	□	□	□	□	□					□	Yes
Bachir Boumaza	1927	□	□	□	□	□		□				No
Ahmed Mahsas	1923	□	□		□							No
Tahar Zbiri	1930	□	□		□		□	□	□	□		No
Mohammedi Said	1912	□	□	□		□			□			?
Mohand oul Hadj	1910	□	□			□			□			No
Khatib Youssef	1935		□			□			□	□		No
Mohammed Tayebi	1918		□		□	□			□			Yes
Salah Boubnider	1927		□		□	□			□			No
Bouhadjer Benhaddou			□		□	□			□			?
Mohammed Yahiaoui			□		□				□			Yes
Ahmed Boudjenane	1921		□				□					Dead
Ahmed Bencherif	1927		□				□		□			Yes
Ahmed Draia			□				□					Yes
Abderrahmane Bensalem			□				□					Yes
Said Abid	1933						□					Dead

		Yes
Chadli Bendjedid	1930	Yes
Abdallah Belhouchet	1927	Yes
Abdelkader Moulay (Chabou)	1927	Yes
Mohammed Ben Ahmed	1928	?
Salah Soufi		

¹ Average date of birth is 1927.

KEY   PB   1st or 2nd Political Bureau
      CC   Central Committee
      Min. Minister under Ben Bella
      Dep. Deputy, 1st or 2nd Assembly
      Op. Opposed Ben Bella in some overt way

      Mil. Held military position under Ben Bella
      TE   Top elite
      Wil. Led a *willaya* during war
      EMG Member of *Etat Major Général* of ALN during war
      Ouj. Part of "Oujda group"

over by members of the Council of the Revolution. The remaining fourteen ministers, however, were not members of the Council of the Revolution, but rather were either carry-overs from Ben Bella's cabinet (five cases), new recruits (seven cases), or, in one case, a minister in an early Ben Bella government who had left in 1963. Of the ministers who were also on the Council of the Revolution, three were Military men, two Revolutionaries, and one Radical. Of those who had previously been ministers, all five were Intellectuals, generally with technical competence. Of the newly recruited ministers, four were technically trained Intellectuals, two were more theoretically inclined leftist Intellectuals with links to the trade unions, and two were young Military officers. The one Minister from Ben Bella's first cabinet was a Revolutionary with the unusual credentials of being the only *chef historique* of the revolution to retain even symbolic power as Minister of State. Compared to earlier cabinets, Boumedienne's government was more dominated by Intellectuals and less so by men who had been deeply involved in prerevolutionary nationalist movement. Few ministers other than some of the Military men and the Intellectuals Zerdani and Ali Yahia, both of whom were close to the UGTA, had any basis of support outside the elite.

Boumedienne's first cabinet was also, on the average, composed of younger, better educated men than had been found in previous governments. The newly appointed ministers contrasted sharply with those who had already served as ministers under Ben Bella. The experienced ministers were, in comparison to the new recruits, slightly older, likely to come from Oran (Boumedienne's appointees were primarily from Constantine), less likely to have received university education, and more likely to have held a top political position during the war for independence. The new ministers by their background and education seemed to reflect the regime's stress on technical competence, economic development, and efficiency. Despite Boumedienne's own strong Arab-Islamic training, his ministers were nearly all educated in French schools and were quite cosmopolitan. Table 12.2 summarizes the available information on the members of Boumedienne's first cabinet.

Collegial Decision-Making?

Soon after the coup which removed Ben Bella from power, Boumedienne made it clear that decentralization and granting of

	Ministry	Region of Birth	Date of Birth	Level of Education	Min.	BB Gov. Role				Rev. Role	
						CC	BP	Dep.	Op.	TE	Mil.
H. Boumedienne	President and Defense	Const.	1932	Univ.	□	□	□			□	□
R. Bitat [1]	State	Const.	1926	Elem.	□		□			□	
A. Medeghri	Interior	Oran	1934	Univ.	□	□	□	□	□		
A. Bouteflika	Foreign Affairs	Oran	1937	Sec.	□	□	□	□	□		
M. Bedjaoui	Justice	Oran	1929	Univ.	□						
B. Boumaza [1]	Information	Const.	1927	Sec.	□	□	□	□			□
A. Mahsas [1]	Agriculture	Algiers	1923	Sec.	□	□	□	□	□	□	□
A. Taleb	Education	Const.	1932	Univ.						□	
B. Benhamouda	War Veterans	Const.	1929	Univ.	□	□		□			□
A. Kaid [1]	Finance	Oran	1927	Sec.	□	□		□	□	□	□
N. Dellici	Commerce	Algiers	1928	Univ.	□						
B. Abdesselam	Industry	Const.	1928	Univ.	□						
L. Saadouni	Habous	Const.	1923	Univ.	□						
M. Hadj Smain [1]	Reconstruction	Const.	1921	Sec.	□	□		□			
A. Ali Yahia [1]	Public Works	Kabylia		Univ.	□	□		□			
T. Heddam	Health	Oran	1921	Univ.		□		□			
A. Zerdani [1]	Work	Const.	1934	Sec.		□		□			
A. Bennahmoud	Youth-Sports	Const.	1929	Univ.		□					
A. Zaibek	Posts-Telecomm.	Algiers	1923	Univ.	□						
A. Maaoui	Tourism			Univ.	□						

KEY

BB Gov. Role	Ben Bella Government Role
Rev. Role	Revolutionary Role
Min.	Minister
CC	Central Committee
PB	Political Bureau
Dep.	Deputy
Op.	Opposition, expressed overtly
TE	Top Elite

[1] By the end of 1968 this minister had changed his position in some way. By late 1966, Bitat had become Minister of Transport, Boumaza, Mahsas, and Hadj Smain entered opposition abroad, Ali Yahia became Minister of Agriculture. In 1968 Zerdani and Ali Yahia were replaced by two new ministers, Mazouzi and Tayebi. Also, Kaid exchanged positions with Cherif Belkacem, the head of the FLN.

greater authority to ministers and prefects would be part of the government's new policy. On July 12 decrees were issued abolishing the highly centralized structures of the Ben Bella period whereby the ministers of Finance, Information, and Interior had come under the direct control of the President. A month later a new set of decrees defined the patterns of organization of the ministries.

In the Council of Ministers, as in the Council of the Revolution, it seemed as if a more collegial system of decision-making was the approved model. Collegiality, however, while perhaps the best guarantee against elite disaffection, might have the inevitable drawback of hindering any decision-making at all by requiring a degree of consensus on goals and policies that did not yet exist. The deviations from collegiality, namely a return to a more centralized structure or a trend toward more autonomy for the various parts of the political system, were well known to Algerian political leaders from earlier experience. Excessive centralization, after all, had been a major cause of the coup which had brought these men to power. Consequently it would be difficult to move immediately in that direction without risking a second use of force. Virtual autonomy of various units within the system seemed a more plausible arrangement if collegial decision-making should fail. The danger in this case, however, was that decisions made by relatively autonomous ministers, Party leaders, or regional military commanders could easily conflict with one another.

The political choices facing the new regime in summer 1965 did not seem particularly attractive. Increased centralization could lead to a second use of violence by dissident elite members, collegiality could easily become synonymous with stagnation unless consensus could be created, and autonomy ran the risk of uncoordinated policies leading to serious conflicts over the use of scarce resources.

Faced with these dilemmas, the new Algerian political elite seemed to opt for a collegial system which allowed considerable autonomy for the army and for the ministers. The one element within the elite which appeared to have no precise role, namely the ex-guerrillas and *willaya* leaders, was also the group which might be expected on the basis of previous behavior to oppose policies or practices which excluded them from power. Evidence for this inference was ample, since Mohand oul Hadj, Tayebi, Sawt al Arab (Boubnider), Khatib Youssef, and Si Moussa had all violently opposed Ben Bella or Boumedienne at some time in the recent past. How could these men, with their prestigious revolutionary past contributing to their demands for influence, be accommodated within a political system composed largely of professional military men and technically competent Intellectuals? The rather unconvincing answer to this query was that they would be responsible for reorganizing the almost nonexistent FLN.

A Role for the Party?

On July 17 the Council of the Revolution announced the formation of a *Secrétariat Exécutif du* FLN, composed of Cherif Belkacem as *coordinateur,* and of four ex-*willaya* commanders who had actively opposed Ben Bella, namely Mohand oul Hadj, Salah Boubnider, Khatib Youssef, and Mohammed Tayebi. The *coordinateur* of the *Secrétariat Exécutif* was a close ally of Boumedienne, under whom he had served in Morocco. The others were the men in charge of the anti–Ben Bella *willayas* 2, 3, and 4 during the crisis of summer 1962.[19]

The role of the FLN under Ben Bella had never been particularly clear. When Khider was Secretary General, Ben Bella had stressed the important role of the state, but when he in turn became Secretary General, the Party's role, in theory, became that of directing and controlling state activities. Boumedienne, it seemed in an early speech, favored a limited role for the Party, stating that

The FLN will be a dynamic, *avant-garde* revolutionary Party, functioning according to the rules of democratic centralism, and consisting of tested militants. Its task will be, in conformity with the Tripoli Program and the Charter of Algiers, that of orienting, animating and supervising [*contrôler*], but not that of administering or substituting itself for the State.[20]

In addition to the small *Secrétariat Exécutif,* the Party eventually developed a more complex structure. Below the level of the *Secré-*

19 Boubnider and Tayebi, during the crisis of the summer, had both claimed the leadership of *willaya* 2 (North Constantine). In what was known as the "coup of Constantine," Tayebi ousted Boubnider, only to have him reinstated as head of political affairs, leaving Tayebi in charge of military matters. Tayebi then held several posts, including director of National Security and Ambassador to Cuba, and finally seems to have been imprisoned by Ben Bella.

20 Boumedienne speech, July 7, 1965, reprinted in *Actualités et Documents,* July 1965. In addition, an article in *Révolution Africaine,* July 24, 1965, p. 4, criticized the FLN under Ben Bella for not having acted as an "animator." Rather the FLN, ". . . little by little was detracted from its true mission and was transformed into an administrative organ and into a parallel administrative hierarchy, losing itself in daily minor interventions in the machinery of the State."

tariat Exécutif a *Direction centrale* was formed, which consisted of about twenty members. The members of the *Direction centrale* each had functionally defined duties, such as responsibility for the press, for mass organizations, for liaisons with liberation movements, and so forth. While many of these men were virtually unknown for their past activities, the majority had been either deputies to the National Assembly, members of the Central Committee of the FLN, or both, under Ben Bella. Ben Bella's first minister of Education was also included.[21]

Others associated with the leadership of the Party, but not made members of the *Direction centrale,* were the *chargés de mission* and, at the departmental level, the *commissaires nationaux* and the *commissaires nationaux adjoints.* These posts were in large part also occupied by ex-deputies or members of the Central Committee, including a number of individuals who had violently opposed Ben Bella and had been expelled from the Party.[22] Thus, while the Party had few explicitly defined functions, it did nonetheless absorb or provide political positions for ex-deputies or Central Committee members from the secondary elite, and it did offer symbolically important posts to the potentially dissident ex-guerilla leaders. The Party did not, however, immediately develop into a powerful organization capable of mobilizing mass support for the regime.

The Search for Stability: Integration or Autonomy?

In brief, within a month of the coup of June 19, 1965, three distinct political institutions had been created to replace those which formed under Ben Bella's rule. The Council of the Revolution, with "supreme authority," consisted almost exclusively of Military men,

---

[21] The entire membership of the Direction Centrale of the FLN during 1966–1967 has never been made public. The closest approximation to the complete list follows, with CC (Central Committee) or dep. (deputy to the National Assembly) indicating earlier position under Ben Bella: D. Bendimered, H. Djafari, (dep.), O. Boudaoud (dep., CC), A. Benhamida (dep., CC and minister), M. Bouarfa, M. Meghraoui (dep.), H. Saci (CC), M. al Mili, Djelloul Malaika (dep.), A. Merouche, T. Seddiki, Y. Maghrebi, M. Hachem (CC), M. Zouaoui (dep.), T. Ouattar, A. Benkedadra (dep.).

[22] Central Committee members Messadia, Louai, and Boubekeur became *commissaires nationaux,* Ould Brahim became *commissaire national adjoint,* and Hamel, Mahiouz, Seddiki, Bouroughaa, Abadou, Chibane, Rais, Chebila, Moulay Brahim, and A. Belaid were named *chargés de mission.* Deputies Yalaoui, Abdelwahab, Guezzen, Krimi, and Rebbah were likewise selected as *commissaires nationaux,* and Boucherit, Abada, Souissi, and Benkherouf were made *chargés de mission.*

half of whom were guerrilla leaders (*maquisards*) and about half of whom were more professionally trained officers. The Council of Ministers, termed the "executive power" of the regime, was primarily made up of Intellectuals in charge of economic and social matters and Military men in control of key Ministries such as Defense, Foreign Affairs, and Interior. Lastly, the Party was restructured, with the ex-*willaya* colonels plus one close associate of Boumedienne at the head of the *Secrétariat Exécutif*.[23]

No single individual could be found in all three of these new institutions, thus some check on excessive concentration of power was provided. In order to permit reasonably effective functioning of these institutions, each one was also relatively homogeneous in terms of its membership. Thus, the three major elements of Boumedienne's coalition—the Intellectuals, the *maquisards*, and the professional Military—were each represented in some part of the political system, but no more than two of these elements were to be found in any single institution. (See Figure 12.1.)

Whereas Ben Bella had sought stability by including all elements of his coalition in virtually every institution, thereby apparently hoping to achieve an informal system of checks on the power aspirations of any one group, Boumedienne sought rather to form relatively homogeneous subsystems, with the Council of the Revolution playing something of the role of arbitrator among the various elite groups.[24]

Capacity for Decision-Making

Despite the instability that characterized the more than two and one-half years that Ben Bella was in power, a number of important decisions were made which affected the nature of the political system and the political process. For example, elections were held for two National Assemblies and to approve Ben Bella as nominee for

[23] In addition to these three institutions, the roles of prefect, of secretary general within various ministries, and of ambassador all provided positions for influential members of the political elite, such as Abdallah Fadel, Mohammed Mazouzi, Boualem Oussedik, Salah Mebroukine, Omar Ouseddik, Zirout Amine, Ali Kafi, and Tayeb Boulharouf.

[24] P. J. Vatikiotis, "Tradition and Political Leadership: The Example of Algeria," *Middle Eastern Studies*, Volume 2, No. 4, July 1966, has argued that two dominant leadership styles can be seen in traditional Muslim Algerian culture. One, the *za'im*, or strong leader model, is best represented by Ben Bella's rule, whereas *shura*, or consultation, better describes Boumedienne's practices.

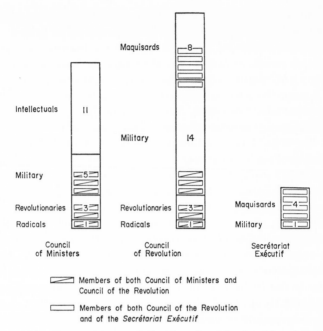

Figure 12.1   Composition and Overlapping Membership of Political
Structures, July 1965

President. In addition, a constitution was written and adopted, and
a Party Congress was held which created new institutions for the
FLN. Among Ben Bella's announced goals for creating new political
structures, however, two were never acted upon, namely the holding
of communal elections and administrative reform at the departmental level.[25]

Ben Bella's economic and social policies likewise showed that
many decisions were made, whatever their merits. All *colon*-owned
land was nationalized, a rather chaotic system of agricultural and
industrial self-management was instituted, and an impressive effort
to educate more children was made. In two areas progress was less
apparent. Arabization of education, a frequently mentioned goal of
the government, advanced slowly. Only the first year of elementary
school was fully Arabized under Ben Bella. Agrarian reform, aimed
at reducing large-scale private landowning, was a second goal that
was often articulated but never acted upon. In general, however,

[25] The rate of turnover in prefects during Ben Bella's incumbency was
remarkable. For 16 departments there were more than 200 prefects named in
little more than 2 years, an average for each department of a new prefect nearly
every 2 months.

Ben Bella's system of concentrated power led to many initiatives and new policies in the political, economic, and social fields.

But while displaying some capacity for adopting new policies, Ben Bella failed to retain the allegiance of important top elite members who might have helped to implement those policies. Relations among the various segments of the political elite under Ben Bella were rather confusing, but in general it can be said that the top elite rapidly became alienated from Ben Bella's authoritarian rule. The secondary elite,however, as represented by the national organizations such as the UGTA, the UNEA and the UNFA, eventually became quite supportive of Ben Bella's policies.[26] While losing the allegiance of Liberals, Revolutionaries, Radicals, and eventually many of the Military, Ben Bella sought to reinforce his authority by sponsoring the aspirations of organized groups within the secondary elite. The result was a great deal of instability in the top ranks of government and frequent outbreaks of politically inspired domestic violence. Ben Bella, however, succeeded in appearing as a popular leader for whom massive audiences of peasants and workers would endlessly applaud.

The new regime created under Boumedienne differed in many respects from that of Ben Bella. Boumedienne, for example, did not actively seek to establish rapport with the masses, and his speeches were given in classical Arabic with little emotion.[27] His government, while supported by a large number of the top elite, met with reserve or hostility from the UNEA (*Union Nationales des Etudiants Algériens*), UGTA (*Union Générale des Travailleurs Algériens*), and even the UNFA (*Union Nationale des Femmes Algériennes*). During the first two and one-half years of Boumedienne's tenure in office, one did not have the impression that many decisions were made, but elite stability was high and incidences of political violence were relatively rare. On issues such as Arabization and agricultural reform, little was changed from the Ben Bella period, though one additional year of primary education was Arabized in 1966–67.[28]

[26] This is not surprising since *autogestion* favored the workers, educational policies benefited the students, and Ben Bella's speeches vigorously supported women's rights.

[27] During Boumedienne's first televised speech the camera focused on the microphone and his face was never shown. See Jean Lacouture, "L'après–Ben Bellisme," *Le Monde*, July 14, 1965.

[28] A comparison of other economic and social policies under the two regimes would be most useful. It would seem that economic growth, largely due to exports of oil and gas, took place more vigorously under Boumedienne than during Ben Bella's years as President. The analysis here, however, will focus primarily on political developments.

Whereas Ben Bella had held elections, adopted a constitution, and held a Party Congress, Boumedienne's government seemed almost unconcerned with formal political structures apart from those created immediately after the coup. Nonetheless, an early statement of intention did define governmental priorities as follows: (1) reform of the Party, (2) holding a Party Congress, (3) elaboration of a new constitution, (4) communal and national elections, (5) social and economic reforms.[29] At the end of 1968 only one of these policies, that of holding communal elections, had actually been carried out. A second task, that of reforming the Party, was the major political goal for 1968 and 1969. Thus, while Boumedienne's collegial system of authority was rather stable, it gave no evidence of possessing great capacity for reaching decisions. It often seemed, in fact, that the price of stability was indecision. This was not, it may be added, for lack of pressures to solve the serious economic situation throughout the country. Rather, it seemed as if the consensus needed to agree on reforms was lacking within the elite.

Organized Interests: Students and Workers

The new regime's relations with the trade union and the students were marked by considerable tension and hostility during the first three and one-half years of Boumedienne's rule. The UNEA, and in particular its Paris section, had opposed the coup, and students had been responsible for virtually the only pro–Ben Bella demonstrations after June 19, 1965. On September 28 the Party installed the first of several *comités exécutifs* of the UNEA, and the following month an ex-president of the UNEA, Houari Mouffok, was arrested. In February 1966, and again in February 1968, student demonstrations took place to protest the Party's interference in student affairs. It was not until November 1966, with the release of Mouffok, that the first clash between students and the regime was temporarily resolved.[30] Future conflicts with the students, however, were not long in coming.[31]

[29] Bachir Boumaza in a press conference, August 14, 1965.

[30] Still, in November 1966, at the university ceremonies beginning the academic year, when Boumedienne entered a hall filled with students there was almost no applause to be heard apart from that of the diplomatic corps. A tract distributed on November 18, 1966, by the "real" UNEA leaders strongly appealed for more autonomy for the student union.

[31] During February 1968 the students at the University of Algiers undertook a lengthy strike to protest the attempts of the Party to name the leaders of the student union. Earlier, on May 1, 1967, a number of students were arrested

The regime's dealings with the UGTA were likewise strained, but there was less overt conflict than with the students. Initial cautious approval of the June 19 coup gave way to full UGTA support of the regime in a speech by Oumeziane, the UGTA president, on September 5, 1965. By March of the following year, however, tensions had increased and issues of the UGTA journal, *Révolution et Travail,* were not allowed to appear for many months. During the summer of 1966 relations seemed to have worsened, but by the end of the year several UGTA members held as prisoners were released. Once again, however, future difficulties could be anticipated from this element of the politically active population.[32]

Conflicts Within the Top Political Elite

If relations between the national organizations, mainly the UNEA and the UGTA, and the Boumedienne government had been characterized by considerable overt hostility, disaffection within the top elite seemed more limited to specific types of individuals.[33] The first wave of opposition came from the left, mainly from the more or less Marxist Intellectuals among Ben Bella's advisers. On August 2, 1965, a tract distributed in Algiers announced the creation of a clandestine opposition party, the *Organisation de la Résistance Populaire* (ORP). Ex-Political Bureau member Zahouane was one of the promoters of this party. Less than a week later a collaborator of Zahouane, the Intellectual Mohammed Harbi, was arrested for printing antigovernment tracts.[34] Shortly thereafter the editor of

by the regime, and a few days before that, at a rally supporting the Viet Cong, such signs as "No Socialism without Democracy" were prominently displayed.

[32] *Le Monde,* February 4–5, 1968, p. 8, announced that Oumeziane had been dropped as head of the UGTA, but in late 1968 he was still in that post. At the Third UGTA Congress in May 1969, Oumeziane was replaced as Secretary General but remained on the Executive Committee.

[33] Representative opinions of Boumedienne and his regime gathered during 1966 and 1967 from members of the political elite ranged from mild enthusiasm to cautious skepticism and hostility. Several individuals praised Boumedienne's personal qualities, particularly his modesty, his willingness to consult others and his pragmatic approach to problems. Some also approved of Boumedienne's stress on Algerian socialism within an Arab-Islamic context as opposed to Ben Bella's more universalistic definition of socialism. Those who opposed Boumedienne, of course, stressed that he had no popular mandate, that his regime was "militaristic," and that it furthered the ambitions of a single "clan" rather than serving the interests of all Algerians.

[34] Boumedienne in his interview with *Al Ahram,* October 8, 1965, claimed that he had no intention after the coup of arresting Harbi or Zahouane, but that he had warned them not to break the law. This they promptly did by distributing clandestine tracts of the ORP.

Révolution Africaine, Amar Ouzegane, a one-time head of the Algerian Communist Party, was dropped from his post. The wave of repression against opposition from the left, associated as it was by an anticommunist press campaign, culminated in September with the arrest of Zahouane, as well as that of Bachir Hadj Ali, another ex-communist.[35] With the arrests of many leaders of the ORP, opponents of Boumedienne began to organize abroad. In April 1966 the *Organisation Clandestine de la Révolution Algérienne* (OCRA), led by ex-Political Bureau member Ait al Hocine and by Mohammed Lebjaoui, was founded. This group seemed to consist of moderate pro–Ben Bellists who called for a return to legality and constitutional practices. Other opposition movements formed, and often disintegrated, around such prestigious figures as Khider, Boudiaf (PRS), Krim (MDRA, October 1967), and Ait Ahmed after his escape from prison in June 1966.[36] Whatever their merits or successes, none of these overseas opposition movements seemed capable of overthrowing Boumedienne's government.[37] However, they did provide a haven for dissident Algerian politicians and ocassionally were responsible for strained relations between Algeria and host countries of these clandestine parties. Their audience within Algeria, however, seemed small.

While some elements within the Algerian political elite, especially the Revolutionaries and some Intellectuals, found it impossible to accommodate themselves to the Boumedienne regime, there were considerably fewer defections from the governing coalition under Boumedienne than under Ben Bella. During the first two years of Boumedienne's rule only three ministers joined the opposition (OCRA). One regional military commander (Soufi) was replaced by another member of the Council of the Revolution (Yahiaoui), but remained nonetheless in good graces on the Council. At the head of the Party there were no changes in leadership until December 1967.

---

[35] For a scathing attack on the *pieds rouges* and the *conseillers transhumants* of the Ben Bella period, see A. Khaldi in *Révolution Africaine,* September 4, 1965.

[36] Khider was assassinated in Spain in January 1967. The circumstances of his death are not well known, but his control of large sums of FLN money suggests one plausible motive.

[37] In the spring of 1967 the OCRA, which had been thought to be the most effective of the opposition groups, announced that three recent recruits had resigned, namely Hadj Smain, Boumaza, and Mahsas, all ex-ministers of both Ben Bella and Boumedienne. *Le Mois en Afrique,* February 1967, discusses the various opposition groups.

The three ministers who left Boumedienne's government during August, September, and October 1966 were men who had all been recruited originally by Ben Bella. The Minister of Reconstruction, Hadj Smain, was the first to join the OCRA in the summer of 1966. Then on September 23 the functions of the Minister of Agriculture, Ahmed Mahsas, were significantly reduced, and two days later he announced from Europe that he too had become a member of OCRA.[38] The third minister to defect was Bachir Boumaza, Minister of Information, who on October 8 also joined the OCRA in Europe. Thus, one Intellectual, one Revolutionary, and one Radical left the Boumedienne coalition. The only two members of the Council of the Revolution who could have been considered "civilians" were now in opposition.

The men appointed by Boumedienne to replace these dissident ministers were Intellectuals of considerable talent, both of whom had been closely associated with the UGEMA and the GPRA. Mohammed Ben Yahia, Ben Bella's ambassador to Moscow for some time, became the new Minister of Information. Lamine Khène was named Minister of Public Works, while the incumbent in that Ministry, Ali Yahia, became Minister of Agriculture. None of these ministers was made part of the Council of the Revolution. The Ministry of Reconstruction vacated by Hadj Smain's departure was abolished, but a new Ministry of Transport was created, with the Minister of State, Rabah Bitat, assuming this new position. In short, during October 1966 Boumedienne slightly changed the composition of his government, adding two technically competent and highly educated young men (Ben Yahia was 34 and Khène was 36) to his cabinet, thereby augmenting the dominance of technicians at the expense of the members of the older nationalist elite.[39]

Growing Autonomy and Conflict

The one major policy initiative of the Boumedienne regime in 1966 and 1967 was the holding of communal elections. This repre-

[38] Others who joined the OCRA at this time were Slimane Rebbah, a national secretary of the UGTA, and Amar Ouzegane, past editor of *Révolution Africaine*. See *El Djeich*, November 1966, "Les marionnettes," for a bitter attack on Mahsas and Boumaza.

[39] *Révolution Africaine*, No. 253, December 21–27, 1967, alluded to an interview given by Boumedienne to *Al Ahram* in which a "complete change" of the cabinet was announced for the near future. This did not take place during 1968 or early 1969.

sented the only important reform of political structures since Boumedienne had taken power. It was also one of the few policies carried through to completion through the combined efforts of virtually the entire governing elite. A great deal of effort went into preparing a communal code, drawing up lists of two Party-approved candidates for each of the seats in the 676 communes of the country. Hopes that communal reforms would be followed by similar reforms at higher level were voiced, but no action was forthcoming by the end of 1968. In May 1969, however, departmental elections were held following procedures similar to those used in the communal elections.

The collegial system of decision-making seemed limited in the decisions it could produce. Following the communal elections, the minimal collaboration achieved in the fall and winter of 1966–67 began to decline, and the autonomy of each group within the elite increased. From March 1967 until the end of the year, intraelite conflicts which had remained veiled for nearly two years once again became obvious. The axes of these conflicts were those dictated by earlier patterns of political socialization.

Ironically, the first sign of overt conflict within the *Secrétariat Exécutif* came as the opposition parties abroad were seemingly disintegrating.[40] During April 1967, the coordinator of the *Secrétariat Exécutif*, and a close ally of Boumedienne, Cherif Belkacem, went to Europe for several weeks. While abroad, he was temporarily replaced in his functions by Salah Boubnider, and it was only with some difficulty that an open conflict was avoided.[41]

The Arab-Israeli war of June 1967 momentarily put an end to open expressions of intraelite conflicts, as Algeria adopted an intransigent line toward Israel. But by July new divisions had arisen, polarizing around the issue of *autogestion* and trade union autonomy as opposed to the form of state capitalism practiced by some of the technically trained ministers.[42] Boumedienne, whose role as media-

---

[40] OCRA lost several prominent members in early 1967. ORP on March 22 appealed for unity with the government in the face of a presumed threat from Morocco. When the June 5, 1967, Arab-Israeli war began, OCRA called for a truce with the government. These appeals, however, received no overt response from the government.

[41] See *Le Mois en Afrique*, May 1967, "Algérie: une crise d'autorité."

[42] On July 25, 1967, the UGTA denounced an antiunion offensive. Cherif Belkacem met UGTA leaders soon thereafter in order to prepare the Third UGTA Congress. See also, *Révolution et Travail*, August 15, 1967, which warned against ". . . the continual abandonment of self-management units in favor of national enterprises."

tor in these conflicts was once again apparent, appointed an ad hoc commission to deal with the contention.

The limits on policy formulation in a political system with several relatively autonomous units were revealed a few days later, as the head of the UGTA, Oumeziane, bitterly attacked the Minister of Industry and Energy, Abdesselam, accusing him of wanting to destroy the system of *autogestion*. A second conflict was also reported to oppose Abdesselam to the Minister of Work, Zerdani.[43] A major division seemed to be developing between proponents of two contrasting models of economic organization.[44]

By October 1967 rumors of ministerial changes were heard, and it was reported that the most ardent proponents of *autogestion*, the leftist Intellectuals Zerdani and Ali Yahia, ministers of Work and Agriculture, had presented their resignation.[45] The climax to this conflict came as the ex-guerrilla leaders began to side with the supporters of *autogestion*. On November 1, at the traditional ceremonies commemorating the beginning of the revolution, the *Chef d'Etat Major*, Tahar Zbiri, refused to appear with Boumedienne.[46] Apparently attempts at reconciliation proved futile.

Early in December Boumedienne convened a large meeting of Party members and announced that, because of the ineffective organization of the FLN, 1968 would be "the year of the Party." The *Secrétariat Exécutif* was disbanded, and the Minister of Finance, Ahmed Kaid, assumed sole responsibility for the FLN.[47] Two of the five members of the *Secrétariat Exécutif*, Cherif Belkacem and Mohammed Tayebi, were still in good graces, but the other three old opponents of both Ben Bella and Boumedienne had clearly been singled out for dismissal.[48]

The next act in the intraelite conflicts which had weakened the decision-making capacity of the Algerian political elite for so long

[43] See *Le Monde*, August 4, 1967, p. 5.

[44] See the lengthy article by G. Viratelle in *Le Monde*, September 6, 1967, p. 5.

[45] See, for example, *Le Monde*, November 12–13, 1967. Zerdani had earlier outlined his ideas in a widely published article, "Les tâches de l'édification socialiste dans notre pays," *El Moudjahid*, January 14, 1967, p. 4.

[46] See Boumedienne's comments on the importance of Zbiri's insubordination in *Le Monde*, January 7–8, 1968. *Jeune Afrique*, November 26, 1967, predicted that this dispute would be settled peacefully.

[47] See *Le Figaro*, December 13, 1967. Boumedienne announced an impending purge of the Party as he criticized the FLN for its immobilism. Also see *Le Monde*, December 12, 1967, and *Unità*, December 13, 1967, p. 12.

[48] Cherif and Tayebi were appointed in March 1968 to head the ministries of Finance and Agriculture respectively.

came on the night of December 14–15, 1967, when troops directed by relatives of Tahar Zbiri tried to advance on Algiers in a futile attempt to stage a coup against Boumedienne. While little is known for certain of the circumstances dictating these rash and poorly planned maneuvers, it seems that Mohand oul Hadj, Salah Boubnider, and perhaps Khatib Youssef were involved along with Zbiri.[49] The attempted coup, however, failed to gain the support of other units in the army and was easily, if violently, crushed by the professional soldiers loyal to Boumedienne.[50] In one of the mystery-shrouded events of the week, the commander of the first Military Region and member of the Council of the Revolution, Said Abid, committed suicide.[51] Abid had been thought to be close to Zbiri, and it was also known that he was responsible for Ben Bella's detention. Rumors naturally filled the foreign press as to the circumstances of his death.

Whatever the reality behind the attempted coup, it was clear that Boumedienne's coalition, like Ben Bella's, had not been able to develop accommodative processes which could avoid elite alienation. Collegiality had been partially successful at bringing stability but at the price of indecisiveness. Autonomy had led to conflicts between proponents of different views of how to organize the economy. Finally, an effort to centralize power through the Party had thrown other individuals into opposition. With the attempted coup of December 1967, the theoretically inclined Intellectuals and the *maquisards* seemed to have clearly lost out to the professional Military and the technicians.

In the year following the attempted coup several minor changes were made within the governing structures of the country. In early March three new ministerial appointments were announced. Cherif Belkacem, the former *coordinateur* of the Party, took Ahmed Kaid's position as Minister of Finance and Planning. Another ex-Party leader, Mohammed Tayebi, became Minister of Agriculture and Agrarian Reform. Both of these changes involved reshuffling of in-

---

[49] See *Le Figaro*, December 18, 1967, p. 5, for a detailed, if unverifiable, account of the attempted coup. *Unità*, December 16, 1967, disputed the interpretation that Khatib Youssef supported Zbiri, suggesting, incorrectly, that he might even be named Minister of Health. See also *Le Monde*, December 19, 1967.

[50] Chabou, Zerguini, and Slimane Hoffmann were mentioned by observers as key professional military men who stopped Zbiri's forces. See especially Yves Cuau, *Le Figaro*, December 18, 1967, p. 5.

[51] *Révolution Africaine*, No. 253, December 21–27, 1967, treated Said Abid as a self-sacrificing martyr who could not tolerate the mutiny of troops under his command and thus committed suicide.

cumbent elite members rather than the introduction of new blood into the centers of power. In addition, a new Minister of Work and Social Affairs, Mohammed Mazouzi, an ex-ambassador and former member of the Central Committee, was named. Finally, Mahmoud Guennez was made Kaid's assistant at the head of the Party.

What these changes would mean for Algeria's future was unclear, but early indications were that the greater homogeneity of the governing elite might permit attempts at centralizing power under a reformed FLN.[52] And early evidence likewise hinted that, as in the past, attempts at centralization would bring on protests, particularly from students and labor unions.[53]

Boumedienne's own role within the elite had been a subject of some speculation following the Arab-Israel war of June 1967, and the unsuccessful coup of December 1967 led again to questions of whether Boumedienne would now emerge as a strong leader. Boumedienne had begun to play an active international role in late 1967, and some observers thought that his influence within Algeria would rise. But it would seem that Boumedienne had limited ambitions of capitalizing upon his international position to attain some greater personal authority within Algeria. His complicated personality, as summarized below by Hervé Bourgès, also led to a certain reluctance to play a starring role.

Cut off from the people, surrounded by rivals waiting for him to make a false move, and driven by a temperament whose authoritarian side is matched by a refusal to impose his will on others, Colonel Houari Boumedienne does not really govern Algeria. In the name of collegialism, he leaves affairs of state in hands that are often expert, but not always clean. It is as though his self-effacement in the midst of the ruling group were a substitute for democracy. Obsessed with order and careful never to interfere with a task once it is given, he is incapable of arbitrating or settling administrative conflicts. An enemy of official abuse, he nevertheless depends on a military and police apparatus that is fostering repression and despotism; a stickler for law, he signs orders for judicial reforms that wipe out in a single stroke what was left of justice; as sincere in his convictions as he is

[52] The FLN under Kaid tried to bring the national organizations under Party control. See *Le Monde*, February 4–5, 1968, p. 5.

[53] Student protests at Party attempts to dominate the UNEA were widespread during February 1968. See, for example, *Le Monde*, February 7, 1968. An important interview with Boumedienne was published in *Le Monde*, April 4, 1968, pp. 1–7, in which Boumedienne analyzed the sources of divisions in the FLN up to December 1967 and predicted that a new era of stability was beginning for Algeria. Boumedienne underlined the primary need for reinforcing state authority above all else.

in the promises he makes, he strays from the former and forgets the latter under the pressure of men and events; by nature uncomprising, he never ceases to compromise. Because he is better suited to command than to govern, Boumedienne is a prisoner of his personality, of his past, and of the men around him.[54]

Boumedienne's self-effacement was probably the price to be paid for relative stability within the ruling group. But the effect of strengthening the Party on intraelite relations might be to upset this balance, for if the Party really developed into a new center of power it would be difficult for individual ministers to retain influence within their respective spheres. Unfortunately the willingness of the regime, and of the Party in particular, to allow autonomy and even dissent, was probably set back considerably by an attempt in January to assassinate Ahmed Kaid and by the nearly successful effort in April 1968 to kill Boumedienne. The atmosphere created by these incidents was hardly conducive to tolerance. Indeed, calls for increased vigilance were heard, and the release of political prisoners, announced by the Minister of Justice early in the year, was postponed. But in November the regime did release from prison several of the most important prisoners, including Harbi, Zahouane, Hadj Ali, Ben Alla, Nekkache, and Cherif. Whether this was a prelude to liberalization or a step toward reconciliation with the opposition groups would only be apparent in light of future developments.

One other source of tension which threatened the coherence of the core leadership involved Algeria's relations with France. In spring of 1968, Minister of the Interior Ahmed Medeghri traveled to France in order to try to resolve outstanding problems between the two countries. According to some sources, he assured the French that no further nationalizations of French-owned industries would take place. But later in the year the powerful Minister of Industry, Abdesselam, convinced Boumedienne that it was necessary for Algeria to take over about forty French companies in order to attain greater economic independence. When these nationalizations took place, Medeghri is said to have threatened to resign, but for the next few months little was heard of the conflict, and by the end of the year Medeghri was again appearing in public. Boumedienne once more was portrayed as a mediator in this dispute.

[54] Hervé Bourgès, *L'Algérie à l'épreuve du pouvoir* p. 151. Translated also in William H. Lewis, "Algeria Against Itself," *Africa Report,* December 1967, p. 14.

In the summer of 1968 Algeria was presented with the unwelcome gift of a highjacked Israeli passenger plane, and the embarrassing question of what to do with its Israeli crew and passengers and with the plane itself seems to have also caused some disagreement within the ruling bodies. After a month of delays, however, the Minister of Foreign Affairs was able to convince his colleagues to release the plane and the Israeli passengers and crew, thus showing that Algerians were neither as unreasonable nor as insensitive to world opinion and pressures as some had thought.

The tests of the regime's ability to cope with still-outstanding major problems revolved around domestic reforms and relations with France. Concerning France, the questions of the Algerian workers in France, of Algerian wine exports to France, and of oil policies will prove to be the touchstones of the regime's capacity to achieve major foreign policy goals. Within Algeria, any progress on departmental or national elections, the holding of a full-scale Party Congress, the promulgation of a new constitution, the appointment of a civilian Prime Minister, or the relaxation of control over the mass media would all be significant political acts. In the economic field, the reduction of regional disparities of income, the provision of many more jobs for the unemployed, and a major agrarian reform program would be signs that serious new efforts were under way to improve the difficult economic situation. Good marks might also be won for the regime if the troublesome border disputes with Morocco, and to a lesser degree Tunisia, could be amicably resolved.[55]

While Algeria's future could not be easily predicted in early 1969, for the first time in recent Algerian history the men in power shared rather similar views of the nature of politics and government because of their earlier political socialization. Whether they could produce an integrated political system, capable of coherent and responsive decision-making, was an open question, but it would seem that conditions were more favorable for the new coalition of technicians and professional Military men than they had been for any other group of Algerian leaders. For in one form or another, any Algerian regime would require the support of the army and the talents of the technicians as it faced the tasks ahead.

[55] Boumedienne's trip to Morocco in January 1969 seemed to be an important step toward improving Algerian-Moroccan relations. Such a state visit would have been inconceivable two years earlier.

13

Themes in Algerian Political Culture

Conflict has been endemic within the Algerian political elite, and its consequences have frequently been debilitating. Thus far intra-elite dissension has been traced primarily to divergent patterns of political socialization. No successful political process has yet emerged to accommodate these differences in orientation, nor have authoritative political structures, whether collegial, autonomous, or concentrated under a single leader, proved capable of providing both order and effective policy-making.

While the effects of Algeria's turbulent colonial and revolutionary past have been seen as responsible for creating many of the conflicts within the political elite, it is also possible to see conflict as stemming from more general cultural values and shared orientations.[1] Although the specific nature of elite divisions in Algeria requires a sociological and historical explanation, the relatively high propensity of Algerians to engage in disputes may be clarified by a brief examination of Algerian political culture. Here one finds not only that there is a high degree of conflict among individuals and groups but

[1] Edward Banfield in *The Moral Basis of a Backward Society* has argued that the prevalence of "amoral familism" and distrust of others has made political integration at the local level in Southern Italy very difficult.

also that the personality of each Algerian is marked by deep contra-dictions. As observers have often noted, Algerians are *complexe et complexé*, that is, "complex and full of complexes." Commenting on this aspect of Algerian personality, Abderrazak Chentouf has said:

Algerians are an absolutist people. In their religion this is seen in the adoption of the strict Malekite rite. In language it is seen in the orthodoxy of the Arabized Berber grammarians. This comes from the Berber sense of the absolute. The mentality of Algerians is characterized by the right angle. There are no contours or compromises. During the war this led to an inflation of heroism so that sometimes propaganda had to be toned down. People are now very critical, especially the young people. But what we need is order and efficiency. Young people today are less balanced than my generation, but they also have fewer complexes.[2]

The term "political culture" has recently become fashionable, though the study of political culture has roots in more traditional political studies. A useful definition of political culture is that it consists of the "system of empirical beliefs, expressive symbols, and values which defines the situation in which political action takes place."[3] Political culture, then, is the result of both latent and manifest political socialization. Verba traces the origins of political culture to the influence of nonpolitical experiences in the family, school, and peer group, to direct experience with the political process, and to the impact of unique political events on beliefs.[4]

A common finding in the study of political culture is that elite political culture differs markedly from mass political culture. As Pye has stated, "Those who must deal with power and have responsibilities for the decisions of government invariably develop outlooks on politics different from those of the people who remain observers or marginal activists."[5]

Algerian political culture reflects the impact of both general cultural values and of recent historical experiences—particularly the war for independence—on the men who have entered positions of leadership. Early political socialization has been most influential

---

[2] Interview with Abderrazak Chentouf.
[3] Sidney Verba, "Comparative Political Culture," in Lucian W. Pye and Sidney Verba, eds., *Political Culture and Political Development*, p. 513.
[4] *Ibid.*, pp. 551–560.
[5] Lucian W. Pye, "Introduction: Political Culture and Political Development," *ibid.*, p. 15. Other studies have referred to elite political culture as the "operational code." See, for example, Nathan Leites, *A Study of Bolshevism.* Alexander George summarizes the contents of an "operational code" in his study, "The 'Operational Code': A Neglected Approach to the Study of Political Leaders and Decision-Making," RAND memorandum, RM–5427–PR, September, 1967.

in transmitting shared values that dictate the way in which individuals should interact with one another. These values are central to an understanding of the roots of much intraelite conflict. Later political socialization, particularly the experience of participating in the nationalist movement and in the revolution, has been most important in forming images of the nature of politics and of the role of government. Policy and policy conflicts are best traced to these later experiences.

Values Affecting the Political Process

Intraelite relations in Algeria, as has been amply demonstrated, have been characterized by considerable hostility and mistrust. In Algerian Arabic dialect, the French word *politique* has been borrowed and transformed into *boulitique,* a term which has come to describe the nature of Algerian elite politics. A highly placed Algerian official has defined the practice of *boulitique* as follows: "I try to get you to do something stupid so that I can take your place." [5] It is no surprise, then, that Algerian leaders often behave, and expect others to behave, as if they are constantly maneuvering and scheming to acquire more power.

The prevalence of *boulitique* in the Algerian elite has numerous consequences. Algerian politicans, for example, seem remarkably *méfiant,* a word which connotes even more than the English "mistrustful." *Méfiance* is certainly related to the prevalence of *luttes des personnes,* or personal quarrels. Rarely will an Algerian leader explain a major political crisis as growing out of the conflicting interests or ideologies of the protagonists. Ideology as an explanation of Algerian political behavior is simply not convincing to most observers. Rather, the preferred explanation is virtually always "personal rivalries" or "personality clashes." [7]

Algerian politicians have had sufficient experience with the de-

---

[6] I am indebted to professor Jean Leca of the University of Grenoble for this definition. A longer discussion of *"boulitique"* is found in Malek Bennabi's article, "Politique et 'Boulitique'," *Révolution Africaine,* No. 139, September 25, 1965.

[7] Jean Lacouture has warned against stressing personal quarrels too much in Algerian politics but has nonetheless provided many of the best interpretations of Algerian politics in these terms. In a different vein, Leonard Binder, in "Egypt: The Integrative Revolution," in Lucian W. Pye and Sidney Verba, eds., *Political Culture, pp.* 444–445, argues that ideology is irrelevant in Egyptian politics. Numerous parallels can be found between Binder's conclusions and those presented here.

bilitating consequences of intraelite conflict to see political opposition as generally destructive and illegitimate. While recognizing
that some disagreements are inevitable, Algerian leaders are virtually
unanimous in saying that such differences should only be aired in
private. Public controversy, it is often argued, can only exacerbate
tensions. In the press even gentle satire aimed at administrative
absurdities has met with a hostile reaction from the government.[8]

The dislike for political controversy and the threatening nature
of political opposition have led many Algerian leaders to the belief
that only by creating "homogeneous" ruling groups can one insure
political stability. Ahmed Kaid, a controversial figure who was
named head of the FLN in December 1967, has argued for the value
of homogeneity in some detail. Speaking to the National Assembly
on August 24, 1963, Kaid replied to deputies who had been extolling
the virtues of collective decision-making by saying that collegiality
had never really worked at the top levels of leadership. Furthermore,
he said,

. . . the issue of collegiality leads us to speak of the crises which took place
under the collegial system. . . . We would never have known these crises
which I have mentioned if we had had strong leadership, and especially if
that leadership had been homogeneous! I personally don't care what kind
of constitution we have, I would prefer to leave the Algerian people without a constitution, if only we could give them homogeneous teams of
leaders, men with the same views, the same outlook—little would it matter
all the recriminations they would face . . . ! [9]

In many political systems a high degree of distrust has been found
in intraelite relations.[10] A frequent corollary to the incidence
of widespread distrust is the belief that political relations should
be hierarchically ordered. Thus the potentially disintegrative consequences of distrust are avoided by common submission to higher

[8] In early 1967 a daily column appeared in the official newspaper *El Moudjahid*,
signed by Krikeche, which was often quite biting in its satire on administrative
complexities. It seemed to bring on considerable popular response, as evidenced
by letters to the editor, but after a short while the degree of criticism declined
and only relatively "safe" topics were discussed.

[9] Ahmed Kaid, in *Journal Officiel, Débats Parlementaires*, first year p. 926.
A similar view of the need for "homogeneity" of leadership is found in *Révolution Africaine*, April 25, 1964, in an article by Mohammed Harbi in which
he says that the fight against the enemies of socialism will produce homogeneity.
Otherwise, he says, no unity is possible. The widely echoed criticisms of the
wartime FLN in both the *Tripoli Program* and the *Charte d'Alger* attribute
weaknesses of the FLN to its heterogeneity.

[10] Lucian Pye, "Introduction: Political Culture and Political Development,"
in Pye and Verba, eds., *Political Culture*, p. 22.

authority. In Algeria, however, widespread distrust of one's colleagues in politics has been accompanied by a strong feeling that political relations must be based on equality and reciprocity. The tensions created by the existence of both distrust and norms of equality in Algerian political culture are widely manifest, and it often seems as if one or the other of these dimensions will change and restore some semblance of equilibrium to the perceptual world of Algerian politicians. Thus far, however, distrust and a demand for equality have coexisted in the minds of many Algerian leaders.

The dimension of equality in intraelite relations is expressed most frequently in the demands for collegial rule and for consultation, and in the rejection of the idea of a "cult of personality." For example, when Algerians are asked their opinions of their neighbors, the Tunisians, they will frequently reply that the Tunisians are rather docile and that they submit to authority too readily. President Bourguiba of Tunisia, it is asserted, would never be accepted as a leader in Algeria because he insists on doing everything himself, is arrogant and pompous, has exalted his own role, and has built palaces throughout the country to remind the people of his power. Algerians, it is argued, would never willingly submit to such a hierarchial system of authority.

Reflecting this distaste for authoritarian procedures is the following remark of Brahim Mezhoudi:

One of the major problems of newly independent countries is the single-party system. Human beings aren't saints, they can't be perfect, and it is possible to tempt them or corrupt them. Thus, some checks on their power are needed. In the one-party systems of communist countries a new bourgeoisie has grown up by way of the party. A one-party system is perhaps all right as a transitional stage. But underdevelopment is not just economic, it is also mental. At our present stage of development we need a mass-based single party, not an elite party. Algerians are fighters, and we aren't really mature enough yet not to have recourse to machine guns to solve political problems. It's far better to allow opposition within the party than to force people to turn to arms because they aren't allowed to express their opposition in other ways.[11]

The criticisms most often heard of Ben Bella and also of an earlier leader, Messali Hadj, are that he tried to do too much without consulting others, was striving to develop a "cult of personality," and that he ignored the essential principles of "democratic centralism."[12] Since Boumedienne came to power in June 1965 there

[11] Interview with Brahim Mezhoudi.
[12] Boumedienne has been quoted as saying that there were two great mistakes in Algerian history, Messali Hadj and Ben Bella.

has been virtually no attempt to emphasize the role of a single individual, and nearly all public pronouncements have stressed the collegial nature of the political system. Algeria has moved so far away from the "cult of personality" that Boumedienne rarely appears in public and makes no attempt to appeal personally to the crowds that he does address. Few informed Algerians today know much about the men who govern them. While at times this anonymity of power seems to bewilder the masses, it clearly has made it possible for the regime to avoid many crises which the more personalistic style of Ben Bella had provoked.[13]

Algerians, when asked to explain the particular mixture of distrust and egalitarianism in Algerian political life, will often say that Algerians are "individualistic" and thus they resent authority and are hard to govern. Consequently they both distrust those who have power and demand an equal share of influence for themselves. Individualism, however, as understood in the West, does not seem to be a dominant trait among Algerians. One would find few signs of the innovative behavior, the tolerance for deviance, and the willingness to break with tradition that are commonly associated with the idea of individualism.

What Algerians really seem to be referring to by the term "individualism" is rather the crucial role played by the concept of "honor" in Algerian culture. It would seem that both of the dominant dimensions in Algerian political culture, namely distrust and equality, can be traced to the concept of "honor." [14] Unfortunately, the psychological origins of this value are not well understood, although one familiar with Algerian society would quite likely stress the critical link between honor and male sexual prowess.[15]

[13] During the June 1967 war between Israel and the Arab states, the Algerian masses became politically mobilized for almost the first time since 1965. It was at this time, when Algeria was adopting a hard line toward Israel, that the first spontaneous demonstrations took place in which cries of "Long live Boumedienne" could be heard. A flurry of rumors circulated in the international press that Boumedienne was trying to replace Nasser as head of the Arab world. By the end of 1967 it would have been difficult to find any evidence for this assumption.

[14] Honor has been well discussed by Pierre Bourdieu, "The Sentiment of Honour in Kabyle Society," in J. G. Peristiany, ed., *Honour and Shame: The Values of Mediterranean Society* and Bichr Farès, *L'honneur chez les arabes avant l'Islam.*

[15] Horace M. Miner and George De Vos in *Oasis and Casbah: Algerian Culture and Personality in Change* have attempted to study early psychosexual development of Algerians. The general personality configuration is common throughout the Mediterranean as well as in Latin America, where it is known

Algerians are extremely aware of the influence of honor in their own culture.[16] The war of independence was frequently described as an effort to "regain honor," and colonial domination was often seen as an "attack upon Algeria's honor."[17] Honor is a personal attribute which must be constantly displayed in individual acts and must be defended from attacks by one's equals or superiors. Criticism from others can easily be seen as an attack upon one's honor. Politics being a domain in which criticism is frequent and often personal, one can understand the distrust Algerians often have of other politicians. Discussions and debates can quickly become matters of personal honor. Hence the volatile nature of political discourse and the prevalence of attitudes of *méfiance*.

Honor likewise dictates that an individual should not subject himself willingly to the authority of another person. The independence of the Bedouins is a traditional manifestation of the sense of honor in influencing political behavior. In Algeria, where there is no monarchy or traditional authority to which deference might be seen as proper, members of the political elite insist upon their right to participate as equals in decision-making. If one remains within the system, he will expect to be consulted and allowed to express his opinion. Then even if his view is not adopted his honor will still be intact. If he is ignored or purposely slighted, however, he may try to regain his self-esteem by acts of defiance of authority and refusal to participate in the system.[18]

When differences of opinion can easily become questions of honor, it is no surprise that accommodative political procedures are slow in developing. It seems that honor is the key value which dictates the incongruent stress on both equality and lack of trust in interpersonal relations. Whether the cultural value of honor will subside as more international norms of behavior become familiar, whether the

as "machismo." See Robert Scott, "Mexico: The Established Revolution," in Lucian Pye and Sidney Verba, eds., *Political Culture*, for several suggestions of the influence of "machismo" in Mexican politics which would also be valid for Algeria.

[16] The word for "honor" is the same in both Arabic and Berber, namely *nif* or *naïf*.

[17] One of the psychologically interesting explanations offered by many Algerians of why the revolution began when it did is that Morocco and Tunisia were already fighting France, which made Algerians look as if they were not men, as if they had no honor.

[18] A major criticism of Ben Bella by Mohand oul Hadj, who helped to lead the Kabyle uprising in October 1963, was that Ben Bella, while claiming to respect Mohand oul Hadj, had not consulted him while drawing up the constitution. See *Jeune Afrique*, October 14–20, 1963, p. 8.

demand for equality will give way to an acceptance of hierarchy among new recruits to the political elite, or whether distrust will be replaced by greater confidence in dealing with others is difficult to foresee. For the moment it seems as if Algerians will continue to live with their particular system of values, neither moving dramatically toward a totalitarian system nor developing attitudes more conducive to compromise and bargaining which would permit a fuller development of democracy.

The Proper Scope of Governmental Action

Just as Algerian leaders must learn to live with their conflicting views of intraelite relations, so also are they obliged to try to reconcile fundamentally inconsistent views of the role of government. Largely as a result of experiences during the colonial period and during the revolution, members of the Algerian political elite have acquired a view of politics which includes the belief in the need for a strong central state and at the same time stresses the great importance of the masses of impoverished workers and peasants.

In practice these two images are found in the development of an *étatiste* form of economic organization, often referred to as state capitalism, while at the same time the merits and demerits of self-management or *autogestion* in agriculture and in industry are hotly debated. Likewise during the communal elections of February 1967, the government seemed to be genuinely attempting to introduce a degree of decentralization into the old, highly centralized French administrative methods still in practice. But also it seemed clear that by creating new communal councils the government was hoping to strengthen its own influence in the rural areas and to provide the basis for extending Party control to previously remote areas. Single policies, then, can embody both the image of a decentralized polity governed by the people and of a strong, centralized state.

These unreconciled views of government both stem from an intensely felt nationalism and a less clearly defined attachment to the symbolism and rhetoric, and occasionally also to the content, of socialism. Both nationalism and socialism are relatively new ideas in Algeria. The parents of most men now in power would hardly understand the modern sense of these words, and yet nationalism, in Algeria as elsewhere, has proved to be a powerful force in overcoming particularism and in establishing the basic consensus needed for nation building, especially within the political elite.[19] No Algerian leaders, not even those from minority ethnic groups, have ever claimed to be other than proponents of Algerian nationalism and of complete territorial integrity.

An important manifestation of nationalism in Algerian political culture is seen in the idea that the state has a right to intervene in many areas of national life. In particular the state must control its own resources and territory. While xenophobia is virtually absent in Algeria, there is strong insistence that foreigners should not control Algeria's economic resources and should not influence her internal politics.[20] To guard against either of these eventualities and to insure territorial integrity, Algeria must possess a strong centralized state. One of the major criticisms of Ben Bella was that his image of nationalism was too open to outside influence, especially to that of his Marxist advisers of Greek and Egyptian origins. Boumedienne, for example, in a spontaneous speech before belligerent students in November 1967 stressed this same theme when he promised that free student elections could be held but that the state would never allow "foreign elements" to be elected.[21]

The concern of Algerian leaders for the people at large seems to be in most cases more than revolutionary and socialist rhetoric. Perhaps the best test of the value which the Algerian elite places on improving the conditions of the masses is to be seen in their genuinely impressive efforts in the field of education. Since independence, school enrollment has risen dramatically, and the budget for the Ministry of Education has consistently amounted to about 20 percent of total government expenditures, generally surpassing even the Ministry of Defense.[22]

[19] A useful essay on Algerian nationalism is that of Jean Leca, "Le nationalisme algérien depuis l'indépendence," in Louis-Jean Duclos, Jean Duvignaud, and Jean Leca, *Les nationalismes magrébins*.

[20] Algerian foreign policy may seem to reflect more ideological commitments than does internal policy. Because of its revolutionary past, Algeria can be expected to continue to support other people fighting anticolonial wars. The theme of anticolonialism and antiimperialism is constant in Algerian foreign policy, but the targets of these terms may change. One may expect that Algeria will try to maintain close relations with France as another constant in her foreign policy. Inter-Arab relations and East-West commitments are much more open to fluctuations, as no irreversible choices have been made in these areas, and intelligent diplomacy will probably try to keep options open for the future. The Foreign Ministry, it should be stressed, is staffed with a number of talented young men with very pro-West orientations.

[21] *Révolution Africaine*, No. 247, November 9–17, 1967, gives the text of this remarkable speech on pages 34 and 35.

[22] See, for example, the "Rapport sur le mouvement éducatif," 29th *Conférence internationale sur l'instruction publique*, Geneva, July 1966, especially pp. 13–14. Between 1961–62 and 1966–67, the number of Algerian primary students doubled.

Even in the much more controversial field of women's rights the government has felt obliged to adopt a progressive position supporting the principle of equality for women.[23] While as yet women have not been noticeably successful in breaking the bonds of tradition, it is significant that, during the mobilization of students following the June 1967 Arab-Israeli war, the regime decided to give military training to girls as well as boys.

While in the fields of education and social welfare the Algerian elite has shown a strong concern for the masses, the same cannot be said for the domain of politics. Speeches may constantly underline the decisive role of the peasants in carrying the burden of the revolution, but the elite has been reluctant to allow extensive political participation by the masses.[24] The idea of *autogestion,* or self-management, has nonetheless received considerable praise, and in one form or another most politicians have expressed approval of the idea that peasants and workers should run their own farms or factories. Conflicts have arisen, however, over whether or not *autogestion* can operate profitably, and there has been some tendency for the state to insist on maintaining standards of economic efficiency.[25]

While it is widely believed that the establishment of effective state authority and the beginnings of satisfactory economic growth must precede any moves toward greater citizen participation or decentralization, there is nonetheless a strong belief among many members of the political elite that eventually the masses should play a greater political role.[26] The communal elections of February 1967 were widely heralded as a step toward decentralization and greater opportunity for the exercise of local political influence, but the consequences of these elections are not yet clear. Nonetheless, it seems safe to say that there is a genuine populist element in Algerian political culture, and while the primary manifestations of these values are seen in the social and educational policies of the

[23] See *Révolution Africaine,* March 12–18, 1966, p. 9. *Le Monde,* March 11, 1966, reports the walkout of women during Boumedienne's speech because of the nonprogressive ideas on women's rights which he expressed. On August 27, 1966, *Le Monde* reported that the government had reversed its position and had supported the idea that women should have full rights.

[24] Ahmed Kaid, in a speech before the National Assembly, argued that political democracy was a myth and that what was needed was "economic democracy." *Journal Officiel,* August 24, 1963, pp. 924–925.

[25] See, for example, *Algérie-Actualité,* "Autogestion: la confusion organisée?", March 19, 1967.

[26] It should be stressed that Algeria, unlike many modernizing countries, does not face the difficulty of having to overcome the entrenched power of landed aristocrats or influential traditional leaders in its efforts to concentrate power.

elite, there is also some commitment to the idea of eventual mass political participation as well.

The tensions created by the simultaneous belief in the need for a strong central state and in the ideal of greater decentralization and mass participation have often led to an inability to formulate coherent policies. During 1967 exponents of state capitalism and of the need for centralized control of the economy found an articulate spokesman in the Minister of Industry and Energy, Belaid Abdesselam. At the same time the interests of those who favored *autogestion* and a less *étatiste* economic structure were articulated by the Minister of Work, Abdelaziz Zerdani.[27] The crisis of December 1967 seems to have resulted in something of a victory for Abdesselam's view of a strong centralized state, but even the men who survived that crisis are concerned with improving conditions for the masses. However, the balance to be struck between the need for enforced savings and investment and the desire to distribute more benefits to the masses in order to increase the legitimacy of the regime is difficult to find.[28] Since elements in the political culture of the elite favor both these orientations, the result of these cross pressures is often an extreme caution in decision-making. Such indecisiveness is a viable position for the present, since popular demands for substantive reform remain unorganized, but the extremely high rate of unemployment in Algeria creates a situation in which stagnation may lead to serious disaffection among the masses, particularly among those now being educated for whom no jobs will exist upon graduation.

Algerian elite political culture, then, seems to contain two major sets of partially inconsistent values. Algerian leaders seem often to distrust each other, yet demand equality and reciprocity in their personal relations. In addition, they appear to believe in the need for a strong centralized state free from foreign influence, while at the same time entertaining ideas of decentralized political structures and of workers' self-management committees directing their own affairs. Both these dimensions of political culture have important implications for the major difficulties facing the Algerian

---

[27] See *Le Monde*, September 6, 1967, p. 5.
[28] Boumedienne has consistently stressed that the people would be called on to judge the regime by its acts, not by its rhetoric. The pressures to distribute the product of economic advances rather than reinvest it must be great indeed, for it is clear that the present regime has not acquired "legitimacy" and probably cannot unless citizens perceive greater benefits accruing to themselves. In comparing Ben Bella to Boumedienne, many Algerians simply state, "Nothing has changed."

political elite, namely the problems of concentrating, increasing, and eventually distributing power more widely within the political system.[29]

The aspects of political culture which might seem most compatible with the concentration and expansion of state power are those which underline the role of the state as the dynamic force in economic and social modernization. There is some reason to think that these values are more dominant in the political elite which emerged from the crisis of December 1967 than in any other ruling group since independence. And, having achieved a degree of homogeneity within the elite which has no precedent, the Algerian leaders will probably not seek reconciliation with the Revolutionaries and Politicians now in exile or in opposition.[30]

One can also expect that the army will continue to play an important political role but will probably share power with the technically competent administrative elite. The type of future recruits to politics is difficult to predict, but it may be that local influentials and technically trained administrators will gradually enter positions in the national elite, especially as the emphasis in recruitment on having an unimpeachable revolutionary past is diluted. As yet, however, no individuals have come to play important political roles who did not receive the major part of their political formation during the colonial period or during the revolution.

If the prospects in Algeria for establishing a greater degree of elite unity than has been seen in the past are indeed relatively good, it is not as clear that the political elite will be capable of responding to demands for wider participation by opening the political system to new groups. For the moment the students, and perhaps the workers, are the most articulate of the groups demanding a greater share of power.[31]

[29] These stages of political development have been outlined by F. W. Frey, *The Turkish Political Elite,* pp. 406–419.

[30] A possible exception to this exclusion of wartime political leaders might be the reentry of some of the GPRA ministers and in particular Abdelhafid Boussouf and M'Hammed Yazid, in positions of political influence. Some others now out of politics might return in important economic posts, such as has been the case for Ben Tobbal and Dahlab.

[31] Students around the world have played important roles in bringing about political change. See the essays edited by Seymour Lipset in *Daedalus,* Winter 1968. In February 1968 the Algerian students launched a prolonged strike, asking for more autonomy from the Party and for better conditions at the University. The regime reacted rather moderately, although numerous arrests were made. The students were clearly the most vocal opponents of the new attempts to concentrate power initiated by Ahmed Kaid as head of the FLN.

Because of the elite's populist orientation, it seems probable that efforts to increase the number of students and to improve the social and economic standards of the masses will continue to be made. But these very efforts will quite likely bring new and more organized demands for participation from individuals who aspire to greater social mobility. If the elite values which see opposition and political dissent as illegitimate dominate those values which favor mass participation, then prospects for stable political development seem dim.

All that can be confidently said at the end of Algeria's seventh year as an independent nation is that few irreversible choices as to the nature of the political system have been made. While the past has been filled with instability and intraelite conflict, the sources of that conflict, namely the diverse patterns of political socialization during the colonial period and during the revolution, could easily diminish in importance. If such historically based sources for division and dissension were overcome, Algerian politicians would still likely be left with the more enduring and perhaps conflicting traits of their political culture to orient and guide their behavior in the years ahead.

If it is true that the dominant themes in Algerian political culture revolve around distrust, equality, a strong statist orientation, and a populist bias, it seems clear that the relative importance of these individual values will partly determine the success of the Algerian political elite in facing the problems of creating political authority and in responding to demands for greater sharing of power. There seems to be no a priori reason to exclude the possibility of development toward either a rigid, authoritarian, unresponsive, and bureaucratic state or toward a more pragmatic, relatively tolerant, participant polity.

Whichever system eventually emerges will reflect choices made by the relatively few men who make up the political elite. Whether these men will have the determination to encourage policies that would provide for a broader inclusion of the rest of the Algerian people in the political process is unclear. It does seem, however, that there is nothing in Algeria's present political culture which precludes a gradual development toward a relatively open political system. It is precisely this undetermined quality of Algerian political development which both places responsibility on Algeria's leaders and makes the Algerian case a subject worthy of continued study and concern.

14
Summary and Conclusion

Algerian politics since 1954 have been dominated by severe conflicts among the members of the political elite and by a series of crises of authority. What were the sources of these conflicts? What have the consequences of intraelite dissension been? And what political practices have been adopted to overcome the crises of authority caused by these divisions?

The sources of political conflicts among Algerian leaders seem to lie primarily in the various patterns of elite political socialization during the colonial period and after the revolution began. Members of the Algerian political elite entered politics by several distinctive paths, primarily in reaction to what was perceived as the "politics of failure" at the time of their entry into political life. As each political generation, or as each socially distinct group became aware of politics, it typically reacted against the ongoing political process and sought to create new norms of political behavior.

The Liberals of the 1930's rejected the prospects of becoming Frenchmen at the price of abandoning their own religion. But the policy of assimilation which they pursued was defeated by the failure of the Blum-Viollette proposal in 1938. A younger political generation, the Radicals, rejected the moderate methods of the Liberals,

277

and decided that mass organization and perhaps even violence would bring Algeria closer to the goal of independence. Violence, for the Radicals, was tried, but failed in 1945, and the path of party organization and elections was likewise undermined by the elections of 1948. Like the Liberals, who abandoned their ideal of assimilation in the late 1930's, the Radicals admitted their failure both to work within the colonial framework and to use violence to end the oppressive system.

In reaction to the failures of Liberals and Radicals, a more militant group of Revolutionaries concluded that force alone would bring independence. They also were nearly condemned to failure with the destruction of the *Organisation Spéciale* in 1950. But in a desperate effort to reverse the series of defeats, the Revolutionaries began an armed insurrection on November 1, 1954.

Even the revolution, however, did not provide a clear model for an effective political process upon which all groups could agree. Rather, the revolution exacerbated existing conflicts in two major ways. The revolution, as it progressed, was joined by virtually all prominent leaders of the nationalist movement, including Liberals, Radicals, and Revolutionaries. Old enemies were thus linked in a common cause, but past differences were not so easily erased. Rather, many forces acted to separate these groups even further. For example, leadership came to be divided between interior forces and exterior ones, and between Politicians and the Military. The arrests and deaths of many noted leaders and the disagreements that grew over the terms of negotiations further deepened these divisions.

A second way in which the revolution added to the diversity and differences within the elite was by bringing in new recruits to top political positions. But once again entry into politics was partly a reaction to feelings that the existing leaders of the war were incompetent. Thus, a new generation of Military commanders who had remained apart from the old nationalist struggles became influential and eventually asserted their independence from the other leaders of the revolution. Intellectuals also joined the political elite, perhaps less in defiance of the ongoing political process than from a feeling that their technical or theoretical competence could effectively be used in new roles.

The consequences of having at least five distinctive types of political actors participating in the war for independence were numerous. First, all participants in the revolution could claim the right to positions of power in the postindependence period. Second, the elite was badly divided and extremely heterogeneous, with no single group obviously strong enough to dominate a future political system.

One consequence of the intraelite conflicts that developed during the colonial period and were exacerbated by the revolution was that with independence the FLN immediately disintegrated, primarily along lines indicated by earlier political socialization. Liberals and Radicals opposed one another, as did Radicals and the Military. Revolutionaries, who more than any other group felt responsible for the attainment of independence, fought with each other and with everyone else in efforts to assure prominent power positions for themselves. The crisis of summer 1962 reflected the depth of divisions within the elite and the persistence of hostile orientations toward other political actors derived from earlier political experiences.

The realignment of groups within the elite which brought the crisis to a close was characterized by the search for a large, widely representative coalition of many types of top leaders. A ruling group formed which excluded primarily the Radicals and some of the Revolutionaries and Intellectuals associated with the GPRA. Consequently, Ben Bella came to power with the support of a heterogeneous group. With time this coalition proved too difficult to maintain and a trend toward the development of a "minimal winning coalition" appeared.

The attempts since Algerian independence to solve the problem of authority created by intraelite divisions have taken three forms. The initial phase of seizing power with a broad coalition of prestigious top leaders has twice resulted in early efforts to preserve this heterogeneous elite by adopting accommodative or collegial procedures of decision-making. For Ben Bella this took the form of allowing free debate within the National Constituent Assembly. For Boumedienne, this meant adopting collegial practices within the Council of Ministers and the Council of the Revolution.

Two deviations from this initial conciliatory political style have occurred in Algeria. The first came with Ben Bella's efforts to concentrate power in his own hands. This resulted in widespread disaffection among his one-time colleagues, many of whom expressed open opposition. As the top elite was eliminated, Ben Bella sought for more manageable allies from the secondary elite. Concentrating power meant that decision-making capacity was augmented, and many new policies were adopted, though few were effectively implemented. Finally, however, Ben Bella's authoritarian practices alienated his last supporters, the Military, and he was easily deposed in a model coup.

Boumedienne also came to power with a rather heterogeneous coalition of *maquisards*, Intellectuals, and professional Military officers. The initial heterogeneity of the elite dictated a collegial style of decision-making. This, however, proved unwieldy in practice, and the deviation from the norm this time took the form of the creation of relatively autonomous subgroups within the elite. Ministers, regional military commanders, and party officials pursued their own goals, and conflicts were both inevitable and difficult to mediate. Stability was relatively high, in contrast to Ben Bella's rule, but decision-making capacity, because of the low degree of elite consensus, seemed very low, particularly with respect to political reforms. New recruits to the top elite from the secondary elite were not as common as under Ben Bella.

Finally, this segmented political structure also broke down as elements within the army attempted a coup in December 1967. Following this futile effort the *maquisards* and leftist Intellectuals were largely eliminated from the elite, leaving professional soldiers and technically competent ministers in control of the country. Efforts to concentrate power seemed to be under way in 1968 and 1969, and with a relatively homogeneous group of leaders prospects for creating some degree of elite unity seemed greater than in the past.

One outcome of the process of elite political socialization in Algeria has been the formation of a "political culture" containing several contradictory elements. Intraelite relations, for example, are characterized by both a high level of mistrust and by an expectation that reciprocity and equality will be respected.

A second set of inconsistent orientations involves the images held by Algerian leaders of the proper role of the state. Strong statist orientations exist, growing out of intensely felt nationalism. But also a genuine popular orientation can be found among the political leaders. Many individuals simultaneously are attracted to both the ideals of a strong centralized state and of extensive mass participation and decentralization.

Given these values, Algerian leaders may eventually either create an authoritarian regime, unresponsive to the people, or a relatively open political process which permits considerable mass participation. One result of extreme elite instability has been that few irreversible choices have yet been made as to the nature of the political system, and from this situation stem both the liabilities and the promises of Algerian political development.

Appendix A
Methodology and Interviewing

Information on the political socialization of Algerian leaders was collected in several ways. The most important means for collecting data on beliefs and attitudes of members of the political elite was the interview. Approximately forty interviews were conducted with prominent Algerian leaders during late 1966 and early 1967. Interviews were unstructured, although a set of similar questions about his career in politics was asked of each respondent.

Interviews usually lasted from one to four hours. An interview would begin with a question about how the respondent came to be involved in politics. More precise questions about social background, particularly important experiences and historical events would be introduced at appropriate times. Depending upon what political offices the respondent had held, a set of questions would be asked about what expectations he had held before entering office and how these compared with the reality later encountered. Each person interviewed was asked to explain the origins of the crisis of summer 1962, a question which usually revealed a good deal about political orientations.

In general, most of those who were willing to be interviewed were extremely open and frank in discussing anything other than current politics. The revolution and the Ben Bella period were openly discussed by most interviewees. The fact that the interviewer was an American at a time when relations between the United States and Algeria were particularly strained did not seem to be much of a hindrance except perhaps in reaching incumbents in top governmental positions. The Arab-Israeli war in June 1967 occurred just toward the end of the proposed research period and would have seriously impeded successful interviewing for the remainder of the summer at least. Fortunately most of the interviewing that could be done was completed by then, though a few follow-ups were put off because of these events.[1]

---

[1] For a good discussion of some of these problems of interviewing in developing countries, see Myron Weiner, "Political Interviewing," in Robert E. Ward, ed., *Studying Politics Abroad.*

Some members of each of the five groups within the elite were interviewed, but access to the Military and the Revolutionaries was more difficult than it was to the other groups. Inevitably the nature of the sample of those interviewed influences the type of inferences one can make using these data, but since quantitative statements are generally not based solely on the interviews this bias is hopefully lessened.

The interviews most heavily relied upon in this study were the following:

Abbas, Ferhat; February 17 and 22, 1967 and May 17, 1967
Batel, Sadek; February 6, 1967
Belhocine, Mabrouk; February 3, 1967
Benkhedda, Benyoussef; February 7, 1967
Bentoumi, Amar; December 7, 1966
Bitat, Zohra; October 13, 1966 and November 3, 1966
Boutaleb, Abdelkader; February 16, 1967
Bouzida, Arezki; January 5, 1967
Brahimi, Abdelhamid; January 6, 1967
Chentouf, Abderrazak; November 29, 1966
Cheriat, Abdallah; March 17, 1967
Chibane, Abderrahmane; February 23, 1967 and March 10, 1967
Dahlab, Saad; April 13 and 25, 1967
Fantazi, Belkacem; March 13, 1967
Gaid, Mouloud; April 27, 1967
Guerroudj, Abdelkader; February 28, 1967 and April 18, 1967
Haroun, Mohammed; February 15 and 27, 1967
Mammeri, Mouloud; March 7, 1967
Mezhoudi, Brahim; December 20, 1966 and February 2, 1967
Al Mili, Muhammad; January 10, 1967
Mohammedi Said; December 11, 1966
Ouamrane, Amar; May 12, 1967
Ramage, Paul; February 2, 1967
Rebbani, Nefa; March 10, 1967
Yazid, M'Hammed; March 6, 1967

For a more complete sample of the political elite, it was possible to gather information on age, education, region of birth, and history of political participation. This information was collected for virtually all the top elite and for about half the secondary elite. Data were drawn from documentary sources, interviews, biographies and autobiographies, and various secondary studies of Algerian politics.

While some gaps also remain in these data, particularly with regard to the Military, most prominent Algerian political leaders are included in this sample.

In addition to information on social backgrounds and political careers it was possible to gather some behavioral data. The most extensive source of this type of information is in the form of voting records and quantitative measures of speaking (in column inches and frequency) in the National Assembly. This information is used in Chapter 10 to illustrate the failure of the Assembly to provide the institutional setting for the development of a conciliatory political process. Deputies belonging to the five major groups within the political elite can be seen to act quite differently in terms of opposition and participation within the Assembly. Some links, then, between political socialization and political behavior can be illustrated with quantitative measures.

The methodological problems accompanying any empirical research that selects the individual as the unit of analysis in an attempt to understand the workings of a larger political system are found in this study.[2] Aggregating data about individuals in order to talk of groups and systems is always difficult, but by focusing considerable attention upon linkages among individuals within the elite, generalizations about larger units can be made with increased confidence. An equally serious methodological problem is that sometimes the data used to support general hypotheses are incomplete, but until the Algerians themselves are willing to divulge information which could fill these gaps one must live with such deficiencies. The most important group for which data are often lacking is, of course, the Military.

[2] Lucian Pye, in *Political Culture and Political Development,* edited by Lucian Pye and Sidney Verba, p. 9, proposes the idea of political culture as a partial means for handling the problem of aggregation, since it refers to the study of individuals but stresses their links to others in the system. A fuller discussion of this "micro-macro" dilemma is found in Heinz Eulau, *The Behavioral Persuasion in Politics.*

Appendix B

The Algerian Political Elite: Tenure in Top Positions, 1954-1968

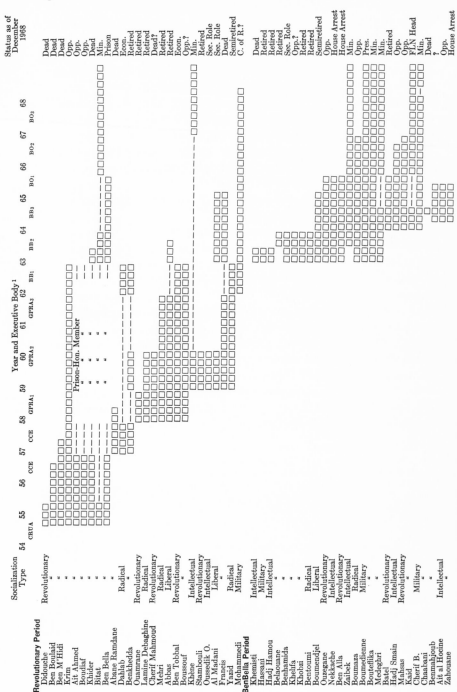

Mohand oul Hadj — Maquisard — Opp.
Khatib Youssef — " — Opp.
Zbiri — " — Opp.
Mendjli — Revolutionary — C. of R.?
Cherif A. — Intellectual — House Arrest
Boudissa — " — Retired
Amrani — Intellectual — Econ.
Ghozali — " — Econ.
Dellici — " — Min.
Heddam — " — Min.
Bedjaoui — " — Min.

Boumedienne Period

Boubnider — Maquisard — Opp.
Said Abid — " — Dead
Ali Yahia — Intellectual — Opp.
Zerdani — " — Opp.
Boudjenane — Military — Dead
Belhouchet — " — C. of R.
Chabou — " — C. of R.
Ben Ahmed — Maquisard — C. of R.
Bendjedid — Military — C. of R.?
Soufi — Maquisard — C. of R.?
Benhaddou — " — C. of R.
Bencherif — " — C. of R.
Draia — Military — C. of R.
Yahiaoui — " — C. of R.
Tayebi — Maquisard — Min.
Bensalem — Military — C. of R.
Taleb — Intellectual — Min.
Masoui — " — Min.
Abdesselam — " — Min.
Saadouni — " — Min.
Benmahmoud — Military — Min.
Benhamouda — " — Min.
Ben Yahia — Intellectual — Min.
Mazouzi — Military (?) — Min.

KEY

□□□□□□□ Period of incumbency. One □ equals about three months.
– – – – – – Period between top elite positions.
Opp. In opposition to the government.
Econ. In an important role in the economy as head of state-owned company.
Sec. Role In a minor political role, ambassador, Party official, etc.
Min. Minister in the Boumedienne government in early 1969.
C. of R. Member of the Council of the Revolution in early 1969.
? Current status uncertain.

1 July 1954, Nine leaders of CRUA
August 1956, 1st CCE
August 1957, 2d CCE
September 1958, 1st GPRA
January 1960, 2d GPRA
August 1961, 3d GPRA
September 1962, BB, 1st Ben Bella Government
September 1963, 2d Ben Bella Government
December 1964, 3d Ben Bella Government
July 1965, Council of Revolution and (BO), 1st Boumedienne Government
October 1966, Partial change in Boumedienne Government
December 1967, Partial change after attempted coup

285

Appendix C
Tenure in Top Political Roles, 1954-1968

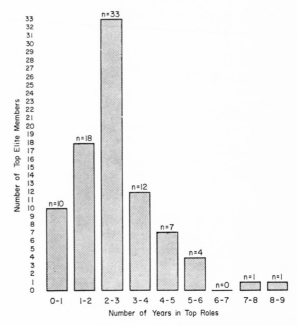

Note: Only 10 of 86 incumbents of top political roles interrupted their tenure in office.

Appendix D

The Members of the Comité des 22 and the Leadership of the CRUA, 1954

The Committee of Twenty-two [1]	1968 Position
Badji Mokhtar	Dead
Belhadj Abdelkader (Kobus) (?)	Dead. Executed as traitor by ALN
Belouizdad Athmane	Deputy after independence, minor Party official
Ben Abdelmalek Ramdane	Died on November 1, 1954
Ben Alla Hadj (?)	House arrest
Benaouda Mostefa	Military attaché, Paris
*Ben Boulaid Mustapha	Dead
*Ben M'hidi Larbi	Dead
Ben Tobbal Lakhdar	President of the *Sidérurgie* complex, Annaba
*Bitat Rabah	Minister of Transport since October 1966
Bouadjadj Zoubir	Unknown. Perhaps Party official
Bouali Said	Dead
Bouchaib Ahmed	Deputy after independence, now in Party
*Boudiaf Mohammed	Opposition, PRS
Boussouf Abdelhafid	Semiopposition
*Didouche Mourad	Dead
Habachi Abdesalem	Administrative position
Mellah Ali (colonel Si Cherif)	Dead
Merzougui Mohammed	Unknown
Nechati Mohammed	Unknown
Suidani Boudjemaa	Dead
Zighout Youssef	Dead

The CRUA Leadership.[1] The 22 plus:	
*Ait Ahmed Hocine	Opposition, FFS
Abane Ramdane (?)	Dead. Executed during war
*Ben Bella Ahmed	Prison since June 19, 1965
*Khider Mohammed	Died January 1967, in exile in Spain
*Krim Belkacem	Opposition, MDRA
Lamine Debaghine Mohammed (?)	Unknown
Ouamrane Amar	Owns gas station, Algiers

[1] Names followed by (?) are those of men who are not universally recognized as members of these bodies. Names preceded by * are those of the nine *chefs historiques*. One source adds Abdelkader Lamoudi as a member of the *Comité des 22* and excludes Abdelkader Belhadj (Kobus).

287

Appendix E

The Members of the first CNRA, August 1956[1]

Full Members	Alternate Members
*Abane Ramdane	*Benaouda Mostepha Amar (?)
Abbas Ferhat	*Ben Tobbal Lakhdar
Ait Ahmed Hocine	Ben Yahia Mohammed
Ben Bella Ahmed	Boussouf Abdelhafid
Ben Boulaid Mustapha	*Cherif Mahmoud
Benkhedda Benyoussef	Chihani Bachir
*Ben M'Hidi Larbi	*Dhilès Slimane (?)
Bitat Rabah	Idir Aissat (?)
Boudiaf Mohammed	Francis Ahmed
Dahlab Saad	Lebjaoui Mohammed (?)
Khider Mohammed	Mahsas Ahmed
*Krim Belkacem	Mehri Abdelhafid
Lamine Debaghine Mohammed	*Mellah Ali
Al Madani Tewfik	*Mezhoudi Brahim
*Ouamrane Amar	*Mohammedi Said
Yazid M'Hammed	Temmam Abdelmalek
*Zighout Youssef	Thaalbi Tayeb

[1] The list of members of the first CNRA was published in *El Moudjahid*, No. 4, November 1956, and included eight pseudonyms for security reasons. Some of these have been positively identified in the present list, but a small number remain somewhat uncertain. Names followed by (?) are those of probable but not confirmed members of the CNRA. Salah Louanchi is also mentioned as an alternate by some sources. Names preceded by an asterisk (*) are those of men who actually attended the Soummam Congress where the CNRA was selected.

Appendix F
The GPRA Ministers

	Position	1968 Status (new incumbents only)
First GPRA September 1958		
Abbas Ferhat	President	Retired
Krim Belkacem	Vice President and Armed Forces	Opposition
Ben Bella Ahmed [1]	Vice President	Prison
Ait Ahmed Hocine [1]	Minister of State	Opposition
Bitat Rabah [1]	Minister of State	Minister of Transport
Boudiaf Mohammed [1]	Minister of State	Opposition
Khider Mohammed [1]	Minister of State	Dead
Lamine Debaghine	Foreign Affairs	?
Cherif Mahmoud	Armaments and Supplies	Dead
Ben Tobbal Lakhdar	Interior	President of *Sidérurgie*
Boussouf Abdelhafid	General Liaisons and Communications	Semiopposition
Mehri Abdelhamid	North African Affairs	Teacher
Francis Ahmed	Economic Affairs and Finance	Dead
Yazid M'Hammed	Information	Semiretired
Benkhedda Benyoussef	Social Affairs	Pharmacist
Al Madani Tewfik	Cultural Affairs	Ambassador to Iraq
Khène Lamine	Secretary of State	Minister of Public Works
Oussedik Omar	Secretary of State	Ambassador to Moscow
Stambouli Mustapha	Secretary of State	?
Second GPRA January 1960		
Abbas Ferhat	President	
Krim Belkacem	Vice President and External Affairs	
Ben Bella Ahmed	Vice President	
Ait Ahmed Hocine	Minister of State	
Rabah Bitat	Minister of State	
Boudiaf Mohammed	Minister of State	
Khider Mohammed	Minister of State	
Mohammedi Said	Minister of State	Council of the Revolution?
Boussouf Abdelhafid	Armaments and General Liaisons	
Ben Tobbal Lakhdar	Interior	
Francis Ahmed	Economic Affairs and Finance	

289

	Position	1968 Status (new incumbents only)
Yazid M'Hammed	Information	
Mehri Abdelhamid	Social and Cultural Affairs	

Third *GPRA* August 1961

Benyoussef Benkhedda	President and Finance	
Krim Belkacem	Vice President and Interior	
Ben Bella Ahmed	Vice President	
Boudiaf Mohammed	Vice President	
Ait Ahmed Hocine	Minister of State	
Ben Tobbal Lakhdar	Minister of State	
Bitat Rabah	Minister of State	
Khider Mohammed	Minister of State	
Mohammedi Said	Minister of State	
Boussouf Abdelhafid	Armaments and General Liaisons	
Yazid M'Hammed	Information	
Dahlab Saad	Foreign Affairs	President of *Berliet*

---

[1] Ben Bella, Ait Ahmed, Bitat, Boudiaf, and Khider were in French prisons during the entire period 1958–1962 but were included as honorary members.

Appendix G
Members of Ben Bella's Three Governments

	Cabinet Post	1968 Position (new incumbents only)
First Government (September 1962)		
Ben Bella Ahmed	President	Prison
Bitat Rabah	Vice President	Minister of Transport
Bentoumi Amar	Justice	Lawyer
Medeghri Ahmed	Interior	Minister of Interior
Boumedienne Houari	National Defense	President and Defense
Khemisti Mohammed	Foreign Affairs	Dead
Francis Ahmed	Finance	Dead
Ouzegane Amar	Agriculture	Opposition
Khobzi Mohammed	Commerce	?
Khelifa Laroussi	Industry and Energy	Opposition [1]
Boumendjel Ahmed	Reconstruction, Public Works	Semiretired
Boumaza Bachir	Work and Social Affairs	Opposition
Benhamida Abderrahmane	Education	Direction Centrale of FLN
Nekkache Mohammed	Health	Prison; released Nov. 1968
Mohammedi Said	War Veterans	Council of the Revolution (?)
Bouteflika Abdelaziz	Youth and Sports	Minister of Foreign Affairs
al Madani Tewfik	Religious Foundations (*Habous*)	Ambassador to Iraq
Hadj Hamou Mohammed	Information	Lawyer
Hassani Mohammed	Posts and Telecommunications	Retired
Second Government (September 1963)		
Ben Bella Ahmed	President	
Boumedienne Houari	Vice President and Defense	
Mohammedi Said	Vice President	
Ouzegane Amar	Minister of State	
Hadj Smain Mohammed	Justice	Opposition
Medeghri Ahmed	Interior	
Bouteflika Abdelaziz	Foreign Affairs	

291

	Cabinet Post	1968 Position (new incumbents only)
Boumaza Bachir	Economy	
Mahsas Ahmed	Agriculture	Opposition
Boumendjel Ahmed	Reconstruction	
Nekkache Mohammed	Social Affairs	
Belkacem Cherif	National Orientation	Minister of Finance and Planning [2]
al Madani Tewfik	Religious Foundations	
Zaibek Abdelkader	Posts and Telecommunications	Minister of Posts
Kaid Ahmed	Tourism	Head of FLN [2]
Batel Sadek	Undersecretary, Youth Sports	Public Accountant

Third Government
(December 1964)

Ben Bella Ahmed [3]	President	
Boumedienne Houari	Vice President and Defense	
Mohammedi Said	Vice President	
Cherif Abderrahmane	Minister Delegated to Presidency	Prison; released Nov. 1968
Bedjaoui Mohammed	Justice	Minister of Justice
Bouteflika Abdelaziz	Foreign Affairs	
Mahsas Ahmed	Agriculture	
Dellici Nourredine	Commerce	Minister of Commerce
Boumaza Bachir	Industry and Energy	
Hadj Smain Mohammed	Reconstruction and Housing	
Boudissa Safi	Work	Trade Union Official
Nekkache Mohammed	Health, War Veterans and Social Affairs	
Belkacem Cherif	Education	
Batel Sadek	Youth and Sports	
Heddam Tedjini	Religious Foundations	Minister of Health
Zaibek Abdelkader	Posts and Telecommunications	
Amrani Said	Administrative Reform	Head of SNED [4]
Ouzegane Amar	Tourism	
Ghozali Ahmed	Undersecretary for Public Works	Head of SONATRACH [5]

---

[1] Laroussi Khelifa was replaced as head of Air Algérie in December 1967.

[2] Ahmed Kaid was made head of the FLN in December 1967, after the removal of Cherif Belkacem.

[3] Ben Bella, in addition to his functions as President in the third government, was directly responsible for the ministries of Finance, Information, and Interior.

[4] SNED stands for Société Nationale d'Editions et de Distribution and constitutes a state monopoly over publishing and importing of printed material.

[5] SONATRACH is the state-owned company in charge of exploration, production, and distribution of petroleum and petroleum products.

Appendix H
Members of the Political Bureau of the FLN

	Concurrent Position	1968 Position
First Political Bureau		
(August 1962)		
Ben Bella Ahmed	President	Prison
Khider Mohammed	Secretary General, FLN	Dead
Bitat Rabah	Vice President	Minister of Transport
Ben Alla Hadj	Vice President of Assembly	House arrest
Mohammedi Said	Minister of War Veterans	Council of the Revolution (?)
Second Political Bureau		
(April 1964)		
Ben Bella Ahmed	President	Prison
Ben Alla Hadj	President of the Assembly	House arrest
Mohammedi Said	Vice President	Council of the Revolution (?)
Boumedienne Houari	Vice President and Defense	President and Defense
Mendjli Ali	Vice President of Assembly	Council of the Revolution (?)
oul Hadj Mohand		Opposition
Mahsas Ahmed	Minister of Agriculture	Opposition
Benmahjoub Omar	Deputy	(?)
Nekkache Mohammed	Minister of Social Affairs	House arrest
Bouteflika Abdelaziz	Minister of Foreign Affairs	Minister of Foreign Affairs
Boumaza Bachir	Minister of National Economy	Opposition
Medeghri Ahmed	Minister of Interior	Minister of Interior
Zbiri Tahar	Chief of Staff of ANP	Opposition
Chaabani Mohammed	Commander Fifth Military Region	Dead
al Hocine Ait	President of *Amicale* in France	Opposition
Zahouane Hocine		House arrest
Youssef Khatib	Deputy	Opposition

293

Glossary

ALN *Armée de Libération Nationale,* the revolutionary army from 1954 to 1962.

AML *Amis du Manifeste et de la Liberté,* a political group formed by Ferhat Abbas in 1944 which united several nationalist tendencies until it was dissolved after the 1945 crisis.

ANP *Armée Nationale Populaire,* the name of the Algerian Army since independence in 1912.

Autogestion "Self-management," a key element in Algerian socialism, which in theory means that peasants and workers manage their own farms or factories.

CCE *Comité de Coordination et d'Exécution,* the first executive agency of the FLN. Five members were named in 1956; in 1957 it had nine.

CNDR *Comité National pour la Défense de la Révolution,* an opposition group formed in 1964 which temporarily grouped together the FFS and the PRS.

CNRA *Comité National de la Révolution Algérienne,* a parliamentary-like body formed in 1956 and reshuffled several times during the war. It acted as the ultimate authority within the FLN.

CNS *Corps National de Securité,* the security forces in Algeria since independence.

Colons The settlers of European origin living in Algeria before independence.

CRUA *Comité Révolutionnaire d'Unité et d'Action,* the group of about thirty men credited with beginning the Algerian revolution.

ENA *Etoile Nord Africaine,* a political movement founded in Paris about 1925 which Messali Hadj soon came to lead as the first nationalist grouping to call for Algerian independence.

Etat Major Général The General Staff of the Army.

FFFLN *Fédération de France du Front de Libération Nationale,* the FLN branch in France during the war which tried to organize Algerian workers and combat the forces loyal to Messali Hadj. It disbanded in 1962 and was replaced by *Amicale* for Algerian workers in France.

FFS *Front des Forces Socialistes,* the primarily Kabyle opposition group formed by Ait Ahmed in September 1963.

FLN *Front de Libération Nationale,* the Algerian revolutionary movement. The name was given by the CRUA and continued as the name for the only legal party in Algeria after independence.

GPRA *Gouvernement Provisoire de la République Algérienne,* the provisional government formed in 1958 in Tunisia, responsible to the CNRA.

Maquis, maquisard *Maquis,* a French word for dense underbrush, came to mean a place of refuge for anti-German resistance movements during

294

World War II. In Algeria, *maquis* referred to the areas of refuge for the guerrilla fighters, and *maquisard* designated the guerrilla himself.

MDRA   *Mouvement Démocratique de la Révolution Algérienne,* an opposition movement formed by Belkacem Krim in October 1967.

MNA   *Mouvement National Algérien,* a movement formed by Messali Hadj in 1955 to counter the FLN.

Moudjahid   The Arab-derived term for guerrillas, literally mujāhid, a fighter in the holy war.

MTLD   *Mouvement pour le Triomphe des Libertés Démocratiques,* a nationalist movement founded by Messali Hadj as a continuation of the PPA after World War II.

ORP   *Organisation de la Résistance Populaire,* an opposition movement formed after the June 19, 1965 coup, which called for the release of Ben Bella, Harbi, Zahouane, and Bachir Hadj Ali from prison. The ORP was generally considered the most leftist of the opposition groups.

OS   *Organisation Spéciale,* the clandestine movement formed by the MTLD in 1947 which prepared for armed insurrection until virtually disbanded in 1950 by the French police.

PCA   *Parti Communiste Algérien.*   Originally the Algerian branch of the French Communist Party, the PCA became autonomous in 1936. Individual PCA members were able to join the FLN during the war, but the party was outlawed after independence.

PPA   *Parti du Peuple Algérien,* a nationalist party formed by Messali Hadj in 1937 as a continuation within Algeria of the ENA.

PRS   *Parti de la Révolution Socialiste,* clandestine opposition party formed immediately after independence by Mohammed Boudiaf.

UDMA   *Union Démocratique du Manifeste Algérien,* a moderate nationalist party formed by Ferhat Abbas after World War II.

UGEMA   *Union Générale des Etudiants Musulmans Algériens,* the FLN-affiliated student organization during the war.

UGTA   *Union Générale des Travailleurs Algériens,* the FLN-affiliated trade union founded during the war and continued after independence.

Ulama   The plural of the Arabic *'ālim,* educated man. In the Algerian context it designates the religious reformers around Ben Badis and his followers from the 1930s on.

UNEA   *Union Nationale des Etudiants Algériens,* the student union since independence, a continuation of the UGEMA.

UNFA   *Union Nationale des Femmes Algériennes,* the FLN-affiliated women's union.

Willaya   One of the six military regions formed at the *Congrès de la Soummam. Willaya* 1 was the Aurès region, 2 was North Constantine, 3 was Kabylia, 4 was the department of Algiers, 5 was Oranie, 6 was the Saharan region. Each *willaya* was led by a colonel of the ALN and enjoyed considerable autonomy during the war.

ZAA   *Zone Autonome d'Alger,* the military organization within the city of Algiers, particularly at the time of the Battle of Algiers and again at independence. *Willaya* 4 claimed the ZAA was under its jurisdiction, but the leaders of the ZAA thought otherwise.

Bibliography

Theoretical and Comparative Studies

Almond, Gabriel A., and Coleman, James S., eds. *The Politics of the Developing Areas*. Princeton: Princeton University Press, 1960.

———, and Powell, G. B., Jr. *Comparative Politics: A Developmental Approach*. Boston: Little, Brown, 1966.

———, and Verba, Sidney. *The Civic Culture*. Princeton: Princeton University Press, 1963.

Apter, David E. *Ghana in Transition*. New York: Atheneum, 1963.

Ashford, Douglas E. *Political Change in Morocco*. Princeton: Princeton University Press, 1961.

Banfield, Edward. *The Moral Basis of a Backward Society*. Glencoe, Illinois: The Free Press, 1958.

Binder, Leonard. *Iran: Political Development in a Changing Society*. Berkeley: University of California Press, 1962.

———. *Politics in Lebanon*. New York: Wiley, 1966.

Brinton, Crane. *The Anatomy of Revolution*. New York: Vintage Books, 1959.

Brzezinski, Zbigniew, and Huntington, Samuel P. *Political Power: USA/USSR*. New York: Viking, 1965.

Centers, Richard. *The Psychology of Social Classes: A Study of Class Consciousness*. New York: Russell and Russell, 1961.

Crozier, Brian. *The Rebels: A Study of Post-War Insurrections*. Boston: Beacon Press, 1960.

Dawson, Richard E., and Prewitt, Kenneth E. *Political Socialization*. Boston: Little, Brown, 1969.

Deutsch, Karl W. *The Nerves of Government*. New York: The Free Press of Glencoe, 1963.

Downs, Anthony. *An Economic Theory of Democracy*. New York: Harper and Row, 1957.

Eckstein, Harry. *Division and Cohesion in a Democracy: A Study of Norway*. Princeton: Princeton University Press, 1966.

Edwards, Lyford P. *The Natural History of Revolution*. Chicago: The University of Chicago Press, 1927.

Eisenstadt, S. N. *From Generation to Generation: Age Groups and Social Structure*. Glencoe, Illinois: The Free Press, 1956.

Eulau, Heinz. *The Behavioral Persuasion in Politics*. New York: Random House, 1963.

Feith, Herbert. *The Decline of Constitutional Democracy in Indonesia*. Ithaca: Cornell University Press, 1962.

Frey, Frederick W. "Democracy and Reform in Developing Societies." Mimeographed. Cambridge: 1967.

————, *The Turkish Political Elite.* Cambridge, Mass.: M.I.T. Press, 1965.

George, Alexander L., and George, Juliette L. *Woodrow Wilson and Colonel House: A Personality Study.* New York: Dover, 1964.

Gordon, Robert A. *Business Leadership in the Large Corporation.* Berkeley: University of California Press, 1966.

Greenstein, Fred. *Children and Politics.* New Haven: Yale University Press, 1965.

Grossholtz, Jean. *Politics in the Philippines.* Boston: Little, Brown, 1964.

Hess, Robert P., and Easton, David. "The Child's Changing Image of the President." *Public Opinion Quarterly,* Winter, 1960.

Hoffer, Eric. *The True Believer.* New York: Mentor, 1960.

Hourani, Albert. *Arabic Thought in the Liberal Age, 1798-1939.* New York: Oxford University Press, 1962.

Huntington, Samuel P. *Political Order in Changing Societies.* New Haven: Yale University Press, 1968.

Hyman, Herbert. *Political Socialization.* New York: The Free Press, 1959.

La Palombara, Joseph, and Weiner, Myron, eds. *Political Parties and Political Development.* Princeton: Princeton University Press, 1966.

Lasswell, Harold D. *Power and Personality.* New York: Viking, 1962.

————. *Psychopathology and Politics.* New York: Viking, 1960.

————, and Kaplan, Abraham. *Power and Society.* New Haven: Yale University Press, 1950.

————, and Lerner, Daniel, eds. *World Revolutionary Elites.* Cambridge, Mass.: The M.I.T. Press, 1965.

————, ————, and Rothwell, C. Easton. *The Comparative Study of Elites.* Stanford: Stanford University Press, 1952.

Leites, Nathan. *Images of Power in French Politics.* Santa Monica: The Rand Corporation, June 1962.

————. *A Study of Bolshevism.* Glencoe, Illnois: The Free Press, 1953.

Lipset, Seymour Martin. *The First New Nation.* Garden City, N.Y.: Anchor Books, 1967.

Marvick, Dwaine, ed. *Political Decision-Makers.* New York: The Free Press, 1961.

Matthews, Donald R. *The Social Backgrounds of Political Decision Makers.* New York: Random House, 1962.

Micaud, Charles A., with Brown, L. Carl, and Moore, Clement H. *Tunisia: The Politics of Modernization.* New York: Praeger, 1964.

Moore, Clement. "La Tunisie après Bourguiba: liberalisation ou décadence politique?" *Revue française de science politique* 17, August 1967, pp. 645–667.

————. *Tunisia Since Independence.* Berkeley: University of California Press, 1965.

Pauker, Guy J. "The Role of the Military in Indonesia," in John J. Johnson, ed. *The Role of the Military in Underdeveloped Countries.* Princeton: Princeton University Press, 1962.

Pool, Ithiel de Sola, ed. *Contemporary Political Science: Toward Empirical Theory.* New York: McGraw-Hill, 1967.

Prewitt, Kenneth, Eulau, Heinz, and Zisk, Betty. "Political Socialization and· Political Roles," *Public Opinion Quarterly* 30 (Winter 1966-67): 569–582.

Pye, Lucian W. *Aspects of Political Development.* Boston: Little, Brown, 1966.

———, and Verba, Sidney, eds. *Political Culture and Political Development.* Princeton: Princeton University Press, 1965.

Riker, William H. *The Theory of Political Coalitions.* New Haven: Yale University Press, 1962.

Rosenberg, Morris. *Occupations and Values.* New York: The Free Press, 1957.

Rustow, Dankwart A. "The Study of Elites: Who's Who, When and How." *World Politics* 18 (July 1966): 690–717.

Scott, Robert E. *Mexican Government in Transition.* Urbana: The University of Illinois Press, 1959.

Shils, Edward. "The Intellectuals in the Political Development of New States." *World Politics,* Vol. 12, No. 3 (April 1960): 329–368.

Singer, Marshall R. *The Emerging Elite: A Study of Political Leadership in Ceylon.* Cambridge, Mass.: The M.I.T. Press, 1964.

Wahlke, John C., Eulau, Heinz, Buchanan, William, and Ferguson, Le Roy. *The Legislative System.* New York: Wiley, 1962.

Ward, Robert E., ed. *Studying Politics Abroad.* Boston: Little, Brown, 1964.

Weber, Max. "Politics as a Vocation." In Gerth, H. H., and Mills, C. Wright, eds., *From Max Weber: Essays in Sociology.* New York: Oxford University Press, 1958.

Weiner, Myron. "Changing Patterns of Political Leadership in West Bengal." *Pacific Affairs,* Vol. 32, No. 3 (September 1959).

———. *Party Building in a New Nation: The Indian National Congress.* Chicago: The University of Chicago Press, 1967.

———. *Party Politics in India: The Development of a Multi-Party System.* Princeton: Princeton University Press, 1957.

Wolfenstein, E. Victor. *The Revolutionary Personality: Lenin, Trotsky, Gandhi.* Princeton: Princeton University Press, 1966.

Studies of Algeria

Abbas, Ferhat. *La nuit coloniale.* Paris: Juillard, 1962.

———. *Le jeune algérien.* Paris: Aux Editions de la Jeune Parque, 1931.

Abdelkader, Abderrazak. *Le conflit judéo-arabe: juifs et arabes face à l'avenir.* Paris: Maspero, 1962.

Ageron, Charles-Robert. "Brève histoire de la politique d'assimilation en Algérie." *Revue socialiste,* no. 95 (March 1958).

———. *Histoire de l'Algérie contemporaine (1830-1964).* Paris: Presses Universitaires de France, 1964.

———. "La France a-t-elle eu une politique kabyle?" *Revue historique,* no. 223 (April-June 1960).

———. "L'Emir Khaled, petit-fils d'Abdelkader, fut-il le premier nationaliste algérien?" *Revue de l'occident musulman,* no. 2, 2ᵉ semestre (1966): 9–49.

———. "Le mouvement 'jeune-algérien,'" *Etudes maghrébines*. Paris: Presses Universitaires de France, 1964, pp. 217–243.

Ait Ahmed, Hocine. *La guerre et l'après-guerre*. Paris: Editions de Minuit, 1964.

Akrouf, Daoud. "Les Amis du Manifeste et de la Liberté." Memoire, Faculté de Droit et de Sciences Economiques, University of Algiers: February 1965.

"Algérie: Pays révolutionnaire du tiers monde." *Démocratie nouvelle*, June 1965.

"Algérie: Une crise d'autorité," *Le Mois en Afrique*, no. 17 (May 1967).

"Algérie: Une opposition vigilante mais divisée," *Le Mois en Afrique*, no. 9 (September 1966).

Annuaire de L'Afrique du Nord 1 (1962), 2 (1963), 3 (1964), 4 (1965). Paris: Editions du Centre de la Recherche Scientifique, 1963, 1964, 1965, 1966.

d'Arcy, François, Krieger, Annie, et Marill, Alain. *Essais sur l'économie de l'Algérie nouvelle*. Paris: Presses Universitaires de France, 1965.

Aron, Robert. *Les origines de la guerre d'Algérie*. Paris: Fayard, 1962.

Ashford, Douglas: *Second and Third Generation Elites in the Maghreb*. Washington: Department of State, 1963.

Azan, Paul. *L'émir Abd el Kader, 1808-1883: du fanatisme musulman au patriotisme français*. Paris: Hachette, 1925.

Bedjaoui, Mohammed. *La révolution algérienne et le droit*. Brussels: Editions de l'Association Internationale des Juristes Democratiques, 1961.

Behr, Edward. *The Algerian Problem*. New York: W. W. Norton, 1961.

Benhabilès, Cherif. *L'Algérie française vue par un indigène*. Alger: Imprimerie Orientale Fantana Freres, 1914.

Benkhedda, Benyoussef. "Contribution à l'historique du FLN." Mimeographed. April 1964.

———. "Contribution à l'historique du mouvement de libération nationale." Mimeographed. April 1964.

Bennabi, Malek. *Memoires d'un témoin du siècle*. Algiers: Editions Nationales Algeriennes, 1965.

———. *Vocation de l'Islam*. Paris: Editions du Seuil, 1954.

Bergheaud, Edmond. *Le premier quart d'heure: l'Algérie des Algériens*. Paris: Plon, 1964.

Bernard, Augustin. *L'Algérie*. Paris: Librairie Felix Alcan, 1929.

Berque, Jacques. *French North Africa: The Maghrib between Two World Wars*, translated by Jean Stewart. New York: Praeger, 1967.

Bessaoud, Mohammed Arab. *Heureux les martyrs qui n'ont rien vu*. Paris: Imprimerie Cary, 1963.

———. *Le FFS: Espoir et trahison*. Paris: Imprimerie Cary, May 1966.

Boualem, Bachagha. *L'Algérie sans la France*. Paris: Editions France-Empire, 1964.

Boudiaf, Mohammed. *Où va l'Algérie?* Paris: Editions Librairie de l'Etoile, 1964.

Bourdieu, Pierre. *The Algerians*. Boston: Beacon Press, 1962.

———. "The Sentiment of Honour in Kabyle Society." In Peristiany, J. G. ed., *Honour and Shame: The Values of Mediterranean Society*. Chicago: The University of Chicago Press, 1966.

Bourgès, Hervé. *L'Algérie à l'épreuve du pouvoir.* Paris: Grasset, 1967.
Brace, Richard M. *Morocco, Algeria and Tunisia.* Englewood Cliffs: Prentice-Hall, 1964.
————, and Brace, Joan. *Algerian Voices.* Princeton: D. Van Nostrand, 1965.
————, ————. *Ordeal in Algeria.* New York: D. Van Nostrand, 1960.
Braestrup, Peter, and Ottaway, David. "In Algeria it's Not 'Yah, Yah, Boumedienne!' but 'Wait and See,' " *The New York Times Magazine,* February 13, 1966.
Bromberger, Serge. *Les rebelles algériens.* Paris: Plon, 1958.
Brown, L. Carl. "The Islamic Reformist Movement in North Africa," *Journal of Modern African Studies* 11 (1964): 55–64.
————. *State and Society in Independent North Africa.* Washington: Middle East Institute, 1966.
Buron, Robert. *Carnets politiques de la guerre d'Algérie.* Paris: Plon, 1965.
Buy, François. *La république algérienne démocratique et populaire.* Paris: Librairie Française, 1965.
Carret, Jacques. "L'Association des Oulama Reformistes d'Algérie," *L'Afrique et l'Asie,* 3ᵉ trimestre, no. 43 (1958).
Chaliand, Gérard. "De Ben Bella à Boumedienne." *Partisans,* no. 23 (November 1965).
————. "L'Algérie au miroir marxiste," *Partisans,* no. 21 (June, July, August 1965).
————. *L'Algérie est-elle socialiste?* Paris: Maspero, 1964.
Charnay, Jean-Paul. *La vie musulmane en Algérie d'après la jurisprudence de la première moitié du xxᵉ siècle.* Paris: Presses Universitaires de France, 1965.
Clark, Michael K. *Algeria in Turmoil.* New York: The Universal Library, 1960.
Confer, Vincent. *France and Algeria: the Problems of Civil and Political Reform, 1870-1920.* New York: Syracuse University Press, 1966.
Courrière, Yves. *Les fils de la Toussaint.* Paris: Fayard, 1968.
Davezies, Robert. *Le Front.* Paris: Editions de Minuit, 1959.
De Card, E. Rouard. *La représentation des indigènes musulmans dans les conseils de l'Algérie.* Paris: A. Pedone, 1909.
Delisle, R. "Les Origines du FLN," *La Nef,* nos. 12-13 (October 1962-January 1963).
Die Algerische Revolution. Stuttgart: Deutsche Verlags-Anstalt, 1963.
Douence, Jean-Claude. *La mise en place des institutions algériennes.* Paris: Fondation Nationale des Sciences Politiques, 1964.
Drif, Zohra. *La mort de mes frères.* Paris: Maspero, 1960.
Duchemin, Jacques. *Histoire du FLN.* Paris: La Table Ronde, 1962.
Duclos, Louis-Jean, Duvignaud, Jean, and Leca, Jean. *Les nationalismes magrébins.* Paris: Centre d'étude des relations internationales, July 1966.
Dusquesne, J. "Au Congres du FLN: Socialisme et Islam," *Revue de l'action populaire,* no. 180, July-August, 1964.
Estier, Claude. *Pour l'Algérie.* Paris: Maspero, 1964.
Fanon, Frantz. *The Wretched of the Earth.* London: Penguin Books, 1967.

Farès, Bichr. *L'honneur chez les arabes avant l'Islam*. Paris: Librairie d'Amerique et l'Orient, 1932.

al-Fasi, Allal. *The Independence Movements in Arab North Africa*. Washington: American Council of Learned Societies, 1954.

Favret, Jeanne. "Le syndicat, les travailleurs et le pouvoir en Algérie," *Annuaire de l'Afrique du nord* 3 (1964).

Favrod, Charles-Henri. *Le* FLN *et l'Algérie*. Paris: Plon, 1962.

Feraoun, Mouloud. *Journal: 1955-1962*. Paris: Editions du Seuil, 1962.

Gaid, Mouloud. *Tarikh al-Jazā'ir al-Musawwar*. Algiers: Maktabah An-Nahdah al-Jaza'iriyyah, 1964.

Gallagher, Charles. "The Algerian Year," Parts 1, 2, 3. American Universities Field Staff Reports, 1963.

———. *The United States and North Africa: Morocco, Algeria, and Tunisia*. Cambridge: Harvard University Press, 1963.

Gillespie, Joan. *Algeria: Rebellion and Revolution*. New York: Praeger, 1961.

Glories, J. "Quelques observations sur la révolution algérienne et le communisme," *L'Afrique et l'Asie*, no. 41, (1958).

Gordon, David C. *North Africa's French Legacy: 1954-1962*. Cambridge: Harvard University Press, 1962.

———. *The Passing of French Algeria*. New York: Oxford University Press, 1966.

Guerin, Daniel. *L'Algérie caporalisée*. Paris: December 1965.

Hadj Ali, Bachir. *L'arbitraire*. Paris: Les Editions de Minuit, 1966.

Hahn, Lorna. "North Africa: A New Pragmatism." *ORBIS*, Spring 1964, pp. 125–140.

———. *North Africa: Nationalism to Nationhood*. Washington: Public Affairs Press, 1960.

———. "Politics and Leadership in North Africa." *ORBIS*, Fall 1965, pp. 729–742.

Halpern, Manfred. "The Algerian Uprising of 1945," *Middle East Journal*, April 1948, pp. 191–202.

———. *The Politics of Social Change in the Middle East and North Africa*. Princeton: Princeton University Press, 1963.

Humbaraci, Arslan. *Algeria: A Revolution that Failed*. New York: Praeger, 1966.

Hurewitz, J. C. *Middle East Politics: The Military Dimension*. New York: Praeger, 1968.

Jammes, René. "Cheikh Ben Badis et la France en avril 1936." *L'Afrique et l'Asie*, no. 57, 1961.

Jeanson, Colette et Francis. *L'Algérie hors la loi*. Paris: Editions du Seuil, 1955.

Joesten, Joachim. *The New Algeria*. Chicago: Follett Publishing Co., 1964.

Johnson, Douglas. "Algeria: Some Problems of Modern History." *Journal of African History* 5 (1964): 221–242.

Julien, Charles-André. *Histoire de l'Algérie contemporaine: la conquête et les débuts de la colonisation (1827-1871)*. Paris: Presses Universitaires de France, 1964.

———. *L'Afrique du nord en marche*. Paris: Juillard, 1952.

Kessel, Patrick and Pirelli, Giovanni. *Le peuple algérien et la guerre.* Paris: Maspero, 1962.

Khelifa, Laroussi. *Manuel du militant algérien.* Lausanne: La Cité Editeur, 1958.

Lacheraf, Mostefa. *L'Algérie: nation et société.* Paris: Maspero, 1965.

Lacoste, Yves, Nouschi, André, et Prenant, André. *L'Algérie, passé et présent.* Paris: Editions Sociales, 1960.

Lacouture, Jean. *Cinq hommes et la France.* Paris: Editions du Seuil, 1961.

——. *De Gaulle.* New York: New American Library, 1966.

Launay, Michel, *Paysans algériens.* Paris: Editions du Seuil, 1963.

Leca, Jean. "Le nationalisme algérien depuis l'indépendence." In Duclos, Louis-Jean, Duvignaud, Jean, et Leca, Jean, *Les nationalismes maghrébins.* Paris: Centre d'Etude des Relations Internationales, July 1966.

Lentin, Albert-Paul. *Le dernier quart d'heure.* Paris: Juillard, 1964.

Le Tourneau, Roger. *Evolution politique de l'Afrique du nord musulmane, 1920-1961.* Paris: Librairie Armand Colin, 1962.

Lewis, William H. "Algeria Against Itself." *Africa Report,* Vol. 12, No. 9, December 1967, pp. 9–15.

——. "The Decline of Algeria's FLN," *The Middle East Journal,* Vol. 20, No. 2, Spring 1966.

Mandouze, André, ed. *La révolution algérienne par les textes.* Paris: Maspero, 1962.

Merad; Ali. "La formation de la presse en Algérie (1919-1939)," *IBLA,* no. 105 (1964).

Merle, Robert. *Ahmed Ben Bella.* Paris: Gallimard, 1965.

Michel, Hubert. "Les institutions politiques de la république algérienne." *Revue de l'occident musulman,* no. 1 (1966).

al Mili, Mubarek. *Tārīkh al-Jazā'ir fī-l-Qadīm wa-l-Jadīd,* vols. 1 and 2. Algiers: Maktabah An-Nahdah al-Jazā'iriyyah, 1963.

Miner, Horace M., and De Vos, George. *Oasis and Casbah: Algerian Culture and Personality in Change.* Ann Arbor: University of Michigan, Anthropological Papers, no. 15 (1960).

Montagne, Robert. "La fermentation des partis politiques en Algérie." *Politique étrangère* 2 (April 1937): 124–147.

Moore, Clement H., and Hochschild, Arlie R. "Student Unions in North African Politics." *Daedalus* 97 (Winter 1968): 21–50.

Murray, Roger and Weingraf, Tom. "The Algerian Revolution," *New Left Review* (London), No. 22, December 1963.

Nouschi, André. *La naissance du nationalisme algérien.* Paris: Editions de Minuit, 1962.

Oppermann, Thomas. *Le problème algérien.* Paris: Maspero, 1961.

Ouzegane, Amar. *Le meilleur combat.* Paris: Juillard, 1962.

Paillat, Claude. *Deuxième dossier secret de l'Algérie.* Paris: Les Presses de la Cité, 1962.

——. *Dossier secret de l'Algérie.* Paris: Le Livre Contemporain, 1961.

Pečar, Zdravko. "L'A.L.N. et la révolution algérienne." *Etudes mediterranéennes,* November 1960.

——. *Alžir do nezavisnosti* (Algeria to Independence). Belgrade: Institut za Izučavanje Radničkog Pokreta, 1967).

"Réforme et élections communales en Algérie." *Maghreb,* no. 20 (March-April, 1967): 5–10.

"Regards sur l'enseignement des musulmans en Algérie (1880-1960)." *Confluent,* June-July, 1963, pp. 596-645.

Remili, Abderrahmane. *Les institutions administratives algériennes.* Algiers: S.N.E.D., 1968.

Rens, Ivo. *L'Assemblée algérienne.* Ph.D. dissertation in Law, University of Geneva, 1957.

Robert, Jacques. "Opposition and Control in Tunisia, Morocco and Algeria." *Government and Opposition* 1, no. 3 (April 1966).

Saadallah, Belkacem. "The Rise of the Algerian Elite, 1900-1914," *The Journal of Modern African Studies* 5, no. 1 (May 1967).

———. *The Rise of Algerian Nationalism (1900-1930),* (Ph.D. dissertation in History, University of Minnesota, July 1965).

Sahli, Mohammed C. *Décoloniser l'histoire.* Paris: Maspero, 1965.

Salah Bey, Anisse. "L'Assemblée nationale constituante algérienne." *Annuaire de l'Afrique du nord* 1, 1962. Paris: Centre National de la Recherche Scientifique, 1963.

Sarrasin, Paul-Emile. *La crise algérienne.* Paris: Les Editions du Cerf, 1949.

Soustelle, Jacques. *Aimée et souffrante Algérie.* Paris: Plon, 1956.

Taleb, Ahmed. *Lettres de prison.* Algiers: Éditions Nationales Algériennes, 1966.

Valin, Raymond. "Socialisme musulman en Algérie." *L'Afrique et l'Asie,* no. 66 (1964).

Vatikiotis, P. J. "Tradition and Political Leadership: The Example of Algeria." *Middle Eastern Studies* Vol. 2, No. 4 (July 1966).

Viollette, Maurice. *L'Algérie vivra-t-elle?* Paris: F. Alcan, 1931.

Wehr, Paul E. *Local Leadership and Problems of Rural Development in Algeria.* Ph.D. dissertation, University of Pennsylvania, 1968.

Yacef, Saadi. *Souvenirs de la bataille d'Alger.* Paris: Juillard, 1962.

Index

Abada, Mohammed, 250
Abadou, Said, 229, 250
Abbas, Ferhat, 22, 26–35, 38, 41, 42, 49, 50–59, 70, 72, 80, 84, 95, 98, 99, 122, 130, 134–137, 141–145, 167–169, 172, 173, 178, 182–186, 194, 198, 199, 216, 223, 234
Abd al Qadir, Emir, 3, 4–5, 31
Abdelkader, Abderrazak, 216
Abdelwahab, M'hammed, 250
Abdesselam, Belaid, 13, 48, 121, 156, 179, 259, 274
Abduh, Muhammad, 36
Abid, Said, 221, 229, 241, 260
Afro-Asian Conference, 233, 237
Age of political leaders, 179, 190, 197, 209, 210, 219, 232
Ageron, Charles-Robert, 10, 30, 31, 61
Agrarian Reform, 252, 253, 263
Ait Ahmed, Hocine, 13, 23, 62, 82, 84, 91, 92, 105, 130, 166, 167, 178, 193, 208, 214, 216, 220, 221, 223, 229, 233, 234
Ait al Hocine, Mohand, 199, 226, 231, 241, 256
Ait Chaalal, Messaoud, 121, 178, 179
Akrouf, Daoud, 50
Algerian Communist Party, 72, 81, 97, 256
Allouache, Ali, 216, 223

Almond, Gabriel, 18, 158, 159
Amicale of Algerian workers in France, 206, 238
Amine, Zirout, 251
Amirouche (Ait ould Hamouda), 115, 138, 139
Amis du Manifeste et de la Liberté (AML), 49–52
Amrani, Said, 63, 231
Apter, David, 159
Arab, Mohammed Bessaoud, 131
Arabic culture, 37, 197
  language, 181
Arab-Israeli War of June 1967, 258, 269, 273
Arabization of education, 252, 253
Armée de Libération Nationale (ALN), 23, 108, 110, 113, 115, 124, 128, 138–143, 146, 167, 172, 178, 211, 218
Armée National Populaire (ANP), 113, 214, 217, 219, 221, 225, 241
Aron, Robert, 10, 31, 40, 51
Arslan, Shakib, 39
Assembly, Algerian (1948), 45, 55, 56, 60
  Algerian National Assembly (1964), 21, 44, 199, 206, 207, 209, 213, 218, 231, 241, 251
  Algerian National Constituent Assembly (1962), 21, 44, 132, 171, 175–203, 216, 217, 251, 267, 279

305